Entrepreneurship and the
Internationalisation of Asian Firms

NEW HORIZONS IN INTERNATIONAL BUSINESS

Series Editor: Peter J. Buckley
Centre for International Business,
University of Leeds (CIBUL), UK

The New Horizons in International Business series has established itself as the world's leading forum for the presentation of new ideas in international business research. It offers pre-eminent contributions in the areas of multinational enterprise – including foreign direct investment, business strategy and corporate alliances, global competitive strategies, and entrepreneurship. In short, this series constitutes essential reading for academics, business strategists and policy makers alike.

Titles in the series include:

Globalizing America
The USA in World Integration
Edited by Thomas L. Brewer and Gavin Boyd

Information Technology in Multinational Enterprises
Edited by Edward Mozley Roche and Michael James Blaine

A Yen for Real Estate
Japanese Real Estate Investment Abroad – From Boom to Bust
Roger Simon Farrell

Corporate Governance and Globalization
Long Range Planning Issues
Edited by Stephen S. Cohen and Gavin Boyd

The European Union and Globalisation
Towards Global Democratic Governance
Brigid Gavin

Globalization and the Small Open Economy
Edited by Daniel Van Den Bulcke and Alain Verbeke

Entrepreneurship and the Internationalisation of Asian Firms
An Institutional Perspective
Henry Wai-chung Yeung

The World Trade Organization in the New Global Economy
Trade and Investment Issues in the Millennium Round
Edited by Alan M. Rugman and Gavin Boyd

Japanese Subsidiaries in the New Global Economy
Edited by Paul W. Beamish, Andrew Delios and Shige Makino

Globalizing Europe
Deepening Integration, Alliance Capitalism and Structural Statecraft
Edited by Thomas L. Brewer, Paul A. Brenton and Gavin Boyd

China and its Regions
Economic Growth and Reform in Chinese Provinces
Edited by Mary-Françoise Renard

Emerging Issues in International Business Research
Edited by Masaaki Kotabe and Preet S. Aulakh

Entrepreneurship and the Internationalisation of Asian Firms

An Institutional Perspective

Henry Wai-chung Yeung

Associate Professor in Economic Geography
National University of Singapore

NEW HORIZONS IN INTERNATIONAL BUSINESS

Edward Elgar
Cheltenham, UK • Northampton, MA, USA

© Henry Wai-chung Yeung 2002

All rights reserved. No part of this publication may be reproduced, stored in a retrieval system or transmitted in any form or by any means, electronic, mechanical or photocopying, recording, or otherwise without the prior permission of the publisher.

Published by
Edward Elgar Publishing Limited
Glensanda House
Montpellier Parade
Cheltenham
Glos GL50 1UA
UK

Edward Elgar Publishing, Inc.
136 West Street
Suite 202
Northampton
Massachusetts 01060
USA

A catalogue record for this book
is available from the British Library

Library of Congress Cataloguing in Publication Data

Yeung, Henry Wai-Chung.
    Entrepreneurship and the internationalisation of Asian firms: an institutional perspective
Henry Wai-chung Yeung.
        p.   cm. — (New horizons in international business)
    Includes bibliographical references and index.
    1. Entrepreneurship—Asia. 2. International business enterprises—Asia.
3. Corporations, Asian. 4. Investments, Asian. I. Title. II. Series.
HB615.Y48 2002
338.8′8′095–dc21   2001033983

ISBN 1 84064 734 5

Printed and bound in Great Britain by MPG Books Ltd, Bodmin, Cornwall

To Weiyu and Kay, and to Peter Dicken who inspires my entrepreneurship in international business studies

Contents

List of figures	viii
List of tables	ix
List of boxes	xii
Preface and acknowledgements	xiii

1. An institutional perspective on entrepreneurship in international business — 1
2. Transnational entrepreneurship in two contrasting Asian contexts: Hong Kong and Singapore — 49
3. City-states and their global reach: outward investments from Hong Kong and Singapore — 103
4. Entrepreneurs in international business — 151
5. Empowered managers: intrapreneurs in international business — 207
6. Conclusion: developing entrepreneurship in international business — 250

References	277
Index	305

Figures

1.1	The institutional structuring of entrepreneurship in specific national business systems	27
1.2	Transnational entrepreneurs and actor networks at different spatial scales	35
1.3	A map of Hong Kong and Singapore	43
3.1	Sectoral distribution of Singapore's direct investment abroad by host region, 1997	114
3.2	Ownership structure of parent companies in Singapore	120
3.3	Sectoral distribution of parent companies in Singapore	121
3.4	Turnover of parent companies in Singapore	122
3.5	Motives of transnational operations by host region	126
3.6	Mechanisms of overseas operations by companies from Singapore	129
3.7	Mechanisms of control over foreign subsidiaries by Singapore companies	132
4.1	Attributes of entrepreneurship described by transnational entrepreneurs	158
5.1	The location of Singapore industrial parks in Wuxi and Suzhou in Jiangsu Province, China	222

Tables

1.1	Entrepreneurship studies in the twentieth century	6
1.2	Entrepreneurship in international business studies	8
1.3	Different views of the entrepreneur	13
1.4	The embeddedness of business firms in their national institutional and ideological structures	22
1.5	Summary table of data collected on Hong Kong and Singaporean transnational corporations	44
2.1	Key macro-economic indicators on Hong Kong and Singapore, 1960–1999	52
2.2	Inward direct investments in Hong Kong by country of origin, 1970–1998	54
2.3	Evolving comparative advantage and major strategies of industrial development in Hong Kong, 1950–1999	56
2.4	Cumulative equity investments in Singapore by country of origin, 1965–1997	59
2.5	Net investment commitments in manufacturing in Singapore by country of origin, 1963–1999	60
2.6	Principal statistics for all establishments in all sectors by number of persons engaged and percentage shares of small and medium enterprises in Hong Kong, 1960–1998	64
2.7	Comparing business systems and entrepreneurship in Hong Kong and Singapore	75
2.8	Local and foreign ownership of selected sectors in Hong Kong, 1960–1998	76
2.9	Local and foreign ownership of selected sectors in Singapore, 1960–1998	77
2.10	Summary of divestments by Temasek Holdings in Singapore	83
2.11	Principal statistics for all establishments in all sectors by number of persons engaged and percentage shares of small and medium enterprises in Singapore, 1960–1998	86
2.12	Financial markets and institutions in Hong Kong and Singapore, 1960–1999	88
2.13	Number of establishments in all sectors and establishment–population ratios in Hong Kong and Singapore, 1960–1997	93

2.14	Distribution of the labour force by activity status in Hong Kong and Singapore, 1957–1999	96
3.1	Estimated flows and stocks of foreign direct investment from Hong Kong to selected host economies	107
3.2	Trade involving Hong Kong's outward processing in Mainland China, 1990–1996	109
3.3	Cumulative outward direct investment from Singapore by country, 1976–1997	110
3.4	Foreign equity investment of Singaporean firms by industrial origin and activity abroad, 1990–1997	113
3.5	A partial list of top TNCs from emerging markets ranked by sales, 1977	116
3.6	The top 25 TNCs from developing countries ranked by foreign assets, 1997	118
3.7	Global geographies of transnational operations by indigenous companies from Singapore and Hong Kong	123
3.8	Importance of different factors of globalisation assessed by indigenous companies from Singapore by region	128
3.9	Modes of foreign entry by 204 indigenous companies from Singapore by host country	131
3.10	Comparison of the characteristics of transnational corporations from Hong Kong and Singapore	134
3.11	Composition of manufacturing exports of three Asian NIEs in the US market, 1989–1992	138
3.12	Agencies of the Singapore state in the regionalisation effort	145
3.13	Assistance schemes and programmes of the Economic Development Board of Singapore	148
4.1	Profiles of transnational entrepreneurs by gender and designation	158
4.2	Influence of home country conditions on the establishment of foreign operations by host region and transnational entrepreneurs	170
4.3	Influence of host country conditions on the establishment of foreign operations by host region and transnational entrepreneurs	171
4.4	Influence of global conditions on the establishment of foreign operations by host region and transnational entrepreneurs	173
4.5	Mechanisms of establishing foreign operations and the role of entrepreneurial vision by transnational entrepreneurs	174
4.6	Case studies of transnational entrepreneurs and their entrepreneurial endowments/resources	188

4.7	Competitive advantages in establishing foreign operations by transnational entrepreneurs	195
4.8	Major problems faced and solutions adopted by indigenous companies from Singapore by region	196
4.9	Attributes of entrepreneurship in overcoming problems in foreign operations by transnational entrepreneurs	204
5.1	Case studies of transnational intrapreneurs from government-linked companies and their entrepreneurial endowments/resources	218
5.2	Case studies of transnational intrapreneurs and their entrepreneurial endowments/resources	220
6.1	Comparison of transnational entrepreneurs and transnational intrapreneurs	256
6.2	Activities by the Trade Development Board to promote Singapore's trade and investments outside Asia 1993–1998	272

Boxes

4.1	The global empire of Kwek Leng Beng and his Hong Leong Group: transnational entrepreneurship and 'triangular family networks'	159
4.2	HKToys, personal networks, and Chinese entrepreneurship	176
4.3	SINFood, the Asian economic crisis, and changing modes of foreign market entry	180
4.4	Managing traditional Chinese family firms across borders: four generations of entrepreneurship in Eu Yan Sang	182
5.1	Teck Wah Paper: trust and intrapreneurship in a Chinese family firm	210
5.2	Suzhou-Singapore industrial park: 'political entrepreneurship' in China	223
5.3	Singapore Telecom: transnational entrepreneurship in a government-linked company	245

Preface and acknowledgements

International business has become one of the most important fields of economic activity in today's globalising world economy. When business firms extend their operations across borders to become transnational corporations, they are often entering into host business environments that are fundamentally different from their home countries in terms of institutional and market structures, industrial organisation, social relations, and cultural practices. To overcome these barriers to globalisation, transnational corporations (TNCs) need actors who are creative, proactive, adaptive, and resourceful in different countries; these are all aspects of transnational entrepreneurship that pushes international business activities beyond just managing across borders. Sometimes, these actors in TNCs are the owners or founding *entre*preneurs themselves. They often participate actively in the establishment and management of foreign operations. More commonly, these actors in transnational operations are *intra*preneurs or professional managers who are neither founders nor owners, but are given much autonomy to initiate new practices and to manage transnational operations. They may be equally entrepreneurial in their approach to ensuring successful cross-border operations. Engaging in international business poses a serious challenge to founders and managers of TNCs. It is clear that an understanding of the nature, *modus operandi*, and performance of these entrepreneurs and/or intrapreneurs is vital to the success of international business operations by any TNC.

If conducting business across national boundaries is rather difficult, it is perhaps even more difficult to write a book about what makes some entrepreneurs more successful in their international business activities. I have always been interested in why some people are more successful than others when they go abroad to establish their businesses. As I read from leading international business journals, I found it hard to accept that most existing studies focus on the firm rather than the individual entrepreneur. The more I read in international business studies, the more disillusioned I got. The outcome of this disillusionment then is this book! I was so frustrated about the lack of attention to entrepreneurs in international business studies that I end up writing a book about it.

Although the intellectual performance of this book remains to be judged by readers, I am indebted to many people and organisations, just like any transnational entrepreneur reported in this book. First of all, I am very grateful to my university, National University of Singapore, for generously funding this research (RP960045 and RP970013). The highly efficient and able research assistance by Wan Menghao and Elen Sia was critical to the completion of this project. My publisher, Edward Elgar Publishing, has also been very encouraging and forthcoming. I must admit that the project was invigorated immediately after a memorable discussion with Mr Edward Elgar in my office in Singapore! An anonymous reviewer has also offered important comments that resulted in significant restructuring and revisions of the original book manuscript. The editorial and marketing team in Edward Elgar has been highly professional. My thanks go to Joanne Betteridge, Julie Leppard, Emma Meldrum, Karen McCarthy and, last but not least, Dymphna Evans. I would like to thank Peter Buckley for putting my book in his highly successful series on New Horizons in International Business.

Moreover, the 'suppliers' of this project, our interviewees, have played an indispensable role in its successful completion. I thank all those corporate executives and relevant people for sharing their views and information generously with us. I hope what I have written about them and their companies does in no way cause any embarrassment or difficulty for them.

Many scholars and researchers have also commented constructively on various portions of the book on various occasions. I thank them all here: Kerstin Sahlin-Andersson, Peter Buckley, Tim Bunnell, Mark Casson, Neil Coe, Peter Dicken, Leo Douw, Ho Kong Chong, Philip Kelly, Lily Kong, Roger Lee, Constance Lever-Tracy, George Lin, Liu Hong, Linda Low, Tai-lok Lui, Luo Qi, Anders Malmberg, Ron Martin, Andrew Marton, Terry McGee, Kris Olds, Rajah Rasiah, Henrik Schaumburg-Müller, Deo Sharma, Erik Swyngedouw, Nigel Thrift, Adam Tickell, Noel Tracy, Eric Tsang, Lai Si Tsui-Auch, Dick Walker, Wang Gungwu, Michael Webber, Brenda Yeoh, and Yue-man Yeung. My friends in the Entrepreneurship Development Centre at the Nanyang Technological University have kindly encouraged my endeavour into their monopoly: Fock Siew Tong and Leo Paul Dana. Mrs Lee Li Kheng has kindly drawn the maps.

Earlier versions of parts of this book have been published elsewhere. I am grateful to the following publishers for their permission to reproduce some materials from articles I previously published in their journals/books. Parts of Chapter 1 were first published in *Review of International Political Economy* (Taylor & Francis, London), Vol. 7(3), pp. 399–432, 2000. Parts of Chapters 2 and 3 first appeared in *Political Geography* (Elsevier Science, Exeter), Vol. 17(4), pp. 389–416, 1998; *International Journal of Urban Sciences* (University of Seoul, Seoul), Vol. 2(1), pp. 24–47, 1998; *Antipode* (Blackwell Publishers, Oxford), Vol. 31(3), pp. 245–73, 1999; and

Competition and Change (Overseas Publishers Association, Amsterdam), Vol. 4(2), pp. 121–69, 2000. Parts of Chapter 4 came from my chapters in David Ip, Constance Lever-Tracy, and Noel Tracy (eds), *Chinese Businesses and the Asian Crisis*, Aldershot: Gower, pp. 87–113, 2000, and in Leo Douw, Cen Huang, and David Ip (eds), *Chinese Transnational Enterprise in Prosperity and Adversity*, Surrey: Curzon, 2001. Parts of Chapter 5 were published in my article in *Political Geography* (Elsevier Science, Exeter), Vol. 19(7), pp. 809–40, 2000.

Finally, my intellectual debt goes to Peter Dicken from the University of Manchester, England. For his crucial role in inspiring my intellectual entrepreneurship, the book is dedicated to him (and his wife Valerie). Of course, as the Chinese saying tells, there is an important woman behind every successful man (and vice versa, I suppose). I am extremely grateful to my wife for tolerating my absence from home to conduct overseas interviews and to present various papers in conferences, and providing me her unfailing support and well wishes that go beyond my wildest imagination. To Weiyu and our new born daughter, Kay, who provide all the joy and excitement for my intellectual projects, I dedicate this book.

Henry Wai-chung Yeung
Singapore
December 2000

1. An institutional perspective on entrepreneurship in international business

> To undertake such new things is difficult and constitutes a distinct economic function, first, because they lie outside of the routine tasks which everybody understands and, secondly, because the environment resists in many ways that vary, according to social conditions, from simple refusal either to finance or to buy a new thing, to physical attack on the man who tries to produce it. To act with confidence beyond the range of familiar beacons and to overcome that resistance requires aptitudes that are present in only a small fraction of the population and that define the entrepreneurial type as well as the entrepreneurial function. This function does not essentially consist in either inventing anything or otherwise creating the conditions which the enterprise exploits. It consists in getting things done. (Joseph Schumpeter, 1942: 132)

INTRODUCTION

Entrepreneurship is a well-known and well-studied phenomenon today. Since the inception of the term *entreprendre* in French in the Middle Ages when it was translated as 'between-taker or go between' (Hisrich, 1990: 209; see also Hébert and Link, 1988), entrepreneurship has received continuous and enormous attention in both scholarly and policy circles. Why then do we need another book on the topic? More specifically, why is a book on entrepreneurship that takes place across borders useful? Consider a businessperson who is confronted with a saturated market in the home country, or another businessperson who stumbles upon an opportunity to expand into foreign markets. It takes great courage and other exceptional qualities, or 'aptitudes' in the words of Joseph Schumpeter, for this person to *act* on these situations and to get things done. This person may be an owner and/or a manager of an evolving transnational enterprise. In the former situation, the businessperson may take the business across borders by establishing another operation or several other operations abroad in order to tap into host country business opportunities. In the latter situation, a new international venture may be formed from the inception of business such that the businessperson has an international business without going through any successive stages of business establishment and internationalisation (cf. Johanson and Vahlne, 1977; Buckley and Ghauri, 1993; Björkman and Forsgren, 1997). In both cases, the businessperson is bound to be confronted with the inherent difficulties of operating in a foreign land of which he or she has *less* information, experience, and knowledge, and faces a different set of institutional contexts. These difficulties of engaging in international business activities can be overcome, sometimes, by sheer luck. But more likely they can only be handled with great initiative and capabilities embedded in the social actor and his/her repertoire of institutional resources and relations.

How then do we account for these rather exceptional phenomena of engaging in cross-border business activities? They are exceptional not because they are relatively rare in today's globalising era. Rather, they are exceptional because these businesspersons have taken an unusual route to organise and produce economic activities in different countries and/or regions. They are clearly *entrepreneurial* in that they have taken extraordinary risks and calculations to engage in businesses differently. In the Schumpeterian tradition, these businesspersons have created 'new combinations' of locating production facilities and/or gaining access to markets in different countries and/or regions. Entrepreneurship is therefore more than the initial quality of owners to start business venturing; more importantly, it is about the exceptional qualities required in the processes of both *creating* and *sustaining* particular business ventures, irrespective of whether these ventures operate across national boundaries. Entrepreneurship is not a 'thing' or 'ingredient' in the making of business firms. To borrow from Schumpeter, entrepreneurship is an everlasting process of 'creative destruction' and reconstruction through which the entrepreneur continually displaces or destroys existing products or methods and organisation of production with new ones.

In this book, these businesspersons are termed *transnational entrepreneurs* because they are engaged in entrepreneurial activities across borders. Not all entrepreneurs, however, can become transnational entrepreneurs. Clearly many existing entrepreneurs fail to establish foreign ventures in their internationalisation processes. The challenge of international business to *transnational entrepreneurship* is the key issue to be tackled empirically in this book. This issue explains why another book on entrepreneurship is needed. Indeed, this is not a book on entrepreneurship *per se*. Entrepreneurship has been extensively theorised and studied in almost every single discipline in the social sciences for over a century now (see recent reviews in Casson, 1990a; Bull et al., 1995; Livesay, 1995; Westhead and Wright, 2000). Instead, this book is about explaining transnational entrepreneurial activities and the internationalisation of Asian firms in their social and institutional contexts. To accomplish this analytical task, I propose an *institutional perspective*[1] on entrepreneurship in international business by arguing that transnational entrepreneurs are not merely driven by historical mechanisms of change. I take a different view of the entrepreneur from Schumpeter (1934: 61) who apparently saw the entrepreneur as 'merely the bearer of the mechanism of change'.

This book takes the conceptualisation of transnational entrepreneurs differently – as businesspersons who take specific proactive action to overcome inherent problems and difficulties associated with international business activities. Their action, however, is both facilitated and constrained by ongoing processes of institutional relations in both home and host countries. These institutional relations may be defined by the social and business networks in which these transnational entrepreneurs are embedded, political–economic structures, and dominant organisational and cultural practices in the home and host countries. Collectively, these institutionalised patterns of social and organisational structuring form different *business systems*. Whitley (1992a: 13) defined business systems as 'distinctive configurations of hierarchy-market relations which become institutionalized as relatively successful ways of organizing economic activities in different institutional environments'. Different business systems are distinctive and enduring ways of structuring market economies that are wide-ranging and long-term in nature. Once established in particular institutional contexts, these business systems may develop considerable cohesion and become resistant to major changes. In this sense, the transnational entrepreneur is conceptualised as more than a bearer of mechanisms of change (cf. Schumpeter). He/she is embedded in ongoing institutional processes that significantly shape, but do not determine, his/her fields of action in different countries of business operations. This institutional perspective is therefore centred on social actors – transnational entrepreneurs themselves, and their embedded structures of institutional relations. In this sense, the perspective aims to resurrect the importance of social actors in entrepreneurship and, to paraphrase Baumol (1968: 66), to give prominence to the Prince of Denmark in the discussion of *Hamlet*. It also gives significant theoretical weight to the role of social and institutional contexts in shaping the outcomes of entrepreneurial activities across borders.

The theoretical focus on entrepreneurship and institutional relations in this book is, however, different from Baumol's (1993) book on entrepreneurship in which he specifically aimed at drawing attention to 'the nature of the institutional arrangements that encourage the exercise of entrepreneurship and that provide incentives for it to take productive directions' (Baumol, 1993: 15). By altering the structure of payoffs or 'rules of the game', Baumol argued that one can redirect the flow of entrepreneurial efforts that are productive to the economy. His theory is therefore primarily concerned with the *supply* of entrepreneurs, not the *processes* of entrepreneurship that remains the key issue of this book. Baumol's economic framework is also deterministic in that he believed that 'the nature and intensity of the productive activities of entrepreneurs are *determined* by current economic circumstances and, in particular, by the relative size of the rewards offered to different allocations of entrepreneurial activity' (Baumol, 1993: 260; my emphasis). This deterministic and, in the words of Granovetter (1985), 'undersocialised' framework of entrepreneurship assumes that prospective entrepreneurs are informed and capable enough to take advantage of differences in the reward systems, thereby ignoring the role of specific historical and/or social circumstances unique to individual entrepreneurs that explain their behaviour.

In the remaining four sections of this introductory chapter, I will first assess whether the study of transnational entrepreneurship can become a new horizon in entrepreneurship and international business studies. Here, I will define the nature of transnational entrepreneurship and identify some of its key attributes and characteristics. The discussion will be situated in the context of the theoretical impasse in entrepreneurship and international business studies. The second section develops an institutional perspective on transnational entrepreneurship. I draw upon the various strands of theoretical literature in the social sciences and integrate them with new theoretical insights from institutional analysis. In particular, I build my institutional perspective upon such concepts as 'business systems' (Whitley, 1992a; 1999), 'embeddedness' (Polanyi, 1944; Granovetter, 1985; Aldrich and Zimmer, 1986; Dacin et al., 1999), and 'networks as strategic resources' (Jarillo, 1988; Ghoshal and Bartlett, 1990; Larson, 1992; Grandori, 1999; Gulati, 1999; Gulati et al., 2000). Collectively, Brüderl and Preisendörfer (1998) have termed this 'the network to entrepreneurship'. This section ends with some key analytical questions for this book. The third section introduces the comparative analysis of transnational entrepreneurship and the globalisation of transnational corporations (TNCs) from two Asian Newly Industrialising Economies (NIEs) – Hong Kong and Singapore. The final section outlines the structure and organisation of this book.

TRANSNATIONAL ENTREPRENEURSHIP: A NEW HORIZON IN ENTREPRENEURSHIP AND INTERNATIONAL BUSINESS STUDIES?

International business activities clearly pose serious challenges to transnational entrepreneurs and their TNCs. These challenges are pertinent in the areas of overcoming barriers in host country political and authority structures, competing and co-operating successfully in host country economic systems, and adapting well to host country social and cultural milieus. Meeting these challenges of international business requires transnational entrepreneurship, defined simply *as the exceptional qualities required in the processes of creating and sustaining particular business ventures across national boundaries by social actors*. These social actors are, of course, defined as *transnational entrepreneurs*. To this effect, I have chosen to use a process definition of transnational entrepreneurship and an agency definition of transnational entrepreneurs (see more in the following section). To understand more about both transnational entrepreneurs and transnational entrepreneurship, we need to revisit decades of entrepreneurship and international business studies. My argument here is that the study of transnational entrepreneurship can offer a new horizon to integrate these two rather disparate strands of theoretical and empirical literature.

Integrating Entrepreneurship Studies and International Business Studies

To date, a theoretical impasse clearly exists in the entrepreneurship and international business studies that are summarised in Tables 1.1 and 1.2. In the twentieth century, entrepreneurship studies have evolved as a distinct and disparate field of intellectual enquiry. In particular, this field of research is associated with studies of entrepreneurship and economic development, entrepreneurship and (international) business venturing, entrepreneurship and business history and ethnicity, and international entrepreneurship. Whereas development economics tends to dominate the sub-field of entrepreneurship and economic development, other social sciences are actively involved in research on business venturing (e.g. management studies), business history (e.g. history), ethnic entrepreneurship (e.g. sociology and anthropology), and international entrepreneurship (e.g. management studies). In Table 1.1, I have assessed the relevance of these sub-fields of entrepreneurship studies for the study of transnational entrepreneurship in this book. First, as a collective body of literature, entrepreneurship studies have illustrated some of the most important dimensions and attributes of entrepreneurship. Second, the literature has shed light on the role of networking in enhancing entrepreneurship. Put in specific social and institutional context (adversarial or encouraging), these studies have shown that entrepreneurship can flourish and prosper. Third, a more recent emphasis of the literature is on the international dimensions of entrepreneurship. This proves to be an extremely fruitful avenue for research in an era of accelerated globalisation. It also helps to bring entrepreneurship studies, which no doubt have a much longer history of existence, closer to

Table 1.1 Entrepreneurship studies in the twentieth century

Themes	Main Disciplines	Major Studies	Analytical Focus	Relevance to Transnational Entrepreneurship
Entrepreneurship and economic development	• Development economics	• Schumpeter (1934) • Baumol (1968; 1990; 1993) • Leff (1978; 1979) • Leibenstein (1966; 1968) • Kirzner (1973; 1985)	• entrepreneurship as a process of creative destruction • the entrepreneur as a disruptive force to create market disequilibrium • the entrepreneur as gap-filler to create X-efficiency and market equilibrium • unproductive entrepreneurship	• definitions of the entrepreneur • the nature of entrepreneurship • historical specificity of entrepreneurship
Entrepreneurship and (international) business venturing	• Management studies	• Rothwell & Zegveld (1982) • Garavan et al. (1997) • Landstrom et al. (1997) • Scaperlanda (1994) • Brush (1995) • Kohn (1989) • McDougall (1989) • McDougall et al. (1994) • McDougall & Oviatt (1996) • Moon & Peery (1997)	• formation and growth of small businesses • technological innovations and international expansion of small firms • strategic change and the performance of international new ventures • entrepreneurial values and the implementation of international new ventures	• international dimension of entrepreneurial activities
Entrepreneurship and business history and ethnicity	• History • Sociology • Anthropology	• J. Brown and Rose (1993) • Aldrich & Waldinger (1990) • Livesay (1995) • B. Wong (1998) • Sloane (1999) • Thornton (1999) • Werbner (1999)	• specific psychological and social attributes of entrepreneurs • ethnic resources and entrepreneurial tendencies	• the social and institutional context of entrepreneurship • the role of networking in entrepreneurship • historical specificity of entrepreneurship
International entrepreneurship	• Management studies	• McDougall (1989) • Birley & MacMillan (1995; 1997) • Hisrich et al. (1997) • Dana (1999) • Thomas and Mueller (2000)	• entrepreneurs in a comparative and international context • entrepreneurship across international boundaries	• comparative analysis • international dimension of entrepreneurial activities

An institutional perspective on entrepreneurship in international business   7

a relatively young sub-field of management studies – international business studies.

International business studies have grown significantly in the past four decades since Stephen Hymer's path-breaking theoretical work (see Table 1.2). There are now a number of theoretical perspectives in international business studies. When it comes to the role of the entrepreneur and entrepreneurship in TNC activities, however, received theories in international business studies seem to be rather silent or unfit in explaining the entrepreneurial outcome. This may have something to do with the nature of entrepreneurship studies itself, i.e. lack of precision and largely driven by inductive studies. There are, however, at least three emerging areas in international business studies that hold promise for integrating entrepreneurship and international business studies: the entrepreneurial decision model of TNCs, corporate entrepreneurship and subsidiary initiatives, and the impact of TNCs on domestic entrepreneurship.

In Table 1.2, I have outlined the relevance of these three areas of international business studies for the study of transnational entrepreneurship. First, the entrepreneurial decision model of the TNC is likely to inform my conceptualisation of the nature of the transnational entrepreneur as a social actor *in control of resources in different countries* (see the next section). Second, the study of corporate entrepreneurship and subsidiary initiatives has demonstrated the need for proven resources within the TNC. This further testifies the relevance of a resource-based view of transnational entrepreneurship (Penrose, 1995; Garnsey, 1998), a theoretical point consistent with my definition of the transnational entrepreneur later in this chapter. Finally, studies of TNC impact on host countries have shown the importance of understanding the institutional context of host countries in which TNC subsidiaries are located. This focus on the host country institutional context is relevant to the institutional perspective on transnational entrepreneurship to be developed later in this chapter. It is also important to our understanding of what exactly shapes the entrepreneurial processes of those subsidiaries.

Despite decades of entrepreneurship research since Richard Cantillon, Joseph Schumpeter, and others (see recent collections in Casson, 1990a; 1995; Livesay, 1995; Low and Tan, 1996; Westhead and Wright, 2000), we still know very little about the real *actors* and their behaviour in these TNCs. First, entrepreneurship studies tend to assume that the entrepreneur will behave and act in the same manner irrespective of the geography of his/her business operations. In this literature, there seems to be no difference in the social, political, and economic contexts of different countries in which an entrepreneur operates. Indeed, most entrepreneurship studies are primarily uni-locational in their spatial unit of analysis. Only very limited studies have

Table 1.2 Entrepreneurship in international business studies

Themes	Main Disciplines	Major Studies	Analytical Focus	Relevance to Transnational Entrepreneurship
Entrepreneurial decision model of transnational corporations	• Economics	• Casson (1982; 1985; 1990b)	• the entrepreneur as a specialist in making judgmental decisions • international business activities as a result of entrepreneurial decisions and information asymmetry	• the role of exceptional qualities in the entrepreneur to overcome risks and uncertainties in international business
Corporate entrepreneurship and subsidiary initiatives	• Strategic management • International business studies	• Birkinshaw (1997; 2000)	• dispersed corporate entrepreneurship • focused corporate entrepreneurship • subsidiary initiatives as dispersed corporate entrepreneurship • the role of proven resources in enhancing subsidiary initiatives	• entrepreneurial activities at the subsidiary level • the role of intrapreneurs in TNC subsidiaries • the role of resources to intrapreneurship
Impact of transnational corporations on domestic entrepreneurship	• Development studies • International business studies	• Jesudason (1989) • H. Tan (1991) • DiConti (1992) • R.A. Brown (1994)	• crowding out of domestic entrepreneurship by foreign TNCs • potential spin-off and linkages from TNCs to promote domestic entrepreneurship	• the role of host country institutional contexts in shaping the impact of TNCs on domestic entrepreneurship • the role of TNC subsidiaries in developing intrapreneurship of host country nationals

been done to offer a comparative analysis of entrepreneurship in different countries (e.g. DiConti, 1992; Birley and MacMillan, 1995; 1997).

Second, most entrepreneurship studies tend to focus on the actors in their *domestic* setting.[2] These studies are concerned with the role of entrepreneurs in innovations, new business start-ups, and the economic development of their home countries. As concluded by McDougall and Oviatt (1996: 36), the internationalisation of new ventures 'does not appear to be a simple matter of applying established strategies and procedures developed for a domestic arena. Successful internationalization appears to be accompanied by changes in venture strategy'. Although certain theories in entrepreneurship studies have been proposed to explain the internationalisation behaviour of entrepreneurs (e.g. Oviatt and McDougall, 1994; Scaperlanda, 1994), the research field is still very much in its infancy, with little direct emphasis on the entrepreneur. Even Casson's (1990b: 44, 82) theory of entrepreneurship in international business focuses on the innovative capabilities of the entrepreneur by arguing that 'the scale of international business activity is inextricably linked to the innovativeness of the source economy . . . To explain fully the size and timing of FDI across source countries, it is therefore necessary to explain the rise and decline of entrepreneurial activity within such countries'. The theory is concerned with how crucial aspects of home country culture are incorporated into the TNC through the decision-making activities of its entrepreneurs, rather than through the entrepreneurs themselves.

With a few exceptions (e.g. McDougall, 1989; McDougall et al., 1994; McDougall and Oviatt, 1996; 2000; Birkinshaw, 1997; 2000; Moon and Peery, 1997), entrepreneurship research has little interaction with mainstream research on international business and organisational behaviour. The latter is preoccupied with *the firm* as the central unit of analysis. One needs only a glance at most articles in recent issues of major international business studies journals[3] to realise that the unit of analysis is overwhelmingly the firm and the TNC, not the human actor and the entrepreneur. This heavy bias towards firm-level analysis reflects the methodological individualism of most international business studies in which predictive statistical tools are used to quantify international business activities. Human actors and entrepreneurs do not seem to have a place in this quantitative methodology, perhaps because their behaviour and action cannot be consistently quantified and predicted. The net result is that the baby has been thrown out with the bath water altogether. We end up with highly 'scientific' studies of global corporations *without* human actors and entrepreneurs. For example, Hébert and Link (1988: 158; see also Ripsas, 1998) reflected on the reasons why the entrepreneur has been squeezed out from modern mainstream economics through the introduction of mathematics to economics:

Since there was not then, and is not now, a satisfactory mathematics to deal with the dynamics of economic life, economic analysis gradually receded into the shadows of comparative statics, and the entrepreneur took on a purely passive, even useless, role.

In one of the earliest contributions to the study of international entrepreneurship, McDougall (1989; also McDougall et al., 1994; McDougall and Oviatt, 1996; 2000) focused almost exclusively on international new venture firms and compared their strategic behaviour and industry structure with domestic new ventures. Firm-specific and industry-specific factors were presented as the critical dimensions to explain and differentiate firm behaviour. There was neither a theoretical nor an empirical role for the individual entrepreneurs who have propelled the firms into an international arena. This is not surprising because as recently as 1994, transnational entrepreneurship (or international entrepreneurship) was still considered as an 'even newer thrust of research activity' in international business research (Wright and Ricks, 1994: 699). Moon and Peery (1997: 11) also argued that '[e]ntrepreneurship is very important in international business. There are some noteworthy, new international ventures that, from inception, seek to derive significant competitive advantage from the use of resources and the sale of outputs in multiple countries'.

In short, while entrepreneurship research tends to ignore entrepreneurs in international business, studies of international business and organisational behaviour focus overtly on the nature and organisation of TNCs at the expense of those actors and individuals who are creating and managing the worldwide network of transnational corporations – the entrepreneurs and intrapreneurs themselves. As noted by Livesay (1995: xi), the entrepreneur is 'an individual at work in the private sector of the economy, not a department of a firm, nor a government agency, though both of these may attempt to produce entrepreneurial results'. The lack of integration and cross-fertilisation between entrepreneurship studies and international business studies has been the main obstacle to a fuller understanding of the nature and processes of transnational entrepreneurship. A casual online keyword search of the Social Sciences Citation Index published by the Institute for Scientific Information is instructive here. In 1988 and 2000, there were respectively 1070 and 1319 articles published in about 1600 journals that contain the keywords 'entrepreneurship' and 'entrepreneurs' (http://www.isinet.com/products/citation/citssci.html, accessed on 13 December 2000). Only 6 and 11 articles contained respectively such keywords as 'transnational entrepreneurship'[4] and 'transnational entrepreneurs'. A further 42 and 68 articles contained the keywords 'international entrepreneurship'[5] and 'international entrepreneurs'. These crude statistics show that while a lot has been published on entrepreneurship and entrepreneurs *per se* during the past decade, the fields of 'transnational entrepreneurship' and/or 'international entrepreneurship' are still emerging and relatively young in the historiography of entrepreneurship studies (see also Hébert and Link, 1988; Casson, 1990a; Chell et al., 1991; Livesay, 1995; Westhead and Wright, 2000). How then should we define transnational entrepreneurs and transnational entrepreneurship? Without knowing our subject of analysis, how can we proceed to conduct a comparative study of transnational entrepreneurship in different Asian economies and/or countries?

The Terminological and Conceptual Jungle of Entrepreneurship Studies

Though I have offered a very simple set of definitions in the introduction to this section, defining the nature of transnational entrepreneurship is never easy for at least three reasons. First, it is always problematical to define the term 'entrepreneur'. As noted by Baumol (1993: 7; original emphasis):

> Any attempt at rigid definition of the term *enterpreneur* will be avoided assiduously here, because whatever attributes are selected, they are sure to prove excessively restrictive, ruling out some feature, activity, or accomplishment of this inherently subtle and elusive character.

Baumol (1993: 8) defined the entrepreneur in such a way as to encompass all non-routine activities by those entrepreneurs 'who direct the economic activities of larger or smaller groups or organizations'.

Second, the definition of the entrepreneur and entrepreneurship has become such a terminological jungle that virtually anyone can plant his/her own tree. Most existing definitions of entrepreneurship are based on either the *outcome* of entrepreneurial activity or *process* based on the creation of new enterprises or organisations. This state of definitional chaos has led to Bull and Willard's (1995: 2) claim that '[w]riters in the field of entrepreneurship seem somewhat obsessed with defining the word "entrepreneur"... The term has been used for more than two centuries, but we continue to extend, reinterpret, and revise the definition. We suggest that this desire to invent a better definition has misdirected research efforts away from a useful theory of entrepreneurship'. Instead, they suggested the adoption of Schumpeter-based concepts of the entrepreneur.

Third, very different views of the entrepreneur exist in different academic disciplines.[6] To a large extent, this divergence in disciplinary views of the entrepreneur results from 'disciplinary closure' as evident in Leff's (1979: 58) remark in his review of the problem of entrepreneurship in economic development:

Sociologists and psychologists may be better able to answer such questions as the social conditions and personality traits that affect the capacity for bearing risk and uncertainty. But economists are needed to take account of the economic conditions under which preferences are transformed into actual investment behavior.

There are basically six views of the entrepreneur. In historical sequence these are: (1) the 'great person' school; (2) classical and neoclassical economics; (3) psychology; (4) sociology; (5) management; and (6) intrapreneurship (see Table 1.3). The *'great person' school* takes the entrepreneur as an exceptional individual who is born with certain entrepreneurial tendencies and attributes. This individual is viewed as possessing special abilities and traits that enable him or her to make entrepreneurial decisions. From a macroeconomic perspective, the concentration of entrepreneurs is simply a random process of birth and death of entrepreneurs. These entrepreneurs are associated with the rapid proliferation of start-up firms in a particular economy.

In *classical and neoclassical* economic models, the firm is essentially 'entrepreneurless'. The role of the entrepreneur has been relegated in neoclassical economics to an indivisible and non-replicable input. Baumol (1968: 66; footnote 2) famously observed that '[t]he theoretical firm is entrepreneurless – the Prince of Denmark has been expunged from the discussion of *Hamlet* . . . There is one residual and rather curious role left to the entrepreneur in the neoclassical model. He is the indivisible and non-replicable input that accounts for the U-shaped cost curve of a firm whose production function is linear and homogeneous. How the mighty have fallen!'. Interestingly, this observation remains in his 1993 book (Baumol, 1993), indicating the marginalisation of the subject in mainstream economics during the 1970s and the 1980s. In his important theoretical contribution to entrepreneurship in economic theory, Casson (1982: 9) recognised this gap in economic theory right at the beginning:

> It may be said quite categorically that at the present there is no established economic theory of the entrepreneur. The subject area has been surrendered by economists to sociologists, psychologists and political scientists. Indeed, almost all the social sciences have a theory of the entrepreneur, except economics.

More recently, Baumol (1995: 17; original emphasis) made another apparently contradictory observation that 'their *does* exist a body of entrepreneurship theory in economics. It even provides a rich store of insights pertinent both for the understanding of behavior and for the formulation of policy'.

The *psychological view* of the entrepreneur was popularised by McClelland's (1961) study and his concept of *n*-achievement (see Low and

Table 1.3 Different views of the entrepreneur

Views of the Entrepreneur (in historical sequence)	Focus	Assumption	Behaviour and Skills	Situation
'Great person' school	• born with intuitive ability and traits and instincts	• entrepreneurship is born and pre-given	• intuition, vigour, energy, persistence, and self-esteem	• start-up
Classical and neoclassical	• innovation	• entrepreneurship is doing rather than owning	• innovation, creativity, and discovery	• start-up and early growth
Psychological	• unique values, attitudes needs and characteristics	• people behave in accordance with their values values	• personal risk-taking, need for achievement	• start-up
Sociological	• family and environmental dynamics	• early childhood influences affect career decision	• shared resources and networks	• start-up
Management	• planning, organising, leading and control	• entrepreneurs can be developed and trained	• production planning, people organising, capitalisation and budgeting	• early growth and maturity
Intrapreneurship	• venture teams within organisations • development of independent units to create, market, and expand services	• entrepreneurs effect change within organisations, lead to organisational building and become managers	• alertness to opportunities, maximising decisions	• maturity and change

Sources: Garavan et al. (1997: Figure 2.1); Bridge et al. (1998: Table 2.1).

MacMillan, 1988; Hisrich, 1990; Chell et al., 1991; Bridge et al., 1998). In this view, several classical dependent variables defining the entrepreneur have been uncovered: the need for achievement, risk-taking propensity, and locus of control. The entrepreneur is seen as someone who possesses experience, flexibility of thought, high norms, long-term view, progressive outlook, self-reliance, and attitudes of deliberation (Casson, 1990b: 57–8). Numerous clinical experiments and statistical tests have been conducted in order to ascertain specific traits and personality of entrepreneurs. Does it mean then that only certain people can be entrepreneurs? Gartner (1988) argued that this limited view of the entrepreneur is not very useful. As noted by Moon and Peery (1997: 15), 'anybody can become an entrepreneur, if he or she can create supernormal values in any area of business with an appropriate strategy'. This view of the entrepreneur is consistent with Schumpeter's (1934) original argument that an entrepreneur ceases to be one if he/she does not create value through 'new combinations' or, in today's terminology, continuous innovation.

The *sociological view* of the entrepreneur has its origin in Max Weber's [1904] (1992) theory on the origin of the entrepreneurial spirit as a cultural account of individualism and the Protestant ethic. Sociological studies of entrepreneurship are particularly prominent in the area of ethnic entrepreneurship (see Aldrich and Waldinger, 1990; Thornton, 1999). Two models have been advanced to explain the relatively high incidence of entrepreneurial activities among certain ethnic groups. The misfit model explains why immigrants tend to be unable to fit into the labour market in the host economies, thereby propelling these immigrants to start their own businesses. The disadvantage model puts the blame on the inherent bias in the economic structures of the host economies and shows how these systematic biases force certain ethnic groups to venture into businesses. Together with earlier models in psychology, these sociological models of ethnic entrepreneurship have found some audience among economists. Concluding their empirical study of patterns of self-employment in the USA between 1968–1987, Evans and Leighton (1989: 532) noted that '[t]he sociological and psychological literature on entrepreneurship contains many insights that economists might consider incorporating in their models'.

The last two views of the entrepreneur are found mostly in management literature. It is sufficient to point out that entrepreneurship is conceptualised as value creation activities by management scholars:

> Entrepreneurship can now be formally defined as an activity of creating supernormal values for individuals, organizations, and society by increasing *reward minus risk*, i.e., increasing reward, reducing risk, or both. (Moon and Peery, 1997: 8; original emphasis)

On the other hand, the management view on intrapreneurship was first popularised by Pinchot (1985) and subsequent studies of corporate entrepreneurship (Duncan et al., 1988; Guth and Ginsberg, 1990; Hisrich, 1990; Fulop, 1991; Block and MacMillan, 1993; Mosakowski, 1998; Barringer and Bluedorn, 1999; Mourdoukoutas, 1999).

The Nature of Transnational Entrepreneurship

In this book, I define a *transnational entrepreneur* as a social actor capable of bearing risks and taking strategic initiatives to establish, integrate, and sustain foreign operations. This transnational entrepreneur is more than a bearer of mechanism of change at the abstract level. He/she has internalised certain exceptional qualities (cf. the psychological view) and his/her strategic action is facilitated by the repertoire and network of resources in which he/she is embedded (cf. the sociological view). A transnational entrepreneur is therefore defined by three interrelated attributes that must be simultaneously present in the entrepreneurial process: (1) control of resources in different countries (e.g. capital, information, and knowledge); (2) capabilities in strategic management in different countries (e.g. innovative and creative deployment of resources); and (3) abilities to create and exploit opportunities in different countries. This process-driven definition of transnational entrepreneurship points at its time- and place-dependent nature. An entrepreneur may not forever be an entrepreneur because he or she may lose entrepreneurship over time or in different places. This time- and place-specificity of entrepreneurship has already been recognised by Schumpeter (1934: 78) and Baumol (1990: 894).

In the first place, the *control of resources* in different countries allows a transnational entrepreneur to overcome the inherent disadvantage of engaging in international business activities when competing with incumbent competitors in the host countries. The use of the word 'control' is intentional here to avoid the necessary implication that control means ownership. A transnational entrepreneur can effectively control certain sets of resources without actually owning them. For example, a transnational entrepreneur may obtain particular information or knowledge about a potential market opportunity through personal contacts or other means. This intangible and tacit knowledge cannot be clearly defined and is not accompanied by particular ownership. The 'network factor' becomes very important here because strong social and business networks can serve as the institutional foundations for transnational entrepreneurship. Social and political institutions significantly shape the attitudes and behaviour of transnational entrepreneurs. These networks and institutions provide the necessary strategic infrastructure to enable the success of these transnational entrepreneurs.

Transnational entrepreneurship is a *process* because it evolves from experience and learning gained through progressive involvement in foreign operations. Through these cross-border operations, transnational entrepreneurs not only learn how to deal with unexpected contingencies in the host countries, but also develop deeper understanding of the realities of these host countries.

Moreover, the utilisation of these cross-border resources is certainly a risk-taking act. In this sense, I disagree with Schumpeter's (1934: 137) view that the entrepreneur is not necessarily a risk-bearing person, but rather the capitalist is the risk-bearer. Since there are opportunity costs associated with the control of cross-border resources by transnational entrepreneurs, there are risks involved in different combinations of utilising and exploiting these resources. Of course, not all risk-taking is good, at least from a firm's point of view. But transnational entrepreneurs must have certain inherent capabilities in absorbing calculated risks, i.e. the kind of risks that generate potential gain. This risk-taking behaviour is particularly critical because operations in a foreign land are often filled with uncertainties and potential business risks. In fact, the risk-taking capacity of an entrepreneur tends to increase with his/her experience with the host countries (see my empirical analysis in Chapters 4 and 5).

This definitive attribute of the transnational entrepreneur, however, excludes most managers of TNCs who do not control resources in different countries. As shown below, some managers of TNC subsidiaries abroad have taken specific initiatives to create 'new combinations' through strategic deployment of their available resources and information/knowledge repertoire. They are conceptualised as 'transnational intrapreneurs' who are professional managers empowered to manage transnational operations.[7] This empowerment may come from the founding entrepreneurs themselves through a process of socialisation. It may also be institutionalised within the organisation itself when top management from headquarters delegates power and control to professional managers abroad. This creates what are known as 'intra-firm' networks that tend to facilitate headquarters' control and co-ordination of overseas subsidiaries through informal mechanisms. The role of heterarchy in encouraging intrapreneurship in international business operates through the flattening of corporate hierarchy. Geisler (1993: 55) argued that '[i]n the new amorphous organization, the middle managers are again in the middle of affairs. This time they function less as linking mechanisms in a vertical flow and more as central focuses for multidirectional interfaces with internal as well as external stakeholders, such as clients and suppliers'.

Second, not everyone who controls resources in different countries can be a transnational entrepreneur because he or she may not be able to deploy

An institutional perspective on entrepreneurship in international business 17

these resources effectively to establish and sustain cross-border operations. A necessary condition to define a transnational entrepreneur is *capabilities in strategic management* in different countries. Once again, a new market entrant can only succeed in a foreign country if he or she deploys available resources *differently* from competitors in the host countries and/or from other countries. This attribute of transnational entrepreneurs explains why they are able to break away from routinised patterns and norms of business activities found among domestic competitors. Baumol (1968: 65) noted that an entrepreneur is 'the Schumpeterian innovator and some more. He is the individual who exercises what in the business literature is called "leadership." And it is he who is virtually absent from the received theory of the firm'. How then does a transnational entrepreneur 'get things done' differently in host countries? These are empirical issues that will be addressed further in later chapters.

Third, since transnational entrepreneurship refers to ongoing processes of successful foreign business venturing, it is important to appreciate a transnational entrepreneur's *abilities to create and exploit opportunities* in different countries. Indeed, the existence of opportunities and their differential exploitation are the central assumptions in Holmes and Schmitz's (1990) economic model of entrepreneurship. It is therefore one thing to control and deploy resources effectively in different countries, but quite another thing to explain why only certain international business ventures are successful and sustainable over time. I believe this contextual factor has something to do with *foresight* in foreign ventures. This aspect is important at least from the perspective of strategic management and transaction cost economics. As Williamson (1999: 1089) acknowledged, '[t]ransaction cost economics ascribes foresight rather than myopia to human actors'. The factor also distinguishes domestic entrepreneurship from transnational entrepreneurship because an entrepreneur is often well entrenched in his/her domestic market. There is a strong sense of inertia against venturing abroad, given his/her comfortable home market share. A transnational entrepreneur therefore needs to possess strong vision and foresight in order to position the future of his/her firm in an era of global competition. Though often assisted by professional analysts and strategists, he/she must be able to identify market opportunities abroad and tap into them. This relentless search for direct investments in foreign markets is important in today's global economy because market presence remains the fundamental drive for an entrepreneur to venture abroad, whether he/she runs a manufacturing or a service firm. If successful, this transnational entrepreneur will enjoy 'first-mover' advantages unavailable to other firms and their actors. Every foreign venture, therefore, may appear as a new business start-up synonymous with the process of new firm formation so well documented in most entrepreneurship studies. The difference here, of course, is that once a foreign venture is established, a transnational entrepreneur must continue to resolve operational and management problems in a business context that is often fundamentally *different* from his/her home country.

TOWARDS AN INSTITUTIONAL PERSPECTIVE ON TRANSNATIONAL ENTREPRENEURSHIP

The institutional perspective on entrepreneurship in international business therefore assumes that transnational entrepreneurs and intrapreneurs must be endowed with control of resources, capabilities in strategic management, and abilities to create and exploit opportunities in different countries. As transnational entrepreneurship refers to the exceptional qualities required in the processes of creating and sustaining particular business ventures across national boundaries by social actors, my analytical tasks are (1) to explain both the sources and variations of *entrepreneurial endowments* (resources and capabilities) enjoyed by transnational entrepreneurs and (2) to explain how these transnational entrepreneurs *capitalise* differently on their endowments through cross-border business ventures. In its essence, an institutional perspective on transnational entrepreneurship postulates that significant variations in institutional structures of home countries explain variations in the *entrepreneurial endowments* of prospective transnational entrepreneurs. Institutional structures are defined as enduring and organised sets of relations among 'prevailing institutions dealing with the constitution and control of key resources such as skills, capital, and legitimacy' (Whitley, 1999: 5). These institutional structures form established systems of economic co-ordination and control in specific market and non-market economies. They inherently shape the logics governing economic decision-making, actions, and the market processes through establishing and enforcing conventions, values, views, norms, practices, and the so-called 'rules of the game'.

Once embedded in these transnational institutional structures, transnational entrepreneurs should be better able to *exercise* their home country endowments in the host countries. This important difference between the home country endowments of transnational entrepreneurs and their abilities in exercising these endowments explains why domestic entrepreneurs from the same home countries may experience differential entrepreneurial outcomes even if they operate in the same host countries. Similarly, this differential ability to exercise home country endowments due to differential embeddedness in cross-border actor networks can also explain why a transnational entrepreneur from a home country with weaker institutional structures (e.g. a restricted home market) may perform better in the same host country *vis-à-vis* a transnational entrepreneur from another home country with stronger institutional structures (e.g. a more competitive home market). There is therefore a place for individual entrepreneurs and their actor-specific initiatives in this institutional perspective on transnational entrepreneurship. Through their actor-specific cross-border networks, some domestic entrepreneurs are more predisposed to become transnational entrepreneurs by successfully establishing and sustaining their foreign operations. Their entrepreneurial action, however, is constrained by home country endowments that are explained by variations in home country institutional structures.

These are the basic theoretical premises of my institutional perspective on transnational entrepreneurship that will be explained in greater detail in the following subsections. Casson (1990b: 44–5) noted that an institutional perspective on entrepreneurship can provide 'a vision of the firm as a coalition of individuals who have contracted to fill prescribed roles within an institutional structure. The creative activity of the firm stems ultimately from the co-operative creativity of the individuals within it'. Instead of starting with the internal attributes of the entrepreneur, my institutional perspective begins its analysis with comparative institutional structures in home and host countries. It then proceeds to analyse the entrepreneurial capacities of individual actors in international business – the transnational entrepreneur – and their embeddedness in cross-border actor-specific networks. These transnational entrepreneurs and intrapreneurs draw upon resources and endowments from the cross-border institutional structures in which they are embedded. This process of embedding in transnational institutional structures is known as the institutionalisation of transnational entrepreneurship.

Varieties of Capitalism and the Institutional Structuring of Business Systems

It is beyond the scope of this book to explain different varieties of capitalism and their business systems[8] (see Whitley, 1992a; 1992b; 1999; Berger and Dore, 1996; Whitley and Kristensen, 1996; 1997; Crouch and Streeck, 1997; Hollingsworth and Boyer, 1997; Porac and Ventresca, 1999). Suffice to argue that variations in institutional structures and business systems significantly explain the sources and variations of resource and capability endowments enjoyed by transnational entrepreneurs from different home countries. The divergent forms of capitalism can be explained by their different configurations of institutional structures and their different institutional structuring of organisational forms. An example is the late twentieth century British economy, which had strong international capabilities in financial services and architecture but relatively weak ones in complex assembly manufacturing and construction. Another similar example is the strength of the Japanese economy in complex assembly manufacturing (e.g. automobiles and electronics), but not so much in precision engineering or media businesses.

In his formulation of a more general approach to economic development and competitiveness, Lazonick (1991; see also Chandler, 1990; Whitley, 1999) highlighted three varieties of capitalism in accordance with their variations in the *configurations of economic institutions and competitive strategies*: proprietary (e.g. the UK), managerial (e.g. the USA), and collective (e.g. post-war Japan). Proprietary capitalism is dominated by vertically and horizontally specialised firms that co-ordinate their inputs and outputs through market contracting (see also Sako, 1992). These firms have little distinctive organisational capacity to pursue innovative strategies and typically delegate control over labour processes to skilled workers who are managed through piecework-based reward systems. Managerial capitalism, in contrast, is dominated by large, vertically integrated and often horizontally diversified firms run by salaried managers organised into authority hierarchies (Chandler, 1977; 1990; cf. Best, 1990; Sabel and Zeitlin, 1996). These firms often developed their own innovation capabilities through establishing R&D laboratories and competed for much of the early twentieth century through innovation-based strategies for mass markets. They also tend to exert strong managerial control over work processes through formal rules and procedures and mechanisation. High levels of managerial integration in such firms do not extend to the manual workforce, or to suppliers and customers. Finally, collective capitalism exhibits even higher levels of organisational integration of economic activities through extensive long-term collaboration between firms in business groups and networks, both within sectors and across them. Additionally, integration within firms is greater in this form of capitalism because loyalty and commitment between employer and employee extend further down the hierarchy than in either of the other two types. This investment in manual workers is crucial to the development of innovative organisations since it encourages employees to improve products and processes on a continuing basis.

How then do these different configurations of capitalism shape the organisation of economic co-ordination and control systems? This diverse *institutional structuring of organisation systems* is evident in the substantial variations in ownership patterns, business formation and co-ordination, management processes, and work and employment relations across countries and/or regions. For example, the ways in which industrial capitalism developed in Britain, Denmark, and Germany differ significantly as a result of variations in their political systems and the institutions governing agricultural production and distribution. To a large extent, the structure and practices of state agencies, financial organisations, and labour-market actors in these countries continue to diverge and to reproduce distinctive forms of economic organisation (Whitley, 1999). Table 1.4 provides a summary of the embeddedness of business firms in their national institutional and ideological structures. I shall extend my analysis here by considering each aspect of this institutional structuring of organisation systems.

First, *ownership patterns of firms* in particular countries can be significantly structured by pre-existing institutions in those countries. These pre-existing institutional arrangements may control sources of capital and other initial inputs to production in ways that promote or discourage private entrepreneurship and private ownership of business establishments. Late industrialising countries, for example, typically have poorly developed capital and stock markets. The lack of capital and other inputs to production (e.g. human resources) has often led to strong involvement of the state in early industrialisation in these emerging countries (see the case of Hong Kong and Singapore in Chapter 2). In other industrialised economies, however, significant variations in state policies and industrialisation processes may shape the behaviour of national firms in terms of their corporate financing (e.g. reliance on capital markets) and corporate governance patterns (see Table 1.4). American firms, for example, have significantly shorter-term shareholding and higher reliance on capital markets than German and Japanese firms.

Second, institutional arrangements may influence the patterns of *business formation and co-ordination*. This is important insofar as entrepreneurship studies are concerned because business formation and venturing have been key research focuses in these studies. In countries with highly competitive markets institutionalised through specific deregulation policies and the establishment of market procedures, firms tend to be established by private entrepreneurs on the basis of their perceived benefits from 'new combinations' of production, marketing, and distribution methods. Recent empirical studies of technological innovations based on patent data have shown that the conditions of home countries influence levels and trends of R&D activities, and technological innovations among national firms. The technological activities of global corporations are firmly rooted in home countries, as indicated by the location and nature of R&D activities. These firms derive their firm-specific technological advantages from home country institutional environments (Cantwell, 1989; 1995; Lundvall, 1992; Patel, 1995).

Based on patenting records of some 686 of the world's largest firms from 1981 to 1986, Patel and Pavitt (1991: 11) concluded that 'in spite of

Table 1.4 The embeddedness of business firms in their national institutional and ideological structures

	United States	Germany	Japan	Ethnic Chinese
Institutional Structures				
1. Political institutions	• liberal democracy • divided government • highly organised interest groups	• social democracy • weak bureaucracy • corporatist organisational legacy	• developmental democracy • strong bureaucracy • 'reciprocal consent' between state and firms	• often hostile or unfavourable host country environment • strong centralisation tradition in China • merchant insecurity
2. Economic institutions	• decentralised, open markets • unconcentrated, fluid capital markets • anti-trust tradition	• organised markets • tiers of firms • bank-centred capital markets • universal banks • certain cartelised markets	• guided, bifurcated, difficult to penetrate markets • bank-centred capital markets • tight business networks/cartels in declining industries	• family-based corporate organisation • networks of small and medium firms • strong inter-personal relationships and business networks
3. Dominant economic ideology	• free enterprise liberalism	• social partnership	• technonationalism	• familialism
TNC Structures and Strategies				
1. Direct investment	• extensive inward and outward	• selective/outward orientation	• extensive outward • limited competition from inward	• extensive outward
2. Intra-firm trade	• moderate	• higher	• very high	• moderate
3. R&D	• fluctuating and diversified • innovation oriented	• narrow base/process, diffusion orientation	• high, steady growth • high-tech and process orientation	• low, but recent growth • product adaptation • customer-based innovation

4. Corporate governance	• short-term shareholding • managers highly constrained by capital markets • risk-seeking, financial-centred strategies	• managerial autonomy except during crises • no take-over risk • conservative, long-term strategies	• stable shareholders • network-constrained managers • take-over risk only within network/aggressive market share-centred strategies	• long-term shareholding • control within family members • constrained by family ideology • more reliance on 'network capital'
5. Corporate financing	• diversified, global funding • highly price sensitive	• concentrated, regional funding • limited price sensitivity	• concentrated, national funding • low price sensitivity	• diversified, network funding • high price sensitivity

Sources: Based on Pauly and Reich (1997: Tables 1 and 4); Yeung (1997a; 1997b; 1998b).

considerable variations amongst the large firms based in different countries, their technological activities remained far from globalised'. Moreover, entrepreneurs in highly competitive industries and markets are more prone to risk-taking behaviour because of perceived payoffs from market-driven processes (see Baumol, 1993). In countries with highly regulated markets and strong state ownership of firms and industries, however, private entrepreneurship tends to be inhibited and the formation of business establishments tends to occur in sectors and industries in which there is least state involvement. In other words, private entrepreneurship serves as 'gap-filler' to improve the overall efficiency of the economy. This is very much an argument in support of Leibenstein's (1966) X-efficiency theory of entrepreneurship (see also Landa, 1991).

In terms of business co-ordination, firms in competitive market economies are more likely to engage in arm's-length transactions and to hold adversarial relationships with customers and suppliers. This is a story well told in theoretical terms by transaction costs economics (Williamson, 1975; 1985). It is interesting, however, that there are still substantial variations in these business co-ordination and control mechanisms among competitive economies in the world today (Hamilton and Feenstra, 1995; Biggart and Guillén, 1999; Feenstra et al., 1999). In countries where ownership and control of firms are more interconnected, firms co-operate as well as compete, and where they are able to share risks with financial partners, it becomes highly difficult and problematic to define precisely the boundaries of firms (hierarchies) and markets. This apparently disorganised structuring of markets and hierarchies (e.g. in Continental Europe) contrasts sharply with their institutional counterparts from the Anglo-American world (Whitley, 1999). In economies that are significantly dominated by state involvement, business co-ordination and control tend to evolve in the forms of business groups, conglomerates, and networks (see Chapter 2). These organisational forms and processes are characterised by co-operative relationships with customers and suppliers based on trust and social ties.

Third, different configurations of home country institutional arrangements have important implications for *intra-firm management* and/or *entrepreneurial processes*. The institutionalisation of capital markets in the USA, for example, has put tremendous pressures on top management to seek short-term returns and to practise financial-centred corporate strategies. Under this condition of capital market discipline, strategic management tends to be much tighter in resource allocation within the firm, and long-term investment in productive and/or innovative activities may be discouraged. Financial management becomes the primary instrument of intra-firm management among most American companies. In contrast, in countries practising 'co-operative capitalism', stable and enduring relationships between banks, firms, and the state tend to encourage strategic behaviour and long-term investments by corporate managers. More resources can be devoted to those activities that promise to generate future returns. Intra-firm management is less based on financial returns *per se* and more managerial autonomy is granted except during financial or other crises.

Fourth, enduring patterns of institutional arrangements in specific countries may shape *work and employment relations* (capital–labour relations) that have serious implications for entrepreneurship. Sociological models of ethnic entrepreneurship (misfit and disadvantage models) are highly powerful in explaining the structural outcome of entrepreneurial activities among ethnic immigrants and groups in the host countries. Work and employment relations here refer to the extent and mode of owner control, the delegation of work control to skilled workers, and the location of organisational segmentation boundaries (Whitley, 1999). In the case of Britain, this segmentation primarily occurs between generalist top managers and managerial specialists, as well as between skilled maintenance workers and unskilled operatives (Braverman, 1974; Thompson, 1989). In the USA, it remains concentrated between college-educated managers and manual workers. In Japan, it occurs between male, core employees and female, temporary workers as well as between large firms and their subcontractors. In addition, the extent of organisational integration of employees and long-term interdependence between employers and employees can explain variations in private and corporate entrepreneurship and business culture (see Chang and Kozul-Wright, 1994; Tiessen, 1997; Daly, 1998).

An Institutional Analysis of the Emergence of Transnational Entrepreneurship

Business systems are difficult to reconfigure unless there are significant changes in the dominant institutions on which these business systems are built (Whitley, 1994; 1998; 1999). How then can entrepreneurship emerge from these institutional arrangements? How do these structures provide budding entrepreneurs with the endowments and/or resources that form the initial foundation on which entrepreneurial activities are based? There are clearly different levels of institutional structuring of entrepreneurship. Whereas *national* institutional structures tend to explain the challenges of international business to transnational entrepreneurs, *cross-national* institutional structures (e.g. transnational business networks) explain the dynamics and practice of transnational entrepreneurship. These important theoretical questions are addressed by an institutional analysis of the emergence of transnational entrepreneurship in this and the next subsections.

Whereas this section examines national institutional structures and their influence on domestic entrepreneurship, the next section examines the institutionalisation of transnational entrepreneurship through the enrolment of entrepreneurs into transnational institutional structures.

In Figure 1.1, I have mapped out the institutional structuring of entrepreneurship in specific national business systems. As explained earlier, an entrepreneur must be endowed with at least some resources to be able to act *differently* in the competitive marketplace. These entrepreneurial endowments and resources are often nationally based in that they are embedded in national business systems and are structured by pre-existing institutional arrangements. This geographical specificity of entrepreneurial endowments and resources explains why some countries tend to produce more entrepreneurs and entrepreneurial activities.[9] But then why are some entrepreneurs from the same sectors and same home countries more actively and successfully engaged in international business activities than others? I will explain this variation in the institutionalisation of transnational entrepreneurship in the next section. As a prelude, such a difference among domestic entrepreneurs from the same sectors and same home countries can be explained by their differential access to transnational institutional structures. How then do individual entrepreneurs from the home countries benefit from their entrepreneurial endowments and resources? Figure 1.1 points out that these endowments can be divided into at least five dimensions: (1) information asymmetry; (2) risks and opportunities; (3) finance and capital; (4) experience in business and/or management; and (5) relationships with customers and/or suppliers.

Information asymmetry is one of the most important entrepreneurial endowments enjoyed by emerging entrepreneurs. In a world of perfect information and rationality of economic action, entrepreneurship simply does not exist because returns to entrepreneurial activities are not sufficient to warrant such activities. If we take Casson's (1982) definition of the entrepreneur as a specialist in taking judgmental decisions in resource allocation, then information asymmetry is a precondition for such an entrepreneur to exist and to make supernormal profit. Why then does such a situation of information asymmetry arise? From the transaction costs economics perspective (see Williamson, 1975; 1985), there are two conditions leading to information asymmetry. The first condition is bounded rationality: '[t]he capacity of the human mind for formulating and solving complex problems is very small compared with the size of the problems whose solution is required for objectively rational behavior in the real world' (Simon, 1957: 198; emphasis omitted). Economic actors have cognitive or perceptual limitations and therefore cannot have perfect rationality as assumed in neoclassical economics. Their economic actions are

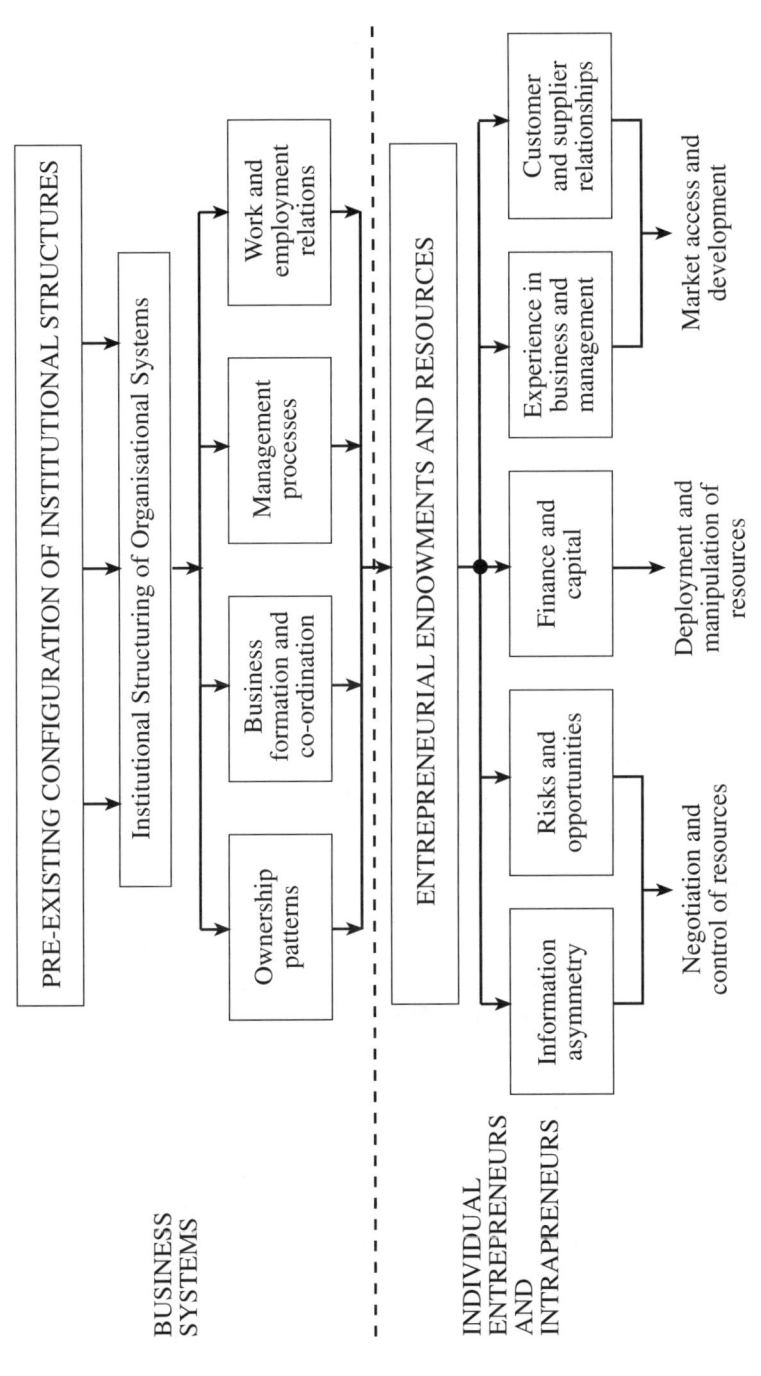

Figure 1.1   The institutional structuring of entrepreneurship in specific national business systems

'*intendedly* rational, but only *limitedly* so' (Simon, 1961: xxiv; original emphasis). Higher transaction costs must be borne in discovering information and negotiating contracts.

The second behavioural factor is information impactedness. In a contract, the distribution of information is never equal in both parties. This asymmetrical distribution of information among the exchanging parties is called information impactedness. Information impactedness is particularly acute when the question of buyer uncertainty arises. Buyer uncertainty refers to the situation in which the goods or services exchanged are intangible so that only the producer (and seller) has access to the information on the quality and other specific attributes of the goods and services. The buyer therefore has to face serious uncertainty with regard to the quality and attributes of the goods and/or services. Information impactedness, accompanied by buyer uncertainty, may cause substantial transaction costs in negotiating and enforcing contracts.

Taken together, certain institutional structures tend to increase information asymmetry. This is a point well recognised by institutional economists and will not be repeated here. It is sufficient to note that in countries with high state control and intensive intra-business group transactions, such information asymmetry is most likely to be high (see Figure 1.1). What then does this high information asymmetry contribute to entrepreneurial activities? I am not concerned here with transaction costs and alternative governance structures between markets and hierarchies. This is the analytical focus of transaction costs economics that seeks to explain 'the comparative costs of planning, adopting, and monitoring task completion under alternative governance structures' (Williamson, 1985: 2; emphasis omitted). Rather, I am concerned with how such information asymmetry stimulates or inhibits entrepreneurial activities. In institutional economics, an entrepreneur is responsible for choosing institutional arrangements and subsequently determining the boundaries of the firm. The *raison d'être* of the entrepreneur is not ownership, but negotiation and control (Casson, 1985: 173).

With hindsight and empirical evidence (see Chapters 4 and 5), it is possible to argue that high information asymmetry tends to encourage social actors who have access to information, to be entrepreneurial and to capitalise on this information. The control of such resources as information is important because it defines directly who can be an entrepreneur. This explains why entrepreneurship continues to thrive under imperfect market conditions and restrictive institutional contexts. In these institutional contexts, those entrepreneurs endowed with specific information are most likely to engage in entrepreneurial activities. For example, a former employee of a large business conglomerate that has business contracts with the state may get hold of an important piece of information through his/her interaction with state officials (e.g. a potential procurement order). This employee may quit the salaried job and set up his/her own business to capitalise on that piece of actor-specific information. Of course, whether he/she will eventually become an entrepreneur depends on a number of other factors. But the initial information provides an important precondition for the entrepreneurial activity to take place.

Obviously, countries with high information asymmetry tend to pose greater *business risks and opportunities* as well, precisely because not every actor is aware of such information and business opportunities. Risks and business opportunities are entrepreneurial endowments because they directly shape the tendencies for social actors to engage in entrepreneurial activities. We can infer from an institutional context the nature of risks and business opportunities for entrepreneurial activities. Such business risks and opportunities tend to be significantly lower in a business system that has highly stable ownership patterns and work/employment relations (see Figure 1.1). First, stable ownership patterns imply that takeover risk is low and market domination by large firms tends to endure. There is therefore little scope for further entrepreneurial activities to fill market niches – a situation of market saturation. Second, stable work and employment relations further discourage entrepreneurial activities as employees are well paid and lack strong incentives to seek self-employment outside the corporate sector. Japan is an example of this phenomenon of employment-stifled entrepreneurship. One may argue, however, that it may well be the lack of entrepreneurship that explains stable ownership and employment relations in some countries. This is clearly not a chicken-and-egg question because if one follows the logic of my institutional arguments, then entrepreneurship has to be an *outcome* of institutional rigidities and inflexibilities, not the other way round (see an empirical discussion of Singapore in Chapter 2).

On the other hand, some countries or regions have highly unstable ownership and employment patterns institutionalised by the lack of co-operation between financiers and industries, and the lack of strong industry associations and trade unions. Risks and opportunities are correspondingly much higher in these institutional contexts. They tend to encourage entrepreneurship because of greater potential payoffs to engaging in entrepreneurial activities. The Silicon Valley phenomenon in California exemplifies this phenomenon of high risks and high return in a rather unique historical and institutional context (Scott, 1988; 1998; Saxenian, 1994; Storper, 1997; Cooke and Morgan, 1998). Its historical context as an R&D centre for the US Department of Defense serves to facilitate an agglomeration of highly skilled technologists. Its institutional context in proximity to centres of learning within California (the location of Stanford and Berkeley nearby) also enhances its entrepreneurial culture.

Granted institutional contexts of information asymmetry and high risks, it still does not necessarily mean that entrepreneurship will emerge. For entrepreneurship to thrive in these contexts, two other sources of entrepreneurial endowments are required. The first endowment is *finance and capital*. Although both Schumpeter (1934) and Casson (1985) argued that the *raison d'être* of the entrepreneur is not ownership, the realisation of entrepreneurial profits requires significant financial and capital support. This is particularly the case in the early stages of the entrepreneurial process. Having gained access to a particular piece of information and learnt the potential payoff of such a high-risk venture, an entrepreneur needs finance and capital to start the venture. In a corporate setting, an intrapreneur needs financial support from top management to put the initial entrepreneurial ideas into practice. The issue here is that certain institutional contexts tend to engender better access to finance and capital. They are therefore more favourable to entrepreneurship. In a business system with a well-developed capital market in favour of business start-ups and venture capital, entrepreneurship tends to flourish. The USA is a good example of a well-established capital market with different tiers of stock markets and venture capitalists.

In business systems with poorly-developed capital markets, entrepreneurship may still thrive if other sources of finance and capital are available and substitute for the lack of well-developed capital markets. This is particularly a problem for developing countries that exhibit high information asymmetry and high risks of business venturing. How then do we explain the fact that entrepreneurship tends to be stronger in certain developing countries? One explanation rests with the availability of finance and capital outside what we normally define as capital markets in these developing countries. In particular, studies of ethnic entrepreneurship inform us that social networks serve as an important source of finance and capital for prospective entrepreneurs who pool together these resources from their social and family ties (see also Birley, 1985; Nafziger, 1986; Hamilton, 1991; Yeung, 1998a). The existence of this 'network capital' is an important substitute for well-developed capital markets to enhance entrepreneurial activities. Its existence can be explained by the peculiar institutional structures in some of these developing countries in which family businesses may be the dominant form of business formation and co-ordination mechanism (see Figure 1.1). The management process in these family businesses facilitates the pooling together of resources within the 'family'.

Another important entrepreneurial endowment is *experience in business*. Contrary to McClelland's (1961) claims, entrepreneurship is not born with an entrepreneur, nor can it be taught. It must be learnt through experience. Prior experience in business is a critical determinant of the capabilities of an entrepreneur to capitalise on information asymmetry and to make appropriate judgmental decisions (see Figure 1.1). As explained earlier, these decision-making capabilities are an important aspect of defining a transnational entrepreneur. The acquisition of experience and learning in different business systems is related to several institutional structures: dependence on foreign firms, centralised bureaucratic management, the role of education in national development, and so on. In a business system dominated largely by foreign firm presence (see DiConti, 1992), entrepreneurial training is still possible if appropriate institutional structures are in place. Amin and Thrift (1994: 15) defined this availability of appropriate institutional structures as 'institutional thickness', which refers to 'the combination of actors including inter-institutional interaction and synergy, collective representation by many bodies, a common industrial purpose, and shared cultural norms and values'. Institutional thickness determines the success of specific places/regions in the global economy because global processes can be 'localised' in some places, to become the basis for self-sustaining growth at the local level. In general, foreign firms may transfer knowledge and skills to local managers. They may also facilitate local entrepreneurship through spin-off subsidiaries and development of supplier linkages (see more below).

On the other hand, entrepreneurial experience can be stifled in an institutional context characterised by high levels of centralised and bureaucratic management process. As explained earlier, this intra-firm management pattern tends to dominate in business systems that have well-established corporate procedures and management practices. Once these corporate norms and management philosophies are in place, they are difficult either to change or to transform. This management rigidity in highly centralised and bureaucratic firms tends to inhibit entrepreneurship both within and outside the firm. As managers are given little autonomy or mandates to develop specific business units, they often feel frustrated and unable to contribute to an entrepreneurial spirit in the firm. If they leave the firm to start their own businesses, they tend to lack entrepreneurial experience, particularly in the areas of strategic deployment of endowments and resources.

The role of education in national development is also important in shaping entrepreneurial experience. Though entrepreneurship cannot really be taught in courses, (continuous) education does play a fairly important role in developing certain analytical and, perhaps, decision-making skills amongst students. Coupled with real life experience in strategic management, these students are in a better position to explore and exploit opportunities, and to tap into resource endowments. National educational curricula, however, differ significantly across countries. Some curricula are driven by the underlying political ideologies of the state and are therefore unfavourable to promoting entrepreneurship (e.g. in Communist countries). Other curricula encourage freethinking and critical analytical skills among students. These curricula tend to favour the development of entrepreneurial tendencies.

The above four dimensions of endowments provide an institutional foundation for entrepreneurship to emerge in specific business systems. As shown in Figure 1.1, individual entrepreneurs may be endowed with information and opportunity, but they also need capital and knowledge to deploy these endowments to maximise their entrepreneurial profits. As these entrepreneurs enter into the market process, typically through establishing business ventures, they are confronted with the reality of dealing with customers and suppliers. Their *relationships with customers and suppliers* therefore play a fairly important role in determining their entrepreneurial outcomes. As different institutional contexts tend to favour different forms of such relationships (i.e. co-operative vs. competitive), it becomes important to understand how these different forms of relationships with customers and suppliers shape entrepreneurial outcomes (see also Tomer, 1998a; 1998b). In co-operative capitalism, the institutional structures are arranged in such a way that firms do not compete against each other directly. Rather, their embedded networks are in direct competition. Such is the experience of Japanese *keiretsu* and Korean *chaebol* (Yeung, 1999a; 2000a; 2000b).

Market access may pose a serious challenge to potential entrepreneurs because of guided, bifurcated, and difficult-to-penetrate networks. An entrepreneur who is able to establish strong and trustworthy relationships with customers and suppliers is more likely to succeed in such an institutional context. This is because inter-firm relations in these networks are governed more by quality and trust than by prices *per se*. The existence of trust is also very important in a network of business relationship because trust 'is pivotal to the economy, and not merely to social relations' (Etzioni, 1988: 7). Trust can be defined as some sort of mutual understanding through which interacting parties in a group are expected to avoid opportunism and to promote welfare among members of the group/network. It allows better information flows to enhance entrepreneurial activities. Trust is constitutive of social life because disputes and clashes can be effectively resolved through such shared understandings. Trust promotes co-operative relationships at all levels (Sabel, 1993; Smith et al., 1995; Uzzi, 1997; 1999). It is not subject to economic cost and benefit analysis (cf. Williamson, 1985; 1993; Nooteboom, 1996; 1999). Gulati (1995; 1998) and Gulati and Gargiulo (1999) found that firms with prior ties with one another do not normally enter into equity-based alliances because they trust each other and such trust minimises the possibility of opportunistic behaviour on which transaction costs arguments rest. Trust relations can therefore substitute for hierarchical contracts based on equity ownership in many exchanges and serve as an alternative control mechanism. Entrepreneurship can thrive on trusting relationships with customers and suppliers.

The Institutionalisation of Transnational Entrepreneurship

If an entrepreneur is endowed with all of the above dimensions of entrepreneurial resources and is capable of deploying them for entrepreneurial gain in a particular institutional context, does it necessarily mean that he or she is able to engage successfully in international business activities? A simple answer from my institutional perspective is negative, because of different home and host country institutional contexts in such aspects as the role of the state, financial systems, skill development and control systems, and trust and authority systems. This raises a fundamental theoretical question. Though pre-existing national institutional configurations structure the nature and processes of entrepreneurship domestically, these institutional arrangements are unable to determine the success of domestic entrepreneurs in their internationalisation processes. Here lies the basic difference between my institutional perspective and existing theories of international entrepreneurship (e.g. Casson, 1985; 1990b; McDougall et al., 1994; Scaperlanda, 1994; Birkinshaw, 1997; Moon and Peery, 1997). Most of these theories explain the modes and market functions of internationalisation among entrepreneurs. They do not explain why only some domestic entrepreneurs internationalise and become successful transnational entrepreneurs. To answer this question, we have to examine the institutionalisation of transnational entrepreneurship through enrolment of these transnational entrepreneurs into cross-border institutional structures. This enrolment serves to help transnational entrepreneurs to build complex and innovative institutional arrangements at the organisational level to overcome inherent cross-national institutional differences and hence their difficulties in engaging in cross-border business activities.[10] These organisational arrangements, embedded in different institutional contexts in home and host countries, are relatively enduring and influential over time, resulting in significant first-mover advantages linked to these transnational entrepreneurs and intrapreneurs. In other words, the enrolment of entrepreneurs in transnational institutional structures is a necessary precondition for them to operate across borders.

Gradual transformations in national institutions and business systems can occur through the two-way enrolment and enticement of entrepreneurs into transnational actor networks at different spatial scales (see Yeung, 2000b). Institutional change is made possible when these entrepreneurs are capable of tapping into the knowledge structures and resources in transnational actor networks. This transnational access to knowledge and resource structures allows specific domestic entrepreneurs to become transnational entrepreneurs through taking up international business activities. In this sense, cross-border actor networks serve as strategic resources to enable transnational entrepreneurship.[11] Using case studies, for example, McDougall et al. (1994) found that some entrepreneurs of international new ventures are more alert to the possibilities of combining resources from different national markets and have access to 'proprietary networks' as their key competitive advantage.

What then is the geographical scale and scope of transnational entrepreneurs and their actor networks? As shown in Figure 1.2, there are at least three types of actor networks among transnational entrepreneurs: global networks, national networks, and national/international networks. For heuristic purposes, each bounded circle in Figure 1.2 represents a relatively distinct business system and each point in these circles represents an actor (i.e. a transnational entrepreneur). Through linkages developed by globalisation tendencies (see below), these actors in different business systems are enrolled into actor networks at different spatial scales and complexity. Actor A, for example, is enrolled into global networks directly with actors in all other business systems and indirectly with actors in two business systems via actor D. Its network relationship with actor D is at the national level with a primary aim to reach out to actor D's global networks. This relationship is known as national/international actor networks. Actor A represents the most globalised actor in Figure 1.2; the same applies to its business system, which bears a mixture of characteristics from different business systems. Actor B (e.g. a local retailer), however, is primarily enrolled into national actor networks and remains very much embedded in national business systems. On the other hand, actor C is enrolled exclusively into global networks (e.g. an export-oriented manufacturer serving the global market). Figure 1.2 is a much-simplified construction of the complex nature and characteristics of transnational entrepreneurship. But it does demonstrate a very important point: that the enrolment of transnational entrepreneurs into actor networks at different spatial scales (represented by various links between actors) is capable of effecting dynamic changes to existing nationally-based business systems. This process helps to institutionalise transnational entrepreneurship among a specific group of domestic entrepreneurs who have access to these actor networks.

How then, specifically, are transnational entrepreneurs enrolled into and influenced by actor networks elsewhere? There are at least three interrelated mechanisms through which this enrolment into transnational actor networks is made possible: (1) engaging with global managers and financiers in

An institutional perspective on entrepreneurship in international business 35

THE GLOBAL ECONOMY

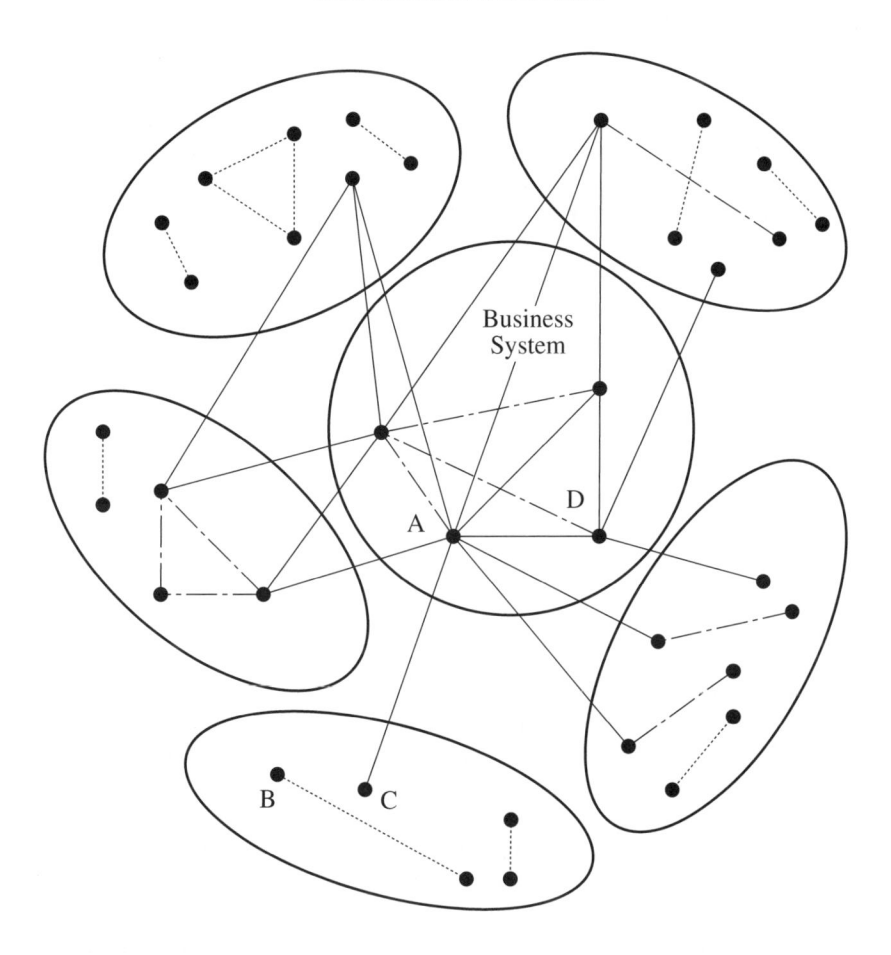

●————● global networks
●— - —● national/international networks
●··········● national networks

Figure 1.2 Transnational entrepreneurs and actor networks at different spatial scales

international business and finance; (2) participating in international media and research on business activities; and (3) gathering knowledge and experience through international educational institutions. First, though Whitley (1994; 1998) argued that the consequences of globalisation for national business systems and firms are limited, it is by no means clear that these limited effects of globalisation do not represent a long-term process of changing dynamics of these business systems. In particular, the two-way globalisation of firms between countries and regions implies that key actors in one business system are compelled to learn new management and business practices from their competitors, suppliers, customers, and so on. At the same time, these actors need to undo some of their previous learning and practices in order to compete effectively against foreign competitors abroad as well as on their home turf. It is true that this process of business contacts between East and West occurred long ago (e.g. during Meiji Japan in the mid-nineteenth century; see Westney, 1987; Hamilton, 1997), but the sheer scale, scope, and speed of these cross-border contacts today make them highly influential in the changing dynamics of national business systems.

This process of *organisational learning through international business and international finance* occurs in several ways. For example, domestic entrepreneurs may appoint actors from other business systems to manage their domestic and foreign operations. These global managers are often endowed with significant experience in managing transnational operations in national economies with distinctive business systems. Their involvement in firms embedded in different national business systems may reshape the norms and practices in these organisations (see Reich, 1991 for the case of Sony; Mair, 1994 for the case of Honda). Domestic entrepreneurs may also pick up organisational knowledge and practices in host countries through cross-border operations (see Mathews and Snow, 1998 for the case of Acer from Taiwan). These knowledge and practices can originate from their intensive interaction with customers and suppliers in the host countries or from their previous employment in foreign firms. Actor networks are formed between these transnational entrepreneurs and their customers, suppliers, and competitors on a global scale, facilitating inter-personal information and knowledge flows and organisational adaptation. For example, Tsang (1999a; 1999b) examined the international human resource management practices of Singaporean companies in China and found that expatriation has an important function of knowledge transfer and training.

On the other hand, actor networks in international finance represent one of the most influential mechanisms for effecting dynamic changes in national business systems. This is because, for those domestic entrepreneurs in search of financial resources from outside their home countries and/or regions, it is important to secure the consent and recognition of global financiers for good governance and return to investments. In other words, these domestic entrepreneurs are increasingly influenced, if not governed, by the norms and rules of the global financial markets. These global financiers are leading bankers, fund managers and brokers. They are often based in major global cities that serve as command centres of global investments (Sassen, 1991). The successful enrolment of domestic entrepreneurs into these global financial actor networks is imperative in an era of intensified competition, greater financial requirements for expansion and investments, and higher risks associated with excessive reliance on domestic finance. To ensure that global financial elites are comfortable with their financial positions and obligations, domestic entrepreneurs are required to follow certain accounting standards and business norms in global capital markets. This necessity for securing global finance provides a key force to effect dynamic changes in home country business systems (see below).

Second, this quest for global finance requires domestic entrepreneurs to come to terms with actors in *international media and research on business activities*. This is because today's global financial system is increasingly characterised by a broader array of actors than just bankers and financiers. As Thrift and Leyshon (1994: 301; emphasis added) argued, 'money, the international financial system, and international financial centres' have simply '"detraditionalized" over the last 30 years or so . . . because of the breakdown of state authority and its replacement by *more diffuse* sources of governance'. Such detraditionalisation is accentuated by the enormous task of understanding, managing and communicating global economic change in a more reflexive manner. This is a style of understanding, managing and communicating that draws a broader array of *actors* into playing a significant (albeit variable) role in materially and discursively constructing the multiple economic systems that make up the global economy (Thrift, 1996; Hollingsworth, 1998). Actors in international media and research houses play an increasingly important role, reflexively producing texts and information about national business systems that can significantly hinder or facilitate their actors' access to global finance.

For example, top international financial newspapers (e.g. *The Financial Times*), magazines (e.g. *Fortune*) and media (e.g. CNN and CNBC), credit-rating agencies (e.g. Standard and Poor's), stockbroking firms and other research houses (e.g. Morgan Stanley) regularly produce reports on specific national entrepreneurs and firms (and, sometimes, national economies). The 'consumers' of these texts are key actors in the global financial industry and international business, including investment bankers, fund managers, brokers and so on. The successful enticement of these global actors into favourable assessments of domestic entrepreneurs and firms requires these actors to enrol themselves into global actor networks in international media and research activities (see Olds and Yeung, 1999 for the case of Cheung Kong Holdings and Hopewell Holdings from Hong Kong). Not only are domestic entrepreneurs participating in producing such texts (and countertexts) through setting up their own credit-rating firms, stockbroking houses, and so on, some of them are also opening their doors to welcome global actors to 'inspect' their operations. Such processes of enrolment and enticement have major implications for the changing norms and practices of these entrepreneurs and their firms and, perhaps eventually, their national business systems.

Third, a growing trend among today's entrepreneurs is that most if not all of them have spent part of their educational life in institutions located abroad (e.g. in North America, Western Europe, and Australia). Most significantly, the *globalisation of business knowledge* is linked to the emergence and, perhaps, domination of top business schools located in North America and Western Europe (see Thrift, 1998; 1999; Wenger, 1998; 2000). Entrepreneurs in Asian family businesses, for example, now face the challenge of professionalising their management and business practices. Other entrepreneurs in Asia's non-family businesses are also active in organisational re-engineering and management restructuring to prepare for global competition. These processes of professionalisation are driven both by internal and external factors. Internally, more patriarchs in family firms have allowed their heir-apparent to be educated in top business schools abroad. Exposed to professional management training in these business schools, the eventual return of these successors to family businesses contributes to the changing dynamics of national business systems in two ways. On the one hand, personal contacts and relationships developed by these successors abroad potentially widen the social and geographic scope of their nationally- or ethnically-based business networks when external members are 'brought' or socialised into these formerly exclusive business networks. Key domestic entrepreneurs thus not only are enrolled into global financial actor networks with their friends and acquaintances from business schools, but also sometimes actively entice these actors into their own networks in the home countries and/or regions. This process of enrolment and enticement implies that the concept of exclusive national business networks should be broadened to a larger degree to include non-family and non-Asian members (see Mitchell, 1995 and Olds, 1998; 2001 for the case of a Chinese business network in Vancouver). On the other hand, the return of a professionally-trained family heir represents an important step towards the professionalisation of domestic family business. When the heir eventually takes over the family business, he/she tends to adopt a much more open view towards the involvement of professionals in the management of the family firm.[12]

Enrolling into transnational actor networks enables a domestic entrepreneur to control resources, to exercise strategic management, and to create and exploit opportunities in different countries. These complex and innovative institutional arrangements at the organisational level also enable transnational entrepreneurs to overcome inherent cross-national institutional differences and therefore their difficulties in engaging in cross-border business activities. In the first place, the enrolment of transnational entrepreneurs in global financial actor networks is critical to gaining access to global capital markets to finance cross-border operations. As international business activities incur significant risks by virtue of the disadvantage of being 'foreign' or 'outsiders' (Hymer, 1976; Hu, 1995), having access to global capital markets facilitates the funding of these cross-border operations and thereby the likelihood of their successful completion. Other resources that transnational entrepreneurs can obtain from their enrolment into cross-border actor networks include information about business risks and opportunities, and trustworthy joint venture partners or allies in the host countries.

Moreover, a transnational entrepreneur can gain significant international business knowledge and experience from his/her enrolment into actor networks elsewhere. This knowledge and experience can greatly facilitate the entrepreneur's strategic decision-making and management capabilities that define the successful entry and subsequent integration of cross-border operations. A transnational entrepreneur embedded in very strong actor networks in the host countries is likely to perform better than another entrepreneur from the same home country without such strong networks. Similarly, the same well-connected transnational entrepreneur is more likely to have access to better business opportunities and to be able to exploit these opportunities. The enrolment into actor networks at different spatial scales, therefore, is a key mechanism for explaining why and how some transnational entrepreneurs choose to operate in foreign markets, and why some entrepreneurs are more successful than others in engaging in international business activities. It also institutionalises the processes of transnational entrepreneurship by providing an international business dimension to such entrepreneurial processes. How then do these theoretical ideas and concepts inform my comparative study of transnational entrepreneurship in Hong Kong and Singapore?

Key Analytical Questions in this Book and Its Potential Contributions

Building upon an institutional analysis of entrepreneurship in international business, this book focuses on *the interaction between transnational entrepreneurs and their embedded structures of social and institutional relations in home and host countries*. Cross-border operations are seen as an outcome of this interaction between agency and structure – a process of structuration. Three key questions form the analytical backbone of this book:

(1) Why do some entrepreneurs choose to operate in foreign markets, irrespective of whether they are in the same industries or home countries?

This analytical question is important because certain home country institutional contexts tend to engender international business activities by transnational entrepreneurs. Whereas they are able to explain why some *firms* go international (e.g. transaction costs economising or exploitation of firm-specific resources, and so on), international business theories are unable to explain why some entrepreneurs from some industries or home countries tend to go international. This is because transnational entrepreneurship, as defined above, goes beyond economic analysis. At the *individual* level, transnational entrepreneurs do not necessarily act according to predictions in economic models of entrepreneurship. It should be noted, however, that these economic models are not developed to explain individual entrepreneurial behaviour anyway. Rather, their scale of analysis rests upon the entrepreneurial firm or entrepreneurship in the economy as a whole. One of the key implications of the institutional perspective developed earlier is that it is possible to understand how different configurations of institutional structures can enhance or discourage transnational entrepreneurship. By understanding these institutional configurations, we are able to explain better international business behaviour of transnational entrepreneurs.

(2) How do some entrepreneurs operate abroad?

This question certainly falls outside the analytical orbit of economic theories of entrepreneurship. Only management theories have accumulated sufficient analytical lenses to resolve the mystery of the internationalisation process. I argue, however, that although they are able to explain well the internationalisation processes of the firm (e.g. Johanson and Vahlne, 1977; Buckley and Ghauri, 1993; Björkman and Forsgren, 1997), international business theories are unable to explain the processes of internationalisation by specific transnational entrepreneurs, which are better explained by organisational analysis. To a large extent, this overt focus on firm-level processes in international business studies reflects their methodological bias towards large-scale data collection and analysis, and the influence on them of economic models of the firm. Organisation studies, on the other hand, sometimes pay serious attention to the role of social actors in organisational processes. This may be explained by the strong presence of sociological analysis in organisation studies. This book takes an actor-oriented scale of analysis and seeks to understand and explain how transnational entrepreneurs establish, integrate, and sustain their operations in different host countries.

(3) Why are some entrepreneurs more successful than others in international business?

After understanding why and how some entrepreneurs operate abroad in foreign markets, it is important to differentiate those enterpreneurs who eventually become transnational entrepreneurs through successful establishment and sustainable operations. Again, international business theories are able to explain the performance of specific firms in their internationalisation processes, not their entrepreneurs. Such explanations need to draw upon insights from entrepreneurship studies, strategic management, and institutional analysis. This last analytical question is crucial in defining which people actually become transnational entrepreneurs and the nature of their transnational entrepreneurship. By identifying those more successful entrepreneurs, we are able to isolate a specific group of transnational entrepreneurs and to explain why they are more successful than other domestic entrepreneurs.

How then does my study of transnational entrepreneurship contribute to new horizons in international business studies? One may even ask how is this institutional perspective different from existing theories in entrepreneurship and international business studies? Does it offer any new insights into existing theories of entrepreneurial behaviour and international business activities? First, the theoretical impasse between entrepreneurship and international business studies is rather deep-seated. This book aims to circumvent this impasse by *integrating concepts* from both disparate areas of study. I believe this integration is important because entrepreneurship studies and international business studies have gone their separate ways as a consequence of different theoretical influences (e.g. the social sciences in entrepreneurship studies vs. economics in international business studies) and methodological practices (e.g. qualitative case studies in entrepreneurship studies vs. quantitative statistical analysis in international business studies).

Second, this book aims to make a modest contribution to international business studies by developing an *institutional perspective* on entrepreneurship in international business and by examining how this perspective can be applied to an empirical investigation of transnational corporations. This institutional perspective is novel in at least two ways: (1) an analysis of structuration between agency and structure and (2) comparative and multi-country studies. The need for an analysis of the interaction between transnational entrepreneurs and their institutional contexts has been explained above. It suffices to say that most entrepreneurship and international business studies do not take into account explicitly the institutional contexts of entrepreneurial behaviour and/or processes when they operate across borders. Even fewer of them consider cross-border operations as a consequence of the interaction between transnational entrepreneurs and their structures of social and institutional relations. Furthermore, in order to shed light on how different configurations of institutional structures in home countries shape the entrepreneurial tendencies of transnational entrepreneurs, we need *comparative studies* of transnational entrepreneurship in different home countries. This is precisely one of the empirical contributions of this book. I have chosen two Asian economies (Hong Kong and Singapore) with very similar historical background and economic development, but very different structures of social and institutional relations. As my empirical analysis in Chapters 2 to 5 will show, transnational entrepreneurship in these two city-states exhibits very different nature, attributes, and trajectories. Similarly, transnational entrepreneurs from these two economies have also significantly different patterns of internationalisation.

A COMPARATIVE STUDY OF TRANSNATIONAL ENTREPRENEURSHIP IN HONG KONG AND SINGAPORE

Before ending this chapter with an outline of the entire book, it is appropriate to introduce the comparative study of transnational entrepreneurship in Hong Kong and Singapore that provides its empirical basis (see Figure 1.3). Two empirical studies of transnational operations of Hong Kong and Singaporean firms were conducted in sequence. The first study on Hong Kong firms was conducted during 1994 and 1995 (see Yeung, 1995; 1998a). The earlier study examined the peculiar role of entrepreneurship in Hong Kong, given the virtual absence of state involvement in Hong Kong's outward investment. This theoretical and empirical work has direct relevance to the second study in which the experience of Singaporean TNCs serves as an interesting case study for comparison. The second study on Singaporean firms was conducted between 1997 and 1999 (see Yeung, 1999b). Both empirical studies aimed to examine the role of entrepreneurship in the internationalisation of transnational corporations from city-

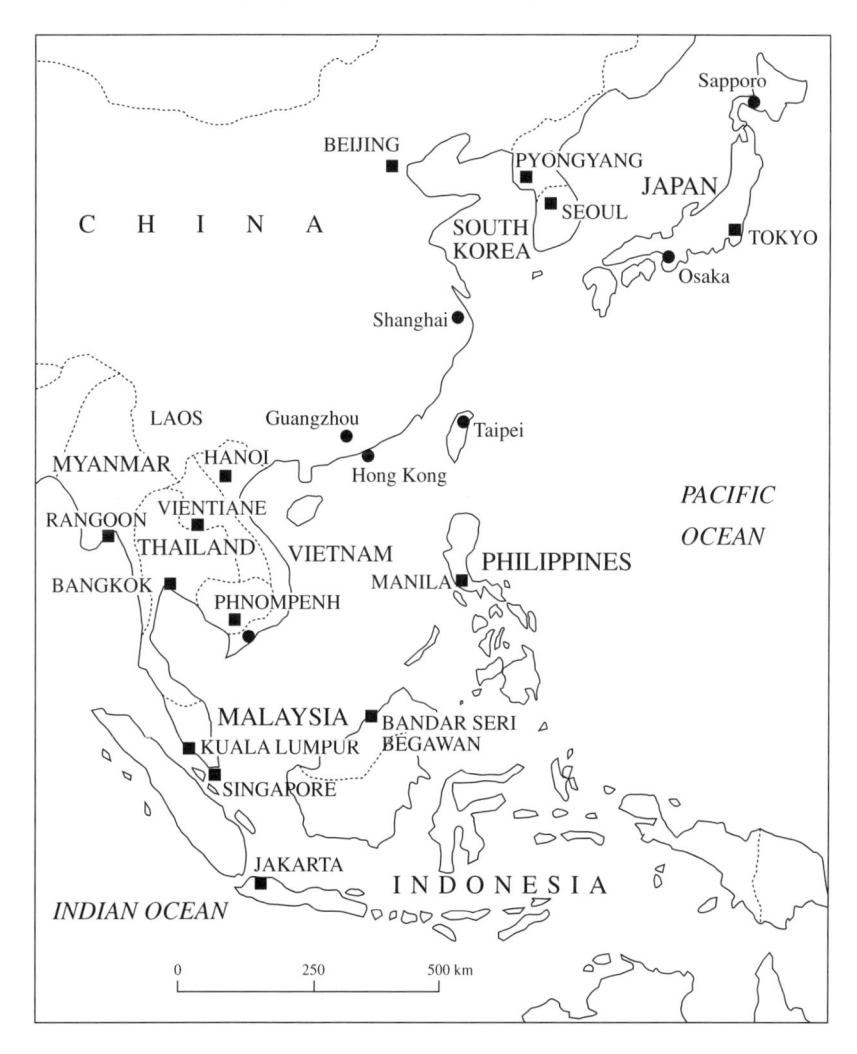

Figure 1.3   A map of Hong Kong and Singapore

states. On the one hand, structural changes in the Hong Kong economy since the 1970s and the opening of China since the late 1970s have created significant opportunities for Hong Kong firms to operate across borders and to establish themselves in the Asian region. On the other hand, the Singapore government has been calling for greater regionalisation of domestic firms since the early 1990s. There have been sustained efforts to promote the establishment of an 'external wing' to Singapore's domestic economy.

All primary data on transnational entrepreneurs from Hong Kong were collected through personal interviews with top executives from parent TNCs in Hong Kong (HKTNCs) and their subsidiaries in Southeast Asia (see Table 1.5). In Hong Kong, the author contacted some 182 headquarters of HKTNCs from an incomplete master directory that was compiled from various published sources and validated through telephone calls. Subsequently, 111 personal interviews were conducted with top executives from these parent HKTNCs, representing a 61 per cent response rate. In four Southeast Asian countries (Indonesia, Malaysia, Singapore, and Thailand), another 63 personal interviews with local top executives were completed from a sample of 103 Southeast Asian subsidiaries and/or affiliates of HKTNCs (61 per cent response rate). The industrial distribution of these 111 parent HKTNCs includes services (59 per cent), manufacturing (38 per cent) and construction (3 per cent). This large database also contains transcripts of personal interviews with top executives from 41 HKTNCs and (some of) their Southeast Asian subsidiaries and/or affiliates, and transcripts of some additional 19 personal interviews with the headquarters only.

Table 1.5 Summary table of data collected on Hong Kong and Singaporean transnational corporations

	Parent Firms		Foreign Affiliates	
	Hong Kong	Singapore	Hong Kong	Singapore
Effective survey population	182	788	103	NA
Actual response	111	203	63	56
	(61.0%)	(25.8%)		
Number of personal interviews	93	194	63	56
Number of interview transcripts	60	134	41	50
Number of top executives[a]	89	114	63	54
	(80.2%)	(75.5%)	(100%)	(96.4%)

Note: [a] Top executives are defined as chairmen, managing directors, CEOs/COOs, presidents, executive directors, directors, senior vice-presidents, and general managers.

Source: Author's interview data.

Empirical data on transnational entrepreneurship in Singapore are derived from a survey of the globalisation of 203 Singapore-based transnational corporations (SINTNCs) (see Table 1.5). At the initial stage of this project, we compiled basic corporate information on some 1246 Singapore TNCs in the database. This information was gathered from various business directories and company reports between November 1997 and January

1998. Of these 1246 companies, 340 companies had only correspondence information in China. As such, they could not be used for our survey in Singapore. Moreover, the database included 84 foreign TNCs in Singapore that were subsequently discarded in accordance with the requirements of the research project. Altogether, only 822 companies in our database fulfilled the preliminary requirements of being Singapore-incorporated TNCs. At the end of the survey in Singapore in January 1999, another 34 companies were disqualified because they either had been closed down ($n=11$) or had no foreign subsidiaries and investments ($n=23$). This means an *effective* population of 788 Singapore TNCs for our corporate survey in Singapore through which we have successfully interviewed 203 parent companies, representing a 25.8 per cent response rate (see Table 1.5). This relatively low response rate is attributed to the ongoing 1997/1998 Asian economic crisis that made top executives concentrate on their businesses, and therefore reduced their willingness to participate in our research project. Of these 203 Singapore TNCs, some 151 have subsidiaries and/or affiliates in China.

To execute our survey, we adopted a personal interview method in international business research (see Yin, 1994; Yeung, 1995). The main advantage of this survey method is that it allows the researchers to probe more deeply the processes and mechanisms of international business operations and provides much flexibility both in the conduct of data collection and in subsequent analysis. In this regard, we conducted face-to-face interviews with all but nine Singapore TNCs. Each interview took about one to one-and-a-half hours. Although the questionnaire served as the main focus in each interview, we often attempted to go beyond the questionnaire and requested the interviewees to explain certain issues in greater depth. All except 69 interviews were taped and subsequently transcribed. To date, our project has yielded a database with detailed information on the global reach of these 203 Singapore TNCs and an archive of qualitative information on some 134 of them. The second stage of the research involved personal interviews with subsidiaries and affiliates of Singapore TNCs in Hong Kong and China during May–June 1998. In contrast to the corporate survey in Singapore, I did not use any questionnaire during all interviews. Instead, these interviews were completely unstructured and virtually all taped. Their duration ranged from one hour to several hours. I managed to interview the top executives of 29 Singaporean firms in Hong Kong SAR and 13 in Guangdong province and 14 in Jiangsu province, China. Of these 56 personal interviews, 50 were taped and transcribed to provide the qualitative information for this book.

Case studies are presented in Chapters 4 and 5 to *illustrate* the nature and processes of transnational entrepreneurship in Hong Kong and

Singapore. They are meant neither as empirical proofs nor for wider generalisations. The analysis of the case studies in these chapters follows Eisenhardt's (1989), Yin's (1994), and Numagami's (1998) approach in which analytical explanations are sought. Because of the huge amount of qualitative information obtained through personal interviews in both studies, the selection of case studies becomes very important in order to minimise sampling bias. Most case studies presented in Chapters 4 and 5 are drawn from the Singapore sample for several reasons. First, I have published elsewhere the complete analysis of all 111 cases of HKTNCs that examines their organisation and mechanisms of transnational operations (Yeung, 1998a). The inclusion of some case studies of HKTNCs is meant for comparative purposes. Second, case studies of SINTNCs are chosen on the basis of the following criteria: (1) completeness of information; (2) sectoral representation; and (3) geographical representation. In some cases, I personally interviewed top executives from the parent companies in Singapore, and their foreign affiliates in Hong Kong and China. This rich information from two sides of the transnational operations allows us to cross-verify data from individual respondents. It also enables a better representation of transnational entrepreneurship when all participants are given an opportunity to voice their opinions.

THE STRUCTURE OF THE BOOK

Taken together, this book aims to offer a new horizon in international business studies. Chapter 2 sets the empirical context for subsequent empirical chapters by examining broader institutional environments in Hong Kong and Singapore. It aims to situate later discussion of transnational entrepreneurship in Hong Kong and Singapore in the context of different state–society relations. Chapter 3 then describes trends of outward investments from Hong Kong and Singapore. Some characteristics of Hong Kong and Singapore-based transnational corporations are discussed. Another section examines the political economy of outward investment from Hong Kong and Singapore by reviewing state–society and state–business relationships in these two city-states.

Chapter 4 applies the institutional perspective developed in this chapter to an Asian context. In particular, I examine the transformations of domestic entrepreneurs from Singapore into transnational entrepreneurs. My main argument is that these transnational entrepreneurs are well endowed with networking skills and capabilities that enable them to participate actively in cross-border business networks. The institutional environment in Asia also favours the strategic formation and implementation of such networks. The next section analyses how these transnational entrepreneurs organise and manage their cross-border operations, and to what extent this organisation of transnational operations is related to their entrepreneurial tendencies.

Chapter 5 analyses another important group of actors in international business – transnational intrapreneurs. I define transnational intrapreneurs as those professional managers who are strongly empowered to establish and manage foreign operations. Though they may not own any operation in an equity sense, they are often bestowed with substantial autonomy in transnational management. Based on empirical data, I analyse several possible explanations: (1) the personality of intrapreneurs; (2) trust and relations between these intrapreneurs and top management, who can be entrepreneurs themselves; and (3) the host institutional environment which necessitates entrepreneurial managers. The chapter begins with a quantitative analysis of the profile and experiences of transnational intrapreneurs interviewed in Singapore. These individual characteristics are then discussed in the context of broader institutional relations in which these transnational intrapreneurs are embedded. Qualitative case studies are presented to shed light on various issues related to transnational entrepreneurship, in particular the formation and the early success of their transnational ventures. Their social relations with top management in headquarters are also analysed. The final section analyses how these transnational intrapreneurs organise and manage their cross-border operations.

Chapter 6 aims to draw some lessons from a comparative analysis of transnational entrepreneurs and intrapreneurs for developing transnational entrepreneurship. The opening section compares and contrasts the findings on entrepreneurs and intrapreneurs in this study. Some lessons are drawn in relation to developing entrepreneurship in international business, and some policy implications for Asian business are also discussed.

NOTES

1. This institutional perspective draws upon recent theoretical developments in institutional and evolutionary economics (e.g. Nelson and Winter, 1982; Williamson, 1985; 1986; Hodgson, 1988; 1994; 2000; North, 1990; Williamson and Winter, 1991; Aoki, 2001), organisational analysis (e.g. Zucker, 1987; DiMaggio and Powell, 1991; Whitley, 1999; Lovas and Ghoshal, 2000), new economic sociology (e.g. Granovetter and Swedberg, 1992; Smelser and Swedberg, 1994), regional development studies (e.g. Storper and Salais, 1997; Cooke and Morgan, 1998), and economic geography (e.g. Amin and Thrift, 1994; Clark et al., 2000).
2. Ethnic entrepreneurship is one exceptional area of entrepreneurship study that by definition is concerned with how different ethnic immigrants survive and adapt to host country conditions (see a comprehensive review in Aldrich and Waldinger, 1990).
3. These journals include *Journal of International Business Studies*, *Management*

International Review, International Business Review, Journal of World Business, Thunderbird International Business Review, and, related journals, *Academy of Management Review*, *Academy of Management Journal*, *Strategic Management Journal*, and *Journal of Management Studies*. See a recent special research forum in *Academy of Management Journal*, Vol. 43(5) and an introduction by McDougall and Oviatt (2000).

4. The term 'transnational entrepreneurship' is sometimes used in studies of transnational communities. For example, Kyle (1999) examined the entrepreneurial development of a transnational trade diaspora of Ecuador's indigenous Otavalan merchants. The term was used to represent a case of 'entrepreneurial transnationalism', defined as transnational activities that are regular or occupationally related. This definition of transnational entrepreneurship is clearly different from the one adopted in this book.

5. McDougall (1989: 388) defined international entrepreneurship as the development of international new ventures or start-ups that, from their inception, engage in international business, thus viewing their operating domain as international from the initial stages of the firm's operation. Defined in such terms, international entrepreneurship is qualitatively different from transnational entrepreneurship because it is concerned primarily with international new venture formation. More recently, however, McDougall and Oviatt (2000: 903; emphasis omitted) have re-defined international entrepreneurship as 'a combination of innovative, proactive, and risk-seeking behavior that crosses national borders and is intended to create value in organizations'.

6. For an excellent historical survey of the genesis of entrepreneurship studies since Richard Cantillon, see Hébert and Link (1988) and Ripsas (1998). For a critical analysis of the sociology of entrepreneurship studies, see Dery and Toulouse (1996), and for a recent analysis of the demand- and supply-side perspectives in entrepreneurship research, see Thornton (1999).

7. For a comparison of the characteristics of entrepreneurs and intrapreneurs, see Hisrich (1990: Table 3).

8. Whitley's (1992a; 1999) comparative business systems approach is different from Casson's (1990b) systems view of international business and production because the business systems approach goes beyond describing institutional differences by providing causal explanations of these differences. For a critique from an international business perspective, see Casson (2000: Chapter 10).

9. Readers may notice that my arguments about the geography of entrepreneurial endowments and resources are similar to Porter's (1990) diamond model of the competitive advantage of nations. There are, however, at least two differences. First, whereas Porter was primarily concerned with the national scale of analysis, my arguments are related to specific entrepreneurs who draw upon their nationally-based endowments and resources. Second, the endowments and resource pools in my perspective may result as much from co-operation as from competition. They are therefore some kind of 'intermediate inputs' to transnational entrepreneurial processes.

10. I am not concerned here with explaining why a transnational entrepreneur internationalises. This is a question best answered by existing international business theories of FDI (foreign direct investment) and transnational corporations.

11. This institutional view of networks as strategic resources has some links with resource-based views of strategic management (Jarillo, 1988; Ghoshal and Bartlett, 1990; Gulati, 1999; Gulati et al., 2000).

12. For an example of a successfully professionalised Chinese family firm, Li & Fung from Hong Kong, see Fung (1997) and Magretta (1998). This is certainly not the same phenomenon as predicted in the existing literature on Asian family firms, where paternalism, nepotism, personalism, and fragmentation are widely believed to be the key characteristics of their organisational rigidities (e.g. Redding, 1990; M. Chen, 1995; Fukuyama, 1995).

2. Transnational entrepreneurship in two contrasting Asian contexts: Hong Kong and Singapore

> Both Hong Kong and Singapore develop their economies in specific historical contexts shaped by the interactions between domestic institutional factors and the world economy. Indeed, any rigorous research on the topic must start from a recognition of the historical structuration of the opportunity of rapid economic growth through export-oriented industrialization and the local response to such an opening of opportunity in the global economy. (Chiu et al., 1997: 8)

> We did not have a group of ready-made entrepreneurs such as Hong Kong gained in the Chinese industrialists and bankers who came fleeing from Shanghai, Canton and other cities when the communists took over. Had we waited for our traders to learn to be industrialists we would have starved. (Singapore's Senior Minister Lee Kuan Yew; quoted in his memoirs Lee, 2000).

INTRODUCTION

This chapter sets the empirical context for the next three chapters by examining the broader institutional structures of Hong Kong and Singapore. Though the book does not aim to provide a fully comparative analysis of entrepreneurship in these two newly industrialised economies, it aims to situate later discussion of transnational entrepreneurship in the context of different state–society relations and economic development trajectories in Hong Kong and Singapore. My argument here is that different home country business and institutional structures have shaped the rationality and behaviour of transnational entrepreneurs and intrapreneurs from Hong Kong and Singapore.

This chapter compares key institutional features of economic development in both city-states. I am concerned more with identifying, and less with explaining, their distinctive pathways to development. There are major similarities and differences between Hong Kong and Singapore. Both city-states are very similar in their geography, population, and colonial history. But they also differ substantially in their post-war development trajectories. The most visible dimension is the relatively laissez-faire economy in Hong Kong and the significant domination of the developmental state in the Singapore economy. Although both political economies have generated similar patterns of economic growth (as evident in major macroeconomic indicators), they have created very different dominant forms of economic organisation in relation to business organisations, industrial structures, labour organisations, and capital markets. These differences in their business systems are no doubt attributable to the differential role of the state and entrepreneurship in both economies.

COMPARING TRAJECTORIES OF POST-WAR ECONOMIC DEVELOPMENT IN HONG KONG AND SINGAPORE

In just over a century, Hong Kong and Singapore have been transformed from small fishing villages into major international financial and commercial centres in the Asia-Pacific region, serving as major springboards to building further economic relations with other regional economies. Table 2.1 provides some macro-economic indicators for both Hong Kong and Singapore from 1960 to 1999. The two city-states have experienced tremendous growth during this period. Whereas Hong Kong's real GDP growth seems to have slowed down from 11.2 per cent in the 1960s and the 1970s to 3.5 per cent in the 1990s, Singapore experienced a less dramatic decline in its pattern of growth from 12.7 per cent in the 1960s to 9.1 per cent in the 1990s. Within nearly four decades, Hong Kong's real GDP at 1990 prices rose twelve-fold from HK$62 billion in 1961 to HK$734 billion in 1998. More significantly, Singapore's real GDP at 1990 prices increased more than twenty-fold from S$5.8 billion in 1960 to S$126.8 billion in 1999. On a per capita basis, both city-states are clearly ranked among some of the most advanced industrialised economies. At per capita GNP incomes (adjusted for purchasing power parity) of US$25295 and US$20763 respectively in 1998, Singapore and Hong Kong were ranked eighth and twenty-third richest economies in the *2000 World Development Indicators* (http://www.worldbank.org/data/wdi2000/index.htm; accessed on 16 May 2000). In 1999, the World Economic Forum ranked both Singapore and Hong Kong as the first and third most competitive economies in the world (http://www.weforum.org/reports_pub.nsf; accessed on 16 May 2000).

The Rise of Hong Kong's Laissez-faire Economy

With hindsight, it is evident that the influx of emigrant industrialists from Shanghai and other parts of China during and after the civil war in the late

1940s provided a favourable starting point for Hong Kong's infant industries, particularly in the textile and garment industries (S.L. Wong, 1988; Choi, 1994; Redding, 1994; Hamilton, 1997; Yu, 1997; 1998; Meyer, 2000). Of similar historical significance to Hong Kong were the Korean War and the US embargo against China in the early 1950s during which Hong Kong suffered seriously because of its over-dependence on China trade. Manufacturing industries were thus held to be the future of the colony. The following two decades became the first phase of Hong Kong's industrialisation. In 1961, manufacturing accounted for almost 40 per cent of Hong Kong's total labour force (Table 2.1). This share grew to 43 per cent in 1970. Manufacturing employment increased rapidly at 4.2 per cent during the 1960s, representing 0.9 per cent above the average growth of labour force. By 1970, manufacturing became the single largest contributor (31 per cent) to Hong Kong's GDP. Clothing, textiles, electronics, plastics, and metal products were leading manufacturing industries. In 1973, they accounted for 61 per cent of all establishments, 76 per cent of manufacturing employment, 74 per cent of gross output and 73 per cent of value-added (Industry Department, various years a). This first phase of Hong Kong's industrialisation was also facilitated by inward investment from Japan and the USA. Table 2.2 shows that in 1970, the stock of inward foreign direct investment (FDI) at historical costs was HK$7.4 billion and accounted for 32.2 per cent of Hong Kong's GDP at current prices. Japan and the USA were two largest foreign investors in Hong Kong's manufacturing industries, in particular electronics and machinery industries (Henderson, 1989a; 1991a).

Since the early 1970s, Hong Kong has undergone a drastic process of industrial restructuring (E.K.Y. Chen, 1989; E.K.Y. Chen et al., 1991; Y.P. Ho, 1992; Chiu et al., 1997; Yu, 1997; Meyer, 2000; Yeung, 2000c). During this second phase of economic development, service industries have come to dominate the developmental trajectories of the burgeoning economy. Table 2.1 shows that as early as 1970, some 35 per cent of GDP came from trade and finance. The 1980s and early 1990s witnessed the third phase of structural change in Hong Kong's economy with the continuing dominance of the financial sector and the development of Hong Kong as a co-ordinating centre of manufacturing activities. Local manufacturing firms relocated their manufacturing activities to nearby locations in China whereas their parent firms in Hong Kong remained as management centres to co-ordinate increasingly complicated networks of production and activities. This process of 'industrial hollowing' has taken place since the early 1980s and intensified since 1987 when the Pearl River delta and other special economic zones were opened in China (Tuan and Ng, 1995a; Ng and Tuan, 1996).

This trend resulted in a drastic decline in manufacturing industries and

Table 2.1 Key macro-economic indicators on Hong Kong and Singapore, 1960–1999

Hong Kong	Annual Growth Rate (%)					Annual Figures (Prices in HK$)				
	1961–70	1970–80	1980–90	1990–98	1961	1970	1980	1990	1998
Population ('000)	2.6	3.0	1.1	2.2	3130	3937	5110	5674	6687
GDP (at 1990 prices)	11.2	11.2	8.2	3.5	62.0bn	131.5bn	294.2bn	559.5bn	734.0bn
Manufacturing	–	6.5	3.8	–6.0	–	40.6bn	69.6bn	98.4bn	45.5bn
Trade	–	13.1	11.2	2.8	–	25.8bn	62.9bn	140.7bn	176.2bn
Finance	–	22.3	6.1	7.3	–	19.6bn	67.7bn	113.1bn	187.9bn
Other	–	9.7	11.0	6.3	–	45.5bn	94.0bn	207.3bn	324.3bn
GDP per capita	7.0	7.7	6.1	1.7	$19558	$33217	$61282	$102121	$117602
Gross capital formation	7.6	20.7	4.6	9.5	17.7bn	31.1bn	102.0bn	153.8bn	285.2bn
Exchange Rate (US$)	–0.1	–0.9	4.7	–0.1	5.776	5.705	5.130	7.801	7.745
Inflation rate (%)	–	–	–	–	1.0	–	–	7.1	2.8
Total exports	16.6	13.4	18.0	3.4	32.8bn	87.1bn	215.0bn	639.9bn	836.5bn
Re-exports	9.9	27.2	48.1	8.2	8.3bn	16.5bn	65.8bn	414.0bn	719.5bn
Domestic exports	18.8	10.1	4.7	–5.4	24.5bn	70.6bn	149.2bn	225.9bn	117.0bn
Total imports	10.0	13.3	14.6	2.3	57.2bn	114.3bn	281.7bn	732.9bn	887.1bn
Total labour force ('000)	3.3	2.0	2.5	–1.3	1191	1583	1939	2471	2181
Manufacturing	4.2	2.9	–1.7	–7.2	476	677	892	730	257
Trade	3.9	13.2	7.5	1.8	131	182	447	815	947
Finance	–	35.3	10.5	5.1	–	26	127	273	398

Table 2.1 (cont.)

	Annual Growth Rate (%)				Annual Figures (Prices in S$)				
Singapore	1961–70	1970–80	1980–90	1990–98	1960	1970	1980	1990	1999
Population ('000)	2.4	1.5	2.3	2.9	1646	2075	2414	3016	3894
GDP (at 1990 prices)	12.7	12.4	9.3	9.1	5.8bn	13.9bn	32.9bn	66.5bn	126.8bn
Manufacturing[a]	12.7	16.5	8.6	7.8	0.29bn	3.29bn	9.26bn	18.0bn	32.1bn
Trade	10.7	8.5	8.1	10.2	0.72bn	2.74bn	5.29bn	10.0bn	20.2bn
Finance & Business	16.8	12.4	13.9	14.3	0.27bn	2.56bn	6.04bn	15.3bn	29.6bn
Other	9.5	12.0	8.1	9.4	1.02bn	5.31bn	12.3bn	23.3bn	44.9bn
GNP per capita	10.2	22.7	11.8	7.5	$1330	$2825	$9882	$22693	$39721
Gross fixed capital formation (1990 prices)	–	16.0	8.1	10.9	–	4.6bn	12.7bn	21.6bn	45.2bn
Exchange Rate (US$)	–	–2.9	–1.5	–0.5	–	3.094	2.094	1.745	1.666
Inflation rate (%)	–	–	–	–	0.3	0.4	8.5	3.4	0.4
Total exports[b]	6.5	70.1	17.9	14.1	2.77bn	4.76bn	34.1bn	95.2bn	229.4bn
Re-exports	–	–	12.2	17.1	–	2.92bn	13.9bn	32.5bn	88.0bn
Domestic exports	–	118.9	19.2	14.1	–	1.83bn	20.2bn	62.8bn	151.3bn
Total imports	10.6	52.9	12.3	9.6	3.48bn	7.53bn	46.5bn	109.8bn	215.4bn
Total labour force ('000)	3.5	6.5	3.4	2.4	471.9	650.9	1115.3	1537.0	1911.6
Manufacturing	8.5	12.5	2.9	–0.9	74.1	143.1	339.2	447.4	409.0
Trade	3.1	5.4	3.5	2.0	114.2	152.6	243.0	337.5	404.5
Finance & Business	1.7	20.9	8.8	8.8	21.7	25.8	85.0	167.2	314.9

Notes:
[a] Data for 1960 are at 1968 prices. Annual growth rates for the 1960–1970 period are calculated based on 1968 prices for both 1960 and 1970.
[b] Data for 1960 refer to 1964. Data for 1964 and 1970 are at current prices. Data for 1980, 1990 and 1998 are at 1990 prices.

Sources: http://www.info.gov.hk/censtatd/eng/hkstat/index1.html; accessed on 16 May 2000; http://www.singstat.gov.sg; accessed on 17 May 2000a; Census and Statistics Department (1969; 1998); Industry Department (various years a) and Department of Statistics (various years a).

Table 2.2 Inward direct investments in Hong Kong by country of origin,

	Inflows								
Country	1995	1996	1997	1998	1970	1980	1985	1990	1991
ASIA									
Mainland China	31.9	39.2	51.9	20.2	2.1	0.4	2.9	3.3	3.7
Japan	110.7	81.5	65.9	0.6	3.2	3.5	3.3	9.8	11.0
Singapore	18.2	21.4	23.8	0.5	–	–	0.2	0.3	0.5
Thailand	–	–	–	–	–	–	–	–	–
EUROPE									
France	–	–	–	–	–	–	–	–	–
Germany	–	–	–	–	–	–	0.2	0.8	0.9
Italy	–	–	–	–	–	–	–	–	–
Netherlands	–	–	–	13.2	–	–	0.5	1.2	1.4
Switzerland	–	–	–	–	–	–	0.3	0.5	0.4
United Kingdom	24.8	26.6	34.2	8.3	–	–	1.1	2.2	1.9
USA	24.4	25.1	32.6	6.6	2.0	3.5	5.7	9.5	9.6
British Virgin Islands	53.2	58.1	99.2	30.3	–	–	–	–	–
Bermuda	23.2	20.9	19.1	20.7	–	–	–	–	–
Others	107.0	120.0	142.4	14.0	–	–	1.4	3.5	5.0
Total	393.3	392.7	469.0	114.4	7.4	7.4	15.5	30.9	34.4
Ratio to GDP at current prices (%)	36.5	32.9	35.4	9.0	32.2	5.2	5.7	5.3	5.1
Percentage in non-manufacturing sectors (%)	–	–	–	93.0	0.0	0.0	0.0	0.0	0.0

Note: [a] Data before 1994 refer to the manufacturing sector only.

Source: Census and Statistics Department (various years a; various years b; 2000b) and Industry Department (various years b).

the emergence of service activities in Hong Kong.[1] Tuan and Ng (1995b: 72), for example, found that 'Hong Kong has substituted exports from its cross-border operations for exports from local enterprises. A service-dominated economy with industrial management of plants crossing the border as a core of its manufacturing sector seems to be a fact today'. By 1980 and 1998, the share of the two sectors in GDP had increased respectively to 45 per cent and 50 per cent (Table 2.1). In the same years, manufacturing's share in GDP had declined to 16 per cent and 6.2 per cent. Over a period of almost three decades, trade and financial services have emerged as the two leading sectors of Hong Kong's economy. Today, clothing, textiles,

1970–1998 (HK$billion)

FDI Stock[a]							Net Assets				
1992	1993	1994	1995	1996	1997	1998	1993	1994	1995	1996	1997
4.1	4.4	96.0	107.5	114.2	142.4	213.7	120.5	134.1	149.1	174.4	218.6
12.4	13.9	86.9	87.6	94.4	97.9	108.8	147.4	165.6	191.4	283.4	377.0
0.5	0.9	9.6	10.4	10.7	15.5	43.3	9.2	11.9	12.2	11.4	19.7
–	–	–	–	–	–	–	2.2	4.0	3.8	24.2	36.7
–	–	9.9	8.8	7.1	14.5	–	11.9	14.1	13.5	18.5	56.5
–	–	9.2	11.4	9.1	11.4	–	–	–	–	–	–
–	–	–	–	–	–	–	17.4	17.3	18.1	20.6	–
1.7	1.7	9.2	11.0	19.7	27.4	124.5	10.3	10.3	12.3	20.9	51.4
1.1	1.3	11.8	16.8	8.9	9.7	–	–	–	–	–	–
1.8	1.6	146.8	148.9	168.7	184.3	153.4	150.6	164.6	169.2	188.6	216.9
10.1	11.5	64.5	71.7	110.8	128.6	115.5	81.4	87.7	93.5	125.3	164.3
–	–	4.7	2.8	4.8	9.4	542.6	–	–	–	–	–
–	–	–	–	–	–	202.0	–	–	–	–	–
5.5	5.6	65.9	71.6	75.4	91.4	240.2	97.8	103.5	128.9	138.9	186.0
37.3	40.9	514.5	548.6	623.9	732.4	174.4	648.7	713.1	792.0	100.6	132.7
4.8	4.6	50.9	50.9	52.3	55.5	137.7	72.2	70.5	73.5	84.4	100.2
0.0	0.0	92.3	91.7	92.3	93.1	95.1	93.7	93.8	93.9	94.9	95.9

electronics, and machinery and equipment are the largest industries in the manufacturing sector. In 1998, they accounted for 62 per cent of gross output, 57 per cent of value-added and 72 per cent of total domestic exports (http://www.info.gov.hk/censtatd/eng/hkstat/index1.html; accessed on 16 May 2000).

Table 2.3 summarises the evolving comparative advantage and major strategies of industrial development in Hong Kong between 1950 and 1999. Starting with its 'First Industrial Revolution' during the 1950s, Hong Kong's manufacturing sector has been dominated by labour-intensive industries. All major manufacturing industries today are light industries producing consumer goods mostly for export to developed countries. This compares unfavourably with such other Asian Newly Industrialised Economies (NIEs) as Taiwan, Singapore, and South Korea that have already been moving towards the production of more capital- and technology-intensive

Table 2.3 Evolving comparative advantage and major strategies of industrial development in Hong Kong, 1950–1999

Period	External Environment	Comparative Advantages	Major Strategies
1950–1978	• more open global market • closed economy of China	• excellent infrastructure • relatively low wage rate (1950–1970) • well-developed service sector and international banking industry (1970–present)	• Export-oriented growth with passive industrial policy (deliberately market-driven) • strengthen socio-economic infrastructure • gradual diversification of the economy • outward FDI (textiles and services) • promotion of inward FDI for new technology
1979–present 1979–1986	• economic opening of China • e.g. special economic zones	• adjacent/proximate area and cheap labour • outward FDI even available for smaller firms	• outward FDI to China • cross-border processing of manufacturing
1987–present	• e.g. opening of Pearl River Delta regions	• further expanded production frontiers • stepping stone to China	• further diversified FDI to China • expanded cross-border operations, e.g. manufacturing management centre • regional headquarters for foreign firms • re-exports/indirect investment centre from Taiwan to China • retraining of manpower to opt to economic transformation

Source: Tuan and Ng (1995b: Table 4).

products for the global market. For example, based on the factory intensity of manufacturing activities in 1986, Nyaw (1991: 193) worked out that by output value, some 93 per cent of Hong Kong's manufacturing activities could be classified as labour intensive, compared to 60 per cent for Singapore. Compared to other Asian NIEs (e.g. Singapore and Taiwan), labour productivity in Hong Kong's major manufacturing industries was generally lower. Eng (1997) also found that Hong Kong's manufacturing sector has the lowest per capita value-added compared with other major economic sectors. Despite improvement in value-added per person and higher capital intensity in the 1980s, the electronics industry remained less efficient and productive than its counterparts in other Asian NIEs (Hong Kong Industry Development Board, 1991). In 1989, average value-added and output per worker in Hong Kong's electronics industry were US$16 and US$79 respectively, lagging far behind Singapore's levels of US$31 and US$109 (Lui and Chiu, 1994: 64).

In terms of trade, Hong Kong was ranked twenty-seventh among the leading world exporters in 1960, but by 1988 and 1998, its position had risen respectively to tenth and ninth, only below the leading developed countries of Europe, North America and Japan (Ho, 1992: Table 1; http://www.info.gov.hk/censtatd/eng/hkstat/index1.html; accessed on 16 May 2000). Hong Kong's prominent role as an entrepôt in the Asia-Pacific region is clearly shown by the consistent double-digit growth of its exports and imports performance during the 1961–1990 period (Table 2.1). In 1999, the top three domestic exports partners of Hong Kong were the USA (30 per cent), China (30 per cent), and the UK (6.1 per cent), whereas China (44 per cent), Japan (12 per cent) and Taiwan (7.2 per cent) dominated Hong Kong's imports in the same year.

The Emergence of Singapore as a Developmental City-state

Singapore is a city-state strategically located at the southern tip of Peninsular Malaysia in the Southeast Asian region (see Figure 1.3). It has grown from a British colonial entrepôt in the late nineteenth and early twentieth centuries to a modern economic centre specialising in high value-added manufacturing activities and international financial and business services (Régnier, 1991; Huff, 1994; Perry et al., 1997; Low, 1998). As early as 1970, Singapore was ranked second only to Japan in Asia in terms of annual per capital income (Y.M. Yeung, 1973: 6). Between 1959 and 2000, Singapore has achieved impressive growth rates above an annual average of 9.0 per cent. Singapore was a British colony until self-rule in 1959. Until then, British investment in Singapore was very significant, albeit mainly concentrating in the trading and distribution sectors. Tremewan (1994: 10) noted that during the first half of the twentieth century, '[l]ocal capital continued to play a dependent and complementary role to British controlled primary production and trade'.

With independence in 1965 and changing global economic systems, Singapore was able to attract a huge influx of foreign investment that took advantage of Singapore's explicit policies towards export-oriented industrialisation. This reliance on foreign capital worked very well in the first two decades of Singapore's industrialisation by plugging it into the so-called 'new international division of labour' (Fröbel et al., 1980). This strategy of courting foreign capital was perceived as 'essential in view of the weak domestic technological base and the long lead-time needed to transform domestic entrepôt traders and small-scale entrepreneurs into a dynamic industrial entrepreneurial class able to compete in the global market' (Chia, 1997: 32). Unlike Hong Kong, by 1960 manufacturing was still a relatively minor sector of the Singapore economy, accounting for only 13 per cent of total GDP at 1968 prices and 16 per cent of total employment (Table 2.1). By 1970, however, these ratios rose respectively to 24 per cent and 22 per cent as a consequence of rapid industrialisation in Singapore. The ratios increased further to 28 per cent and 30 per cent in 1980. Since 1970, manufacturing has been the single most important sector in the island economy.

Given this early developmental strategy, the Singapore economy was, and still is, heavily dependent on foreign investment. As shown in Table 2.4, the share of foreign investment in Singapore's GDP rose steadily from 5.3 per cent in 1965 to 17 per cent in 1970 and 52 per cent in 1980. By the early 1970s, for example, Singapore had become a preferred offshore assembly location for foreign semiconductor manufacturers (Scott, 1987; Henderson, 1989b). K.C. Ho (1993: 54) estimated that between 1968 and 1976, output in the electronics industry grew from about 0.5 million units to 1.7 million units. About 90 per cent of this output was exported. Similar to the experience of Hong Kong, this increase was supported by an expanding labour force as the proportion of labour in electronics manufacturing expanded from 3.1 per cent in 1968 to 17.3 per cent in 1976.

The 1970s and the 1980s witnessed a massive expansion of FDI from the USA, Japan and European countries (Mirza, 1986; Huff, 1994). As shown in Table 2.5, net foreign investment commitments in Singapore's manufacturing sector grew tremendously from S$88.6 million in 1963 to S$6.3 billion in 1999, representing more than a seventy-fold increase over a period of three-and-a-half decades. This surge in foreign investment in Singapore's manufacturing industries was enlarged further in the post-1985 period when Japanese investment supplemented inflows from the USA, the UK, the Netherlands, and Germany. Just prior to the recent 1997/1998 Asian

Table 2.4 Cumulative equity investments in Singapore by country of origin, 1965–1997 (S$million)

Country	1965	1970	1974	1980	1985	1990	1991	1992	1993	1994	1995	1996	1997
USA	23.0	343.0	1082.0	2551.5	6170.0	9951.8	11108.4	11731.0	13356.7	14325.9	17048.6	19812.9	24922.1
Australia	–	–	–	403.9	593.9	3033.8	3122.8	3158.0	3315.8	3552.6	3380.5	3531.2	3632.7
EUROPE	85.0	406.0	997.0	4814.9	7688.7	16272.0	18414.7	18299.5	20455.2	25307.2	29781.1	37368.2	44038.8
United Kingdom	–	199.0	424.0	3432.8	4365.2	6951.4	8238.1	7310.7	8086.1	9149.3	10453.5	13063.5	16083.2
Germany	–	3.0	107.0	421.6	565.2	902.1	1008.1	1054.0	1093.0	1339.1	1936.0	2031.0	1868.0
Netherlands	–	183.0	420.0	253.1	877.2	4349.6	4623.2	4498.2	4470.6	4631.7	4765.7	7335.3	8259.3
Switzerland	–	–	–	505.1	1415.4	2362.3	2537.6	2766.4	3480.4	5834.8	7250.0	9180.9	10960.3
ASIA	49.0	–	–	4679.0	9068.2	20324.3	21435.3	23448.8	26202.8	30033.7	33364.7	37883.0	41938.0
Japan	–	68.0	354.0	1420.6	3261.3	11271.6	12449.1	13813.4	14721.5	16919.2	18817.0	21645.8	23518.6
Hong Kong	–	–	–	1707.0	2352.8	4220.8	4187.4	4522.9	5021.6	5018.2	5348.0	5998.4	6038.2
Taiwan	–	–	–	61.6	82.0	254.1	284.7	390.2	571.4	790.9	1006.8	1214.7	2024.9
ASEAN	–	–	–	1361.0	3165.7	4338.7	4164.7	4561.5	5408.6	6622.1	7139.0	8041.4	9073.5
Malaysia	–	–	–	1171.4	2784.8	3286.6	3183.6	3525.6	3791.9	4331.1	4712.5	5610.6	6575.3
OTHER COUNTRIES	–	199.0	667.0	553.1	1981.9	8353.3	8829.3	8713.7	9954.7	12624.1	15640.8	17052.8	24429.0
Total (Foreign)	157.0	995.0	3054.0	13002.4	25502.7	57935.2	62910.5	65351.0	73285.2	85843.5	99215.7	115648.0	138960.6
Ratio to GDP at current prices (%)	5.3	17.1	24.3	51.8	65.5	87.2	83.6	80.7	78.9	80.6	83.7	89.7	98.4
Percentage in non-manufacturing sectors (%)	0.0	0.0	0.0	46.7	53.3	60.9	63.7	67.3	67.4	65.2	62.8	63.6	63.4
Total (Foreign and Local)	157.0	995.0	3054.0	34010.8	74644.5	155748.7	173347.6	188915.3	220527.9	262076.9	315421.2	365925.6	418655.1
Percentage of foreign (%)	100.0	100.0	100.0	38.2	34.2	37.2	36.3	34.6	33.2	32.8	31.5	31.6	33.2

Note: Data on 1965, 1970 and 1974 refer to foreign investment in Singapore's manufacturing industries in terms of gross fixed assets.

Sources: Economic Development Board (various issues) and Department of Statistics (various years b).

Table 2.5 Net investment commitments in manufacturing in Singapore by country of origin, 1963–1999 (S$million)

Country	1963	1973	1980	1985	1990	1991	1992	1993	1994	1995	1996	1997	1998	1999
USA	18.3	8.8	505.8	427.3	1054.8	969.2	1201.4	1452.2	2451.7	2075.8	2262.0	2422.6	2293.0	3586.6
Japan	27.2	151.4	139.7	244.1	708.2	713.2	858.0	779.4	913.8	1152.5	1960.4	2030.0	1822.2	1179.9
EUROPE	–	43.9	360.4	201.0	435.3	684.2	618.7	881.8	907.0	1526.3	1389.1	1423.7	1040.0	1138.8
France	–	–	18.8	15.1	60.4	75.2	34.1	124.9	54.0	140.5	59.1	271.5	138.3	96.1
Germany	–	18.4	69.2	20.1	165.7	60.2	106.4	204.6	91.8	183.9	246.4	121.3	522.7	630.7
Italy	0.4	–	45.4	–	–	70.1	26.7	43.3	38.9	12.8	53.9	175.0	89.9	84.8
Netherlands	2.5	0.6	1.0	75.2	72.6	216.2	43.1	7.7	175.6	391.4	517.8	384.7	44.0	187.0
Sweden	3.2	21.0	53.6	14.9	7.1	1.2	19.3	5.0	–	–	–	–	24.3	8.4
Switzerland	5.3	–	35.8	4.7	32.7	12.6	63.1	66.3	11.4	13.2	60.1	25.2	153.8	26.4
United Kingdom	3.7	1.9	129.5	69.4	89.9	186.5	305.5	357.8	525.1	771.6	397.6	445.1	8.5	91.7
Other	–	2.0	7.1	1.6	6.9	62.2	20.6	72.3	10.2	12.9	54.2	0.9	58.5	13.7
Hong Kong	8.0	–	23.0	1.2	5.2	30.3	6.2	16.0	–	–	–	–	–	–
OTHER OR UNKNOWN	20.0	20.0	170.1	14.4	14.4	64.2	48.8	47.5	54.9	97.8	104.8	85.5	58.4	351.8
Total (Foreign)	88.6	224.1	1199.0	888.0	2217.9	2461.1	2733.0	3177.0	4327.4	4852.4	5716.2	5963.8	5213.6	6257.1
Total (Foreign and Local)	–	295.9	1421.6	1120.4	2487.4	2934.0	3481.0	3922.6	5764.6	6809.1	8085.1	8488.4	7829.4	8037.4
Percentage of foreign (%)	–	75.7	84.3	79.3	89.2	83.9	78.5	81.0	75.1	71.3	70.7	70.3	66.6	77.8
Total in GFA (Foreign)[a]	157.0	3054.0	–	–	32814.8	35669.7	39168.2	43613.4	47546.2	52104	56767	67503.4	70409.8	–
Total in GFA (Foreign and Local)	–	–	–	–	41496.8	45508.9	49771	55730.9	60867	66851	74106	87081.7	91478.3	–
Percentage of foreign (%)	–	–	–	–	79.1	78.4	78.7	78.3	78.1	77.9	76.6	77.5	77.0	–

Notes: [a]GFA refers to Gross Fixed Assets. Data for 1963 and 1973 refer to 1965 and 1974.

Sources: Economic Development Board (various issues) and Department of Statistics (various years a).

economic crisis, Japanese FDI in Singapore's manufacturing industries (S$2.0 billion) came very close to US FDI (S$2.3 billion). In 1999, nevertheless, American investments in Singapore's manufacturing sector surged further ahead of those of Japan and were worth almost three times as much as Japanese investments. Throughout the 1980s and into the early 1990s, Singapore attracted over 10 per cent of all FDI received by destinations outside the OECD (Perry et al., 1997: 15). As an assessment of the importance of foreign capital in Singapore's economy, Huff (1995: Table 6) estimated that foreign investment contributed some 22 per cent and 26 per cent of the gross domestic fixed capital formation (GFCF) during the 1970–1979 and 1980–1992 periods respectively. This ratio of foreign investment to GFCF is certainly one of the highest among the Asian NIEs. In 1997, Singapore played host to 16 190 foreign TNCs, over 300 of which were in the manufacturing sector (Department of Statistics, 2000: xi).

Since the 1980s, there has been a qualitative shift in the nature of foreign investment in Singapore as the island economy has grown from an offshore manufacturing base to a regional control and co-ordination centre. Table 2.4 shows that in 1980, non-manufacturing FDI accounted for about 47 per cent of total foreign equity investment in Singapore. By 1990 and thereafter, this ratio grew to 61 per cent and above, indicating the rapid growth of FDI into Singapore's service industries. Perry et al. (1997: 15) observed two major influences behind this transformation in FDI activities. First, the emergence of a 'regional focus' in the corporate strategy of many TNCs has resulted in the decentralisation of an extended range of business functions to enable fuller exploitation of the Southeast Asian regional market than had previously been attempted. The focus of investment in Singapore has not changed from low production costs, but rather it has changed the use made of different locations. Second, the regional decentralisation of foreign investment to nearby countries occurs in response to increasing labour costs, and unavailability of land and other factors of production. Singapore is well positioned at an apex in the emerging regional divisions of labour to assume importance as a distribution, testing, design, and administrative centre for production that is spatially dispersed amongst a new 'periphery' of lower-cost countries (e.g. Indonesia, Malaysia, Thailand, and the Philippines). The launching of various incentive schemes in Singapore since 1986 represents the main policy instrument for Singapore to compete for the location of regional headquarters (Dicken and Kirkpatrick, 1991; Perry, 1992; 1995; Perry et al., 1998a; 1998b; Yeung, 1998b; Yeung et al., 2001).

By the late 1980s, the Singapore government began to realise the limits of capital accumulation within Singapore and the need to expand its global reach in search of new sites for continuous capital accumulation (Yeung and Olds, 1998; Yeung, 1999c). Singapore faced increasing competition and rivalry for foreign capital because of the availability of more favourable investment locations in nearby countries. In short, the global competition for investment had stepped up significantly by the late 1980s and the early 1990s. This fear of long-term limits to growth was later transformed into an official argument for building an 'external wing' to Singapore's economy in the early 1990s.[2] This outward developmental strategy, in particular, is one that no city government would ever pursue. City governments instead focus on attracting inward investment flows. They express little concern with facilitating the regional (Asia-Pacific) or global 'reach' of firms situated within their territorial boundary. This relatively recent departure in Singapore's economic development strategies underscores the role of the developmental state in steering the Singapore economy and domestic corporate activities. The next sections examine how the colonial state in Hong Kong and the newly independent state in Singapore strove hard to fashion a developmental model of their own.

THE NATURE OF COLONIAL INFLUENCE IN HONG KONG

Although some of the following points have been well developed in the East Asian developmental state literature (e.g. Deyo, 1987; Amsden, 1989; Haggard, 1990; Wade, 1990; Appelbaum and Henderson, 1992; Weiss, 1998), none of them has adequately addressed the role of the state in Hong Kong's economic development.[3] Instead, they seem to have skipped Hong Kong in their discussion and prefer instead to accept the laissez-faire interpretation of the colonial state in dominant neoliberal writings (e.g. E.K.Y. Chen, 1979; 1984; Sung, 1991; Y.P. Ho, 1992; Berger and Lester, 1997; Enright et al., 1997). In a review of post-war economic development published in the late 1980s, the Hong Kong government listed seven 'interlocked' and 'reinforced' factors to explain Hong Kong's economic development (cited in Sit and Wong, 1989: 43):

1. the existence of the free port and free trade;
2. a convertible currency and free movement of money;
3. the long accumulation of commercial and financial experience;
4. Hong Kong's favourable location and good communications;
5. the hard work and entrepreneurial instincts of the population;
6. the flexibility of the labour market; and
7. government policies, including relatively low taxation and a prudent fiscal policy.

The last factor seems to be perhaps most crucial in explaining Hong Kong's success in transforming itself from a fishing village to an Asian NIE. Among neoclassical economists (e.g. E.K.Y. Chen, 1984; Cheng, 1995; Enright et al., 1997), the key explanation of Hong Kong's economic development and structural change is no doubt the role of laissez-faire capitalism in which the colonial state adopted a 'positive non-intervention' stance towards industrial and economic development (see K.Y. Yeung, 1991). For example, the share of government consumption expenditure was stabilised between 7 and 9 per cent throughout the 1961–1999 period (E.K.Y. Chen, 1984: 10; http://www.info.gov.hk/censtatd/eng/hkstat/index1.html; accessed on 16 May 2000). There were also no foreign exchange controls, no foreign trade restrictions, and no central banking system. The colonial state believed in neutrality in budgetary policy and the inappropriateness of fiscal policy because of the openness of the Hong Kong economy and the high marginal propensity to import. This belief can be explained by the *perceived* notion that any increase in government expenditure through fiscal policies would only increase output and employment in countries other than Hong Kong. The state's 'positive non-intervention', according to neoclassical economists, has produced positive results in terms of economic growth and low unemployment (Table 2.1). It remains unclear how 'positive non-intervention' is linked to the wider political practice of the colonial state (see also Choi, 1994; Chiu, 1996; Lui and Chiu, 1996; Chiu et al., 1997; Meyer, 2000).

To a large extent, the features of Hong Kong's manufacturing production system and its unique trajectory of economic development described above were shaped by a particular economic ideology of the colonial government – neoliberalism. The Hong Kong government followed an export-orientated industrialisation strategy in the post-war period. The regulatory environment was relatively lax in the 1950s and 1960s when the Hong Kong economy started to take off and Western economies faced rising regulation. Under a generally acknowledged laissez-faire economic approach, such liberal fiscal and monetary measures as tax incentives and free capital mobility were implemented to stimulate industrial and economic development. During its early phase of industrialisation, a manufacturing system based on labour-intensive industries and small and medium enterprises (SMEs) was developed to promote rapid economic growth and full employment. To date, Hong Kong's manufacturing production system is rather unique in that it has thrived on flexible forms of organisation and transaction, but has neither a pre-existing path of extensive mass production nor a wide adoption of craft labour processes (Eng, 1997). Table 2.6 provides some principal statistics for all sectors in Hong Kong from 1960 to 1998. It is clear that SMEs make very significant contributions to all sectors in Hong Kong. In 1973, SMEs accounted for over 98 per cent of all

Table 2.6 Principal statistics for all establishments in all sectors by number of persons engaged and percentage shares of small and medium enterprises in Hong Kong, 1960–1998[a]

Year	Size of establishments	Number of establishments Mfg	Trade	Finance	Number of persons engaged ('000) Mfg	Trade	Finance	Compensation of employees (HK$billion) Mfg	Trade	Finance	Gross output/Turnover (HK$billion) Mfg	Trade	Finance	Value added (HK$billion) Mfg	Trade	Finance
1960	Total	4784	5	585	215.9	—	19.8	—	—	—	—	—	—	—	—	—
1973/74	1–99	23805	54752	—	296.2	242.6	—	2.4	—	—	11.5	—	—	4.1	—	—
	100–199	638	64	—	88.7	9.0	—	0.8	—	—	4.4	—	—	1.5	—	—
	200–999	456	32	—	177.4	12.8	—	1.7	—	—	9.8	—	—	3.5	—	—
	1000 and above	52	—	—	91.4	—	—	0.9	—	—	4.3	—	—	1.8	—	—
	Total	24951	54848	1228	653.7	264.5	34.2	5.9	—	—	29.9	—	—	10.8	—	—
	% by SME	98.0	99.9	—	58.9	95.1	—	54.2	—	—	53.2	—	—	51.9	—	—
1980[b]	1–99	46610	60804	2366	557.5	274.5	18.7	12.7	6.0	0.9	63.0	186.5	11.1	17.2	16.5	1.6
	100–199	1048	104	9	138.4	14.6	2.4	3.5	0.7	0.1	21.3	20.8	0.7	5.3	2.1	—
	200–999	616	56	2	219.4	20.4	1.5	5.5	0.7	—	39.8	21.5	—	9.8	2.5	—
	1000 and above	49	3	—	80.8	3.9	—	2.0	—	—	12.7	—	—	4.0	—	—
	Total	48324	67943	2387	996.1	327.2	22.6	23.8	7.4	1.0	136.8	228.8	11.8	36.3	21.1	1.6
	% by SME	98.6	89.6	99.5	69.9	88.4	93.4	68.1	90.5	100.0	61.6	90.6	100.0	62.0	88.2	100.0
1990	1–99	50611	140827	5152	462.3	549.2	31.5	29.8	38.5	5.1	164.1	1096.8	44.8	46.5	89.7	3.2
	100–199	786	253	64	104.3	33.8	8.9	8.1	4.4	2.2	53.4	112.5	19.6	14.1	12.4	0.9
	200–999	396	136	31	151.0	49.6	17.9	12.7	5.3	3.0	84.4	77.5	12.2	25.0	11.0	0.9
	1000 and above	30	8	—	45.0	17.7	—	4.0	1.1	—	20.3	16.9	—	6.7	1.9	—
	Total	51823	141224	5247	762.6	650.3	58.4	54.5	51.1	10.3	322.2	1321.0	76.6	92.2	117.9	5.0
	% by SME	99.2	99.9	99.4	74.3	89.7	69.2	69.5	84.0	70.9	67.5	91.5	84.1	65.7	86.6	82.0

1998[c]																
1–99	22076	173494	6952	152.1	710.8	39.6	19.9	82.1	15.1	105.2	1972.4	81.6	31.7	191.8	14.3
100–199	204	309	66	27.1	39.1	9.2	5.0	10.5	4.5	33.4	211.0	64.6	9.2	22.9	3.7
200–999	137	166	52	49.6	60.5	39.8	10.1	14.4	16.7	65.4	224.6	66.3	21.0	26.3	9.9
1000 and above	14	12	–	22.8	24.4	–	5.0	3.0	–	26.5	34.6	–	9.0	4.1	–
Total	22431	173978	7071	251.7	834.8	88.6	40.1	133.8	36.4	230.5	2861.9	212.5	70.8	287.0	28.0
% by SME	99.3	99.9	99.3	71.2	89.8	55.1	62.3	69.2	53.8	60.1	76.3	68.8	57.8	74.8	64.3

Notes:
[a] Small and medium enterprises are defined as any enterprise with an employment of fewer than 200. In the service sector, the employment size for an SME is defined as fewer than 100.
[b] Data on manufacturing refer to 1981.
[c] Data on trade and finance refer to 1997.

Sources: Census and Statistics Department (various years a; various years c).

establishments in the manufacturing and trade sectors. They also employed respectively 59 per cent and 95 per cent of all persons engaged in manufacturing and trade activities. By 1990, SMEs in the manufacturing sector became more important in terms of their employment (74 per cent), compensation of employees (70 per cent), gross output (68 per cent) and value-added (66 per cent). Although these ratios declined slightly by 1998, an indication of Hong Kong's maturing economy, SMEs have remained highly important to Hong Kong's manufacturing industries. The same observation can be applied to the trade and financial sectors as well.

Hong Kong's manufacturing sector, however, lacks a 'developmental' network of SME subcontractors. In Japan and Taiwan, most SMEs are also subcontractors for large manufacturing establishments. There is an intimate subcontracting relationship between large and small enterprises that tends to promote intense inter-firm flows of information, technological know-how, and management skills, contributing to industrial dynamism and global competitiveness. In Hong Kong, the subcontracting practice within the SME sector has been held to be a major reason behind the flexibility and price-competitiveness of local manufacturing industries. Most subcontracting relationships between large firms and SMEs, nonetheless, are merely 'mechanical market-response' or 'commercial subcontracting' (Sit and Wong, 1989; Lui and Chiu, 1996; Berger and Lester, 1997; Eng, 1997). The relationship between a contractor and its subcontractor is often temporary, and remains at arm's-length, consisting of transactions with simple *ad hoc* buying and selling of a good or service in response to price differentials between in-house production and external subcontracting. Many subcontractors also become 'shock buffers' to absorb fluctuations both in volume and nature of the products demanded in the world market. In their 1987 survey of 294 SMEs in Hong Kong, Sit and Wong (1989: 188) found that some 71 per cent of the 76 SMEs having subcontracting relationships regarded these relationships as very unstable and irregular. There is thus very little flow of technical, market and management information, and assistance between contractors and subcontractors. The latter have much less to contribute to technological innovation and economic stability than their counterparts in Japan and Taiwan.

Since the late 1970s, however, the Hong Kong economy and its manufacturing industries have been subject to global competitive pressures from other Asian NIEs and developing countries. Hong Kong has also faced rising protectionism in many developed countries with which it has trading relationships. Before 1997, the colonial state responded by maintaining its neoliberal stance towards economic development and industrial transformation. It believed that neoliberalism provided the best tool to manage the laissez-faire economy because it safeguards financial and commercial interests and the continual influx of foreign capital into Hong Kong. The rapid rise of trade and finance since the late 1970s should be understood in this political–economic context. In 1980 and 1990, trade and finance contributed to around 45 per cent of real GDP in Hong Kong, up from only 35 per cent in 1970 (Table 2.1). By 1998, this ratio increased further to 50 per cent and finance emerged as the single largest contributor (HK$188 billion) to Hong Kong's GDP (see Crawford, 2001). Inward FDI stock also increased dramatically from HK$16 billion in 1985 to HK$1.7 trillion in 1998 (Table 2.2).

Why did the colonial state in Hong Kong not practise a more interventionist approach to economic development (cf. Singapore)? The answer rests with its relations with the British government and capitalists in Hong Kong and the UK. The post-war state in Hong Kong is best described as a 'bureaucratic colonial state'. It had several distinctive characteristics: first, there was an obvious merging of the roles of the bureaucrats and the politicians. Hong Kong's political system prior to 1 July 1997 consisted of three elements: the governor, the Executive Council, and the Legislative Council. The governor was appointed by London and became part of the Colonial Office. His main task was to maintain the status quo and prosperity of Hong Kong. The two councils served as advisory bodies to the governor but had no binding power on him. As a result, neither council was accountable to the Hong Kong people until direct elections of some members of the Legislative Council were held in September 1991. Second, its colonial bureaucratic nature and the class interest that it was supposed to serve bound the state in Hong Kong. Choi (1994: 47) described the colonial government as 'highly bureaucratised, and perhaps efficient in carrying out orders [from London], but it is also equally conservative, rigid, and extremely unwilling to initiate change without intense social pressure'. Third, the colonial state believed firmly in free trade and laissez-faire policies as encapsulated in neoliberalism to serve the interests of their colonial masters and British capitalists. This strict adherence to neoliberalism in Hong Kong during almost the entire twentieth century is particularly interesting because it diverged from the welfare state practised in Britain in the immediate post-war period up to the 1970s.

Another interesting observation is that the neoliberal economic ideology of the colonial state in Hong Kong was originally linked to the mercantile orientation of the entrepôt in the immediate post-war period. For example, trade was so much the insignia of British colonialism that colonial officials were blinded to any alternative future for Hong Kong other than as a free port within the British Empire. Even though the industrialisation programme had been taken up in the immediate post-war period, Governor Grantham did not see the need for any fundamental change in Hong

Kong's economic structure. During an address delivered to the Legislative Council in 1949, he maintained that the future of Hong Kong lay in trade, not industries: 'Trade is the life blood of this Colony . . . I am proud of being Governor of a Colony of shopkeepers' (cited in Choi, 1994: 49).

How then did commercial and business interests shape the neoliberal economic ideology of the colonial state? To shed light on this issue, we have to examine the historical relationship between business and politics in Hong Kong. By selectively co-opting leading business and commercial elites into the governance process, the colonial state succeeded in maintaining the status quo while absorbing conflicts of interests among different social groups. The state did this through appointing unofficial members into the Legislative and Executive Councils. Writing on business and politics in Hong Kong, S.L. Wong (1993: 489) explained that:

> In the post-war period, a free market economy flourished under authoritarian rule in Hong Kong. Economic freedom existed without political democracy. Through appointments, the colonial administration coopted prominent businessmen into the political system and gave them a strong voice in the formulation of public policies.

For effective governance, the colonial ruler needed the co-operation of the local, and predominantly Chinese, trading elite. The elite incorporation process is a prime example of wealth marrying with power. The elite first became successful in business and then was invited to join the Councils. The domination of the business elite class in the Legislative and Executive Councils was so indisputable that '[b]y the time manufacturing industry was ready to "leap ahead" in the 1950s, the state's alliance with the dominant commercial–financial bourgeoisie was supported by a dense institutional network of consultation, representation, and communication, inducing a coalescence of interests between the two parties' (Chiu, 1996: 238). For example, in 1951, all of the eight 'unofficials' in the Legislative Council were director, chairman or manager of at least one of the major corporations in the colony (Choi, 1994: 53). None of them were representatives of the growing industrial class. During the early period of Hong Kong's industrialisation, the industrial class lacked a seat in the Councils and hence a significant voice and influence on the colonial state.

By 1965, some 37 per cent of the seats of all the Councils (Executive, Legislative, and Urban) were still occupied by businessmen, the largest majority being British expatriate (Davies, 1989: 48). The British *taipans* or capitalists used to have a powerful voice in the economic policies of the colonial state. A minority of Chinese business elites was firmly established in the Chinese community. But their presence and influence in the Councils was restricted to areas not involving 'fundamental significance' (Choi,

1994). Representatives from the industrial class accounted for only 19 per cent of these Chinese unofficials in the Legislative Council. The colonial government, for example, was able to dismiss lightly repeated calls for a protective tariff to help manufacturers in the 1950s. The protection was deemed particularly necessary in the local spinning sector against imports of yarn and other textile materials (S.L. Wong, 1988).

In the ensuing two decades, the domination of commercial and business interests in the two councils was weakened. By 1986, professionals and labour representatives made up the same number of seats as business voices in the Councils. The idea of business domination in the councils was still deeply ingrained in the minds of the Hong Kong people. In a survey conducted between 1988–1989, S.L. Wong (1993: 505) found that the majority of 2239 intellectuals (59.2 per cent) in Hong Kong (sample defined as graduates of local universities and polytechnics) still thought that business leaders in Hong Kong had too much influence in political affairs. A phenomenon, however, did occur in the balance of power between foreign (mainly British) capital and Chinese capital in favour of the latter. In his analysis of interlocking directorships among major British *hongs* or trading companies and their involvement in the colonial state, G.K.K. Wong (1991: 135ff) observed the declining influence of British capital since the 1970s. He noted that by the mid-1980s, even the leading British *hong*, Jardine Matheson, feared being taken over by Chinese property tycoons.

As evident above, the decline of British capital in Hong Kong largely coincided with structural changes in Hong Kong's economy towards the deindustrialisation of the colonial economy. Choi (1994: 50) argued that 'the conservative nature of the bureaucracy was not amenable to self-motivated and long range interventionism. The outcome was a piecemeal approach reflecting a crisis/response pattern in its industrial policy'. During this period, Hong Kong's manufacturing industries had undergone drastic and painful restructuring in response to global economic changes and competitive pressures from other Asian NIEs and developing countries (see also Sum, 1995; Yeh and Ng, 1994; Leung and Wu, 1995; Martinsons, 1998; Jessop and Sum, 2000). The colonial state, however, continued to practise neoliberalism in favour of financial and commercial capital. The 1980s and the 1990s therefore witnessed the emergence and domination of financial and commercial interests in Hong Kong's economy (Table 2.1).

THE DEVELOPMENTAL STATE IN SINGAPORE

As a comparative case, the developmental state in Singapore was much more active in inducing industrial restructuring during the same period (see

Chiu et al., 1997; Yeung and Olds, 1998; Yeung, 1999c). Toward the mid-1970s, the low-cost and export-oriented industrialisation strategy in Singapore faced increasing pressures because of contradictions in the labour market where labour remained low in skill and productivity. Relatively low wages also made it difficult to sustain Singapore's export-led industrialisation because of insufficient mass consumption.[4] The state responded by implementing a 'corrective' wage policy in the belief that artificially low labour costs in previous years had distorted the real market value of Singapore's scarce labour and contributed to a high dependence of the economy on labour-intensive production established by foreign firms. In 1979, the National Wage Council (NWC) recommended considerable increases in wages, including a basic monthly pay increase of S$32 for all workers, plus an additional 7 per cent of the existing worker's wage (Rodan, 1989: 144). It also recommended that employers pay an extra 4 per cent per worker into their national compulsory saving scheme (CPF). A Skills Development Fund (SDF) proposed to aid upgrading of labour skills was to be financed by imposing on employers a levy of 2 per cent or S$5 for each employee receiving S$750 or less per month. Four industrial sectors (electrical and electronics, food, beverages and tobacco, industrial machinery, and chemicals, petroleum and pharmaceuticals) experienced the greatest changes and impact.

This 'Second Industrial Revolution' in Singapore was aimed at shaking out inefficient users of labour by raising wages to induce a rationalisation of production that could take several forms. Some labour-intensive foreign manufacturers subsequently relocated their production facilities to other low-cost countries (K.C. Ho, 1993; 1994). Others moved up the technological ladder by upgrading their value-added activities and automating their operations in Singapore. During this restructuring process, labour was required to work three shifts round the clock to offset the high fixed costs of capitalisation, and there was a need to maintain flexible production arrangements. Another dimension of labour market restructuring in the 1980s was the increasing participation of foreign workers in Singapore's labour force (K.C. Ho, 1993; 1994). Firms were more willing to employ foreign labour because such labourers were perceived to have more positive work attitudes (including willingness to work extra hours and night shifts), higher education levels and relative youth. Between 1975 and 1979, the foreign labour force constituted one-third of the growth in the work force. Between 1980 and 1984, foreign workers accounted for more than half of the work force increase in Singapore. The original position of the state in the late 1970s and early 1980s was to view foreign workers as a temporary stopgap measure. But by the late 1980s, this view was replaced by one that allowed for a carefully controlled intake. The state thereafter developed foreign worker policies that are more indirect, using the foreign worker levy and quotas to constrain the growth in the number of foreign workers. The size of the levy and quotas not only differ for skilled and unskilled workers, but also vary between different industries. These foreign worker policies, however, generally favour high-tech and high value-added foreign firms in Singapore (Hui, 1997; Coe and Kelly, 2000), as indicated in their relative ease in getting foreign worker approval and quotas.

How then do we explain the power of the state in Singapore to implement such painful restructuring policies? To understand state–business relations in Singapore, one has to unpack the political economy of its post-war development. The rise of the developmental state in Singapore is influenced, to a certain extent, by immediate post-independence experience and subsequent political development. The ascent of the People's Action Party (PAP) to power in 1959 and its enduring power in politics and government since independence in 1965 has given birth to a developmental state in Singapore, with national economic development the primary goal of the PAP government for the past 30 or more years. The Singapore economy was very dependent on entrepôt trade for basic livelihood and employment under the British administration. Trade alone accounted for up to one-third of GDP at factor cost in 1957 (Rodan, 1989: 48) and 31 per cent of real GDP at 1968 prices in 1960 (Table 2.1). The development of manufacturing industries became the top priority of the newly elected PAP in the immediate post-1959 period. As a consequence, Perry et al. (1997: 7) observed that 'the state gives much greater priority to transforming economic conditions than it does to changing aspects of the social order'. The First Development Plan, covering the period 1961–1964, focused on the provision of new jobs and the promotion of economic development (Y.M. Yeung, 1973). During the 1960s, a grave employment problem arose with the departure of the British administration and military and the rapid rate of population growth. The PAP's manifesto explained that only through the promotion of manufacturing industries could Singapore's existing and prospective unemployment be addressed. The PAP was apparently aware of the fundamental political, social, and economic implications of unemployment and the remedy for it (Rodan, 1989).

The Singapore economy inherited by the PAP from the British administration, however, was weak in industrial bourgeoisie and lacked any significant manufacturing base. Indigenous entrepreneurship was not strong enough financially to shoulder the huge burden of industrialising Singapore. Moreover, the PAP-ruled state was suspicious of indigenous capitalists for fear of their pro-communist and pro-China attitudes

(McVey, 1992; Menkhoff, 1993). Régnier (1993: 308) perceptively explained that for social, economic and political reasons, 'Lee Kuan Yew [leader of PAP and Prime Minister] deliberately neglected and even distrusted the developmental capacity of local Chinese entrepreneurs, infant though they might have been in the early 1960s'. The resource-deficient small city-state subsequently chose to rely on foreign capital to gain quick economic growth in order to legitimise its political domination. Although impressive economic records were achieved in the following four decades, indigenous entrepreneurship and domestic capital were rather disadvantaged and not given sufficient room to grow. Rather, foreign capital was given a privileged place to grow in the Singapore economy (see more below).

In a developmental state, the preoccupation with economic development must be supported by the establishment of an elite economic bureaucracy to 'guide' the market as argued by Johnson (1982) and Wade (1990). In 1961, the Economic Development Board (EDB) of Singapore was established as a one-stop investment promotion agency to assist foreign firms in their operations in Singapore.[5] Working closely with the Ministry of Trade and Industry, the EDB has since played a key role in shaping the Singapore economy through its efforts to solve the unemployment problems, promote investment, train manpower and develop the industrial sector (Low et al., 1993). It must be emphasised, however, that until recently, the main concern of the EDB has been attracting foreign (preferably global) firms to invest in Singapore. Generous incentive schemes were offered to foreign firms to compensate for the lack of competitive advantage in Singapore during its early phase of industrialisation (e.g. the Pioneer Industries Ordinance in 1959 and the Economic Expansion Incentives Act in 1967). The establishment of the Jurong Town Corporation (JTC) in 1968 provided another institutional boost to the state's strategy of relying on foreign capital. The JTC was primarily responsible for the construction and management of industrial estates, the first of which was located in the Jurong area. These industrial estates were intended to provide low-cost production sites for foreign manufacturing firms. Since its establishment, the JTC has planned, developed and managed more than 6000 hectares of industrial land, of which over two-thirds has remained under its ownership (Perry et al., 1997: 158). Together, both statutory boards have worked hard to attract large inflows of foreign investment into Singapore throughout the past three decades (see Tables 2.4 and 2.5).

As well as creating institutional structures, the state also employed other measures to make Singapore more attractive to foreign investment. K.C. Ho (1994: 48) noted that 'as an NIE operating in a turbulent world with many manufacturing location options, [Singapore] can survive successfully only if state intervention structures local and regional conditions to fit the requirements of international capital'. First, the state regulated the labour market by disciplining the labour force with the Trade Union (Amendment) Bill in 1966 and the Employment Act along with the Industrial Relations (Amendment) Act in 1968 (Rodan, 1989; Huff, 1995; 1999; Yeung, 1999c). The 1966 Trade Union (Amendment) Act had a significant impact on the subsequent development of labour movements. This powerful act turned against organised labour, declaring strikes and other industrial action illegal unless approved through secret ballot by a majority of a union's members. In essential services, strikes were banned altogether. The Trade Union Ordinance was amended to outlaw sympathy strikes and allow the Labour Minister to bar the formation of a federation of unions in essential services. The Employment Act of 1968 further altered the conditions of service and remuneration of employees when the standard weekly working hours were increased and public holidays and leave were reduced. The act resulted in considerable savings to employers in direct and indirect payments to labour. The Industrial Relations (Amendment) Act, 1968, also expanded the prerogatives of the management by barring such issues as promotions, transfers, retrenchments, dismissals, reinstatements, and work assignments from union negotiation. These constitutional measures greatly weakened the scope for industrial action and marked the arrival of corporatism in Singapore. As Rodan (1989: 93) noted, 'one thing was abundantly clear: militant trade unionism was finished in Singapore. Labor was now part of the corporate structure of the Singapore state.' These labour market regulations resulted in the creation of a highly disciplined and depoliticised labour force in Singapore, allowing its smooth entry into the peripheral role of the emerging new international division of labour spearheaded by global corporations.

Another attribute of Singapore's developmental state is the close alliance of the PAP and the state bureaucracy. Since the first general election for a fully elected legislative assembly in Singapore in 1959, the PAP has not lost to any single opposition party, thus ensuring a continuous domination of party ideology and preoccupation with economic development. There has been a virtual monopoly of political power by the PAP in Singapore since its independence and this creates a stable (albeit repressive) political environment and a significant space for closer party–state alliance (Hill and Lian, 1995; Hamilton-Hart, 2000). To a certain extent, the PAP has become the state and has a significant role in 'guiding' developmental policies. The state bureaucracy, on the other hand, serves the general interests of Singapore exceptionally well by formulating development policies that enable the proliferation of foreign firms and state-owned enterprises.

DOMINANT FORMS OF ECONOMIC ORGANISATION IN HONG KONG AND SINGAPORE

What then are the impacts of the peculiar political economies in Hong Kong and Singapore on their dominant forms of economic organisation? As argued in Chapter 1, the pre-existing configurations of institutional structures and state–society relations have a significant role in shaping domestic business systems in which dominant forms of economic organisation endure for a relatively long period of time (see Figure 1.1). These business systems contribute to the entrepreneurial endowments and resources for thriving transnational entrepreneurs to internationalise their domestic operations or to go international right from the start of their business activities. In the following subsection, I describe and assess the dominant forms of economic organisation in Hong Kong and Singapore in relation to ownership patterns and capital markets. The next subsection explains business formation and co-ordination, management processes, and work and employment relations in Hong Kong and Singapore. Table 2.7 presents a summary of these key attributes of the dominant forms of economic organisation in a comparative context and shows their potential impact on the extent of entrepreneurship in Hong Kong and Singapore, also to be discussed in the next subsection.

Ownership Patterns: Private versus Foreign/Public

There are significant and yet crucial differences in the ownership patterns of the two city-state economies. Tables 2.8 and 2.9 show the extent of local and foreign ownership of the manufacturing, trade, and finance sectors in Hong Kong and Singapore between 1960 and 1998. In general, foreign firms play a less important role in Hong Kong's economy, whereas they are particularly dominant in Singapore's corporate sector. In Hong Kong, foreign firms made up only around 1 per cent of total manufacturing establishments between 1980 and 1998. Although their contributions to the total number of workers, compensation, gross output, value added, and fixed investments are not as pronounced as their counterparts in Singapore, these foreign firms accounted for disproportionately higher percentages in all five categories of industrial production. Trends in Table 2.8 also indicate that foreign firms are playing an increasingly important role in Hong Kong's manufacturing sector over time. From a modest contribution of less than 15 per cent of total employment, compensation, gross output, and value added in 1980, these foreign firms were responsible for over 20 per cent in all categories except total employment (15 per cent) in 1998.

Table 2.7 *Comparing business systems and entrepreneurship in Hong Kong and Singapore*[a]

Business Systems	Hong Kong	Singapore
Ownership patterns	• Fairly low presence of foreign-owned affiliates (+) • Insignificant presence of state-owned enterprises (+) • Strong presence of (Chinese) family-owned enterprises (+) • Large presence of small and medium enterprises and flexible production networks (+)	• Large presence of foreign-controlled enterprises (−) • Significant presence of state-owned enterprises (now government-linked companies) (−) • Domination of large firms and their affiliates (−)
Capital markets	• Large presence of foreign and local banks (+) • Very active stock market (+) • Informal channels of capital available (+)	• Large presence of foreign and local banks (+) • Active stock market (+) • Very high rates of forced individual savings (−)
Business formation and co-ordination	• High firm birth (+) • Strong reliance on relationships in venture formation (+)	• Low firm birth (−) • Some reliance on relationships in private venture formation (+)
Management processes	• Existence of both professional and family management styles in large enterprises (?)	• Professional management in large enterprises (+) • Bureaucratic management in government-linked companies (−) • Family management in SMEs (?)
Work and employment relations	• High preference for self-employment and ownership (+) • Labour markets oriented towards the private sector (+) • Lack of unionism (−) • Performance-based appointments in top local companies (+)	• High preference for self-employment and ownership (+) • Large employment absorption capacity of foreign firms and the government sector (−) • Lack of unionism (−) • Political appointments of top executives in government-linked companies (−)

Note: [a] The sign in parentheses represents the direction of the impact on domestic entrepreneurship. A plus sign represents positive impact and vice versa for a negative sign. A question mark represents ambivalent impact.

Table 2.8 Local and foreign ownership of selected sectors in Hong Kong, 1960–1998 (50% equity as cut-off and in HK$billion unless otherwise specified)

Industries	1960 Total	1970 Total	1980 Total	1980 Foreign (%)	1985 Total	1985 Foreign (%)	1990 Total	1990 Foreign (%)	1998 Total	1998 Foreign (%)
Manufacturing[a]										
Establishments	4784	16507	52566	0.9	49140	0.8	51823	1.2	22431	1.5
Workers ('000)	215.9	549.2	1031	7.5	908.5	7.3	762.6	9.5	251.7	14.9
Compensation	–	–	21.8	8.6	34.0	8.5	54.5	12.2	40.1	20.7
Gross output	–	–	116.5	13.4	177.0	11.9	322.2	17.0	230.5	27.3
Value added	–	–	30.8	12.7	50.3	10.7	92.2	16.1	70.8	25.9
Fixed investments	–	–	–	18.5	5.4	16.3	12.3	22.7	8.9	23.2
Trade[b]									[1997]	
Establishments	131.0	54848	67943	–	–	–	141224	–	173978	1.1
Workers ('000)	–	264.5	327.2	–	–	–	650.3	–	834.8	9.0
Compensation	–	–	7.4	–	–	–	51.1	–	133.8	–
Turnover	–	–	228.8	–	–	–	1321.0	–	2861.9	–
Value added	–	–	21.1	–	–	–	117.9	–	287.0	–
Finance (except banks)									[1997]	
Establishments	585	585	2387	–	–	–	5247	–	7071	7.3
Workers ('000)	19.8	19.8	22.6	–	–	–	58.4	–	88.6	18.3
Compensation	–	–	1.0	–	–	–	10.3	–	36.4	–
Receipts	–	–	11.8	–	–	–	76.6	–	212.5	–
Value added	–	–	1.6	–	–	–	5.0	–	28.0	–

Notes:
[a] Data on foreign contributions for 1980 refer to 1983.
[b] Data on 1970 refer to 1974. Data on foreign contributions for 1997 refer to 1995.

Sources: Census and Statistics Department (various years a; various years c).

Table 2.9 Local and foreign ownership of selected sectors in Singapore, 1960–1998 (50% equity as cut-off and in S$million unless otherwise specified)

Industries	1960 Total	1970 Total	1974–75 Total	1974–75 Foreign (%)	1980–81 Total	1980–81 Foreign (%)	1990 Total	1990 Foreign (%)	1997–98 Total	1997–98 Foreign (%)
Manufacturing			[1975]		[1980]				[1998]	
Establishments[a]	548	1747	2385	22.0	3355	24.9	3703	23.4	4004	20.8
Workers ('000)	27.4	120.5	191.5	52.0	285.2	58.5	351.7	58.9	352.3	50.5
Compensation	66.8	397.6	1180.5	55.0	2526.9	58.5	6852.2	61.3	11768	56.2
Gross output	465.6	3891.0	12610	71.3	31658	73.7	71333	75.9	121433	77.3
Value added	142.1	1093.7	3411.1	62.7	8521.9	67.4	21607	72.7	29627	73.3
Direct exports	164.3	1523	7200.7	84.1	19173	84.7	47000	85.8	75530	88.3
Capital expenditure[b]	9.8	421.3	622.6	64.6	1861.9	74.6	4184.4	70.7	37246	67.8
Trade[c]			[1975]		[1981]				[1997]	
Establishments	–	–	21208	–	35251	4.7	40147	6.0	51337	13.1
Workers ('000)	–	–	124.5	–	172.8	15.6	211.0	21.0	265.3	29.1
Compensation	–	–	698.2	–	1676.0	34.3	4191.5	39.6	9055.1	49.3
Turnover	–	–	22334	–	64264	42.5	179856	63.1	371978	74.1
Value added	–	–	2369.4	–	4993.0	39.2	10338	50.4	19249	52.3
Number of companies	–	–	–	–	8196	20.7	15259	23.9	37225	19.3
Shareholders' equity	–	–	–	–	5491.9	34.5	15871	38.6	36730	41.8
Fixed assets	–	–	–	–	3491.5	36.4	1552	36.3	26705	36.1
Equity investments[d]	–	–	1406.7	25.4	4553.7	40.1	13195	51.0	37550	44.4

Table 2.9 (cont.)

Finance	[1974]		[1980]		[1997]	
Establishments	1327	–	2330	18.3	2724	18.0	5499	26.4
Workers ('000)	19.3	–	28.1	40.1	11.7	41.0	18.7	25.7
Compensation	223.0	–	541.9	49.8	386.4	44.4	1256.5	35.9
Receipts	272.0	–	2177.2	57.0	1006.0	62.6	2859.9	41.3
Value added	272.0	–	2177.2	57.0	1006.0	62.6	2859.9	41.3
Number of companies	–	–	2010	22.3	3763	30.5	11914	20.7
Shareholders' equity	–	–	9867.2	17.5	62578	24.7	178458	27.8
Fixed assets	–	–	1237.2	34.9	6424.6	20.7	15348	22.5
Equity investments[d]	1306.1	14.4	10515	22.2	72552	36.9	18249	29.2

Notes:
[a] In 1964 and 1970, 7.9% and 11.7% of respectively 965 and 1626 total establishments were majority or wholly foreign-controlled.
[b] Data for 1998 refer to net fixed assets.
[c] Data for 1980 refer to 1981.
[d] Data for 1974–15 refer to paid-up capital.

Sources: Department of Statistics (various years b; various years c; various years d; 1992; 2000). Data on trade and finance for 1980–81, 1990, and 1997 are from unpublished data supplied by the Department of Statistics, 9 June 2000.

The growing importance of foreign firms, however, should be understood in the context of Hong Kong's rapid deindustrialisation in the 1980s and the 1990s. One may argue that this trend reflects the broader sector shift of many previously Hong Kong-owned manufacturers into the service sector through the relocation of their manufacturing operations across the border to mainland China and southward to Southeast Asia (Cheng et al., 1998; Yeung, 1998a). In Hong Kong's non-manufacturing sector, foreign firms are likely to play a more important role. As noted earlier in Table 2.2, foreign firms in Hong Kong's non-manufacturing sector contributed to over 90 per cent of inward FDI stock and net assets between 1993 and 1998. In the financial sector, however, foreign firms made up only about 7 per cent of total establishments and 18 per cent of total employment in 1997. These figures indicate that the rise of trade and finance as major industrial destinations of inward investments into Hong Kong does not necessarily lead to the domination of foreign firms in these two sectors. Local private and public listed firms remain highly important in both sectors.

Another key component in Hong Kong's economy is the role of private ownership in virtually all sectors (Table 2.7). As explained earlier, the colonial government did not take an active interventionist approach to Hong Kong's economic development. There were consequently no state-owned enterprises in Hong Kong, although there were some monopolies in specific sectors (e.g. electricity and telecommunications). Instead, the Hong Kong economy has been driven largely by the private sector. In this regard, it is important to note that there is a strong presence of (Chinese) family-owned enterprises in Hong Kong's economy. In 1994, Chinese family firms controlled 123 companies listed on the Hong Kong Stock Exchange with an aggregate market capitalisation of US$155 billion and total assets of US$173 billion (Wu and Duk, 1995: Table 3; Au et al., 2000; Yeung, 2000d; Yeung and Olds, 2000). An estimate reported in the *Far Eastern Economic Review* (10 February 2000: 42) shows that about 70 per cent of all publicly listed firms in Hong Kong are family-controlled. Furthermore, as Table 2.6 has shown, small and medium enterprises constitute the major component of Hong Kong's industrial organisation. These ownership patterns in Hong Kong's corporate sector have important implications for domestic entrepreneurship (see next section).

On the other hand, there is no doubt that Singapore depends heavily upon foreign investments for its industrialisation and economic development (Table 2.7). In 1980, foreign interests controlled some 66 per cent of Singapore's total corporate assets in all sectors of Singapore's economy, valued at S$223 billion (Department of Statistics, 1992: Table 2). By 1989, this ratio of foreign control of Singapore's total assets (S$685 billion) rose to 73 per cent, although the ratio decreased to 58 per cent of total assets

(S$1949 billion) in 1997 (Department of Statistics, 2000: Table 6). In terms of equity investments (see Table 2.4), foreign-controlled companies accounted consistently for over 30 per cent from 1980 to 1997.

In terms of industrial distribution, foreign ownership is most conspicuous in Singapore's manufacturing sector. As mentioned earlier, foreign capital contributed significantly to net investment commitments in Singapore's manufacturing sector from the 1970s onwards. In 1973, the share of foreign interests in Singapore's net investment commitments was 75 per cent (Table 2.5). This ratio rose to an all-time high of 89 per cent in 1990, although it remained at over 70 per cent for most of the ensuing years in the 1990s. Table 2.5 also shows that foreign interests accounted for over 70 per cent of gross fixed assets in Singapore's manufacturing sector during the 1990s. In terms of some principal statistics, the extent of foreign ownership of Singapore's manufacturing sector is even more striking. In 1966, foreign investment represented some 45 per cent of total gross fixed assets in manufacturing (Rodan, 1989: 99). By 1975, foreign-controlled firms in Singapore's manufacturing sector were responsible for 52 per cent of total employment, 55 per cent of remuneration, 71 per cent of gross output, 63 per cent of value-added, 84 per cent of direct exports, and 65 per cent of capital expenditure (Table 2.9). In the next two decades, Singapore's industrialisation was characterised by a shift towards high value-added manufacturing activities. This trend is indicated in the growing domination of foreign firms in Singapore's manufacturing sector in terms of gross output, value-added, and direct exports from 1975 to 1998. In 1998, although they accounted for only 21 per cent of total establishments, foreign firms contributed to 77 per cent of gross output, 73 per cent of value added and 88 per cent of direct exports.

In other non-manufacturing sectors, foreign firms are not much less dominating either. Table 2.9 shows that during the 1980–1997 period, foreign interests contributed to over 30 per cent of shareholders' equity and fixed assets and over 40 per cent of equity investments in Singapore's trade sector. In the financial sector, foreign firms are slightly less influential, accounting for over 20 per cent of shareholders' equity, fixed assets and equity investments during the same period. It should be noted here that the 50 per cent equity cut-off point adopted by Singapore's Department of Statistics (1992; 2000: 18) is very high for both trade and finance sectors. In these sectors, many foreign firms are often able to exercise effective management control without majority ownership (see Aharoni, 1993; Sauvant and Mallampally, 1993; Nachum, 1999). If we take 10 per cent equity as the cut-off point as adopted by the Census and Statistics Department (various years b) in Hong Kong, the extent of foreign control of Singapore's trade and finance sectors should be much higher.

Another very important feature of Singapore's industrial organisation is the significant role of government-linked companies (GLCs) that were previously established as state-owned enterprises for specific developmental purposes (Table 2.7). In the early years of Singapore's independence, the state took up a heavy responsibility for the provision of public infrastructure through major state-owned enterprises. Many state-controlled statutory boards were established to provide roads, electricity, transport and communication services for the nation. State-owned enterprises spun-off from these statutory boards sowed the seeds for the domination of GLCs in the regionalisation drive since 1993 (see Chapter 3). In fact, public investment in the industrial sector started as early as 1963. Seven public enterprises in manufacturing were established: Sugar Industry of Singapore Ltd., National Grain Elevator Ltd., Singapore Textile Industries Ltd., United Industrial Corporation Ltd., Singapore Polymer Corporation Pte Ltd., Jurong Shipyard Ltd., and Ceramics (M) Pte Ltd. (Rodan, 1989: Table 3.2). Most of these enterprises were established to respond to perceived large domestic markets. Rodan (1989: 77) argued that this trend reflected 'the government's thinking that the question of industrial structure should not be left solely to the market – especially given the absence of a domestic industrial bourgeoisie of any consequence'.

Temasek Holdings was set up on 25 June 1974 to hold and manage the Singapore government's S$345 million equity invested in 36 companies (*The Straits Times*, 25 June 1999: 74). It served as a holding company to monitor the activities of its companies, to collate all the information of various government investments and to keep the Minister for Finance and the Cabinet informed about the performance of these companies. Its present chairman, S. Dhanabalan, who was a former Cabinet minister, recalled that 'there was no supervisory function [for Temasek Holdings]. Each company had its own management who were accountable to its own board . . . The Government's main interest was to make sure the right people were in charge and after that the management was to chart its own course. That approach carried on in Temasek' (quoted in *The Straits Times*, 25 June 1999: 74–5). By 1979, Temasek Holdings had adopted a new and more active approach: (1) to provide focus and direction to its companies; (2) to foster closer co-operation among the companies; (3) to seek out new investments; and (4) to consider mergers with profitable companies. By 1983, the state had directly invested in 58 diverse companies with a total paid-up capital of S$2.9 billion. These companies in turn wholly or partially owned some 490 firms in Singapore (Huff, 1995: 1428). Some of these large state-owned enterprises have grown significantly since then and become today's major GLCs spearheading the Singapore economy (e.g. the Keppel Group and the Sembawang Group).

During the 1980s and 1990s, Temasek Holdings began to shed its stake in non-strategic and viable companies through public listing and other forms of divestment. The main purpose then was to promote market mechanisms and to allow the private sector to play a bigger role in the Singapore economy. Through privatisation since the late 1980s, many former large state-owned enterprises have now been listed in the Stock Exchange of Singapore (Singapore Airlines, Keppel Corporation, Sembawang Holdings, and so on). Singapore Airlines, as one of the most successful local corporations, constituted as much as 5 per cent of Singapore's GDP at its peak. These former state-owned enterprises have since been known as GLCs because the state still retains significant influence over their management control, primarily through four state-owned holding companies – Temasek Holdings, Singapore Technologies, MinCom Holdings, and MND Holdings.

Today, the public sector and GLCs account for about 60 per cent of Singapore's GDP (Ministry of Finance, 1993a: 39; see also Singh and Ang, 1998). As of 31 May 1999, the market capitalisation of first-tier public listed GLCs controlled by Temasek Holdings alone was S$88 billion or 25 per cent of total market capitalisation of the Stock Exchange of Singapore. The share of Temasek Holdings in these GLCs amounted to S$47 billion or 13 per cent of total market capitalisation (*The Straits Times*, 25 June 1999: 74). Table 2.10 lists companies that were divested by Temasek Holdings between 1985 and 1998. It should be noted that six GLCs in Table 2.10 had a combined market capitalisation of S$164 billion by the end of 1999. Some of the GLCs are top players in their respective industries: Singapore Telecom (telecommunications), Keppel Corporation (shipyard and infrastructure), SembCorp Industries (shipyard and marine industries), DBS Groups Holdings (banking and property development), Singapore Airlines (airlines), Neptune Orient Lines (shipping), and Singapore Technologies (high-tech manufacturing). There may also be companies controlled by Temasek Holdings that are not included in the table.

In more recent years, Temasek Holdings started to invest in new strategic or risky ventures and in companies that would bring foreign skills and technology and access to foreign markets. When the regionalisation programme was launched in 1993, Temasek Holdings supported the Singapore government's long-term policies by co-investing with private companies abroad and by asking its companies to go regional, in particular in China and in Indonesia (see case studies in Chapters 4 and 5). Its role remained as a *facilitator* to provide more focused direction to subsidiaries and associated companies and to foster closer co-ordination and co-operation among its companies. In 1998/99, Temasek Holdings experienced winds of

Table 2.10 Summary of divestments by Temasek Holdings in Singapore

Companies	Date of Divestment	Share of Government (%) Before	Share of Government (%) After	Market Capitalisation (end of 1999) (S$ billion)
Cerebos Pacific	November 1985	45.0	0.0	—
Natsteel (relinquished controlling interest)	September 1986	19.7	8.2	—
United Industrial Corporation	September 1986	10.9	0.0	—
SNP Corporation (1st company on SESDAQ)	January 1987	100.0	63.0	—
Neptune Orient Lines	Nov 1988 – Dec 1993	63.0	49.0	S$18
Singapore Airlines	May 1987 – June 1993	62.0	32.6	S$21
	December 1985	77.0	63.0	
	June 1987	63.0	56.3	
Chemical Industries (FE)	July 1987	22.9	0.0	—
Acma Electrical Industries	January – March 1988	12.2	0.0	—
Hitachi Electronic Devices (Pte) Ltd	August 1988	15.0	0.0	—
Yaohan Singapore Pte Ltd	November 1988	15.0	0.0	—
Philips Petroleum Singapore Chemicals	December 1988	25.0	0.0	—
Keppel Corporation	Jan 1989 – June 1993	58.5	31.7	S$30
Denka (S) Pte Ltd	March 1989	20.0	0.0	—
The Polyolefin Company (S) Pte Ltd	April 1989	25.0	0.0	—
Ethylene Glycols (S) Pte Ltd	April 1989	50.0	0.0	—
Petrochemical Corporation of Singapore Pte Ltd	April 1989	20.0	0.0	—
Singapore Telecom	November 1993	100.0	89.2	S$38
	July 1996 – March 1998	89.2	78.2	
SembCorp Industries	—	—	57.9	S$29
DBS Groups Holdings	—	—	15.5	S$28
PSA Corporation	—	—	100.0	—
Singapore Technologies	—	—	100.0	—
Media Corporation of Singapore	—	—	100.0	—
Singapore MRT	—	—	100.0	—
Singapore Power	—	—	100.0	—

Sources: The Straits Times (25 June 1999: 74; 29 April 2000: 62).

change and has become more proactive in governing its companies in order to nurture world-class companies through effective stewardship and commercially-driven strategic investments. There are two reasons underlying this strategic change in corporate governance. First, one of the controversial issues for corporate governance in Singapore was the unwieldy diversification by some GLCs both in Singapore and abroad before the Asian economic crisis of 1997/1998. Temasek Holdings chairman S. Dhanabalan remarked again that 'we have made it clear to Temasek companies that while we have no objection to them diversifying into other areas, we want them to discuss with us and convince us that they need to go in that direction' (quoted in *The Straits Times*, 25 June 1999: 1).

Second, a recent report by the Committee on Singapore's Competitiveness (Ministry of Trade and Industry, 1998) has called for an active role by GLCs in spearheading the development of more world-class companies from Singapore. The reorientation of Temasek Holdings, as a key holding company of most GLCs, towards more proactive corporate governance is therefore timely. Temasek's chairman noted that 'we have to strike a balance. I don't want to give the impression that we are going to be very intrusive in our stewardship role' (quoted in *The Straits Times*, 25 June 1999: 1). Changes planned or implemented include: (1) closer monitoring of the diversification plans of GLCs to ensure that they capitalise on what they know best; (2) specifying performance benchmarks to ensure they focus on the correct targets; (3) limiting the terms of the chairmen and directors to ensure fresh thinking prevails at the top; and (4) keeping separate the appointments of the chairmen and the chief executive officers to ensure that their boards retain an objective view of proposals brought before them by senior management.

The immediate consequence of this significant domination of foreign firms and GLCs in Singapore's economy is that most of its industries and sectors are organised around large firms, irrespective of their local or foreign ownership. As shown in Table 2.11, SMEs account for an overwhelming majority of the total number of establishments in all sectors throughout the 1960–1998 period. But their contributions to the Singapore economy vary significantly by industry and sector (Department of Statistics, 1997). In the manufacturing sector, SMEs are less important than large firms (controlled by foreign firms and GLCs) in terms of their contributions to employment, remuneration, gross output, and value-added. In all these four categories, the relative contributions by SMEs declined during the 1960–1998 period. This decline is most significant in terms of gross output (from 65 per cent in 1960 to 21 per cent in 1998) and value-added (from 56 per cent in 1960 to 24 per cent in 1998). Meanwhile, SMEs continue to thrive in the trade sector, experiencing an increase in percentage shares in both total employment and remuneration during the 1980–1997 period. The decline of their contributions to turnover and value-added during the period is also not as significant as their counterparts in the manufacturing sector. In the finance sector, SMEs maintain their relatively dominant role throughout the 1974–1997 period which witnesses their growing shares in total employment and remuneration. Moreover, the majority of growing SMEs in Singapore, defined as those gaining employment and output/sales between 1984 and 1994, operated as private limited companies. Together, they constituted 42 per cent of the total population of 8712 growing SMEs that were 11 per cent foreign owned in 1994.

Capital Markets

Both Hong Kong and Singapore are major international financial centres today (Wu and Duk, 1995; Chiu et al., 1997; Wu, 1997; Crawford, 2001). The existence of favourable capital markets is very important for the formation of entrepreneurial endowments and resources (Figure 1.1). As shown in Table 2.12, both Hong Kong and Singapore have relatively high ratios of banks per 1000 population, although Hong Kong's ratios are consistently double those of Singapore. These banks in all forms, ranging from fully licensed banks and deposit-taking banks to offshore banks, provide critical financial resources for entrepreneurship to thrive in the two city-states. In terms of bank loans, there are significant variations in their industrial orientation and sector preferences. In Hong Kong, the financial system is characterised by an institutional separation of finance and industry (Chiu, 1996). There was a relatively low proportion (less than 20 per cent in Table 2.12) of bank loans granted to manufacturing industries in the early phase of Hong Kong's industrialisation, as compared to Singapore (and Taiwan and Korea). This is not surprising because the colonial government did not participate directly in banking activities. By 1998, the manufacturing sector accounted for only 4.8 per cent of total bank loans in Hong Kong, as compared to general commerce (9 per cent) and financial industries (12 per cent).

In Singapore, state-owned enterprises participated directly in the capital accumulation process through the provision of credits and loans, subsidisation of labour costs, and expansion of land supply. There was a high degree of integration between the financial sector and the manufacturing sector in Singapore's early phase of industrialisation. The Singapore government established the Development Bank of Singapore in 1968 as an industrial bank to provide long-term financing for the nascent industrial sector. This had a tremendous 'demonstration effect' on Singapore's

Table 2.11 Principal statistics for all establishments in all sectors by number of persons engaged and percentage shares of small and medium enterprises in Singapore, 1960–1998[a]

Year	Size of establishments	Number of establishments Mfg	Trade	Finance	Number of persons engaged ('000) Mfg	Trade	Finance	Compensation of employees (HK$billion) Mfg	Trade	Finance	Gross output/Turnover (HK$billion) Mfg	Trade	Finance	Value added (HK$billion) Mfg	Trade	Finance
1960	1–99	497	—	—	15.3	—	—	32.2	—	—	254.2	—	—	65.4	—	—
	100–199	26	—	—	3.4	—	—	8.5	—	—	49.9	—	—	13.7	—	—
	200 and above	25	—	—	8.7	—	—	26.1	—	—	161.5	—	—	63.1	—	—
	Total	548	—	—	27.4	—	—	66.8	—	—	465.6	—	—	142.1	—	—
	% by SME	95.4	—	—	68.2	—	—	60.9	—	—	65.3	—	—	55.7	—	—
1970[b]	1–99	1534	19182	1294	45.6	—	11.7	123.4	—	122.2	1117.3	—	2083.9	303.8	—	—
	100–199	111	126	33	15.2	—	7.7	45.4	—	100.5	628.3	—	2482.2	173.2	—	—
	200–499	65	—	—	20.1	—	—	71.0	—	—	558.9	—	—	179.9	—	—
	500 and above	37	—	—	39.6	—	—	157.8	—	—	1586.6	—	—	445.9	—	—
	Total	1747	19308	1327	120.5	—	19.3	397.6	—	222.7	3891.0	—	4566.1	1093.7	—	—
	% by SME	94.2	99.3	97.5	50.5	—	60.4	42.5	—	54.9	44.9	—	45.6	43.6	—	—
1980	1–99	2845	38057	2288	79.4	171.9	16.1	663.2	1411.2	309.5	6228.4	53447	15072	1830.9	3876.5	1454.6
	100–199	254	180	42	35.8	43.4	12.0	316.2	581.1	232.4	3146.1	12559	4332.4	873.3	1902.0	722.6
	200–499	154	—	—	48.5	—	—	418.1	—	—	5994.7	—	—	1476.2	—	—
	500 and above	102	—	—	121.5	—	—	1129.5	—	—	16289	—	—	4341.6	—	—
	Total	3355	38327	2330	285.3	215.3	28.1	2526.9	1992.3	541.9	31658	66006	19405	8521.9	5778.6	2177.2
	% by SME	92.4	99.5	98.2	40.4	79.9	57.2	38.8	70.8	57.1	29.6	81.0	77.7	31.7	67.1	66.8
1990	1–99	3047	43214	2709	86.5	204.6	7.6	1650.8	2965.7	259.4	11020	116521	4676.6	3689.8	6292.4	425.6
	100–199	329	241	15	45.5	60.7	4.1	924.7	1253.4	126.9	7660.2	21379	6692.0	2417.1	2997.6	580.4
	200–499	200	—	—	61.9	—	—	1260.8	—	—	15837	—	—	4827.0	—	—

500 and above	127	–	–	157.8	–	3015.9	–	36817	–	10673	–			
Total	3703	43455	2724	351.7	265.3	11.7	6852.2	4219.1	386.4	71333	137901	11369	21607	9289.9	1006.0
% by SME	91.2	99.4	99.4	37.5	77.1	64.8	37.6	70.3	67.1	26.2	84.5	41.1	28.3	67.7	42.3
1998[c] 1–99	3354	51128	5474	98.3	222.6	12.1	3051.4	6799.7	907.4	15984	261344	9225.7	4358.8	12284	1894.9
100–199	331	217	25	46.6	42.7	6.6	1488.5	2244.7	322.7	9486.9	110650	15178	2624.9	6875.6	942.2
200–999	271	–	–	104.9	–	–	3718.1	–	–	38768	–	–	10319	–	–
1000 and above	48	–	–	102.5	–	–	3510.0	–	–	57194	–	–	12325	–	–
Total	4004	51345	5499	352.3	265.3	18.7	11768	9044.3	1230.2	121433	371994	24404	29627	19160	2837.1
% by SME	83.8	99.6	99.5	41.1	83.9	64.7	38.6	75.2	73.8	21.0	70.3	37.8	23.6	64.1	66.8

Notes:
[a] Small and medium enterprises are defined as any enterprise with an employment of less than 200. In the service sector, the employment size for a SME is defined as less than 100.
[b] Data on trade refer to 1993 and data on finance refer to 1974.
[c] Data on trade and finance refer to 1997.

Sources: Department of Statistics (various years c; various years d; various years e).

87

Table 2.12 Financial markets and institutions in Hong Kong and Singapore, 1960–1999 (HK$ and S$million)

Hong Kong

	Growth Rate (%)					Annual Figures				
	1961–67	1967–80	1980–90	1990–98	1961	1967	1980	1990	1998
Number of banks	3.9	54.0	4.0	−1.0	59	75	415	599	544
Per 1000 population	–	–	–	–	1.9	1.9	8.1	10.6	8.1
Total bank loans (HK$)	–	157.2	41.3	20.4	–	5401	124287	689369	1957752
Manufacturing (%)	–	–	–	–	–	19.8	10.7	7.2	4.8
General commerce	–	–	–	–	–	31.4	25.9	10.8	9.2
Financial industries	–	–	–	–	–	3.1	5.3	15.2	11.8
Transport & comm.	–	–	–	–	–	4.1	9.3	6.0	5.4
Construction	–	–	–	–	–	16.4	15.5	15.7	21.3
Individuals	–	–	–	–	–	13.1	19.7	30.0	37.4
For business	–	–	–	–	–	5.3	5.1	3.2	1.2
Prime rates (%)	–	–	–	–	6.0	7.5	13.5	10.5	9.94
Stock market turnover	−11.2	2232	18.3	54.4	1414.2	305.2	95684	288715	1701112
Ratio to GDP at current prices (%)	–	–	–	–	19.0	2.0	67.5	49.6	134.2

Singapore

	1962–70	1970–80	1980–90	1990–99	1962	1970	1980	1990	1999
Number of banks	–	–	4.1	0.9	–	–	97	141	154
Per 1000 population	–	–	–	–	–	–	4.0	4.7	4.0
Total bank loans (S$)	21.8	75.7	16.9	15.5	731.1	2167.7	20206.9	57696.4	147178
Manufacturing (%)	–	–	–	–	12.8	34.1	21.6	31.0	7.9
General commerce	–	–	–	–	51.6	31.3	39.3	23.7	13.5
Financial industries	–	–	–	–	6.7	3.6	10.4	17.2	14.3
Transport & comm.	–	–	–	–	2.7	1.5	6.4	3.0	2.5

							1998
Construction	–	–	–	–	2.6	8.4	9.3	22.3	39.8
Individuals	–	–	–	–	–	13.1	7.0	13.4	14.7
Prime rates (%)	–	–	–	–	–	8.00	13.60	7.73	5.80
Stock market turnover	–	85.9	51.9	11.4	–	746.9	7806.1	36756.0	74479.4
Ratio to GDP at current prices (%)	–	–	–	–	–	12.9	31.1	55.3	52.7
Contributions to central provident fund (S$)	45.7	124.4	19.3	13.7	30.6	156.4	2296.0	7174.2	16000.4
Ratio to GCF at current prices (%)	–	–	–	–	9.6	7.0	19.7	29.5	33.9

Sources: See Table 2.1 except for Singapore, Monetary Authority of Singapore (various years).

banking sector. A report by the director of the Development Bank of Singapore in 1969 observed that 'some banks are now beginning to grant term loans of, say, up to five years to industries. This step may have been taken as a result of the establishment of the Development Bank of Singapore. The provision of term loans may lead to opportunities for the more lucrative short-term financing. Unless banks want to lose business to Development Bank of Singapore, which also provides short-term loans, it may be to their interest to consider giving term loans to manufacturers' (quoted in Chiu et al., 1997: 47–8).

In 1962, bank credit to the manufacturing sector in Singapore accounted for only 13 per cent of total loans and advances to customers. This ratio continued to rise, to 21 per cent in 1967 and 34 per cent in 1970, and contrasted very favourably with the situation in Hong Kong (Table 2.12). In the early phase of Hong Kong's industrialisation, a committee was set up by the Governor in January 1959 to consider the establishment of an industrial bank to ease problems of credits and capital faced by industrialists. However, the committee was comprised of government officials, bankers and traders who eventually decided against the idea of an industrial bank in Hong Kong (Chiu, 1996). Lui and Chiu (1994: 59) thus argued that this separation between finance and industry in Hong Kong's financial system 'discourages restructuring strategies which require heavy capital investment and encourages capital-saving strategies, especially for the smaller firms'. The same phenomenon persisted in the 1980s and the 1990s so that Hong Kong's manufacturers lacked sufficient credits and loans for restructuring and upgrading to higher value-added activities.

Another interesting phenomenon in Hong Kong and Singapore is that as both economies mature over time, the proportion of bank loans given to construction and private individuals for property purchase and mortgages has increased dramatically. In the late 1960s, construction and individuals in Hong Kong and Singapore accounted for respectively about 30 per cent and 22 per cent of total bank loans. By 1998/1999, this ratio increased to 59 per cent for Hong Kong and 55 per cent for Singapore. The proportion of bank loans granted to individuals for business purposes in Hong Kong was reduced from 5.3 per cent in 1967 to a meagre 1.2 per cent in 1998. Meanwhile, the maturing of both economies as major international financial centres is evident in extremely vibrant stock-markets that provide alternative finance to budding entrepreneurs. Measured by their ratios to GDP at current prices, the stock-market in Hong Kong clearly stands out as much more active than its Singapore counterpart. Singapore's stock-market had a head start in 1970, measured in terms of both absolute turnover and ratio to GDP. Hong Kong's stock-market caught up rapidly from the 1980s onwards. By 1998, both stock-markets became major platforms for entrepreneurial companies to secure investment funds and market recognition.

One very important difference in the financial system between Hong Kong and Singapore is the role of the Central Provident Fund (CPF). The establishment of the Central Provident Fund Board in Singapore was intended to provide long-term security to its members and to initiate a compulsory national savings scheme to finance national development plans. From an initial rate of contribution of 5 per cent of gross monthly salary, the CPF rates rose steadily over time to 25 per cent just before the 1985 recession and subsequently decreased to about 15–20 per cent. As shown in Table 2.1, gross domestic capital formation in Singapore grew substantially during the 1970–1999 period. Measured in terms of their ratio to gross capital formation at current prices, contributions to the CPF increased significantly from 7 per cent in 1970 to 35 per cent in 1999. In other words, some one-third of total national capital formation in Singapore today comes from the compulsory individual savings scheme. The effect of this state-enforced savings scheme is manifested in the channelling of a large share of potential investment capital from private capital markets to the CPF Board and other state-owned sectors, making it very difficult for private entrepreneurs to obtain the necessary capital for domestic and overseas expansion. From this perspective, some researchers argue that the saving–investment process of Singapore has 'crowded out' local entrepreneurship (e.g. Tan, 1991).

THE EXTENT OF ENTREPRENEURSHIP IN HONG KONG AND SINGAPORE

What then is the impact of these rather different institutional configurations and structuring of business systems in Hong Kong and Singapore on indigenous entrepreneurship? To sum up these institutional differences, the Hong Kong economy is characterised by rapid deindustrialisation and significant private-sector initiatives in the commercial and financial sectors. Most establishments in Hong Kong are family-owned SMEs that are organised through flexible production and business networks. As the capital market in Hong Kong has a large number of banks and an active stock-market, aspiring entrepreneurs are well positioned in these entrepreneurial endowments and resources in Hong Kong. In contrast, large foreign firms and GLCs dominated Singapore's economy. Today, the manufacturing sector remains highly important to Singapore's economy and is significantly dependent on foreign investments. Privately-owned firms are active in Singapore's trade and finance sectors, although their contributions are not as significant as those of their counterparts in Hong Kong. The capital market in Singapore is characterised by a relatively good presence of banks and an active stock-market. However, very high rates of forced individual savings have reduced entrepreneurial endowments and resources for private individuals. Instead, the state sector takes on the role of an entrepreneur in its own right, establishing formerly state-owned enterprises and spearheading the development of the Singapore economy.

Measuring Entrepreneurship in Hong Kong and Singapore

How do these different configurations of entrepreneurial endowments and resources shape the processes of business formation and management, and work and employment relations in Hong Kong and Singapore? Some broad statistics on both city-states indicate their differential extents of entrepreneurship. Table 2.13 summarises the *number of establishments* in all sectors and establishment–population ratios in Hong Kong and Singapore from 1960 to 1997. It is clear that Hong Kong's industrialisation took place during the 1960s and the 1970s when the number of manufacturing establishments grew dramatically, from 4784 in 1960 to 52 566 in 1980. By 1980, there were 10.3 manufacturing establishments per 1000 population in Hong Kong, an almost seven-fold rise since 1960. Since the 1980s, Hong Kong's industrialisation has been overtaken by the rise of the service economy. Establishments in both trade and finance almost tripled between 1980 and 1997, whereas manufacturing establishments shrank by over 50 per cent during the same period. The establishment–population ratios in both trade and finance also doubled during the 1980s and 1990s. The overall number of existing local companies indicates that Hong Kong's deindustrialisation in the 1980s and the 1990s did not inhibit the entrepreneurial activities of its population. Instead, Hong Kong's total establishment–population ratio increased over four-fold from 16 per cent (81 206) in 1980 to 73 per cent (474 517) in 1997. In Singapore, the manufacturing sector continued to experience modest growth between 1980 and 1997, alongside a rapid proliferation of establishments in trade and finance particularly in the 1990s. The total number of existing local companies also increased substantially during the same period. In 1980, there were a total of 15 279 establishments in all sectors and 6.3 establishments per 1000 population in Singapore. By 1997, the total number increased almost five-fold to 73 662 and the ratio tripled to almost 20 establishments per 1000 population.

On the basis of the statistics presented in Table 2.13,[6] one may argue that entrepreneurship thrives much better in Hong Kong than in Singapore. Hong Kong consistently has higher establishment–population ratios than Singapore, in virtually all sectors and benchmark years (Table 2.7). The

Table 2.13 *Number of establishments in all sectors and establishment-population ratios in Hong Kong and Singapore, 1960–1997*

Hong Kong	Annual Growth Rate (%)				Annual Figures					
	1960–73	1973–80	1980–90	1990–99	1960	1967	1973	1980	1990	1997
Manufacturing										
Total	30.1	13.8	−0.1	−6.5	4784	10234	24951	52566	51823	24925
Per 1000 population	–	–	–	–	1.5	2.6	5.9	10.3	9.1	3.8
Trade										
Total	–	1.4	12.0	2.9	5	9	54752	60804	140827	173494
Per 1000 population	–	–	–	–	–	–	13.0	12.1	24.8	27.0
Finance										
Total	7.9	11.8	10.9	4.3	585	–	1228	2387	5247	7071
Per 1000 population	–	–	–	–	0.2	–	0.3	0.5	0.9	1.1
Number of new local companies incorporated										
Total	54.3	20.6	9.8	4181	11631	31292	81206	265452	474517	
Per 1000 population	–	–	–	–	0.2	0.3	1.3	2.9	4.6	7.6
Number of existing local companies										
Total	46.3	19.9	20.6	9.8	4181	11631	31292	81206	265452	474517
Per 1000 population	–	–	–	–	1.3	3.0	7.4	15.9	46.8	73.0

Table 2.13 (cont.)

Singapore	1963–70	1970–80	1980–90	1990–97	1963	1970	1980	1983	1990	1997
Manufacturing										
Total	27.3	8.4	0.9	1.7	548	1747	3355	3662	3703	4195
Per 1000 population	–	–	–	–	0.3	0.8	1.4	1.4	1.2	1.1
Trade										
Total	–	–	7.8	29.6	–	–	8196	11413	15259	51345
Per 1000 population	–	–	–	–	–	–	3.4	4.3	5.1	13.7
Finance										
Total	–	–	1.5	12.7	–	–	2330	3099	2724	5499
Per 1000 population	–	–	–	–	–	–	1.0	1.2	0.9	1.5
Number of new companies incorporated										
Total	–	–	0.02	4.6	–	–	6486	1162	6503	8918
Per 1000 population	–	–	–	–	–	–	2.7	0.4	2.2	2.4
Number of existing companies										
Total (local)	–	–	8.0	19.6	–	–	15279	20906	28693	73662
Per 1000 population	–	–	–	–	–	–	6.3	7.8	9.5	19.7
Foreign-controlled	–	–	9.9	10.8	–	–	4159	6156	8686	16190

Sources: See Table 2.1. Department of Statistics (1992; 2000).

extent of entrepreneurship is particularly evident in both manufacturing and trade sectors. In the manufacturing sector, Hong Kong has a much greater number of establishments per 1000 population between 1960 and 1990. In the trade sector, the establishment–population ratios in Hong Kong were consistently three or more times that of Singapore between 1980 and 1997. The same trend may be observed in terms of both number of new local companies incorporated and the total number of existing companies. During the 1980–1997 period, Hong Kong experienced significantly greater growth in both ratios than Singapore.

On the other hand, a slightly different impression of entrepreneurship may be evident in *work and employment relations* in Hong Kong and Singapore. Table 2.14 presents the distribution of the labour force by activity status in Hong Kong and Singapore. While both economies experienced a decline in the proportion of their labour force in the categories of self-employment between the late 1950s and the late 1990s, there is a slight increase in the proportion of their labour force as employers during the same period. This indicates the maturing and corporatisation of both economies. However, it should be noted that Singapore has a modestly higher proportion of its labour force in the self-employment category. In 1957, some 17 per cent of Singapore's labour force was self-employed, compared to 10 per cent in Hong Kong in 1961. In 1999, Singapore had a higher proportion of its labour force in both self-employment and employer categories than Hong Kong. These broad statistics on the activity status of the labour force tend to indicate higher entrepreneurship in Singapore.

In terms of employment relations, the labour market in Hong Kong is predominantly oriented towards the needs of the private sector, in particular indigenous firms. In contrast, Singapore's labour market is oriented towards foreign and public sectors. In fact, the state maintains its influence in GLCs through a small group of politically loyal senior civil servants appointed to their boards of directors. A recent study, for example, has identified a group of 13 persons each of whom were members of at least 18 boards of directors, mainly drawn from top civil service posts and with government careers starting in the 1950s and 1960s (quoted in Perry et al., 1997: 127). Moreover, both economies seem to be lacking in strong unionism, which favours entrepreneurial activities. There was a remarkable lack of unionism in Hong Kong with less than 20 per cent of all employees belonging to unions (Lui and Chiu, 1994: 58; Chiu et al., 1997; Snape and Chan, 1997). Trade unions have been more concerned historically with acting as welfare organisations for their members than with improving their wages and working conditions (Henderson, 1991b). Capitalists were given a free hand in restructuring their production and relocating their operations abroad.

In Singapore, trade unions are organised by the National Trade Union

Table 2.14 Distribution of the labour force by activity status in Hong Kong and Singapore, 1957–1999 (%)

Hong Kong	Growth Rate (%)				Annual Figures				
	1961–66	1966–82	1982–90	1990–98	1961	1966	1982	1990	1998
Self-employed	–	–	–	–	10.2	13.2	8.9	5.2	4.7
Employers	–	–	–	–	4.7	–	4.1	5.3	5.2
Employees and workers	–	–	–	–	83.3	83.1	86.5	88.4	89.6
Unpaid family workers	–	–	–	–	1.7	3.7	2.3	1.1	0.5
Total number ('000)	3.3	8.9	1.6	2.0	1212.0	1454.7	2364.5	2711.5	3201.0

Singapore	1957–70	1970–80	1980–90	1990–99	1957	1970	1980	1990	1999
Self-employed	–	–	–	–	17.4	17.1	10.8	6.5	7.8
Employers	–	–	–	–	3.7	2.8	3.9	4.5	5.7
Employees and workers	–	–	–	–	73.7	76.5	82.8	87.5	85.4
Unpaid family workers	–	–	–	–	5.1	3.6	2.5	1.6	1.1
Total number ('000)	3.1	6.0	3.4	2.7	455.2	650.9	1077.1	1485.8	1885.9

Sources: See Table 2.1 except for Singapore, see Department of Statistics (various years f; various years g).

Congress and industrial action is banned under the 1966 Trade Union (Amendment) Act. The political defeat of labour in Singapore was crucial to its early industrialisation. In a first move towards this goal, three labour organisations were brought together in late 1965 to ratify a 'Charter for Industrial Progress'. They were the National Trade Union Congress, the Singapore Manufacturers' Association, and the Singapore Employers' Federation. Under this Charter, 'all partners in the industrialization program, worker, employer, government, must pool their efforts and strive for a continuing increase in productivity and output in all enterprises' (quoted in Rodan, 1989: 91). The appeal of the Charter was consistent with ideological notions of self-sacrifice for the collective good and economic problems being above class interests that were promulgated by the dominant political party, the People's Action Party (PAP) headed by the then Prime Minister Lee Kuan Yew. Through its political influence in the tripartite National Trade Union Congress, which comprised representatives from the PAP government, labour, and capital, the state was able to deny labour unions their traditional role as legitimate interest groups and to corporatise labour into the management needs of the state.

Institutional Structuring of Entrepreneurship in Hong Kong and Singapore

How then do we account for these differences in entrepreneurial tendencies in Hong Kong and Singapore? I do not pretend to explain all subtle differences in their entrepreneurial tendencies. Nor do I intend to give an absolute quantitative assessment of entrepreneurship in both economies. There are real dangers in using aggregate statistics to give a definitive assessment of entrepreneurship in Hong Kong and Singapore. In their comparative assessment of entrepreneurship in Hong Kong and Singapore, Lee and Low (1990: 11) concluded that 'the evidence regarding entrepreneurship in the aggregate is therefore mixed. It is not at all clear that, in terms of numbers, entrepreneurship in Singapore is less than that in Hong Kong'. I intend to point out, however, the major institutional differences in both city-state economies that may influence the extent of entrepreneurship (see Table 2.7). It may well be argued that the practice of neoliberalism by the colonial state and the effective blockade of local Chinese in the political system have together contributed to the rise of domestic entrepreneurship in Hong Kong. In contrast, the active intervention of the developmental state in Singapore in virtually all spheres of economic and social life has left little room for the growth and development of local entrepreneurship. Instead, the state has replaced local business elites as the leading 'entrepreneur' of Singapore's economy. I will now explain each of these institutional processes as they unfold in Hong Kong and in Singapore.

In Hong Kong, the Chinese business system is the dominant mode of business operations. The spirit and ethos of capitalism in Hong Kong have produced socially, culturally, and politically specific business systems (Lau and Kuan, 1988; Redding, 1990; 1995; 1996; S.L. Wong, 1995; Yu, 2000). Ethnic Chinese industrialists in Hong Kong are known for their entrepreneurship and higher propensity to engage in risky business and overseas ventures. The arrival of industrialists and entrepreneurs from mainland China after the communist takeover in 1949 contributed significantly to the early process of rapid industrialisation and economic development in Hong Kong. The peculiar neoliberal political economy in Hong Kong had several consequences for transnational entrepreneurship in Hong Kong. First, the private sector assumed a leading role in Hong Kong's economic development from the take-off of its industrialisation in the 1960s. This strong role of the private sector in Hong Kong has contributed to the proliferation of entrepreneurial activities in Hong Kong in all sectors. Many Hong Kong entrepreneurs have strong business experience through self-employment or as employers before they turn into transnational entrepreneurs. As argued in Figure 1.1, this prior experience in business and management is highly important in gaining market access and development through transnational activities. Many of these nascent transnational entrepreneurs have also developed a strong home economy presence prior to their internationalisation.

Second, the lack of direct state intervention in Hong Kong's industrialisation and economic development processes has contributed to the growth of domestic companies in both large firm sectors and small firm networks. This dual existence of large and small companies in all sectors of the Hong Kong economy facilitates the development of strong competitive advantage among domestic enterprises. The presence of strong SME production networks also underscores the importance of customer and supplier relationships in Hong Kong's production system. As indicated in Figure 1.1, these networks of relationships are important aspects of Hong Kong's entrepreneurial endowments and resources.

Third, the financial system in Hong Kong, while biased against the manufacturing sector, is highly favourable for the development of the service sector, particularly commerce, business, and financial services. The experience of many Hong Kong entrepreneurs in these service industries also better enables them to deploy and manipulate financial resources for transnational activities. Since information and risks are highly important in these service industries, Hong Kong entrepreneurs are well endowed with capabilities in the negotiation and control of resources in the presence of a business environment characterised by information asymmetry, high risks, and high returns.

In Singapore, while the Chinese business system is also present to a certain extent, there are significant variations in the institutional structuring of this business system (Table 2.7). During the late nineteenth century, Southeast Asia absorbed many Chinese emigrants who left mainland China for perceived better opportunities elsewhere (Lim and Gosling, 1983; Hodder, 1996; Lim, 1996; 2000; Lynn, 1998; Chan, 2000). This minority group of ethnic Chinese (except in Singapore where the Chinese have remained as the major ethnic group) has maintained its century-long contacts and relations with contemporaries elsewhere in the Asia-Pacific region. These contacts and relations form the organisational basis of ethnic Chinese business firms in Singapore where a similarly high level of entrepreneurship can be observed among ethnic- and family-based Chinese business networks. This phenomenon partially accounts for the dominance of ethnic Chinese in the business and commercial sectors of Singapore and most other Southeast Asian economies.

There are important qualifications, however, to these entrepreneurial tendencies in Singapore. Notably, a large proportion of local investments, particularly in the manufacturing sector, came from foreign firms, and GLCs and their various subsidiaries. The role of indigenous private enterprises in Singapore's industrialisation is rather limited. It is also difficult to expect this economically marginal group of local private enterprises to spearhead the Singapore economy. The majority of Singaporeans have become contented with their job security and are less willing to take specific kinds of risks to launch new business ventures (Ray, 1994; Teoh and Foo, 1997). As Senior Minister Lee Kuan Yew noted, 'we have built up too comfortable life for Singaporeans. But the people who want to be comfortable are the people who are not going to be rich. So, you've got to decide whether you want to try and get the jackpot, or you just live a quiet, peaceful life' (quoted in *The Straits Times*, 11 July 1996). Instead, the state was committed to rapid industrialisation and economic development with the assistance of a rapid influx of foreign investment. To achieve such objectives within a short period of time, the state had to focus on policies favourable to attracting foreign capital. It was apparently unavoidable that interest groups, particularly local business elites, were excluded from the political process. Huff (1995: 1431) noted that the state's 'decision to rely for economic development on MNEs [multinational enterprises] and state-owned enterprises allowed Singapore's local business elite largely to be excluded from the decision-making process'.

This process of exclusion not only handicapped the development of indigenous entrepreneurship, but also partially accounted for the late entry of indigenous Singaporean firms in the regional and global marketplaces. Instead, the state has taken a leading role in the recent regionalisation drive (see the next chapter). If the private sector cannot provide the necessary capital and entrepreneurial skills, the state will do so without any hesitation. In this regard, Lee and Low (1990: 167) argued that 'economic deregulation and liberalisation may not be sufficient to encourage growth and competition without political and social liberalisation as well. The overpowering nature of state entrepreneurship has to be dismantled with a greater sincerity from the government to achieve a relaxation of the socio-political environment. While the red tape and administrative stumbling blocks are being scrutinised at various committee levels to make business among local entrepreneurs more spontaneous, it is the psychological barrier that must be broken down between the policy-makers and the indigenous entrepreneurs. Somehow, a more open and transparent relationship, where both parties are more trusting and on a more equal footing, must be developed'.

CONCLUSION

As important 'twin cities' in the Asia-Pacific region, Hong Kong and Singapore share many similarities in their history and geography. Both city-states have experienced tremendous growth and development in the past four decades. One would therefore expect that their economies share many similar features in their institutional structures and business systems. Based on extensive data on the economic structures and business systems of both economies, this chapter has shown that Hong Kong and Singapore are indeed very different global metropolises. On the one hand, Hong Kong was, and is still, governed by neoliberal laissez-faire economic ideologies that favour the role of private entrepreneurship in economic development and the emergence of a service economy oriented towards commerce, finance, and business services. On the otherhand, Singapore shares the same recent orientation towards the service economy. But it arrived at this stage of economic development via very different processes of institutional structuring. In the immediate aftermath of independence, the Singapore state chose a developmental ideology through which extensive state intervention in the national economy was legitimised. The developmental state also favoured foreign investment as the key impetus to its industrialisation programme. The net outcome of this initial institutional choice is the very significant domination of foreign firms and government-linked companies in Singapore's economic landscape today. In this peculiar business system, there is, in short, not much room for private entrepreneurship to flourish.

The extent to which these entrepreneurial tendencies in the domestic settings of Hong Kong and Singapore can be translated into action when indigenous entrepreneurs and their firms internationalise into foreign countries remains unclear. One may argue that an economy with a strong presence of indigenous entrepreneurship (i.e. Hong Kong) may be able to produce many transnational corporations that are both entrepreneurial and competitive in the global economic platform. One may equally argue, however, that an economy with fewer entrepreneurs and endowed with fewer entrepreneurial resources (e.g. Singapore) can produce a different genre of transnational entrepreneurs. This is because many domestic private individuals go international to compensate for the lack of business opportunities in their home country. These budding transnational entrepreneurs become more entrepreneurial and competitive when they go abroad.

To what extent are these preliminary speculations on the nature and extent of transnational entrepreneurship valid? This will be the key empirical question to be tackled in Chapters 4 and 5, which examine critically the processes of internationalisation by transnational entrepreneurs and intrapreneurs, and the resources that facilitate these processes of transnational entrepreneurship. Before I proceed to analyse the extent of transnational entrepreneurship in Chapters 4 and 5, it is necessary to examine the trends and characteristics of outward investments and transnational corporations from Hong Kong and Singapore in the next chapter.

NOTES

1. It is useful to situate this manufacturing decline in the context of the emergence of Hong Kong as the co-ordination centre of cross-border manufacturing activities. Enright et al. (1997: 21) estimated that more than 6000 manufacturing firms in Hong Kong were reclassified into services firms in 1992 and 1993 alone because of the closure of their Hong Kong factories. The Census and Statistics Department (2000c: 91) reported that in 1998, some 6550 trading establishments in Hong Kong had previously operated as manufacturing firms.
2. In fact, the state's explicit encouragement of outward investment started immediately after the recession of the mid-1980s (Kanai, 1993). Investment measures, however, initially emphasised the globalisation of Singaporean firms into Europe and North America in order to promote a shift to higher value-added activities. They were ineffective because few Singaporean firms were capable of securing a market place in these advanced industrialised countries. For example, both Yeo Hiap Seng Ltd. (a major local food manufacturer) and Singapore Technologies (a state-owned enterprise) had bitter experiences in the USA (see *The Sunday Times*, 2 August 1992; Kanai, 1993). It was not until the early 1990s that the focus of the state was shifted to regionalisation instead of globalisation.
3. The aim of this section is to examine the role of the colonial state in Hong Kong's post-war economic development. I do not intend to discuss the economic policies of the post-1997 Hong Kong SAR government.
4. Another major reason for the low level of mass consumption is the role of the Central Provident Fund through which disposable income is effectively reduced (see below).
5. General information on the Singapore Economic Development Board (EDB) is located

at: http://www.sedb.com.sg/index1.html.
6. One important qualification to the data in Table 2.13 is that they do not indicate the size of establishment. Earlier discussion has already shown that SMEs are much more important in Hong Kong than in Singapore. As a consequence, the data tend to be biased against Singapore and should be viewed in the context of peculiar industrial structures in both economies.

3. City-states and their global reach: outward investments from Hong Kong and Singapore

> We can change our orientation. We can alter our social climate to become more encouraging and supportive of enterprise and innovation. We can enthuse a younger generation with the thrill and the rewards of building an external dimension to Singapore. We can and we will spread our wings into the region and then into the wider world. (Singapore's Senior Minister Lee Kuan Yew; quoted in Economic Development Board, 1993)

INTRODUCTION

Domestic institutional structures and organisation systems not only shape trajectories of national economic development, but also influence the ways through which national economies are articulated into the global economy. Chapter 2 has evaluated the significant differences in the institutional structuring of domestic developmental trajectories in Hong Kong and Singapore. With the exception of some discussion of trade and inward investment flows, however, it offers nothing on how both city-states are actively globalising themselves via promoting outflows of people and capital. The fact that city-states are globalising themselves is not new (Olds and Yeung, 2000). What is surprising, however, is that much of the literature on global cities has paid only lip service to the complex interrelationships between global city formation and the developmental state. This lacuna in the global city literature, to a large extent, is explained by the dependency of the literature on empirical studies of two to three major global cities – London, New York and, occasionally, Tokyo (see Yeoh, 1999; Douglass, 2000).

As reflected in the above quotation from Singapore's Senior Minister, the aim of this chapter is therefore to explore empirically the global reach of two city-states via outward investments. 'Global reach' is defined as the complex processes through which a city articulates itself into and benefits from participation in the global economy. It illustrates how a specific territorial organisation (e.g. the city-state) is able to extend its influence and relations in the global economy through encouraging both inward and outward flows of people, capital, goods and services, and information. It also sets the institutional context of transnational activities by entrepreneurs from Hong Kong and Singapore. While the next two chapters are concerned with specific characteristics and processes of transnational entrepreneurship at the scale of individual actors (see Figure 1.2), this chapter focuses on the national and organisational scales in analysing outward investments from the two city-states.

The chapter is organised into four sections. It first describes trends of outward investments from Hong Kong and Singapore. It then discusses some characteristics of Hong Kong and Singapore-based transnational corporations (TNCs). The third section addresses the political economy of outward investment from Hong Kong and Singapore by examining critically the role of the state in the globalisation of the two city-states. The final section raises some analytical issues for understanding transnational entrepreneurship in Hong Kong and Singapore. This serves as a prelude to the empirical analysis in Chapters 4 and 5.

HISTORICAL DEVELOPMENTS OF OUTWARD INVESTMENTS FROM HONG KONG AND SINGAPORE

In the Asia-Pacific region, Hong Kong has been the leading developing country spearheading the international operations of domestic enterprises and capital. While foreign investments by TNCs based in other Asian Newly Industrialised Economies (NIEs) had their roots in the late 1950s and thereafter, some large Hong Kong-based TNCs (HKTNCs) had emerged as early as the late nineteenth century, in particular those controlled by British capital in Hong Kong (Yeung, 1998a). Some of these British establishments were former colonial trading houses, known as *hongs* locally in Hong Kong and Southern China (e.g. Jardine Matheson, the Swire Group, and the Wharf Group). Some of these *hongs* and commercial firms had also made substantial overseas investment, mostly in then Imperial China and Southeast Asia (e.g. Hongkong and Shanghai Banking Corporation). This was a historical period in which foreign direct investment (FDI) from Hong Kong (HKFDI) resulted primarily from the colonial and expansionist tendencies of the British government and British-controlled HKTNCs.

From 1945 to the late 1960s, we observe moderate changes in the composition of HKFDI abroad. These changes were particularly prominent in terms of increasing ownership and control by indigenous Hong Kong firms. For example, some large textile companies from Hong Kong, owned and operated by emigrant industrialists who had fled Shanghai before the communist takeover of China in 1949, began to venture into Southeast Asia and selected countries worldwide (e.g. South Africa). Some of these textile mills later became the pioneers of integrated textile mills in the host countries (e.g. Malaya). This was also the period in which Hong Kong experienced dramatic changes in its industrial structure and economic development processes (see Chapter 2). Manufacturing industries came to the forefront of the domestic developmental agenda. These internal developments resulted in certain spin-offs of FDI from Hong Kong into, for example, Southeast Asia. Meanwhile, the imposition of voluntary quota restrictions on Hong Kong textiles firms in the late 1950s and the early 1960s by developed countries in Europe and America effectively induced many textile HKTNCs to venture into overseas locations where export quotas were available (Lui and Chiu, 1994).

Since the late 1960s and early 1970s, a number of HKTNCs have emerged and invested in other parts of the world. This was the first phase of major growth of outward FDI by HKTNCs. Manufacturing HKTNCs made a start. Textile and garment and electronics HKTNCs expanded into lower-cost production sites in Southeast Asia and other developing countries because they felt the increasing pressures emerging from industrial restructuring in Hong Kong. Since 1979, China's 'open-door' policy has also attracted a huge influx of Hong Kong firms, ranging from large listed corporations to small family operators in all types of industries and sectors (see Thoburn et al., 1990; Leung, 1993; K.C. Ho and So, 1997). Another major wave of Hong Kong's overseas investment has occurred since the early 1980s when the future of Hong Kong became increasingly uncertain. The consolidation of the Sino-British Joint Declaration in December 1984 (Hong Kong Government, 1984) represented a major watershed in the historical development of HKTNCs and outward FDI flows from Hong Kong. Major companies in Hong Kong began to rethink their future strategies beyond 1997.

Leading Hong Kong companies responded in diverse ways. Within the Asia-Pacific region, a large proportion of HKFDI has now been invested in Mainland China, in particular in Guangdong province. According to Chinese sources,[1] Hong Kong is the largest foreign investor in China and had US$110 billion worth of cumulative realised FDI in China between 1979 and 1998, followed by Taiwan (US$16 billion), the USA (US$16 billion), and Japan (US$8.2 billion). Although an estimated 20–30 per cent of HKFDI in China originates from foreign affiliates in Hong Kong (see Low et al., 1998: 144), this figure is still very significant since Hong Kong is a relatively small economy compared to Taiwan, the USA, and Japan.

UNCTAD (1996: Annex Table 4) recently estimated that outward FDI stock from Hong Kong was US$9.4 billion in 1985 and had reached US$85 billion by 1995. By 1998, this figure rose to US$224 billion or HK$1.7 trillion (Census and Statistics Department, 2000b: Table 4). In 1995, HKTNCs controlled more than 4317 foreign affiliates in host countries (UNCTAD, 1996: Table I.4).

Table 3.1 presents some recent estimated flows and stocks of FDI from Hong Kong to selected host economies. As early as 1984, Malaysia and Singapore were the most important destinations of HKFDI, accounting for 57 per cent of total HKFDI at US$3.8 billion. The next decade saw the rapid emergence of Mainland China as the largest recipient of HKFDI. By 1993, HKFDI in China alone constituted 75 per cent of total HKFDI, at US$49 billion. The Census and Statistics Department (2000b) recently published a set of statistics on outward investments from Hong Kong in 1998. Based on this report, total HKFDI in 1998 was estimated at US$224 billion or HK$1.7 trillion. Its ratio to Hong Kong's GDP at current prices was 137 per cent, a figure far greater than that in Singapore (see below). Some 54 per cent, or US$120 billion, went to four tax havens, i.e. British Virgin Islands (US$93 billion), Cayman Islands (US$13 billion), Bermuda (US$12 billion) and Panama (US$2.9 billion). The remainder, some US$103 billion, went to Mainland China, the UK, the USA, Southeast Asia and other countries. Of this HKFDI not heading towards tax havens, Mainland China accounted for 68 per cent or US$71 billion. During the same period, HKFDI played an increasingly important role in total FDI stock in China, Indonesia, and Thailand. Hong Kong's share of total FDI stock in China increased very substantially from 11 per cent in 1984 to 61 per cent in 1993. Meanwhile, the shares of HKFDI in total FDI stock in Malaysia and Singapore decreased from respectively 14 per cent and 10 per cent in 1984 to 8 per cent and 7 per cent in 1993, indicating the shift in both Southeast Asian economies towards attracting high value-added investments from developed economies.

The sectoral distribution of HKFDI tends to be skewed towards service industries. In 1998, investment holding, real estate and business services (44 per cent) and wholesale and retail trade (12 per cent) contributed 56 per cent of total HKFDI (Census and Statistics Department, 2000b: Table 6). Manufacturing industries only accounted for 9 per cent of total HKFDI. A sample survey of Hong Kong manufacturers conducted by Tuan and Ng (1995a: 154) in 1993 reported that some 85 per cent of them were involved in cross-border operations, 59 per cent of which were located in China. More than 75 per cent of outward FDI by Hong Kong manufacturers in China was geographically located in Guangdong province. In 1998, Guangdong province accounted for 65 per cent of Hong Kong's direct

Table 3.1 Estimated flows and stocks of foreign direct investment from Hong Kong to selected host economies

Host Country	1984	1985	1986	1987	1988	1989	1990	1991	1992	1993	1998
FDI Stock from Hong Kong (US$million)											
China	341	1151	2284	3882	5978	8055	9969	12456	20269	36684	70717
Indonesia	275	272	298	337	393	459	632	876	1192	1442	–
Korea	31	38	46	86	104	116	131	137	150	162	–
Malaysia	1208	1308	1491	1370	1322	1464	1510	1938	2429	2186	–
Philippines	43	48	48	67	126	163	198	239	253	301	1420
Singapore	986	881	765	1000	1197	148	1806	2127	2568	3016	2014
Taiwan	162	181	214	301	418	585	722	825	950	1070	–
Thailand	213	236	273	304	414	637	911	1365	1937	2109	2634
United States	574	576	617	1073	1161	1549	1808	2210	2078	2229	7308
United Kingdom	–	–	–	–	–	–	–	–	–	–	120465
Tax havens[c]											
Total	3832	4692	6036	8420	11113	14509	17689	22171	31827	49200	223938
Ratio to GDP at current prices (%)	11.6	13.4	15.0	17.0	18.9	21.5	23.5	25.7	31.6	42.5	136.9
Hong Kong's Share of Total FDI Stock in Host Countries (%)											
China	11.1	24.4	34.6	43.6	49.4	52	52.5	53.3	59	60.7	–
Indonesia	9.2	8.2	8.3	8.5	8.7	8.8	10	11.2	12.5	12.5	–
Korea	2.8	2.9	2.6	3.6	3.2	2.9	2.8	2.4	2.4	2.4	–
Malaysia	13.5	13.6	14.8	13	11.8	11.3	9.9	10.1	10.2	7.8	–
Philippines	5.6	6.1	5.3	5.5	5.9	6	6.1	6.3	6.3	6.3	–
Singapore	10	8.1	6.1	6.5	6.3	6.7	6.6	6.6	6.6	6.6	–
Taiwan	11.2	10.1	10.1	10.6	11	10.8	10.7	10.7	10.7	10.9	–
Thailand	9.5	9.9	10.2	10.1	10.1	10.8	10.8	13.1	15.4	15	–
United States	0.4	0.4	0.3	0.4	0.4	0.4	0.4	0.5	0.5	0.5	–
Total	2.3	2.5	2.7	2.9	3	3.2	3.4	4	5.3	7.4	–

Notes: [a] They are British Virgin Islands, Cayman Islands, Bermuda, and Panama.
Figures between 1984 and 1993 are estimated by multiplying Hong Kong's shares of total FDI flows or paid-up capital stocks and the value of total FDI flows reported in the balance of payments for each host economy. They are very rough estimates, but are all based on values reported in host economy balance of payments statistics.

Sources: Low et al. (1998: Table 4.2) and Census and Statistics Department (2000b: Table 4).

investments in China, estimated at US$71 billion or HK$548 billion (Census and Statistics Department, 2000b: Table 5). Enright et al. (1997: 11) also found that some 55 per cent of Hong Kong's clothing manufacturers had manufacturing capabilities in China. The majority of these manufacturing operations, however, were in relatively labour-intensive industries. Cheap labour, land costs, and geographical proximity to Hong Kong were the most often cited reasons for these cross-border operations (see also Federation of Hong Kong Industries, 1992). Table 3.2 shows that China's share in Hong Kong's domestic exports over the 1990–1996 period decreased. But the values of items shipped out for further processing and manufacturing in China made up a significant majority of Hong Kong's domestic exports to China. These items also accounted for a significant proportion of imports from China and re-exports of goods of Chinese origin to the rest of the world. While the manufacturing sector accounted for 33 per cent of total HKFDI in China in 1998, investment holdings, real estate, and various business services (28 per cent) and communications (11 per cent) were equally important industrial destinations (Census and Statistics Department, 2000b: Table 7).

On the other hand, FDI from Singapore (SINFDI) was small historically compared to other forms of investments (e.g. portfolio investment).[2] Singaporean firms had neither the financial strength nor any firm-specific advantage to extend their operations abroad. Since the mid-1970s, however, a centrifugal tendency in the Singapore economy has surfaced. Singaporean firms are now investing in other parts of the world in the form of FDI. The Department of Statistics (1991) estimated that at the end of 1976, SINFDI was slightly above S$1 billion. As shown in Table 3.3, this figure had grown to S$1.7 billion by 1981, S$14 billion by 1990 and S$71 billion by 1997. Today, Singapore has become one of the major sources of FDI among the Asian NIEs. It should be noted, however, that much of this outward FDI flow from Singapore originates from Singapore-based affiliates of foreign TNCs. Singapore's dependence on foreign capital for industrialisation has generated sufficient momentum for these very foreign firms to participate actively in the regionalisation effort. As early as 1981, foreign-controlled companies accounted for 48 per cent of Singapore's total direct investment abroad. In 1997, this ratio increased slightly to 50 per cent (see Table 3.3).

Geographically, Singapore's outward FDI has been concentrated in the Asian region (see Table 3.3). During the 1981–1997 period, about 53 per cent of Singapore's outward FDI went to Asian countries. In 1997, Malaysia, China, and Hong Kong were the largest Asian recipients of outward FDI from Singapore. In Europe and North America, the UK emerged as the largest host country, receiving some S$7.7 billion or 11 per

Table 3.2 Trade involving Hong Kong's outward processing in Mainland China, 1990–1996

	1990	1991	1992	1993	1994	1995	1996
Estimated value of outward processing trade (in HK$million)							
Domestic exports to Mainland China	36418	40369	44271	45141	41959	43890	43089
Re-exports to Mainland China	55496	73562	97368	115037	139221	173722	179235
Imports from Mainland China	145103	197384	254013	295203	354912	399567	452890
Re-exports of goods with Mainland China origin (except to Mainland China)	–	221450	299833	364536	422544	492461	552822
Estimated proportion of outward processing trade (in %)							
Domestic exports to Mainland China	79.0	76.5	74.3	74.0	71.4	71.4	72.8
Re-exports to Mainland China	50.3	48.2	46.2	42.1	43.3	45.4	43.2
Imports from Mainland China	61.8	67.6	72.1	73.8	75.9	74.4	79.9
Re-exports of goods with Mainland China origin (except to Mainland China)	–	74.1	78.3	80.8	82.0	82.2	86.0

Source: Census and Statistics Department (1998: Table 3.11).

Table 3.3 Cumulative outward direct investment from Singapore by country, 1976–1997 (S$million)

Country	1976	1981	1985	1986	1987	1988	1989	1990	1991	1992	1993	1994	1995	1996	1997
Asian Countries	–	1289.9	1721.4	1836.5	1908.5	1963.6	1968.4	7013.3	7401.5	9209.3	11480.0	22121.5	27101.2	31714.2	37316.6
ASEAN	–	1078.5	1133.3	1155.8	1180.5	1216.0	1138.4	3567.1	3995.6	4896.7	5933.8	12189.5	16088.2	16874.2	17924.8
Brunei	–	3.7	52.9	50.0	54.2	57.4	56.6	66.2	69.4	88.5	91.2	128.5	92.0	89.9	73.9
Indonesia	–	39.5	65.0	67.7	58.6	59.8	53.3	224.8	267.3	328.1	517.3	2359.9	4030.9	3914.3	5722.2
Malaysia	–	1006.9	971.8	985.6	1008.4	1030.8	971.6	2790.1	3121.1	3916.5	4656.7	8182.3	9715.9	9591.1	8973.7
Philippines	–	18.4	22.4	22.5	14.3	22.5	22.8	97.7	89.7	106.3	230.6	445.2	625.1	1003.8	934.1
Thailand	–	10.0	21.2	30.0	45.0	45.5	34.1	388.4	448.1	457.4	438.1	1073.6	1252.8	1573.0	1219.0
Vietnam	–	–	–	–	–	–	–	–	–	–	–	172.0	371.3	702.1	1001.9
China	–	–	57.6	93.8	101.4	79.1	47.4	239.7	220.0	282.6	444.1	1696.7	2968.2	6414.1	8960.4
Hong Kong	–	181.8	460.7	497.9	539.9	545.2	581.4	2266.2	2368.6	3051.1	4025.6	6655.0	6268.3	5973.6	7257.3
Japan	–	0.3	5.0	6.0	16.1	16.7	33.9	51.8	73.5	75.8	109.4	414.5	465.8	454.9	535.1
Taiwan	–	12.9	32.9	37.8	26.0	54.3	86.0	494.8	287.0	349.5	354.5	524.6	573.2	570.7	657.7
Others	–	16.2	31.9	45.2	44.6	37.5	65.4	393.7	456.7	553.6	612.7	469.1	737.4	1426.6	1981.2
European Countries	–	50.7	89.3	167.2	358.2	303.4	203.4	1095.4	1397.6	1480.2	1549.7	3941.3	5550.8	8754.0	11391.4
Netherlands	–	0.8	12.0	13.8	165.4	111.4	–94.3	656.3	549.6	525.5	467.1	1079.2	1020.8	2422.6	2254.0
United Kingdom	–	49.7	45.9	81.8	48.3	49.3	50.4	300.4	322.3	351.0	360.6	1846.1	3296.5	5021.5	7680.0
Others	–	0.2	31.4	71.6	135.9	134.1	223.9	138.6	525.8	603.7	722.0	1016.0	1233.4	1309.9	1457.4
Australia	–	62.6	176.9	175.6	217.8	166.1	138.3	530.5	570.0	636.5	374.1	1325.3	1448.3	1773.1	1821.2
New Zealand	–	–	–	–	–	–	–	1358.5	1387.3	1332.6	1493.8	2173.4	2118.4	1453.6	1384.5
Canada	–	–	17.6	17.6	17.6	29.0	73.4	–	–	–	–	–	–	–	–
United States	–	31.8	66.1	65.4	69.3	107.7	160.0	689.7	1303.9	1589.5	1755.1	2427.1	2635.2	2628.9	2962.7
Other Countries n.e.c.	–	242.9	185.9	335.4	390.1	424.1	400.2	2934.3	3123.6	3493.1	4587.4	6384.2	7386.3	9212.7	15764.2
Total	1015.1	1677.7	2257.2	2597.7	2961.5	2993.9	2943.7	13621.7	15183.8	17741.3	21240.2	38372.8	46240.2	55536.4	70640.5
Ratio to GDP at current prices	7.0	5.7	5.8	6.6	6.8	5.9	5.2	20.5	20.2	21.9	22.9	36.0	39.0	43.1	50.0

Percentage of non-manufacturing	–	–	–	–	–	–	79.6	76.2	74.4	68.2	77.4	75.4	79.3	81.4
Total (foreign)	–	799.4	585.1	744.1	1125.1	1095.1	989.8	6674.0	8066.5	9605.3	11984.6	18319.5	21982.8	25362.8	34998.2
Percentage of foreign	–	47.6	25.9	28.6	38.0	36.6	33.6	49.0	53.1	54.1	56.4	47.7	47.5	45.7	49.5

Note: Data from 1976–1989 refer to direct investments abroad (D1). Data from 1990–1993 refer to direct investment (D1) plus the reserves of the overseas subsidiaries and associates attributable to these companies. Data from 1990–1993 refer to direct equity investments (D2), which are direct investment abroad (D3) which are D2 plus loans granted to affiliates. Data for 1994–1997 refer to total direct

Source: Department of Statistics (various years h).

cent of total direct investment from Singapore. It is also ranked as the fourth largest recipient of Singapore's foreign investment. In cumulative terms, Singapore is also one of the largest foreign investors in many Asian economies:

- ranked first in Myanmar (1989–1997) and Vietnam (1991–1997)
- ranked second in Malaysia (1975–1997)
- ranked fourth in Indonesia (1967–1997)
- ranked fifth in China (1979–1997)

Of this Asian-focus of Singapore's outward FDI, Malaysia has always been the most important destination country (Yeung, 1998c). Although its lion's share in Singapore's outward FDI declined from 60 per cent in 1981 to 13 per cent in 1997, Malaysia was still the single largest recipient country. This relative decline can be readily explained by the recent 1993 regionalisation drive by the Singapore government through which more investment opportunities in China and Southeast Asia have been opened to Singaporean companies (see the next section). Singapore's investment in China and Indonesia has grown significantly during the 1994–1997 period. Singapore's FDI in China grew over five-fold from S$1.7 billion in 1994 to S$9.0 billion in 1997. Singapore's FDI in Indonesia also more than doubled from S$2.4 billion in 1994 to S$5.7 billion in 1997 (Table 3.3). This growth is in line with the Singapore government's heavy involvement in developing large industrial estates and infrastructural projects in China and Indonesia. In the midst of the Asian economic crisis, however, Singapore's FDI in China dipped 42 per cent to US$1.5 billion for the first six months of 1998 (*The Straits Times*, 28 July 1998). A large amount of Singapore's investment in China is also channelled through Hong Kong, explaining why Hong Kong's figures look rather impressive. The significant four-fold growth of SINFDI in the UK from S$1.8 billion in 1994 to S$7.7 billion in 1997 is accounted for mainly by financial and property investments (see below).

Data on the industrial origin of Singapore's FDI were incomplete and unavailable until recently. Table 3.4 gives an impression of the industrial origin of foreign equity investment from Singapore and shows that the extent of overseas operations differs significantly across various industrial sectors. In terms of sectoral distribution, the financial sector continues to spearhead Singapore's global reach. In 1997, some S$40 billion or 56 per cent of total outward investment from Singapore (S$71 billion) went into this sector. The manufacturing sector accounted for another S$13 billion or 19 per cent. Between 1990 and 1997, financial and manufacturing firms were the two major investors from Singapore by industrial origin. At the

Table 3.4 Foreign equity investment of Singaporean firms by industrial origin and activity abroad, 1990–1997 (S$million)

Industrial Sectors	1990	1991	1992	1993	1994	1995	1996	1997	% Increase 1990–1997
Industrial origin									
Manufacturing	2779.8	3618.7	4545.5	6752.7	10244.7	15241.2	13031.6	14271.7	513.4
Construction	251.3	268.8	326.4	614.0	884.0	837.5	839.1	882.1	351.0
Commerce	993.5	1105.4	1361.9	1220.7	3481.6	4746.5	5280.0	5935.2	597.4
Transport	825.1	401.2	421.8	504.7	2046.8	2435.9	2828.6	4243.0	514.2
Financial	6362.9	7182.8	8194.6	8945.6	16809.0	20546.1	28193.0	39139.9	615.1
Real Estate	1140.9	1119.8	1391.0	1692.8	2327.9	2939.7	2778.7	3360.4	294.5
Business Services	1246.6	1455.9	1469.1	1481.3	2502.3	2744.3	2399.8	2624.9	210.6
Others	21.7	31.4	31.0	28.4	76.4	79.7	185.5	183.4	845.2
Total	13621.8	15184.0	17741.3	21240.2	38372.7	49570.9	55536.3	70640.6	518.6
Activity Abroad									
Manufacturing	2395.0	2901.1	3760.1	4612.7	8979.9	12418.9	11515.3	13161.9	549.6
Construction	69.5	72.3	130.2	199.3	439.0	597.7	556.2	552.8	795.4
Commerce	1504.3	1606.2	1967.1	2067.8	4068.3	5092.0	5208.0	5594.7	371.9
Transport	347.2	244.9	289.8	322.0	1548.4	2097.8	2011.3	2394.3	689.6
Financial	7301.2	8648.0	9752.7	11723.1	19420.8	23845.7	28839.5	39809.0	545.2
Real Estate	1213.1	859.3	962.9	1294.8	2534.0	3610.4	4429.1	5301.1	437.0
Business Services	511.6	605.1	595.3	766.9	1167.9	1359.4	2302.0	3129.5	611.7
Others	279.8	246.9	283.4	253.6	514.4	548.8	675.1	697.2	249.2
Total	13621.7	15183.8	17741.5	21240.2	38672.7	49570.7	55536.5	70640.5	518.6

Source: Department of Statistics (various years h).

114 Entrepreneurship and the internationalisation of Asian firms

end of 1997, they accounted for S$53 billion (76 per cent) of total direct equity investment abroad by industrial origin of investors. While Table 3.3 shows that during the 1990–1997 period, over 68 per cent of SINFDI was consistently in non-manufacturing activities, Table 3.4 demonstrates that construction, transport, and business services were the leading activities abroad for SINFDI.

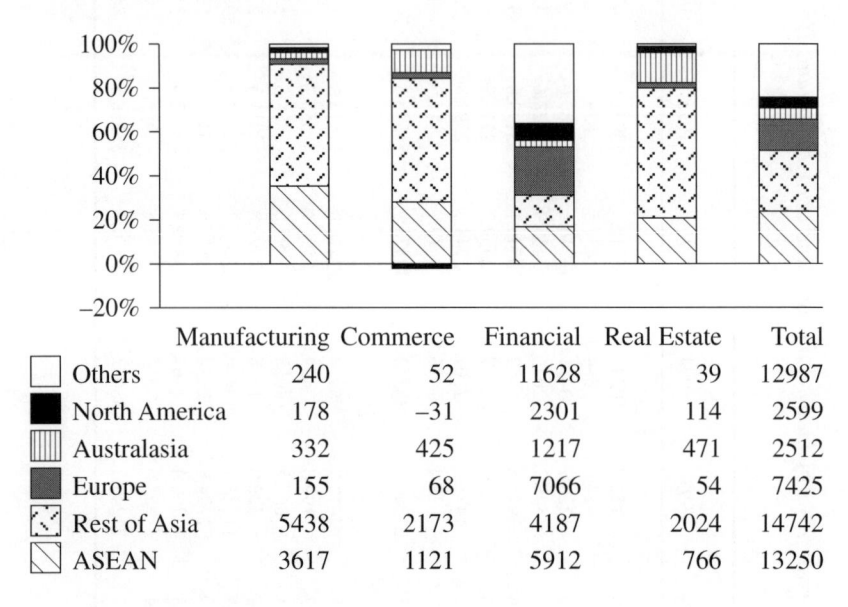

	Manufacturing	Commerce	Financial	Real Estate	Total
Others	240	52	11628	39	12987
North America	178	−31	2301	114	2599
Australasia	332	425	1217	471	2512
Europe	155	68	7066	54	7425
Rest of Asia	5438	2173	4187	2024	14742
ASEAN	3617	1121	5912	766	13250

Source: Department of statistics (various years).

Figure 3.1 Sectoral distribution of Singapore's direct investment abroad by host region, 1997 (S$million)

Figure 3.1 examines this sectoral distribution by host regions. Asia, in particular China and Southeast Asian countries, accounted for an overwhelming majority of manufacturing, commerce, and real estate investments from Singapore in 1996. However, a significant amount of real estate investment also went to Australasia, namely Australia and New Zealand, which emerged as almost equally important to ASEAN. In the financial sector, Europe (the UK, the Netherlands, and Belgium) and 'others' (Netherlands Antilles and Liberia) emerged as the most important destinations.

CHARACTERISTICS OF TRANSNATIONAL CORPORATIONS FROM SINGAPORE COMPARED WITH HONG KONG

The above section has provided a background and overview of outward direct investment from Hong Kong and Singapore, based upon aggregate statistics published by various agencies and authorities. In this section, I report the main findings of the corporate survey and personal interviews conducted with individual companies from Singapore and their overseas subsidiaries (see Chapter 1). I also offer a comparison with findings on the global reach of Hong Kong-based TNCs (HKTNCs) published in an earlier monograph (see Yeung, 1998a: Chapters 4 and 5). These findings present a more detailed and nuanced perspective on Singapore's global reach via cross-border investments by Singapore-based TNCs (SINTNCs). They are also very useful in setting the firm-specific context for my analysis of transnational entrepreneurship among SINTNCs in the next two chapters. After a discussion of their global significance, the following attributes of SINTNCs are considered: (1) ownership and sectoral distribution; (2) global distribution; (3) motives for overseas operations; (4) strategies and mechanisms of overseas operations; and (5) organisation of overseas operations.

Global Significance of TNCs from Hong Kong and Singapore

To begin, it is useful to compare the relative significance of HKTNCs and SINTNCs in the global economy. In their classic paper on 'Third World multinationals', Heenan and Keegan (1979) did not identify the possible role of TNCs from emerging economies as a formidable global competitor. In fact, it was not until the 1960s that the first major wave of FDI by business firms from emerging economies began to surface. A few emerging economies led this early wave of FDI: Hong Kong and South Korea from Asia, and Brazil, Mexico, and Argentina from Latin America. Whereas TNCs from Hong Kong were primarily controlled by private capital, Korean, Brazilian, Mexican, and Argentine TNCs were largely state-owned or government-related enterprises (see Yeung, 1999a). The two groups therefore exhibited rather different patterns and processes of transnational operations. As Table 3.5 shows, most of these early TNCs from emerging economies in 1977 were state-owned enterprises and oriented towards the natural resource sector. For example, virtually all petroleum TNCs from emerging economies were nationalised corporations formerly owned by major global oil companies. By 1997, none of these TNCs had originated from Hong Kong and Singapore, the two resource-scarce city-states that were experiencing rapid industrialisation.

Table 3.5   A partial list of top TNCs from emerging markets ranked by sales, 1977

Ranking (Sales)	Name of TNC	Economy	Industry	Sales (US$million)
1	National Iranian Oil	Iran	Petroleum	22315
2	Petroleos de Venezuela	Venezuela	Petroleum	9268
3	Petrobas	Brazil	Petroleum	8284
4	Pemex	Mexico	Petroleum	3395
5	Haci Omer Sabanci Holding	Turkey	Textiles	2903
6	Hyundai Group	South Korea	Shipbuilding, transportation	2591
7	Indian Oil	India	Petroleum	2316
8	Schlumberger	Neth. Antilles	Scientific equipment	2160
9	Chinese Petroleum	Taiwan	Petroleum	1920
10	Zambia Industrial & Mining	Zambia	Mining and metal refining	1862
11	Lucky Group	South Korea	Petroleum, electronics	1744
12	Steel Authority of India	India	Metal refining	1448
13	Turkiye Petrolleri	Turkey	Petroleum	1377
14	Kuwait National Petroleum	Kuwait	Petroleum	1376
15	Korea Oil	South Korea	Petroleum	1341
16	Samsung Group	South Korea	Industrial equipment	1305
17	Thyssen-Bornemisza	Neth. Antilles	Shipbuilding, farm equipment	1259
18	CODELCO-CHILE	Chile	Mining and metal refining	1231
19	Koc Holding	Turkey	Motor vehicles	1208
20	Philippine National Oil	Philippines	Petroleum	986
21	Daewoo Industrial South	South Korea	Textiles	852
22	Siderurgica Nacional	Brazil	Metal refining	848
23	USIMINAS	Brazil	Metal refining	826
24	General Motors do Brasil	Brazil	Motor vehicles	824
25	Vale do Rio Doce	Brazil	Mining	824
26	Ford Brasil	Brazil	Motor vehicles	759
27	SANBRA	Brazil	Food products	707
28	Industrias Reunidas F. Matarazzo	Brazil	Chemicals, food products, textiles	675
29	Grupo Industrial Alfa	Mexico	Metal refining	603
30	ICC	South Korea	Metal products	581
31	Bharat Heavy Electricals	India	Industrial equipment	525
32	Ssangyong Cement Industrial	South Korea	Chemicals	598
33	Sunkyong	South Korea	Textiles	468

Source: Collated from Exhibit in Heenan and Keegan (1979: 104).

By the late 1990s, however, it is clear that TNCs from emerging economies, in particular Hong Kong and Singapore, had established a significant presence in the global market. Table 3.6 lists the top 25 TNCs from developing countries, ranked by foreign assets in 1997. It must be noted that many of them have made it to the *Fortune 500* top companies in the world (see also Hamlin, 1998). The point here is that many TNCs from emerging economies, particularly Hong Kong (e.g. Jardine Matheson), had humble origins as regional trading and commercial ventures. They had internationalised across national boundaries as early as the late nineteenth century. Their participation in globalisation, however, did not occur until the 1980s when the global economy was increasingly competitive, their organisational capabilities were much more consolidated, and their home governments were serious about growing 'national champions'. Viewed in this context, the globalisation of business firms from emerging economies should be seen as an incremental process through which these firms are becoming significant competitors in the global economy.

Two observations can be made from Table 3.6. First, significantly more leading developing country TNCs are based in Hong Kong than in Singapore. Of the six HKTNCs, indigenous Chinese residents in Hong Kong control only Hutchison Whampoa and New World Development. The rest are controlled by British interests based in London (e.g. Jardine Matheson), Chinese interests based in Beijing (CITIC Pacific), or ethnic Chinese in Indonesia (e.g. First Pacific). The Two SINTNCs, one public-listed and another government-linked, are ranked much lower among the 25 largest TNCs from developing countries. Second, the largest HKTNCs tend to be diversified business entities, whereas SINTNCs are more specialised in particular industries such as food and beverages, and transportation. This sectoral specialisation, as revealed in the survey data below, reflects the broader industrial orientation of both city-state economies.

Ownership and Sectoral Distribution

This section starts with the background and global geographies of 204 indigenous companies from Singapore included in the corporate survey. As shown in Figure 3.2, some 66 per cent of these 204 SINTNCs are *private companies* (sole proprietorships, limited companies, or partnerships managed by professional managers and/or family member). Another 23 per cent of our sample belong to SINTNCs listed on either the main board or SESDAQ of the Stock Exchange of Singapore (SES). The last 11 per cent are made up of government-linked companies (GLCs) most of which are listed in the SES. This sample of SINTNCs is fairly representative of

Table 3.6 The top 25 TNCs from developing countries ranked by foreign assets, 1997 (US$million and number of employees)

Ranking (Foreign Assets)	Name of TNC	Economy	Industry	Assets Foreign	Assets Total	Sales Foreign	Sales Total	Employment Foreign	Employment Total	Index[a]
1/88[b]	Petroleos de Venezuela SA	Venezuela	Oil, Gas and Coal	9007	47148	32502	34801	11849	56592	44.5
2/52[b]	Daewoo	South Korea	Diversified	–	22946	–	18802	–	–	50.8
3	Jardine Matheson	Hong Kong	Diversified	6652	11970	7983	11522	–	175000	75.0
4	First Pacific Co Ltd	Hong Kong	Diversified	6295	11386	7416	8308	40400	51270	74.4
5	Cemex SA	Mexico	Construction	5627	10231	2235	3788	10690	19174	56.6
6	Hutchison Whampoa	Hong Kong	Diversified	4978	15086	1899	5754	17013	37100	37.3
7	Sappi Ltd.	South Africa	Paper	3830	4953	2419	3557	9492	23458	61.9
8	China State Construction Engin Corp	China	Construction	3730	7230	1530	5420	5496	258195	27.3
9	China National Chemicals	China	Diversified	3460	5810	11240	17880	625	8905	43.1
10	LG Group	South Korea	Electronics	3158	15431	5175	17640	32532	80370	30.1
11	YPF Sociedad Anonima	Argentina	Oil, Gas and Coal	3061	12761	911	6144	1908	10002	19.3
12	Petroleo Brasileiro	Brazil	Oil, Gas and Coal	–	34233	–	27946	–	41173	4.4
13	Sunkyong Group	South Korea	Energy, Chemicals	2561	24572	9960	31692	2600	32169	16.6
14	Hyundai Engineering & Construction Co.	South Korea	Machinery	–	8063	–	5405	–	30981	37.6
15	New World Development Co Ltd	Hong Kong	Diversified	2060	14030	800	2580	–	14840	15.3
16	Guangdong Investment Ltd	Hong Kong	Investment	1898	3053	676	924	15080	16500	75.6
17	Citic Pacific	Hong Kong	Diversified	1834	8733	912	2154	8262	11800	44.5
18	PETRONAS	Malaysia	Petroleum	–	20990	–	10055	–	13000	25.9
19	China Shougang Group	China	Diversified	1600	6640	1040	4390	–	218158	16.2
20	Fraser & Neave Ltd	Singapore	Beverages	1578	4273	1230	1912	11461	13131	62.8
21	Samsung Co Ltd	South Korea	Electronics	–	16301	–	13050	–	57817	16.3

22	Singapore Airlines	Singapore	Transportation	1546	9111	3454	4727	2957	13258	37.4
23	Companhia Valedo Rio Doce	Brazil	Transportation	1509	14332	3320	4744	7432	42456	32.7
24	Enersis S.A.	Chile	Electrical Services	–	14281	–	890	–	14366	28.2
25	Acer Group	Taiwan	Electronics	1376	2946	3204	4217	6792	12342	59.2

Notes:
[a] The index of transnationality is calculated as the average of foreign assets to total assets, foreign sales to total sales and foreign employment to total employment.
[b] Data refer to rankings among the world's top 100 TNCs in 1995.

Source: UNCTAD (1999: Table 2).

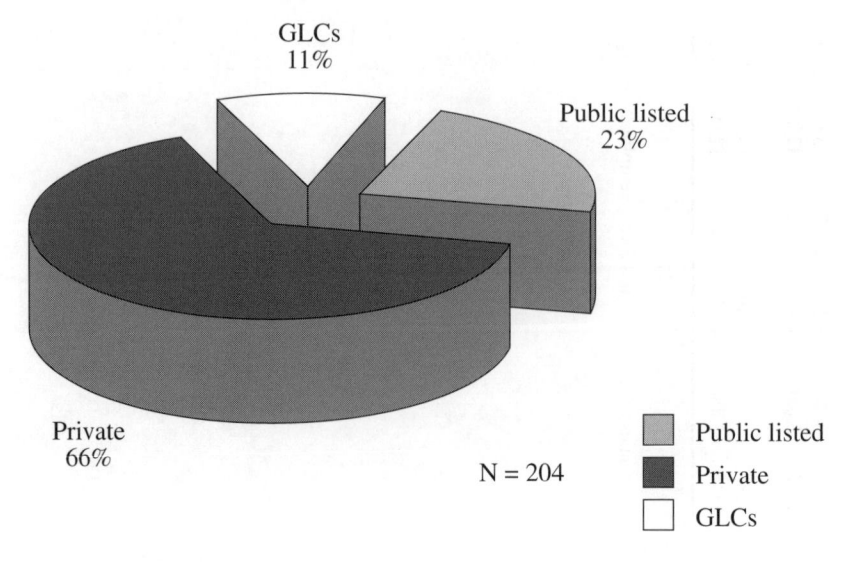

120   *Entrepreneurship and the internationalisation of Asian firms*

```
         GLCs
         11%
                         Public listed
                             23%


    Private                              ▨ Public listed
     66%                                 ■ Private
                    N = 204              ☐ GLCs
```

Source: Author's survey.

Figure 3.2   Ownership structure of parent companies in Singapore

the ownership structure of indigenous companies in Singapore. It compares very well with the ownership distribution of HKTNCs in the earlier survey (Yeung, 1998a). Some 41 of a total of 111 HKTNCs (37 per cent) are listed on the Hong Kong Stock Exchange and the rest belong to private companies (N = 70; 63 per cent). Both sample data sets are therefore very comparable.

In terms of sectoral distribution, Figure 3.3 shows that *manufacturing* SINTNCs account for the largest sub-sample, with over 37 per cent of all 204 companies. As the next important group of SINTNCs in my sample, *other services* include real estate, business services and other services. This is followed by SINTNCs from wholesale and retail trade, transport and communications, and finance. Together, these three service industries contribute 41 per cent of total sample size and surpass the importance of the manufacturing sector. In comparison, the survey on HKTNCs earlier reveals that respectively 38 per cent (N = 42) and 60 per cent (N = 67) of 111 HKTNCs are in the manufacturing and service industries. This sector distribution matches remarkably well that of SINTNCs.

Compared to data provided by the Department of Statistics (various years h) in Figure 3.1, my sample of SINTNCs tends to be biased towards those in manufacturing, commerce, and real estate, and against those in finance. This sampling bias is inevitable because of the *random sampling*

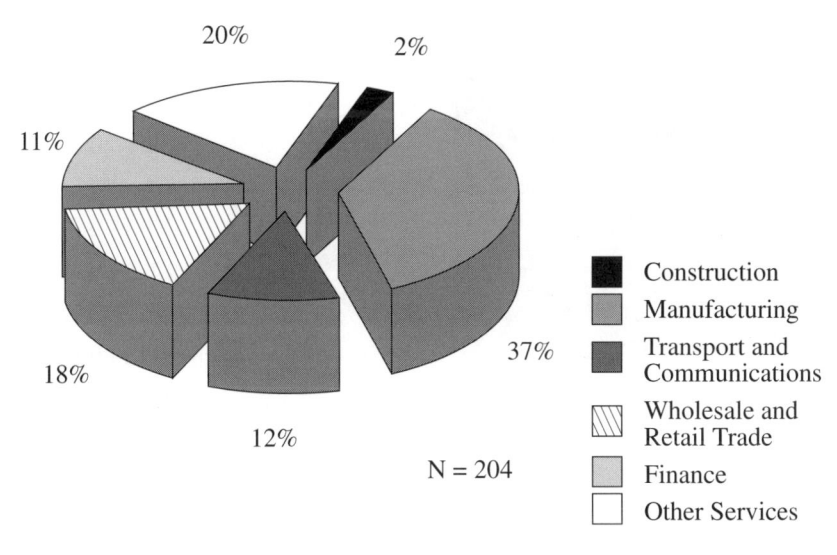

Figure 3.3 Sectoral distribution of parent companies in Singapore

procedure explained in Chapter 1 and the responses from SINTNCs. Another note is that both sets of data are different in their measurements. Whereas the Department of Statistics' sectoral distribution refers to Singapore's direct investment abroad, the sectoral distribution of the sampled SINTNCs is based on actual companies. Similar sectoral bias in favour of the manufacturing sector is also applicable to my survey of HKTNCs. While the Census and Statistics Department (2000b) noted that manufacturing HKTNCs only contributed 9 per cent of total HKFDI in 1998, my survey of 111 HKTNCs comprised 38 per cent of manufacturing HKTNCs.

In addition, Figure 3.4 uses turnover or sales value to measure the corporate size of parent companies in Singapore. Other measurements (e.g. assets and employment size) were also used in the original survey, although they all point towards the same pattern that *large companies* dominate the sample. Some 41 per cent of the sampled 204 SINTNCs have an annual turnover of at least S$50 million. Among these relatively large SINTNCs, 30 per cent have an annual turnover of over S$100 million. These major SINTNCs tend to be GLCs and public-listed companies. Another 59 per cent of the sampled SINTNCs have a turnover of less than S$50 million, indicating the relatively significant role of small and medium enterprises (SMEs) in contributing to Singapore's global reach. Today, SMEs account

Pie chart segments: 30%, 6%, 18%, 35%, 11%

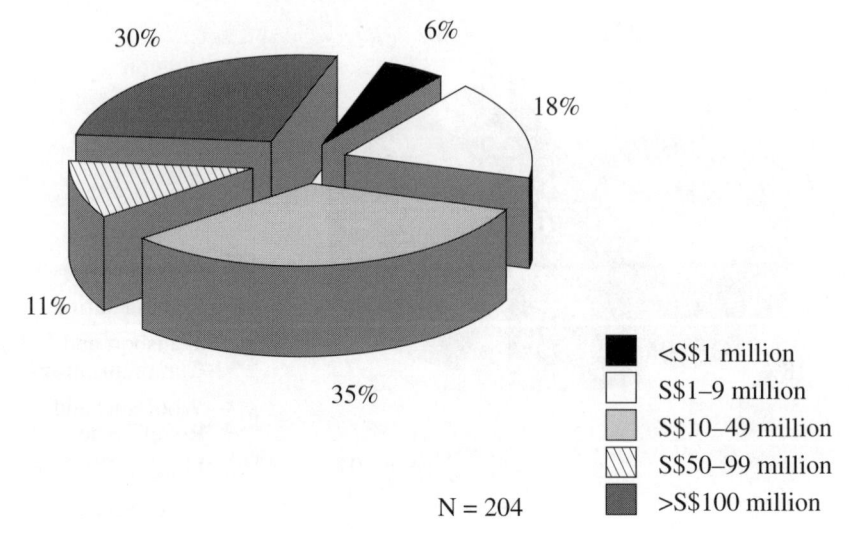

Legend:
- <S$1 million
- S$1–9 million
- S$10–49 million
- S$50–99 million
- >S$100 million

N = 204

Source: Author's survey.

Figure 3.4 Turnover of parent companies in Singapore

for about 94 per cent of the total establishments, 48 per cent of employment, 34 per cent of value-added, and 49 per cent of direct exports in Singapore (Department of Statistics, 1997; see also Chapter 2; Chew and Yeung, 2001).

Global Distributions of SINTNCs

Table 3.7 presents the geographical distribution of the sampled SINTNCs and HKTNCs by five measurements:

- earliest year of establishment
- mean year of establishment
- number of SINTNCs having a presence there
- number of subsidiaries controlled by these SINTNCs
- number of expatriate staff sent by the headquarters in Singapore

With the exception of the Philippines and China, SINTNCs have been operating in most regions and countries of the global economy since Singapore's independence in 1965. Interestingly, SINTNCs established a presence in Europe, North America, and other regions outside Asia as early as the 1950s and the 1960s. Singapore's global reach is therefore *not*

Table 3.7 Global geographies of transnational operations by indigenous companies from Singapore and Hong Kong (percentage in parentheses)

Regions/ Countries	Earliest Year of Establishment	Mean Year of Establishment	Number of TNC Presence	Number of Subsidiaries by Parent Companies	Number of Expatriate Staff from Home Country
SINTNCs					
Southeast Asia	–	–	–	582 (46.0)	354 (41.3)
Indonesia	1943	1987	74 (36.3)	155 (12.3)	235 (27.4)
Malaysia	1910	1985	119 (58.3)	273 (21.6)	49 (5.7)
Thailand	1940	1987	34 (16.7)	52 (4.1)	15 (1.7)
Philippines	1979	1993	37 (18.1)	42 (3.3)	13 (1.5)
Others	1910	1990	45 (22.1)	60 (4.7)	42 (4.9)
East Asia	–	–	–	484 (38.3)	411 (47.9)
China	1975	1992	151 (74.0)	365 (28.9)	372 (43.4)
Hong Kong	1910	1985	61 (29.9)	87 (6.9)	26 (3.0)
Others	1960	1989	26 (12.7)	32 (2.5)	13 (1.5)
Europe	**1950**	**1990**	**35 (17.2)**	47 (3.7)	19 (2.2)
North America	**1967**	**1990**	**33 (16.2)**	48 (3.8)	10 (1.2)
Other Regions	**1958**	**1990**	**57 (27.9)**	103 (8.1)	64 (7.5)
All SINTNCs	*1908*	*1975*	*204 (100)*	*1264 (100)*	*858 (100)*
HKTNCs					
Southeast Asia	–	–	–	411 (38.5)	–
Indonesia	–	–	33 (29.7)	39 (3.7)	–
Malaysia	–	–	53 (47.7)	95 (8.9)	–
Singapore	–	–	92 (82.9)	148 (13.9)	–
Thailand	–	–	58 (52.3)	76 (7.1)	–
Philippines	–	–	31 (27.9)	34 (3.2)	–
Others	–	–	14 (12.6)	19 (1.8)	–
East Asia	–	–	–	431 (40.4)	–
China	–	–	76 (68.5)	251 (23.5)	–
Others	–	–	74 (66.7)	180 (16.9)	–
Europe	–	–	**41 (36.9)**	77 (7.2)	–
North America	–	–	**55 (49.5)**	131 (12.3)	–
Other Regions	–	–	**10 (9.0)**	18 (1.7)	–
All HKTNCs	*1836*	*1965*	*111 (100)*	*1068 (100)*	–

Source: Author's surveys.

a recent phenomenon. Rather, what is new arguably is its intensification and acceleration. This is evident in terms of the mean year of establishment. Most of the 204 sampled SINTNCs had established their overseas operations from the mid-1980s to the early 1990s. This was a period of rapid growth in Singapore's domestic economy after recovery from the 1985–1986 recession. As explained in Chapter 2, Singapore experienced drastic industrial restructuring during the same period that propelled many Singapore companies to relocate their manufacturing operations and to seek new markets elsewhere in the Southeast Asian region and beyond.

The 1993 regionalisation drive (see the next section) clearly had an impact on Singapore investments in China. To date, 151 of the 204 sampled TNCs have established 365 subsidiaries in China. On average, each SINTNC has more than two subsidiaries in China. But the mean year of establishment is only 1992, indicating that at least half of these subsidiaries of SINTNCs in China must have been established after 1992. Malaysia also experiences a high concentration of SINTNC subsidiaries: 119 of the sampled 204 SINTNCs have established 273 subsidiaries in Malaysia. On the other hand, these SINTNCs are not as active in Europe and North America. Fewer than 20 per cent of them have a presence in both major regions and each of them has barely more than one subsidiary in these regions. Based on these findings, it is fair to say that while Singapore's global reach has a long historical root, it is happening to only a limited range of Singapore companies. Most of the SINTNCs in the sample continue to focus on East and Southeast Asia as their centres of business operations, an observation consistent with the investment statistics reported in the earlier section.

In comparison, HKTNCs seem to have a longer global reach, with respectively 37 per cent (N=41) and 50 per cent (N=55) of the sampled HKTNCs having operations in Europe and North America. The figures for the number of subsidiaries in these two regions are also relatively impressive in relation to HKTNCs. About 20 per cent of the 1068 subsidiaries of HKTNCs are located in Europe and North America, compared to only 7 per cent in the case of SINTNCs. Like SINTNCs that operate within Southeast Asia, HKTNCs tend to operate within their home base region in East Asia. A large number of HKTNCs (N=74; 67 per cent) have a presence in East Asian countries outside China, in particular Taiwan. Interestingly, HKTNCs also have an extensive presence in Singapore, further confirming the 'twin-cities' status of Hong Kong and Singapore.

Another important point to be inferred from Table 3.7 is that a disproportionate number of expatriate staff have been sent from Singapore to some of the host countries. In particular, Indonesia and China account respectively for 12 per cent and 29 per cent of all subsidiaries, but they also take up some 27 per cent and 43 per cent of all 858 expatriate staff sent from Singapore. On average, each subsidiary in Indonesia and China has at least one expatriate staff member sent from the headquarters in Singapore. This phenomenon clearly has something to do with the nature of the business environments in these two countries. Indonesia and China have some of the most opaque business rules and uncertain regulations in Asia. This problem necessitates more attention from the headquarters in Singapore through tighter control mechanisms, such as having one or more expatriate staff members from Singapore to manage the local subsidiaries. On the other hand, while the sampled 204 SINTNCs have respectively 47 and 48 subsidiaries in Europe and North America, they have sent only 19 and 10 expatriate staff to manage these subsidiaries in each region. This is explained by the relatively open and transparent business environments and the availability of good quality management executives in these two regions. Geographical proximity explains why Malaysia has a large number of SINTNC subsidiaries (N = 273) and, yet, only 49 expatriate staff have been sent there on a permanent basis.

Motives for Overseas Operations

Having explained the nature and geographies of SINTNCs, I now examine more substantive issues in our understanding of Singapore's global reach. Figure 3.5 summarises the motives for transnational operations by these 204 SINTNCs. Motives for transnational operations are measured by host region because TNCs may venture into different host regions and/or countries for different motives. The next section explains how the strategies of transnational operations vary across different regions and/or countries. It is clear from Figure 3.5 that *market presence* is the single most important motive in driving the globalisation of Singaporean companies. It is measured by three interrelated motives that account for over 60 per cent of responses for all host regions except Europe (50 per cent):

- important growth region in the industry
- serving customers in host regions/countries
- regional coverage of operations

First, many sampled SINTNCs venture abroad because of the belief that the host countries are located in *important growth regions* in the industry. This motive is particularly important in the case of SINTNCs in East Asia and '*other regions*'. Many SINTNCs invest in China on the assumption that

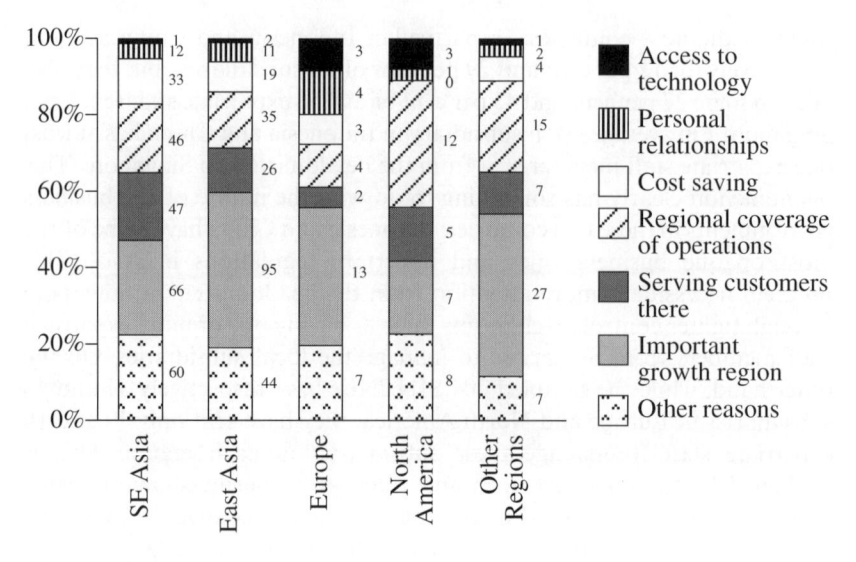

Figure 3.5   Motives of transnational operations by host region

it has the potential to become one of the fastest and biggest growing markets in the world. This explains why China has attracted the highest number of sampled SINTNCs (Table 3.7).

Second, some sampled SINTNCs are prompted by their *local, regional or global customers* to make a presence in the host countries in order to provide them with quality and customised products and/or services. This motive is equally important for both manufacturing and service SINTNCs. For those in manufacturing industries, having a presence in host countries significantly increases their chances of securing contracts as preferred suppliers. This is particularly so for those SINTNCs that are engaged in OEM (Original Equipment Manufacturing) for major global corporations. For those in service industries (e.g. producer services), they have to globalise with their customers in order to serve them better. Banks from Singapore are one good example. Many of them set up branches in Asia and beyond to serve customers from Singapore. Of course, they also tap into potential clientele in the host countries and/or regions.

Third and related, SINTNCs in the sample venture abroad to establish *regional coverage of operations*. In other words, they have to be there in the host countries in order to complete their networks of global operations. This is the most important motive (33 per cent) for SINTNCs to globalise into North America. For manufacturing SINTNCs, venturing into North

America enables them to become a truly global player in their respective industries. Of course, access to technology is also an important motive for high-tech manufacturing SINTNCs to venture into Europe and North America. For service SINTNCs, it is imperative to have a presence in North America because of the global nature of their business. Together, these findings show that market presence is the most important motive for SINTNCs to globalise. In my earlier study of HKTNCs, I found that market presence is similarly the most important motive for their globalisation (see Yeung, 1998a: 118–25).

How do we reconcile the findings in the new international division of labour literature about the predominant role of costs in international production (e.g. Fröbel et al., 1980)? Figure 3.5 shows that whilst a significant motive, cost saving is clearly *not* the most important motive in driving Singapore's global reach. After all, most SINTNCs in our sample are not labour-intensive manufacturers *per se*. Rather, they are high value-added manufacturers or service providers. Production or labour costs constitute only a relatively low proportion of their total operational costs. It is also interesting to note that some SINTNCs are motivated to invest in East and Southeast Asia on the basis of personal relations with local partners and/or customers. In some host countries (e.g. China and Malaysia), ethnicity and social connections seem to have played a role in motivating Singapore investments there (see also Chapters 4 and 5). These findings are also similar to the case of HKTNCs in Southeast Asia (Yeung, 1998a: 110–17). In most industries and host countries, cost saving reasons account for less than 25 per cent of all responses by the 111 HKTNCs.

To verify further these claims, we asked our respondents to evaluate different sets of factors that explain their global reach in *specific regions*. The results are tabulated in the form of mean scores in Table 3.8. The scale of importance of these factors ranges from Very Important [1] to Not Important At All [5]. In other words, the lower the mean score, the more important the factor is.

In home country terms, two factors clearly emerge: (1) entrepreneurial vision of founders and key executives and (2) limited domestic market. The first factor has something to do with the nature of entrepreneurial decisions in the parent companies (see more in Chapters 4 and 5). These entrepreneurs and/or intrapreneurs tend to have a clear vision of what they want to achieve for the company. They have clear corporate missions and strategies to accomplish these visions. In that sense, their companies are much more proactive in globalisation processes. The second factor is related to the lack of market growth potential in Singapore. Many SINTNCs are therefore compelled to expand overseas, a finding consistent with their market-driven motives of globalisation. This finding is also linked to the

Table 3.8 Importance of different factors of globalisation assessed by indigenous companies from Singapore by region

Major Factors of Globalisation (mean score)[a]	Southeast Asia	East Asia	Europe	North America	Other Regions
Home Country Factors					
1. entrepreneurial vision	1.8	1.6	1.9	1.4	1.8
2. diversification of risks	2.7	2.7	2.7	2.9	2.5
3. high (labour) costs of operations	2.8	2.9	4.1	3.9	3.2
4. technological upgrading	4.2	4.0	2.9	2.8	4.0
5. intensified competition	2.3	2.5	2.7	2.6	2.4
6. imited domestic market	2.0	2.0	2.2	2.5	2.2
7. government encouragement	3.9	3.7	3.6	3.9	4.0
Host Country Factors					
1. government incentives	3.8	3.3	4.0	4.2	3.9
2. lower (labour) costs of operations	2.7	2.8	4.3	4.3	3.3
3. marketing strategies	1.8	1.7	1.6	1.7	2.0
4. availability of skilled labour and/or technology	3.1	3.2	2.8	2.7	3.3
5. good local contacts	2.2	2.5	2.7	3.0	2.2
6. familiar operating environment	2.3	2.6	2.9	3.2	2.4
Regional and Global Factors					
1. growing global competition	2.5	2.6	2.7	2.8	2.3
2. rising tariffs and quotas	3.4	3.4	4.3	4.2	3.7
3. tapping potential regional market	1.9	1.9	2.2	2.0	1.9
4. improvement in transport and communication facilities	3.2	3.1	3.4	3.3	3.0
5. globalisation of firms	3.2	3.1	3.3	2.9	3.0

Note: [a] The scale of importance ranges from Very Important [1] to Not Important At All [5].

Source: Author's survey.

role of marketing strategies as the most important host country factor in attracting SINTNCs. Similarly, tapping into potential regional markets is rated as quite important in explaining the global reach of SINTNCs.

Lower costs of operations in host countries are only quite important for SINTNCs operating in East and Southeast Asia. Cost is much less important for those operating in Europe and North America. The same regional variation can also be observed in the assessment of local contacts as a globalisation factor. It seems that more SINTNCs agreed that good local contacts are important in their operations in Asia than in Europe and North America.

Strategies and Mechanisms of Overseas Operations

If market presence is so important in driving the global reach of SINTNCs in our sample, how then do they operate across borders? Figure 3.6 shows the various strategies and mechanisms employed by SINTNCs to establish overseas operations. Respondents from 152 of the 204 sampled SINTNCs shared their experience in overseas operations. Some 21 per cent of them establish their overseas subsidiaries through an *expansion of their existing operations*. Typically, these SINTNCs have prior experience and knowledge of the host countries. This can be achieved through trading activities with customers there and frequent travel by staff to host countries to serve clients.

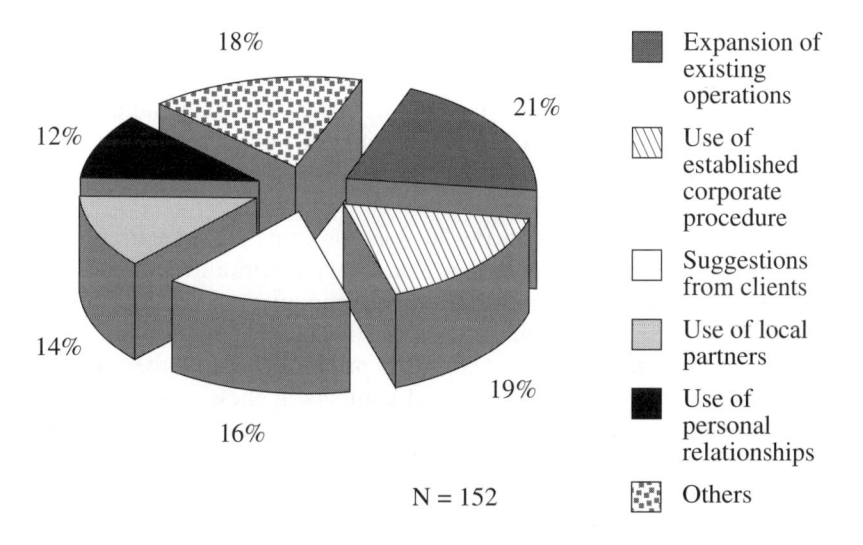

Source: Author's survey.

Figure 3.6 Mechanisms of overseas operations by companies from Singapore

When the need to establish an operation in the host countries arises, these SINTNCs simply expand their existing trading/sales relationships into a full-fledged manufacturing or services subsidiary in the host countries. In this process, some 19 per cent of them make use of *well-developed corporate procedures*, e.g. feasibility studies, consultancy, evaluations by committees, and so on. These procedures are highly relevant for setting up operations in Europe and North America because of their relatively open and transparent business environments. Another 18 per cent also act on suggestions from clients to set up their overseas operations. These suggestions vary from know-how to know-who in host countries. They are important because many of these SINTNCs are not experienced in establishing overseas operations. For example, it is useful to know how to apply for local business licences and who to deal with in order to facilitate globalisation processes.

Another interesting set of mechanisms is *the role of local partners* and *the use of personal relationships* in overseas operations. Together, these two related mechanisms constitute 26 per cent of all responses. Some 93 per cent of respondents agreed that their companies have prior business connections with the host countries. About 50–60 per cent of them have also prior political, family, and social connections with host countries. Among all these different types of connections, business connections are given a mean score of 1.2, indicating that they are highly important in the overseas operations of SINTNCs. These business connections can be further divided into two types: (1) personal contacts and (2) trading and business partners. My earlier study of HKTNCs found a similar role of business connections and local partners in facilitating their Southeast Asian operations (Yeung, 1998a: Table 5.1).

In practice, many host countries in Asia have opaque regulations and strict foreign investment rules. Reliance on local partners and personal contacts becomes an extremely important way to minimise risks in these highly uncertain business environments. Some SINTNCs in my sample have chosen to operate in certain host countries primarily because their owners or top executives have strong personal contacts in these host countries. These local contacts both increase their chances of securing customers and reduce their risks of venturing into unfamiliar host countries. In some Asian host countries, foreign investors are required by law to have local partners. Some SINTNCs therefore activate their prior business and personal contacts in these host countries to become their joint venture partners. Sometimes, these partners become 'sleeping partners' once the ventures have begun. In other cases, local partners play an imperative role in guiding the development of local subsidiaries.

Organisation of Overseas Operations

How then do SINTNCs organise their overseas operations and what are their modes of entry? Table 3.9 shows the different modes of foreign entry by the 204 sampled SINTNCs. Because of their different business environments, we expect these modes of entry to vary across host countries and/or regions. In general, most TNCs prefer *wholly owned subsidiaries* when they engage in globalisation. This is because 100 per cent ownership guarantees full control by the parent companies in home countries. One finding in Table 3.9 is that more than 50 per cent of SINTNCs have established wholly-owned subsidiaries only in countries (e.g. Hong Kong) and regions (Europe and North America) reputed to be open and transparent in their business environments, a finding confirmed in my earlier study of HKTNCs (Yeung, 1998a: 101–3). Operations by SINTNCs in Indonesia, Thailand, and China have the lowest proportion of wholly-owned subsidiaries, an indication of the perception and reality of business environments in these host countries.

Table 3.9 Modes of foreign entry by 204 indigenous companies from Singapore by host country (percentage in parentheses)

Regions/ Countries	Wholly-owned Subsidiaries	Associate Companies	Joint Ventures	Other Modes	Total
Southeast Asia	–	–	–	–	–
Indonesia	21 (30.4)	8 (11.6)	38 (55.1)	2 (2.9)	69 (100)
Malaysia	76 (49.4)	18 (11.7)	54 (35.1)	6 (3.9)	154 (100)
Thailand	10 (28.6)	7 (20.0)	18 (51.4)	–	35 (100)
Philippines	15 (41.7)	2 (5.6)	18 (50.0)	1 (2.8)	36 (100)
Others	19 (45.2)	6 (14.3)	15 (35.7)	2 (4.8)	42 (100)
East Asia					
China	66 (31.0)	14 (6.6)	125 (58.7)	8 (3.8)	213 (100)
Hong Kong	47 (62.7)	6 (8.0)	21 (28.0)	1 (1.3)	75 (100)
Others	12 (46.2)	5 (19.2)	8 (30.8)	1 (3.9)	26 (100)
Europe	21 (61.8)	2 (5.9)	10 (29.4)	1 (2.9)	34 (100)
North America	17 (56.7)	3 (10.0)	10 (33.3)	–	30 (100)
Other Regions	30 (53.6)	5 (8.9)	17 (30.4)	4 (7.2)	56 (100)

Note: There are no statistically significant differences by (1) ownership; (2) sector; or (3) turnover.

Source: Author's survey.

Perhaps because of these host country regulatory constraints, more than 50 per cent of SINTNCs tend to establish *joint ventures* in China, Indonesia, Thailand, and the Philippines. Fewer SINTNCs established joint ventures in Hong Kong, Taiwan, Europe, North America, and Other Regions (e.g. Australia and New Zealand). Once established, parent SINTNCs tend *not* to exercise strict control over their foreign subsidiaries. On average, the mean scores for control, integration, and co-ordination are respectively 2.9, 2.4, and 2.4. These indicate that foreign subsidiaries are relatively autonomous and independent of their headquarters in Singapore.

132   *Entrepreneurship and the internationalisation of Asian firms*

Figure 3.7 shows the various mechanisms of control exercised by the headquarters in Singapore over their foreign subsidiaries. Among these six major control mechanisms, only two are specifically related to the centralisation of corporate control: (1) cost control by the headquarters and (2) central decisions by the headquarters. The rest of the control mechanisms give *substantial autonomy to local managers* at the subsidiary level. These parent–subsidiary control mechanisms are similar to those adopted by HKTNCs and their Southeast Asian subsidiaries (Yeung, 1998a: 147–56). They fall within Birkinshaw's (1997) definition of dispersed corporate entrepreneurship through which foreign subsidiaries experience more strategic choices and are more likely to initiate discrete and proactive undertakings for the benefits of the TNC as a whole (see Chapter 1).

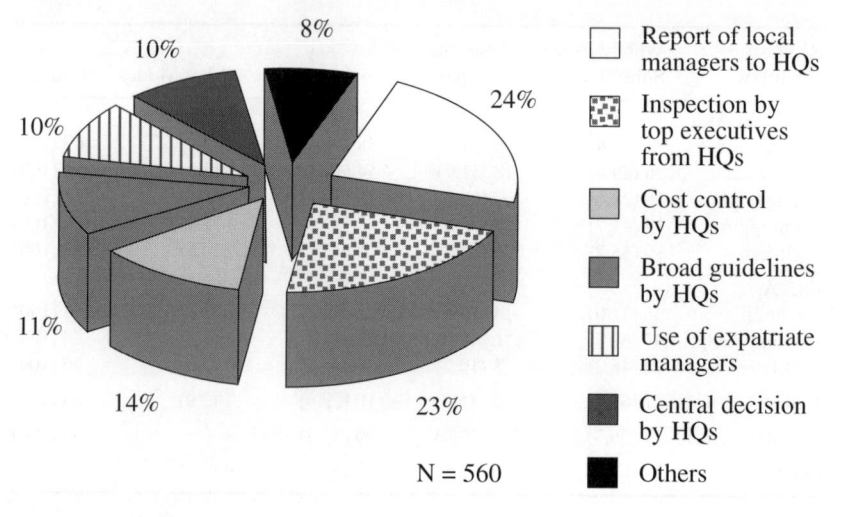

Pie chart data (N = 560):
- Report of local managers to HQs: 24%
- Inspection by top executives from HQs: 23%
- Cost control by HQs: 14%
- Broad guidelines by HQs: 11%
- Use of expatriate managers: 10%
- Central decision by HQs: 10%
- Others: 8%

Source: Author's survey.

Figure 3.7   Mechanisms of control over foreign subsidiaries by Singapore companies

In general, almost half of the top executives from the headquarters visit their foreign subsidiaries at least once every month. This relative autonomy of foreign subsidiaries of SINTNCs may be attributed to two reasons. First, since many SINTNCs operate in relatively opaque business environments in Asia, local subsidiaries need substantial *autonomy* and *flexibility* to succeed in these host countries. This also implies that host country operating environments are often very different from the transparent and open business environment in Singapore. My interviews with top executives from China subsidiaries of SINTNCs certainly confirm this point. Second, many SINTNCs have not yet developed an organisational structure and capability to manage foreign subsidiaries. Sometimes, this is due to sheer lack of experience. In other cases, foreign subsidiaries are seen as *appendages* to the main areas of businesses in Singapore. This issue is taken up further in the analysis of transnational entrepreneurship in the next two chapters.

To understand further the organisation of overseas operations by SINTNCs, we examine their sources of marketing, supply, and technology/expertise by their regions of operations. First, over 60 per cent of the sampled SINTNCs market their products and/or services through *local marketing departments* in their subsidiaries. This high ratio of local marketing shows that few SINTNCs conduct centralised marketing activities at the headquarters in Singapore, a finding consistent with the case of HKTNCs (Yeung, 1998a: Table 5.3). The ratio varies from 60–67 per cent among East and Southeast Asian subsidiaries to 72–75 per cent among North American and European subsidiaries. This shows that SINTNCs tend to give their subsidiaries in Europe and North America more autonomy in marketing products and services for the group.

Second, over 50 per cent of the sampled SINTNCs obtain their supplies of production inputs and/or services through *local production and supply departments* in their subsidiaries, indicating that few SINTNCs reap economies of scale through central purchasing at the headquarters. The ratio varies in favour of subsidiaries in North America (74 per cent) and East Asia (66 per cent). The latter subsidiaries clearly benefit from the availability of local supplies in China, particular in the area of raw materials.

Third, parent SINTNCs seem to play a much more important role in the provision of *technology and/or expertise* for their foreign subsidiaries. Well over 50 per cent of subsidiaries in East and Southeast Asia rely upon direct transfer of product/process technology and expertise developed in parent companies in Singapore. Another 10 per cent of these subsidiaries adapt locally product/process technology developed in parent companies. However, some 30–45 per cent of subsidiaries in Europe and North America develop their product/process technology locally in the host countries. This compares favourably with the fact that only 10–20 per cent of subsidiaries in East and Southeast Asia develop their own technology/expertise locally in the host countries. This finding implies that as a key strategy of their global reach, SINTNCs could well tap into the technological and expertise base of their subsidiaries and other local firms in Europe and North America.

To sum up, there seem to be many similarities and relatively few differences in the nature and characteristics of TNCs from Hong Kong and Singapore. Table 3.10 summarises these similarities and differences. In

Table 3.10 Comparison of the characteristics of transnational corporations from Hong Kong and Singapore

Category	HKTNCs	SINTNCs
Historical trends	• significant investment in Indonesia, Singapore and Thailand • surge of investments in China since the 1980s • fairly extensive presence in Europe and North America	• significant investment in Southeast Asia, particularly Malaysia • recent venture into China in the 1990s • limited presence in Europe and North America
Sector	• majority commercial and services	• majority commercial and services
Size and ownership	• medium to large firms • virtually all private-sector firms	• medium to large firms • significant role of foreign firms and government-linked companies
Entry modes	• majority wholly- or majority-owned	• majority wholly- or majority-owned
Corporate strategy	• market development and presence • regionalisation of operations	• market development and presence • regionalisation of operations
Investment motivations	• significant market-related motives: serving clients, local market presence and growth region • insignificant cost factors • insignificant government incentives	• significant market-related motives: serving clients, local market presence and growth region • insignificant cost factors • significant home country government incentives

Sources: Author's surveys and Yeung (1998a: Table 8.1).

general, both HKTNCs and SINTNCs are intra-regional in their investment scope and geographical distribution. They are also equally well represented in both manufacturing and service industries. When they venture abroad, they tend to engage in wholly- or majority-owned operations, although joint ventures and other co-operative modes may be adopted in certain countries with opaque institutional and regulatory structures. Their strategic orientation tends to be towards market development and building regional networks of operations. Market access and presence becomes the most important factor in explaining their internationalisation. Despite these similarities, however, there are some significant differences in their ownership structures and global significance. Whereas HKTNCs tend to be driven by the private sector and have a relatively significant role among all developing country TNCs, quite a number of SINTNCs are foreign-controlled or government-linked. They are still at a relatively early stage of internationalisation. These structural differences are clearly related to the distinctive political economies of outward investments from both Hong Kong and Singapore. This is the issue for the next section.

THE POLITICAL ECONOMY OF OUTWARD INVESTMENTS FROM HONG KONG AND SINGAPORE

Chapter 2 has revealed that the post-war developmental trajectories of Hong Kong and Singapore are the consequences of very different institutional and dominant forms of economic organisation in the two city-states. Granted the above similarities and differences in outward investments and TNCs from Hong Kong and Singapore, it is useful to relate these similarities and differences to the institutional structures of their home economies. To pre-empt the following analysis, I argue that the state has played an important, albeit differential, role in driving outward investments from both economies. Outward investments and TNCs from Hong Kong may be viewed as an indirect outcome of the passive industrial policies of the colonial states (Yeung, 2000c). Singapore's global reach via outflows of capital and TNCs, however, should be seen as an active and direct consequence of the state's intervention in the national economy (Yeung, 1998d; 1999c; 2000e). Since the launch of its regionalisation programme in 1993, outward investments from Singapore have increased dramatically. The institutional structuring and political economies of specific national business systems are therefore highly relevant to our understanding of their processes of internationalisation.

Outward Investments as a State-driven Phenomenon? Disincentives in Industrial Policies in Hong Kong

It has been argued that outward investments from Hong Kong are an outcome of successive waves of industrial restructuring. Spatial relocation of labour-intensive manufacturing operations to China and Southeast Asia represents an effective defensive strategy for Hong Kong manufacturers to reduce production costs and to compete in the global market (Thoburn et al., 1990; Yeung, 1994a; 1996; 1998a; Berger and Lester, 1997; Yu, 1997; 1998; Enright et al., 1997; Meyer, 2000). As evident in Chapter 2, it is apparent that outward investments from Hong Kong are made possible because of the state's neoliberal economic strategies, which indirectly forced labour-intensive manufacturing activities to relocate their production activities abroad.

The Hong Kong experience, however, differs significantly from other Asian NIEs. First, unlike Taiwan and South Korea, which explicitly restricted capital outflow and encouraged higher capital investment in domestic manufacturing production up to the mid-1980s, the colonial state in Hong Kong did not impose any restriction on FDI by Hong Kong firms. Whereas FDI outflows from other Asian NIEs are means through which the 'developmental states' in these countries build their 'national champions' (Yeung, 1994b; 1999a), FDI outflows from Hong Kong were driven by private initiatives. As evident later in this section, the regionalisation drive in Singapore was explicitly supported by the state and its institutions (e.g. statutory boards and GLCs). Through the regionalisation of Singaporean firms, the state aimed to nurture some 50 large enterprises capable of competing in the regional and global marketplaces. In Hong Kong, however, manufacturing firms were driven out of the domestic economy not by institutional support, but rather by the *lack* of institutional support. It became imperative for these discouraged manufacturers to search for alternative production sites and markets abroad. Outward investments by Hong Kong's manufacturers resulted largely from a defensive strategy to regain cost competitiveness in the global economy.

Second, there is a significant difference in the motives of FDI from Hong Kong *vis-à-vis* other Asian NIEs. Whereas firms from other Asian NIEs globalised to capture more markets and absorb technological innovations in the Triad countries – an offensive strategy – Hong Kong's manufacturing firms largely relocated their labour-intensive operations to China and elsewhere to capture savings in production costs in order to survive, not to lead, global competition. In other words, globalisation helps firms from other Asian NIEs to attain greater market diversification and technological innovation (see Clark and Kim, 1995; Dicken and Yeung, 1999; Yeung,

1999a). This is achieved through the strong impetus provided by the 'institutional fix' of their home country states (e.g. subsidised loans, intergovernmental agreements, tax incentives, and so on). In the case of Hong Kong, without an effective 'institutional fix', globalisation has forced Hong Kong's manufacturing industries to stay labour-intensive and low in technology. Hong Kong firms have been locked into a constant battle for lower production costs *per se* and the perpetuation of labour-intensive manufacturing in Hong Kong.

A point must therefore be made about the impact of horizontal expansion by Hong Kong firms into labour-intensive production in China since 1979 without concomitant capital or technology-deepening in Hong Kong's industrial structure (compared with Taiwan; see Lin and Chen, 1996). E.K.Y. Chen and Wong (1995: 261) have termed this a 'technology stagnation effect' through which the technology transferred from Hong Kong to China does not embody much new knowledge and skills. The technology of the supporting activities conducted by the subsidiaries in China can hardly serve as a stimulus for further technological change back in Hong Kong. Instead, Hong Kong has become 'locked' into labour-intensive manufacturing through outward processing operations in China (Berger and Lester, 1997; Chiu et al., 1997). Tuan and Ng (1995a; 1995b) found that in terms of productivity and factor use, FDI from Hong Kong has not led to capital deepening. Between 1976–1987, they observed high growth rates in labour employment, lower growth rates in capital employment, and slower growth rates in factor intensity and value-added in Hong Kong's manufacturing sector. Between 1980 and 1998, negative growth in Hong Kong's manufacturing labour employment (-1.7 per cent and -7.2 per cent) was registered (see Table 2.1). Although a positive rate of capital employment (2.2 per cent) and an increase in labour productivity of 5.1 per cent per annum occurred, capital productivity decreased by 6.2 per cent and manufacturing value-added decreased by 4.2 per cent per annum. Tuan and Ng (1995a: 167) concluded that 'it is the outward FDI from Hong Kong and the millions of inland labourers working for Hong Kong manufacturers over the border that have made the reduction in local manufacturing labour possible and enhanced/increased labour productivity for the manufacturing sector in Hong Kong during the study period'.

In terms of the composition of manufacturing exports (see Table 3.11), between 1989–1992, only 17 per cent and 27 per cent of Hong Kong's exports to the USA were made up of technology-intensive and high-tech commodities, compared to more than 25 per cent and 38 per cent respectively for Taiwan and South Korea during the same period. The total growth rates of exports for these products were also -2.4 per cent and 0 per cent, compared to significant growth in the exports of the same products from Taiwan and South Korea. Another study of Hong Kong's electronics industry conducted by Hong Kong Industry Development Board (1991) reveals that many electronics manufacturers have been quick in capitalising on the abundant supply of low-wage labour in China through cross-border investments. Some 67 per cent of the 116 companies surveyed have plants in China for the assembly of semi-finished products, finished products, and parts and components. Establishments in Hong Kong, however, continue to concentrate either on those parts of production that are still cost-efficient for local production or on product designs and marketing. They remain largely at the relatively labour-intensive end of electronics production (Lui and Chiu, 1993; 1994; 1996; Yeh and Ng, 1994).

Table 3.11 Composition of manufacturing exports of three Asian NIEs in the US market, 1989–1992 (%)

Asian NIEs	Technology Intensive	High-tech	Chemical Products	Consumer Durable	Machinery Equipment
Hong Kong					
1989	17.73	26.95	31.55	11.43	15.10
1990	17.01	27.03	31.54	12.77	13.76
1991	15.83	27.43	31.72	13.80	12.15
1992	15.53	26.97	30.74	12.53	10.42
1989–92	16.532	7.10	31.39	12.63	12.86
Taiwan					
1989	22.62	30.91	38.25	12.32	18.38
1990	25.96	32.86	40.66	10.70	19.64
1991	27.73	34.32	41.99	10.93	21.33
1992	30.76	38.08	45.75	10.88	23.75
1989–92	26.80	34.04	41.66	11.21	20.78
South Korea					
1989–92	25.44	43.65	50.25	11.76	11.1

Note: Due to multiple classification, sum of horizontal percentages may be greater than 100.

Source: Tuan and Ng (1995b: Table 3).

In short, it can be argued that outward investments by Hong Kong's manufacturing firms were indirectly driven by the neoliberal economic policies of the colonial state. Although these foreign investments and spatial relocation have enabled Hong Kong manufacturers to achieve cost competitiveness in the short term, they have not been accompanied by a greater extent of technological upgrading and market diversification of industries in Hong Kong. There has also not been a significant inter-industry shift within Hong Kong's manufacturing sector towards more high-tech and high value-added activities. Most Hong Kong manufacturers have remained in labour-intensive industries that are extremely susceptible to competitive pressures and market fluctuations. The crisis tendencies of Hong Kong's industrial sector have become increasingly apparent after each round of industrial restructuring that fails to transform Hong Kong into a high-tech manufacturing centre in East Asia. Hong Kong's industrial sector thus remains a likely victim of deindustrialisation in today's era of neoliberalism and global competition. What then is the case of outward investment from Singapore?

The State as a Political Entrepreneur? Singapore's Regionalisation Programme

The state in Singapore has always been hailed as the hallmark of a 'developmental state' that plays an integral role in domestic economic development processes (see Chapter 2). Some researchers have also examined the state's effort in attracting foreign TNCs to assist Singapore's industrialisation programme (Hughes and Sing, 1969; Yoshihara, 1976; Mirza, 1986; Chia, 1993). There is, however, relatively little attention paid to the role of the state in the regionalisation of Singaporean firms (Kanai, 1993; Régnier, 1993; Perry and Yeoh, 2000).[3]

Singapore's regionalisation effort was officially launched in early 1993. I argue that the state in Singapore has not only created favourable conditions for this regionalisation effort, but also taken key initiatives to ensure its success. Since its separation from Malaysia and independence in 1965, the state has been relying on foreign capital to expedite the industrialisation process (see Chapter 2). The island economy took off rapidly in the late 1960s through to the mid-1980s when global economic recession hit Singapore seriously. Singapore experienced its first negative growth in 1985. The mid-1980s saw one of the most serious recessions in its entire history primarily because of global downturn. In what became the blueprint for Singapore's economic development in the late 1980s and 1990s, the report by the Economic Committee in 1986 recognised the vulnerability of Singapore's economy because of its over-dependence on foreign capital and the lack of indigenous entrepreneurship.

In 1989, the Singapore–Indonesia–Malaysia Growth Triangle idea was proposed by the then Deputy Prime Minister Goh Chok Tong in response to drastic industrial restructuring within Singapore and perceived complementarity among the three countries (Perry, 1991; Toh and Low, 1993; K.C. Ho, 1994; K.C. Ho and So, 1997). The idea was based on three premises about industrial location and regional integration. First, the decentralisation of industry to the immediate region will retain greater economic linkages back to Singapore than where decentralisation is widely dispersed. Second, TNCs have well-defined location preferences that can be satisfied by the growth triangle. Third, facilitating the process of decentralisation will simultaneously assist the upgrading of the activities left behind (Perry, 1991: 143). In technical areas, labour and land constraints in Singapore require the relocation of low value-added and labour-intensive production processes to Johor, Malaysia or Riau, Indonesia. Only high value-added manufacturing activities remain in Singapore. In terms of the division of labour by sector, Singapore plays a more important role in services as the regional headquarters (RHQs) for TNCs operating simultaneously in all three locations (see Dicken and Kirkpatrick, 1991; Perry, 1992; 1995; Yeung, 1998b; Yeung et al., 2001). The emergence of a regional division of labour is clear when all three countries contain different comparative advantages and, therefore, play different economic roles in this regional interdependence.

The growth triangle strategy, however, was deemed unable to resolve the dilemma of vulnerability and deep penetration of the domestic economy by foreign capital. The state began to realise the vulnerability of the domestic economy and the absence of indigenous entrepreneurship as a result of the deep penetration of foreign capital and the spectacular presence of state-owned enterprises. Various state policies in the earlier phases of industrialisation had created a situation in which private entrepreneurship was indirectly discouraged. By the late 1980s, the PAP-dominated state had become much stronger politically and economically. The domestic economy had experienced unprecedented growth for several decades. As the global economy became more competitive, Singapore began to realise that heavy reliance on foreign TNCs was no longer useful in attaining its long-term strategic goals. Foreign TNCs do come and go, particularly when the world is becoming more 'borderless' (Ohmae, 1990; cf. Yeung, 1998e). It was necessary for Singapore to respond to this new global competition by developing indigenous economic capabilities that could tap into growth potential in other countries.

One such strategy was to regionalise firms to capture the booming regional market, spearheaded by state-owned enterprises. In order to promote the growth of indigenous private companies, the state decided in early 1993 to build an external dimension to the domestic economy by encouraging both state-owned and private sector enterprises to regionalise their operations. Kanai (1993: 41) noted that 'no matter what Singapore does in terms of business promotion policy, it is an unavoidable fact of modern economic life that Singapore will face keener competition from its neighbors as a center for regional manufacturing or service industry operations. So it would seem better for Singapore to promote the outward regional expansion of its own private sector, and in the process capture for itself some of the benefits of the region's dynamic development'. In doing so, the state believed that the resultant economic structure would be much more resilient in times of recessions. An external economy would also reduce the dependence of Singapore on foreign capital and overseas markets for long-term economic survival. According to a report by the Ministry of Finance (1993a: 14), an external economy could help overcome Singapore's small domestic market and limited resource base, through generating business and economies of scale for companies based in Singapore, making the domestic economy more productive. It would also allow Singaporean firms to contribute to and benefit from the rapid growth of the countries in the region. Singapore need not depend so heavily on developed countries for growth and markets, an external limit that took the state almost three decades to realise. This twin-argument by the state implicitly conforms to Porter's (1990) view that the competitive advantage and wealth of national firms and their home countries are essentially the same. If national firms are competitive abroad, so is the home country in which these firms are incorporated.

There is, however, an apparent contradiction in this regionalisation drive because the real private entrepreneur is missing. The state has therefore assumed the role of an 'entrepreneur' in the regionalisation process through its GLCs and institutional support provided by state agencies and key politicians. State intervention can be a form of entrepreneurial activity through which domestic firms are brought into the regional and global marketplace. A strong state can become an 'entrepreneur' exercising its capabilities in accordance with its national developmental priorities and political ideology. Senior Minister Lee Kuan Yew therefore announced in January 1993 that the state was taking new initiatives to generate a bigger pool of local entrepreneurs and to build up the 'external wing' of the Singapore economy (Régnier, 1993). This national strategic thrust is known as Singapore's 'Regionalisation 2000'. Senior Minister Lee mooted this idea because most advanced industrialised countries have globalised their national firms to tap into resources, talents, and markets in the global economy. The idea is to develop Singapore into a global city with total business capabilities. Singapore can be not only an attractive manufacturing investment location for global TNCs, but also an ideal springboard for them to venture into the Asia-Pacific region (Economic Development Board, 1995). Prime Minister Goh Chok Tong also made it clear that '[g]oing regional is part of our long-term strategy to stay ahead. It is to make our national economy bigger, our companies stronger and some of them multi-national' (reprinted in *Speeches*, May–June 1993: 15).

As shown in the earlier section, however, the extent of Singapore's outward investment was relatively limited before the early 1990s. Singapore's FDI in the 1980s was very biased towards a few major geographical destinations. Compared to other advanced industrialised countries, the proportion of Singapore's FDI to its GNP in the early 1990s was small. For example, Singapore's FDI reached 16 per cent of GNP in 1991, compared to 30 per cent for Switzerland, 36 per cent for the Netherlands and 23 per cent for the UK (Ministry of Finance, 1993a: 20). In 1990, only 2293 (6 per cent) of 36573 companies in Singapore had regionalised their operations (Ministry of Finance, 1993a: 70). Even among the Asian NIEs, Singapore compared very unfavourably in terms of its extent of transnational operations. Moreover, as the earlier section shows, foreign firms in Singapore accounted for more than 50 per cent of outward investment from Singapore in recent years. The role of private sector investment is rather dismal at this beginning phase of regionalisation.

The historical underdevelopment of indigenous entrepreneurship in the private sector has convinced the state that the regionalisation drive cannot be effectively taken up by private sector initiatives only. The state has to take up the role and the risks of spearheading regionalisation in two specific ways: (1) the regionalisation of GLCs and companies set up by statutory boards and (2) 'political entrepreneurship' through which the state opens up overseas business opportunities for private capitalists and negotiates the institutional framework for such opportunities to be tapped by Singaporean firms. In the first place, instead of relying on indigenous entrepreneurs, the state has internalised potential entrepreneurs into state-owned enterprises. This unique approach to economic development has proven successful in its peculiar historical context. Since the mid-1980s, the state has begun to privatise its state-owned enterprises to allow for greater private sector participation and more entrepreneurial activities (see Chapter 2). In this regard, many large state-owned enterprises are now listed on the Stock Exchange of Singapore (e.g. Singapore Airlines, Keppel Corporation, Sembawang Holdings, and so on). In 1993, the public sector and GLCs accounted for about 60 per cent of Singapore's GDP (Ministry of Finance, 1993a: 39). These GLCs have become one of the primary instruments through which the state inaugurates the regionalisation drive.

In principle, the state's involvement in regionalisation through GLCs and other companies set up by statutory boards is run on a commercial basis. With specialised expertise and commercial experience, these GLCs and companies of statutory boards can partner private sector companies and even take the lead in large projects. The state, however, does not take on a greater proportion of the risk than that which the private sector investors of the project are prepared to take. The GLCs and companies of statutory boards are prepared to take the lead only in large infrastructural projects. In most other projects, the private sector entrepreneurs are expected to bear the primary risks and take on the majority stakes.

GLCs are managed under four state-owned holding companies – Temasek Holdings, Singapore Technologies Holdings, MinCom Holdings and MND Holdings. Together with statutory boards, these GLCs serve as partners to private sector companies in overseas ventures by selling their expertise to the private sector; forming joint ventures and consortia; and leading large infrastructural projects (Ministry of Finance, 1993a: 42–3). First, a private company is often unable to undertake an overseas project because of its lack of expertise for some parts of the project. GLCs and statutory board companies may often have the requisite expertise that can be sold to the private sector. Second, the sale of expertise brings limited benefits to the GLCs or statutory board companies. They can make greater use of public sector capabilities by entering into consortia or joint ventures with private sector companies. This form of state participation in the regionalisation drive involves equity stakes in the ventures. The state becomes therefore a 'quasi-entrepreneur'. Third, for large infrastructural projects that require substantial investments and expertise and resources, the GLCs and statutory board companies are ideally endowed with these skills and resources. Most of these projects also have long gestation and payback periods that are unattractive to private sector capital. The state can thus play a leading role by holding majority equity stakes in the joint ventures. Here the state becomes a full entrepreneur in its own right.

Case studies in Chapter 5 show how the state in Singapore has tried to lead the regionalisation drive by taking direct equity stakes in large infrastructural development projects in the region and by employing inter-state relationships to raise the profile and image of its investment projects. For example, Singapore's investment in China increased substantially after October 1990 when diplomatic relations between the two countries were established and the Singapore government made it a top priority to encourage Singapore companies to venture abroad (see Table 3.3). Senior officials from Singapore have made a number of visits to China in recent years to enhance the goodwill and improve the *guanxi* (relationships) between the two countries. Senior Minister Lee himself visited many sites in China to build connections with local governments and officials and to pave the way personally for Singaporean firms, whether GLCs or private companies. A state visit by Prime Minister Goh Chok Tong in 1993 further strengthened the business ties with China at the state level. The Suzhou township project (see Chapter 5), for example, is a commercial proposal riding on congenial inter-state relationships. In this way, the state serves as a facilitator for overseas ventures of both GLCs and private sector companies. Today, some 15 state agencies are involved in the regionalisation effort (see Table 3.12). Their projects are mostly related to infrastructural developments located in Asia.

Though the state in Singapore has taken the lead in the regionalisation drive through GLCs and 'political entrepreneurs', it does recognise the long-term goal of the private sector as the leading force behind regionalisation. The main obstacle to realising such a goal is the underdevelopment of private entrepreneurship in Singapore. In order to promote private entrepreneurship, the state has been offering help to private companies in Singapore through various incentive schemes. In doing so, the state has artificially changed the comparative advantage of regionalisation *vis-à-vis* domestic investment. Some Singaporean companies are lured into regionalisation to take advantage of the state's incentive schemes. But they may not be aware of the full costs of regionalisation since these incentives have changed its comparative advantage to make it favourable to these companies (see some case studies in Chapter 4). The long-term viability of nurturing entrepreneurship through such incentive schemes is therefore questionable. The Ministry of Finance's (1993b) final report pays serious attention to the intangible social dimension of entrepreneurship, and the difference between owner entrepreneurs and manager entrepreneurs.

Small and medium enterprises (SMEs) have been the backbone of many advanced industrialised countries. Among the Asian NIEs, Hong Kong has the most developed network of SMEs, which flourish together with the influx of foreign capital (see Chapter 2). These SMEs from Hong Kong have also extensively engaged in transnational operations in China and the Southeast Asian region (Yeung, 1998a). Based on this principle, the state in Singapore has aimed since the early 1990s, to nurture SMEs into national firms capable of penetrating foreign markets and establishing transnational operations. In fact, the Economic Development Board (EDB) has been assisting local SMEs almost since Singapore's independence in 1965. It was not until the 1985 recession, however, that the state fully recognised the importance of SMEs in surviving economic recessions. Policy initiatives in the post-1985 period were much more concrete than before. In 1986, the EDB initiated the Local Industry Upgrading Programme (LIUP). The SME Master Plan was published in 1989 and the revised Local Enterprise Finance Scheme was announced in 1992. The most important document, however, is the Strategic Economic Plan published in 1991 in which the state sees locally-grown TNCs as one of the strategic tools to achieve fully developed country status by 2000.

In practice, the state has developed through the EDB a wide array of assistance schemes and programmes to accelerate the development of local enterprises at every stage of growth – from cradle to maturity (see Table 3.13). By 1993, there were over 60 such schemes and programmes

Table 3.12 Agencies of the Singapore state in the regionalisation effort

Agency	Profile of Expertise	Country of Projects
Civil Aviation Authority of Singapore	• feasibility studies • planning & design • management consultancy • systems acquisition • operation plans & procedures, training	China, Philippines, Maldives, Pakistan, Fiji
Commercial & Industrial Security Corporation	• training programmes • design, integration & installation of security systems, central alarm monitoring • service & maintenance • key installation security & industrial, commercial & banking security • special projects	Indonesia
Construction Industry Development Board	• construction quality advancement system • quality management systems • training, skills certification	Hong Kong, Brunei, Taipei
Housing and Development Board	• master planning & urban design • architectural design • structural engineering • civil engineering & infrastructural design • CAD & drafting • coastal engineering & reclamation • project management, estate management • upgrading & retrofitting	China, Indonesia, Vietnam

Table 3.12 (cont.)

Jurong Town Corporation	• industrial parks and towns • renewal & redevelopment • integrated land infrastructure • port operation & marine base • land reclamation & marine structures • architecture & industrial building construction • clean rooms & R & D labs • geotechnical investigation, testing, instrumentation • surveying & mapping services • golf courses & management	Indonesia, China, Philippines, Thailand, Vietnam, Kenya, North Africa
Mass Rapid Transit Corporation	• planning, design, procurement, construction, training, operation • railway maintenance	–
Ministry of Environment	• sewerage system, solid waste management, pollution, drainage system • environmental health • quarantine & epidemiology	Indonesia, Malaysia, China, Vietnam
National Computer Board	• computerisation, software development standards & methodologies • software quality management • contracts & facilities management • system development life-cycle management • IT applications, feasibility study & consultancy	–
National Productivity Board	• management consultancy • campaigns, training • administration & research	Botswana, China, ASEAN, Mauritius
Port of Singapore Authority	• terminal operations • engineering & marine services	Indonesia, Italy, Mauritius, Brunei, China, Philippines, Sri Lanka, West Germany

Public Utilities Board	• commercial services • information services • port administration • thermal power plants • urban & rural electrification • water supply schemes • electrical consultancy, contracting & engineering services	Indonesia, Brunei, China, Vietnam, Philippines, Sri Lanka
Public Work Department	• architecture & engineering services • development & management • specialist services • geotechnical & structural • roads & transportation • building, conservation, retrofitting	China, Philippines, Fiji
Singapore Institute of Standards & Industrial Research	• testing & inspection • calibration, certification • design & development • technology transfer, R&D • consultancy & training	Malaysia, Sri Lanka, Philippines
Singapore Telecom	• infrastructural planning • international leased circuits • information systems • ISDN, mobile communication • satellite communication • corporate switched telecom network systems	Saudi Arabia, China, Qatar, Columbia, Japan, Kuwait, Fiji, Zimbabwe, Thailand, Philippines, Brunei, Mauritius, Indonesia, Taiwan, Germany, Madagascar, Marshall Island
Urban Redevelopment Authority	• planning, urban design • development control • architecture, conservation • project services, land management, R&D	Brunei, China

Source: Economic Development Board (1993).

Table 3.13 Assistance schemes and programmes of the Economic Development Board of Singapore

Start-up	Growth	Expansion	Going Overseas
Local Enterprise Computerisation Programme	ISO 9000 Certification	Automation Leasing Scheme	Business Development Scheme
Local Enterprise Finance Scheme	Local Enterprise Finance Scheme	Brand Development Assistance Scheme	Double Deduction for Overseas Investment Development Expenditure
Product Development Assistance Scheme	Local Enterprise Technical Assistance Scheme	Franchise Development Assistance Scheme	Franchise Development Assistance Scheme
R&D Incubator Programme	Local Industry Upgrading Programme	ISO 9000 Certification	Local Enterprise Finance Scheme (Overseas)
Skills Development Fund	Market & Investment Development Assistance Scheme	Local Enterprise Computerisation Programme	Local Industry Upgrading Programme
Venture Capital	Product Development Assistance Scheme	Local Enterprise Finance Scheme	Market & Investment Development Assistance Scheme
	Pioneer Status/Investment Allowance	Local Enterprise Technical Assistance Scheme	Overseas Enterprise Incentive/ Overseas Investment Incentive
	Skills Development Fund	Local Industry Upgrading Programme	
	Software Development Assistance Scheme	Market & Investment Development Assistance Scheme	
	Venture Capital	Pioneer Status/Investment Allowance	
		Product Development Assistance Scheme	
		Skills Development Fund	
		Software Development Assistance Scheme	
		Total Business Plan	
		Venture Capital	

Source: Economic Development Board (1993).

addressing broad spectrum of business needs (Economic Development Board, 1993). The state's target is to nurture 100 such SMEs into major players in the regional economy. First, the Local Enterprise Finance Scheme (LEFS) provides low-cost loans for the purchase of equipment and industrial facilities needed for overseas operations. Second, a number of tax incentives are offered to encourage local enterprises to invest abroad (e.g. the Double Reduction for Overseas Investment Development Expenditure). Third, the Regionalisation Training Scheme (RTS) provides training passes for a core group of key operators, supervisors, and engineers to receive training in Singapore. Companies may apply for a grant from EDB to defray the cost of the Foreign Workers' Levy incurred during their stay in Singapore. Fourth, to establish an overseas presence successfully, local companies often need to develop an understanding of the host operating environment and the range of business opportunities available. They can do so by participating in study missions organised by industry associations or government agencies such as EDB or the Trade Development Board.

CONCLUSION

Together with Chapter 2, this chapter has demonstrated the emerging global reach of Hong Kong and Singapore via outward investments and TNCs since the 1980s and 1990s. This emergence is set within peculiar institutional contexts and political economies that differ between Hong Kong and Singapore. They form the essential elements of an institutional analysis of transnational entrepreneurship developed in Chapter 1. It should now be clear that the business system in Hong Kong is quite different from that of Singapore. Different processes of institutional structuring have also influenced both business systems, resulting in different dominant forms of economic organisation in the two city-states (see Table 2.7). These institutional differences have a significant bearing on the nature and extent of outward investments and TNCs from two economies with similar histories and geographies.

This institutional analysis has so far been set at the national scale, demonstrating the complex interrelationships between national institutional structures and business systems. It remains unclear how these different institutional contexts shape the characteristics and behaviour of individual entrepreneurs and intrapreneurs who take their business operations across borders to become true TNCs. The next two chapters provide an empirical analysis of the nature and processes of transnational entrepreneurship in Singapore. For the purposes of simplicity, I have chosen to divide the discussion into two chapters – each addressing one dimension of transnational entrepreneurship. In Chapter 4, I will start with entrepreneurs who engage in international business and show how they benefit from their entrepreneurial endowments and resources embedded in their home economy. Their abilities to exploit these endowments and resources, however, are dependent on their successful enrolment into actor-specific networks in the host countries. In Chapter 5, I will apply the same analysis to the role of intrapreneurs in international business. The emphasis here is placed on the influence of home country business systems on the attributes and behaviour of these transnational intrapreneurs.

NOTES

1. These data are calculated by summing the cumulative realised FDI values between 1979 and 1996 (Sun, 1998: Appendix A) and in 1997 and 1998 (Ministry of Foreign Trade and Economic Cooperation, various years).
2. The transnational operations of Singaporean firms, in fact, have occurred much earlier than those captured in official statistics. Khong Guan Biscuit Factory, for example, was engaged in biscuit manufacturing in Indonesia during the 1950s (Chan and Chiang, 1994: 108ff). Similar examples of Singaporean manufacturers abroad were Ho Rih Hua's operation in Thailand and the Lau Ing Woon brothers spread into Southeast Asian countries (Chan and Chiang, 1994: 272–75).
3. For other general studies of outward investment from Singapore, see Lim and Teo (1986); Lee (1994); Lu and Zhu (1995); Pang (1995); Tan (1995); Tsang (1999a; 1999b); Okposin (1999); Rajan and Pangarkar (2000).

4. Entrepreneurs in international business

> A strong bias among Asian companies – and a key strength – is entrepreneurship. This is fine when a company is small, but creates special challenges by the time you grow to become a trans-nationally organised corporation. The structure needs to evolve not into a large centralised bureaucracy but into a series of small, relatively independent, entrepreneurial profit centres. (Victor Fung, Chairman of Li & Fung, one of the largest trading companies in Hong Kong, 1997: 222; see also Magretta, 1998)

INTRODUCTION

It should be clear by now that the pre-existing configurations of institutional structures have important implications for transnational entrepreneurship through their impact on entrepreneurial endowments and resources. This chapter extends the theoretical discussion in Chapter 1 and employs the institutional perspective on transnational entrepreneurship to analyse international business activities by Asian entrepreneurs. In particular, I examine the transformations of domestic entrepreneurs from Singapore (and Hong Kong) into transnational entrepreneurs. My main argument is that these transnational entrepreneurs are well endowed with networking skills and capabilities that enable them to participate actively in cross-border business networks and transnational ventures. The institutional environment in Asia also favours the strategic formation and implementation of such networks. In other words, there are intense interactions between individual entrepreneurs and their embedded business systems. These business systems tend to structure and shape the repertoire of entrepreneurial endowments and resources enjoyed by transnational entrepreneurs (see Figure 1.1).

This chapter therefore aims to show how transnational entrepreneurs from Singapore operate across borders to establish successful foreign ventures and to manage peculiar problems associated with these ventures. My empirical analysis is based on the two surveys of indigenous transnational corporations conducted in Hong Kong and Singapore (see Chapter 1). Although there is no intention to prove conclusively the validity of the theoretical framework proposed in Chapter 1, this chapter draws upon various quantitative and qualitative findings to shed light on the nature and role of transnational entrepreneurship in international business activities. The objective is to stimulate further theoretical and empirical studies in entrepreneurship and international business studies.

In analysing the nature and extent of transnational entrepreneurship among social actors, it is necessary to make a distinction between entrepreneurs and intrapreneurs, and analyse them separately in this and the next chapter for two reasons (see also Chapter 1). In the first place, it can be argued that entrepreneurs and intrapreneurs may have different risk-taking behaviour. This difference emanates from their different roles in business formation and venturing. Whereas transnational entrepreneurs are both owners (capitalists) and operators, transnational intrapreneurs are corporate managers who are given the mandate by shareholders or stakeholders to execute business formation and venturing. Transnational entrepreneurs may be able to take more risks and adopt a more innovative approach to cross-border operations, drawing upon their repertoire of endowments and resources (see Figure 1.1). While they may be more capable in strategic management – an essential criterion for transnational entrepreneurship – transnational intrapreneurs are constrained by the very mandate given to them by shareholders or ultimate owners of transnational corporations. They face certain constraints in making decisions in relation to cross-border operations.

Another reason for a separate institutional analysis of transnational entrepreneurs and intrapreneurs is that they may be embedded in different institutional endowments and resources. As explained in Chapter 1 (Figure 1.2), transnational entrepreneurship depends critically on the ability of transnational entrepreneurs and intrapreneurs to enrol into actor networks at different spatial scales. Because of their differential access to capital and management expertise, transnational entrepreneurs and intrapreneurs may operate differently across borders and engage in different business networks. Whereas transnational entrepreneurs tend to build alliances with other firms (inter-firm networks) and non-firm institutions (extra-firm networks) in home and host countries, transnational intrapreneurs tend to exploit their mandates within the TNC (intra-firm networks). In other words, the former group has full control of its business operations and is therefore more likely to engage in external networking with other firms and non-firm institutions. The latter group, however, has to secure its mandates from the parent companies and/or their boards of directors. In the case of government-linked companies (GLCs) from Singapore, transnational intrapreneurs must be particularly careful in ensuring their corporate initiatives do not contradict national economic imperatives (see more in Chapter 5).

Having set up these preambles, this chapter is organised into four sections. The next section explains the institutional structuring of transnational entrepreneurs in Singapore and Hong Kong. The analysis is based on the predominant role of Chinese business systems in Singapore and Hong Kong. Section two analyses transnational entrepreneurs from Singapore and their foreign operations, based on findings from the survey of transnational entrepreneurs. Qualitative case studies are presented in various boxes to shed light on several issues related to transnational entrepreneurship, in particular the formation and the early success of their transnational ventures. The third section examines the role of transnational entrepreneurs in managing across borders. Transnational entrepreneurship is best observed when these entrepreneurs are confronted with severe problems in the host countries and through how they manage to overcome barriers to internationalisation. The concluding section provides a brief summary of the main findings in this chapter.

THE INSTITUTIONAL STRUCTURING OF TRANSNATIONAL ENTREPRENEURS IN SINGAPORE AND HONG KONG

Today, there is no doubt that ethnic Chinese in East and Southeast Asia are well known to be exceptionally entrepreneurial in their domestic economies (Lim and Gosling, 1983; Redding, 1990; Hamilton, 1996; Hodder, 1996; Lim, 2000). In some Southeast Asian countries (e.g. Indonesia and Malaysia), the restrictive 'home' institutional context explains the predominant focus of ethnic Chinese on business activities. Many of these ethnic Chinese abroad have formed formidable 'bamboo networks' embedded in 'particularistic ties and multiplex relationships [that] are likely to figure prominently in situations of imperfect competition' (S.L. Wong, 1988: 109; see also Weidenbaum and Hughes, 1996). Redding (1990: 34) also cautioned that 'explaining networking in terms of *purely* ethnic reasons would be simplistic. There are reasons of hard economic and business expediency as well as ethnic loyalties behind much of this behavior'. The role of home and host country institutional conditions in structuring these entrepreneurial outcomes becomes highly important (see Chapter 1). In other Asian economies dominated by ethnic Chinese, these 'bamboo networks' are constituted not only by fellow Chinese entrepreneurs, but sometimes also by political figures (e.g. in Taiwan and Thailand) and non-Chinese business people (e.g. in Hong Kong and Singapore). Early studies of Chinese capitalism in Asia were exclusively preoccupied with the domestic constitution of these 'bamboo networks' and the complex business practices embedded in these networks.

Since the 1970s, it has become clear that ethnic Chinese entrepreneurs are increasingly spreading their 'bamboo networks' across countries and, sometimes, regions. This process of the globalisation of Chinese business firms is a significant development in the business history of the 'Overseas Chinese'. This is because transnational operations require more than the traditional skills and competitive advantages that ensure the success of these Chinese entrepreneurs in their 'home' countries (see Yeung, 1999d; Yeung and Olds, 2000). Kao (1993: 32) might be right in arguing that 'cross-border investments alone are responsible for turning the *de facto* network of loose family relationships into today's Chinese commonwealth'. But he offered little to explain *why* and *how* such a transformation in the spatial organisation of 'bamboo networks' comes about. Here I would like to argue that transnational entrepreneurship plays a critical role not only in spreading these 'bamboo networks' abroad, but also in transforming them into significant business opportunities. Three attributes of Chinese transnational entrepreneurship are particularly important in facilitating the transnational operations of Chinese business firms: (1) their greater possibility of internalising overseas markets; (2) their trust and goodwill in host countries; and (3) their reliance on transnational social and business networks.

First, transnational Chinese entrepreneurs tend to exhibit a greater tendency towards *internalising foreign markets* through direct investments and other forms of equity investments. Within the Chinese psyche, there is a deep-seated and culturally embedded desire for self-ownership and autonomy in decision-making (Bond, 1986; Redding, 1990). Although the family serves as a significant binding and centripetal force, Chinese entrepreneurs prefer to be their own boss. There is a famous Chinese proverb: 'better be the beak of a cock than the rump of an ox' (cited in S.L. Wong, 1988: 101). It is not surprising that ethnic Chinese are well known for their entrepreneurial spirit. In the context of cross-border operations, this drive towards ownership and control implies that transnational Chinese entrepreneurs are more willing to venture into rather opaque business environments.

Once established, these foreign ventures tend to be less risky under the direct control and management of the entrepreneurs and their trusted lieutenants. These transnational Chinese entrepreneurs are also more likely to take a personal approach to foreign ventures through direct participation in the negotiation stage and subsequently more frequent visits. These aspects of transnational entrepreneurship are particularly useful in host countries with opaque business environments and ineffective corporate governance systems (see case studies below). Direct ownership in highly competitive and open business environments (e.g. North America and Western Europe) requires both transnational entrepreneurship and significant competitive advantages (e.g. brand names, proprietary technology, management expertise, and so on).

Second, there is no doubt that *developing trust and goodwill* form an integral part of Chinese business practice. For aspiring transnational Chinese entrepreneurs, having strong trust and goodwill in the host countries helps to open doors and gain better acceptance by the host business and political communities. There is thus less necessity for complex and detailed contracts to be negotiated because verbal guarantees by a transnational Chinese entrepreneur, well known for his/her trustworthy behaviour, are better than many contracts that lay out all contingencies. This reliance on trust and goodwill rather than just formal contracts is much less common in Western business. Recent research has shown that formal contracts still play the most important role even in co-operative ventures among Western firms (see Willcocks and Choi, 1995; Lewis, 1995; Beamish and Killing, 1997; Doz and Hamel, 1998). Some researchers (e.g. Fukuyama, 1995) argued that in a well-functioning market system, formal contracts enable businesses to be conducted among complete strangers, thereby contributing to greater transparency and economic efficiency.

Trust and goodwill is important for transnational Chinese entrepreneurs not only to penetrate into difficult host countries in Asia, but also to establish themselves successfully in highly competitive business environments. On this latter point, some of today's transnational Chinese entrepreneurs are globalising into North America and Western Europe. Trust and goodwill are significant sources of advantages to enable them to receive good support from bankers and financial analysts, and therefore to gain access to global capital markets. This access to capital and finance also enables a widening of Chinese business networks to enrol strategically non-Chinese actors who function as bridges for transnational Chinese entrepreneurs to enter into these globally competitive markets (see Olds and Yeung, 1999; Yeung, 1999d; 2000b; Yeung and Soh, 2000).

While they may prefer to own and control foreign ventures, transnational Chinese entrepreneurs do not always take an authoritarian approach to these ventures. They often delegate responsibilities to trusted members of their inner circles, who may be relatives. Sometimes, they are non-family members who have been socialised into the entrepreneur's family through a process of 'family-isation', defined as the gradual co-opting of non-family members through personal relationships and marriage alliances (see Chan and Chiang, 1994: 297; Yeung, 2000f). There are at least two reasons for the necessity of 'family-isation'. One reason is that there is simply a shortage of capable family members to take over such key responsibilities as setting up foreign ventures. As Fukuyama (1995: 64) argued, 'a single family, no matter how large, capable, or well educated, can only have so many competent sons, daughters, spouses, and siblings to oversee the different parts of a rapidly ramifying enterprise'. An inevitable result of this succession problem is that most big Chinese family businesses today are stacked with professional managers. One fund manager, for example, noted that 'many of the people who actually run Robert Kuok's businesses are not linked to the family empire. Obviously he has to trust these lieutenants, but he is prepared to delegate' (cited in *The Financial Times*, 5 March 1998).

Another reason for 'family-isation' is that as a rule of thumb in Chinese entrepreneurship, a senior (sometimes a former employer) is obliged to help a junior to set up his/her own business if the latter is proven to be sufficiently entrepreneurial. M. Chen (1995: 53) observed that '[w]hen *guanxi* links two persons of unequal rank or social status, the weaker side usually expects more help than he or she can reciprocate in equal terms'. This unwritten 'cultural rule' is unthinkable in Western business because of culturally-embedded individualism and competitive behaviour (Hamilton, 1994; 1996). Foreign ventures are established to provide opportunities for both business expansion and internalising enterprising employees. We begin to find more competent professional managers being socialised into Chinese family businesses such that over time, they become trusted 'insiders' in these reshaped 'Chinese' business networks.

Third, transnational Chinese entrepreneurs often rely on their *social and business networks* to facilitate foreign ventures, although as argued above, these networks are no longer exclusively Chinese in terms of their ethnic constituency. Studies of ethnic Chinese entrepreneurs from Hong Kong have revealed the importance of personal history and embedded interests in their transnational operations (e.g. M. Chen, 1995; Yeung, 1997a; 1997b; 1998a). The contemporary Chinese people are experienced migrants and tend to form socially organised networks to provide emotional and personal support. Sometimes, family and clan members almost exclusively constitute these social networks. As Kao (1993: 24) argued, '[f]or many generations, emigrant Chinese entrepreneurs have been operating comfortably in a network of family and clan, laying the foundations for stronger links among businesses across national borders' (see case studies below). In other circumstances, transnational Chinese entrepreneurs may rely on their trusted friends and employees to develop business networks across borders. These strong personal relationships with key employees often result in the growth of transnational *intra*preneurs who are empowered by their owners to develop foreign ventures (see Chapter 5). Transnational Chinese entrepreneurs therefore need to take significant risks, and possess foresight in the selection and delegation of transnational intrapreneurs.

TRANSNATIONAL ENTREPRENEURS FROM SINGAPORE AND THEIR FOREIGN OPERATIONS

Profiles of Transnational Entrepreneurs

If Chinese business people tend to engage in cross-border operations, what then are the key attributes of these transnational entrepreneurs? Table 4.1 shows the gender and designations of transnational entrepreneurs, based on the survey of Singaporean firms that have foreign operations. It must be noted that the classification of a respondent into a transnational entrepreneur is based on his/her self-acknowledgement. There are no statistically significant differences between transnational entrepreneurs and non-transnational entrepreneurs in terms of the sectoral distribution, ownership, sales value, and assets of their companies. In Table 4.1, a majority (N = 122; 62 per cent) of the 197 respondents agreed that they are transnational entrepreneurs. In terms of gender distribution, it is statistically significant to find that more transnational entrepreneurs are men. Some 92 per cent of the respondents who described themselves as transnational entrepreneurs are male, compared to only 80 per cent in the case of non-transnational entrepreneurs. This finding is explained by the predominant role of men in Chinese business systems (see S.L. Wong, 1988; Whitley, 1992a; 1999; cf. Whyte, 1996).

Another statistically significant finding is that the positions of the respondents in the SINTNCs are related to the likelihood of them being transnational entrepreneurs. Transnational entrepreneurs tend to be top executives of their companies. In fact, Table 4.1 shows that almost 60 per cent of transnational entrepreneurs are chairmen or CEOs/managing directors/presidents of their companies. However, only 32 per cent of those non-transnational entrepreneurs are holding the same designations. This finding can be explained by the differential entrepreneurial endowments and resources enjoyed by top executives and other corporate managers (see more examples below). As described in Chapter 1 (Figure 1.1), these entrepreneurial endowments and resources comprise tapping into information asymmetry, identifying risks and opportunities, access to finance and capital, experience in business and management, and relationships with customers and/or suppliers.

Figure 4.1 summarises the key attributes of entrepreneurship as described by transnational entrepreneurs in our survey. These attributes essentially define the personality and traits with which a transnational entrepreneur should be endowed. From all 317 responses, it is clear that *strong vision and accomplishment* is the single most important attribute (19 per cent) that must be possessed by transnational entrepreneurs. Together

158   *Entrepreneurship and the internationalisation of Asian firms*

Table 4.1   Profiles of transnational entrepreneurs by gender and designation

Category	Entrepreneur	(%)	Non-entrepreneur	(%)	Total
Gender					
Male	112	91.8	60	80.0	43
Female	10	8.2	15	20.0	134
Total	122	100.0	75	100.0	197
p<0.01; chi-square=5.8; d.f.=1					
Designation					
Chairman	9	7.4	2	2.6	11
CEO/Managing Director/ President	64	52.5	22	28.9	86
Executive Director/General Manager/ Senior Vice President	28	23.0	25	32.9	53
Divisional Manager/ Vice President	14	11.5	14	18.4	28
Others	7	5.7	13	17.1	20
Total	122	100.0	76	100.0	198
p<0.01; chi-square=17.2; d.f.=5					

Source: Author's survey.

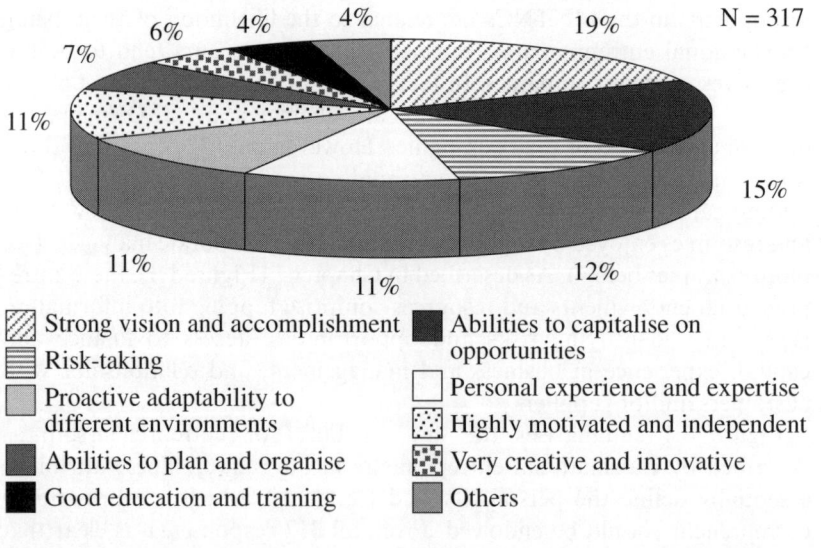

Figure 4.1   Attributes of entrepreneurship described by transnational entrepreneurs

with *risk-taking abilities* (12 per cent) and *abilities to capitalise on opportunities* (15 per cent), these three attributes account for almost half of all responses. They explain the peculiar abilities of transnational entrepreneurs to tap into information asymmetry and to exploit opportunities for cross-border operations (see Figure 1.1). Their importance in driving cross-border operations is clearly seen in the case of Kwek Leng Beng, Chairman of Hong Leong Group in Singapore (see Box 4.1). Kwek not only possesses the key attributes of transnational entrepreneurship above, he is also able to make use of these attributes to advance his global corporate empire. His key transnational projects include the acquisition of the London-based Millennium & Copthorne Hotels via his CDL Hotels International based in Hong Kong and the development of major properties in China via his 'triangular family networks'. The next set of important attributes comprises *personal experience* (11 per cent), *adaptability to different business environments* (11 per cent), and *strong motivations* (11 per cent). The next subsection explains how these attributes of transnational entrepreneurship are put into practice in international business activities.

> **BOX 4.1 THE GLOBAL EMPIRE OF KWEK LENG BENG AND HIS HONG LEONG GROUP: TRANSNATIONAL ENTREPRENEURSHIP AND 'TRIANGULAR FAMILY NETWORKS'**
>
> The story of Hong Leong Group's Kwek Leng Beng is well known (see Yeung, 1998c; 1999f; Backman, 1999). In this case study, I want to show how Kwek's transnational entrepreneurship, as manifested in his meticulous capitalisation on family networks and linkages at a regional scale, has contributed to his successful international business operations in Hong Kong, China, and Britain. The founder of the Hong Leong Group is the late Kwek Hong Png who came to Singapore from Fujian, China in 1928. Over a period of half a decade, he managed to build up a vast business empire starting with trading, then expanding into property, finance, and hotels. The Group's Malaysian branch started in 1963 when the late Kwek Hong Png sent his brother Kwek Hong Lye to Malaya (from which Singapore was soon to separate) to extend the family's operations there (East Asia Analytical Unit, 1995: 332). Over time, the Malaysian family branch has grown substantially into one of the biggest conglomerates in Malaysia, with an annual turnover of US$1.3 billion. It had a strong foothold in Hong Kong's financial industry as its subsidiary, the Guoco Group, controlled the

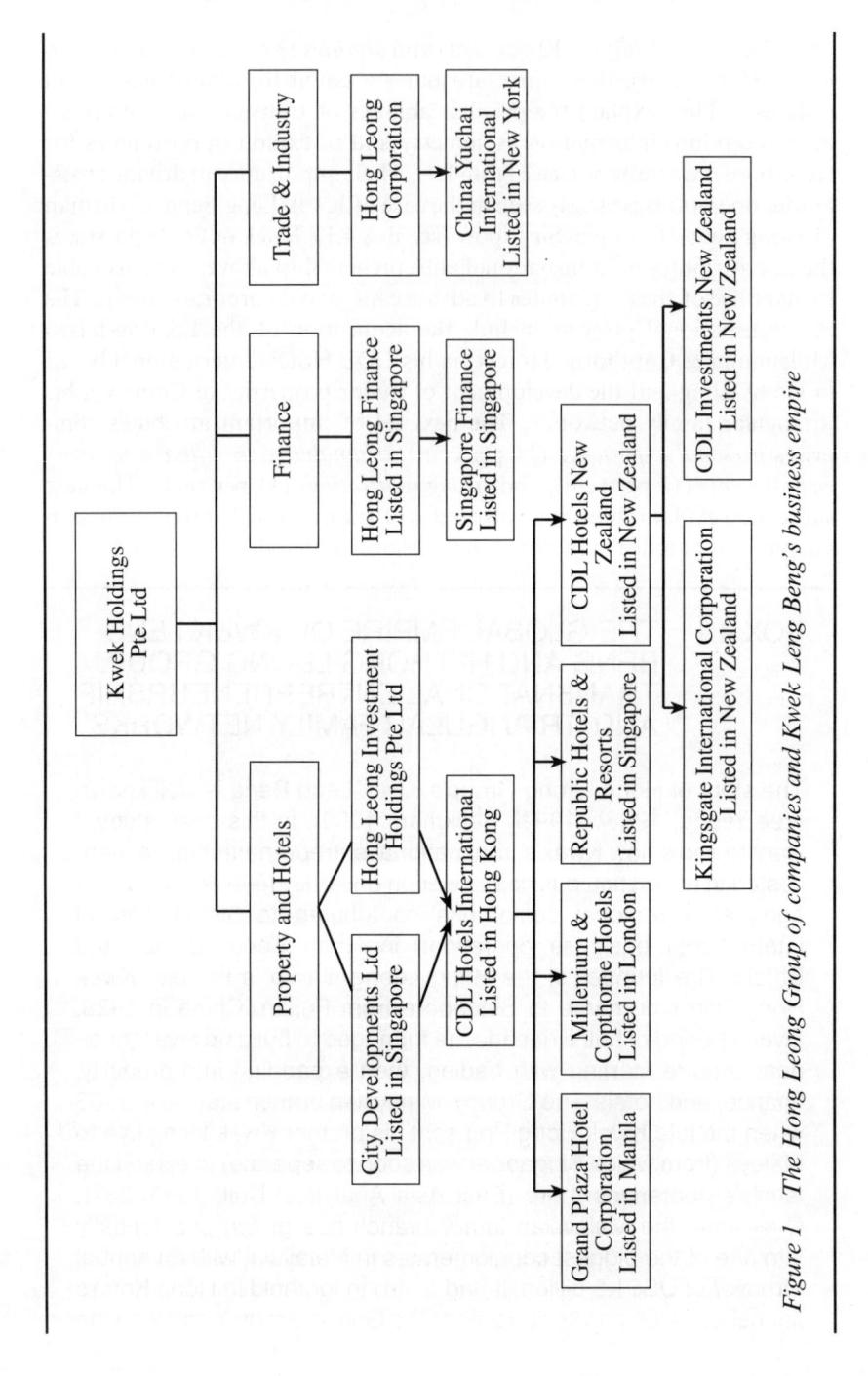

160   *Entrepreneurship and the internationalisation of Asian firms*

Figure 1   The Hong Leong Group of companies and Kwek Leng Beng's business empire

fifth largest local bank in Hong Kong – Dao Heng Bank. When Kwek Hong Lye died in 1996, his son, Quek Leng Chan, took over the Malaysian business.

My focus here is on Singapore's Kwek Leng Beng, son of the late Kwek Hong Png and cousin of Quek Leng Chan in Malaysia. In 1994, Kwek Leng Beng took charge of the Hong Leong Group in Singapore after his father's death. Joining his father's business after finishing his law degree in Britain in 1963, Kwek initiated the takeover of a loss-making listed company (City Developments) in the late 1960s and the early 1970s, and successfully turned it around to become a leading property developer in Singapore. The Hong Leong Group (see Figure 1) is now one of the largest Chinese business groups in Singapore with a market capitalisation value of US$16 billion, an employment strength of 30000 worldwide, and a stable of 300 companies, including 11 listed on various bourses in Singapore, Hong Kong, New Zealand, Manila, New York, and London (*The Sunday Times*, 2 February 1997). Through its private property arm (Hong Leong Holdings) and its industrial company (Hong Leong Corporation), Kwek controls China's largest refrigerator manufacturer (Xin Fei Electric) and New York-listed diesel engine maker China Yuchai International (*The Straits Times*, 9 August 1997: 10).

Since taking over from his father in late 1994, Kwek has developed a voracious appetite for major acquisitions abroad. The Hong Leong Group has recently globalised into the hotel business through its property development arm – City Developments Ltd. CDL Hotels International, controlled by City Developments Ltd. and listed on the Hong Kong Stock Exchange, manages the group's hotel interest. Since the late 1980s, CDL Hotels International has grown tremendously, from owning only 5 hotels in 1989 to 117 in 2000. CDL Hotels International has a hotel empire spanning 13 countries in Europe, the USA, Australia, New Zealand, East and Southeast Asia. In 2000, it was the eight largest hotel owner and operator in the world (http://www.hongleong-group.com.sg/hotels.html; accessed on 27 July 2000). Its success in acquiring hotels on a global scale rests not only with the sheer financial muscle of the Hong Leong Group, but more importantly, with the excellent business acumen and transnational entrepreneurship of its present chairman, Kwek Leng Beng.

What then is so entrepreneurial about Kwek Leng Beng to earn him Singapore's Businessman of the Year 1996? In a rare interview, Kwek said with his characteristic understatement that 'A lot of people say: "You are either born an entrepreneur or you are not. You cannot learn to become one". This is not true' (cited in *The Sunday Times*, 2 February 1997: 2). In fact, Kwek Leng Beng attributed much of his entrepreneurship to his late father Kwek Hong Png:

> It is my strong belief that when you are in it for some time, you can get the feel of it, you get the feel in your guts . . . I have been trained by my old man and I graduated from his university. He had a lot of strengths, which I learnt over the years. I have been the type of person who likes to soil his hands. I have gone through the process, so I understand the A to Z of the business. (Cited in *The Sunday Times*, 2 February 1997: 2)

The three important business principles Kwek learnt from his late father are: (1) never overpay for something, particularly when the market has gone crazy; (2) work hard to realise good profits rather than just plain sailing; and (3) do something in a big way without over-stretching oneself. Kwek's superior skills and entrepreneurial instincts in takeover and acquisitions evolved from his early involvement in the takeovers of City Developments Ltd. in the late 1960s and Singapore Finance in 1979. Both listed companies are major contributors to the Hong Leong Group today. In a series of major hotel acquisitions in the 1990s which enabled CDL Hotels International to become one of the largest global hotel chains, Kwek demonstrated tremendous strength and transnational entrepreneurial acumen. This was not an easy task at all because the transnational entrepreneur needs a lot of experience and good judgement in the absence of complete information about these major assets abroad.

Moreover, Kwek is clearly a risk-taker who does not like to minimise risks by following the crowd. In another interview on why he did not follow the regionalisation strategy of most Singaporean firms, Kwek reflected on his global acquisition trail:

> I think like this: Yes, external wing is good. But when everybody is going to the region, developing properties, that is the time, honestly, I want to sell. I don't follow herd instinct; I fight it . . . It's common sense. A lot of people thought, it's [Asian markets] a pot of gold, if you go, I must go. But if there are five of you building hotels in the same place, then you won't make it, easy to see . . . When I went to London to buy hotels, everybody said, 'this guy is talking rot, talking rubbish', but I did not listen. I smelled the market, I know. (Cited in *The Straits Times*, 20 November 1998: 74)

The Kwek way is not to rely on partners, whether they are from Singapore or in the host countries. Very often, interested parties both within and outside Singapore have asked Kwek for good projects. For example, instead of Kwek being driven by the Singapore government's call for regionalisation since 1993, it is the Singapore government that, through Temasek Holdings, asked Kwek for good projects, came to evaluate Kwek's suggestions and got involved (e.g. the Beijing Riviera residential project). This is how the Hong Leong Group helps government-linked companies (GLCs) from Singapore to regionalise their operations. According to my interview with a key Kwek family member in Hong Kong (11 June 1998), 'they [GLCs] have money, but no expertise in running projects'.

In many ways, Kwek is truly a transnational entrepreneur as defined by the interrelated attributes cited in my survey. First, Kwek has tremendous personal experience and expertise in property development, finance, and hotels. Through his public listed companies in Singapore (City Developments Ltd., Hong Leong Finance, and Singapore Finance) and Hong Kong (CDL Hotels International Ltd), he has demonstrated excellence in both business acumen and financial prudence. All three listed companies showed healthy profits in 1998, despite the ongoing Asian economic crisis. Second, Kwek has strong vision and accomplishment. Since he took over the helm of the Hong Leong Group from his father in 1994, he has expanded the Group to become a Chinese family conglomerate with truly global operations. His CDL Hotels International now has a hotel empire spanning 13 countries in the Triad regions. Third, Kwek is a well-known calculated risk-taker who fights against herd instinct to be the final captor (*The Straits Times*, 20 November 1998). Precisely because of his global hotel acquisition drive since the early 1990s, the Hong Leong Group suffered much less from the 1997/1998 Asian economic crisis. Fourth, Kwek is a highly motivated and independent businessman. Even before the departure of his late father, Kwek was able to implement freely his hotel acquisition strategy. As reported in *The Sunday Times* (2 February 1997: 3):

> Just as the 'old man' [the late Kwek Hong Png] was famous for sniffing out good real estate deals, his son [Kwek Leng Beng] has been credited with an astute eye for choice hotels at bargain prices, often picking them up at rock-bottom prices from receivers. In international hotel circles, Mr Kwek is known as 'a business-cycle bottom fisher' and is reputed to be a decisive and fast buyer.

Last but most importantly, Kwek is not only well connected and resourced, but also capable of capitalising on these family and business networks to develop his foreign ventures. In the case of his businesses in Hong Kong and China, there is clearly a 'triangular family network' for him to exercise his transnational entrepreneurship and to capitalise on its transnational business synergy. This 'triangular family network' involves Kwek Leng Beng in Singapore and Quek Leng Chan, his cousin from Malaysia, as well as Gan Khai Choon, his brother-in-law stationed in Hong Kong. In 1985, Kwek's late father sent Gan, his son-in-law, to set up Hong Leong International (Hong Kong) Ltd and to be its Managing Director, with the intention of investing in both Hong Kong and China. The timing was right because Hong Kong's property market was just recovering from a serious collapse in the period 1982–1984. As Executive Director of the public listed CDL Hotels International in Hong Kong, Gan is also looking after Kwek's hotel businesses in Hong Kong and Taiwan.

So how exactly does this 'triangular family network' work in favour of Kwek's investments in Hong Kong and China? Let us examine just one specific transnational investment by Kwek – the Beijing Riviera residential property development project (see Figure 2). First identified by Gan in 1994, this project is a co-operative joint venture between a Singapore consortium led by Hong Leong Holdings Ltd. and their Chinese partner (Beijing East Suburb Agriculture Industry Commerce United Corporation). The reputation of the project was good from the beginning and it attracted investors from the USA, Europe, Japan, and Taiwan. There were two reasons for this. First, investors were impressed by the involvement of Kwek's Hong Leong Group, which had already achieved worldwide acclaim in its hotel businesses. The participation of Temasek Holdings Pte Ltd, an investment and holding arm of the Singapore government, further boosted the image of the project as a clean and credit-worthy investment. Second, though required by Chinese law, the local Chinese partner did not contribute any equity to the Beijing project. Instead, it guaranteed the project's profitability. It also does not interfere in the decision-making of the project, contributing further to investors' confidence. By June 1998, 50 per cent of the Beijing project had been completed and over 75 per cent of units had been sold. This was quite a remarkable achievement, given the serious downturn in property markets throughout Asia in the midst of its worst-ever crisis.

The division of labour in this 'triangular family network' is rather straightforward, an evidence of intra-family synergy and trust relationships. As shown in Figure 2, Kwek's Hong Leong Group in Singapore owns 51 per cent of the project, split equally between Hong Leong Holdings and its 100 per cent owned subsidiary in Hong Kong, Hong Leong International (HK). In Hong Kong, Kwek taps into his brother-in-law's expertise in, and familiarity with, property development in Hong Kong and China. Kwek also requests operational assistance from his Malaysian cousin, Quek Leng Chan, in two ways (see Figure 2). First, Quek Leng Chan's Dao Heng Bank in Hong Kong handled financial transactions and insurance related to the Beijing project. Dao Heng Bank also arranged purchase loans and financing for buyers. Second, building materials for the Beijing project were acquired through Hong Leong Industries in Malaysia. Together, this 'triangular family network' represents what Gan referred to as 'group total effort' among members of the Kwek/Quek families, and companies of the Hong Leong groups in Singapore, Malaysia, and Hong Kong. Clearly, the Beijing project is not the first time Kwek Leng Beng has sought co-operation from his cousin in developing transnational operations. Kwek recently described his relationship with his Malaysian cousin as 'excellent' and revealed that they are looking for co-operative ventures in the global market:

> We played together, lived together when we were young. We now exchange views on matters we think our companies will have synergies ... It does not take a genius to realise that Singapore Hong Leong and Malaysia Hong Leong can be a real force to be reckoned with internationally. (Cited in *The Sunday Times*, 2 February 1997: 3)

The case of Kwek Leng Beng and his Hong Leong Group therefore shows how a transnational entrepreneur can tap into his cross-border family and business networks to engage in successful foreign ventures.

In consequence, Kwek's transnational entrepreneurship and globalisation strategy paid off in the midst of the Asian economic crisis. All three major listed arms of the Hong Leong Group achieved significant net profits in 1998, a year in which most listed companies in Singapore suffered losses (see Table 1). City Developments Ltd, which controls CDL Hotels International, was ranked seventh most profitable listed company in Singapore in 1998, with a net profit of S$123.7 million. Hong Leong Finance, Singapore Finance, and Hong Leong Asia pocketed a net profit of

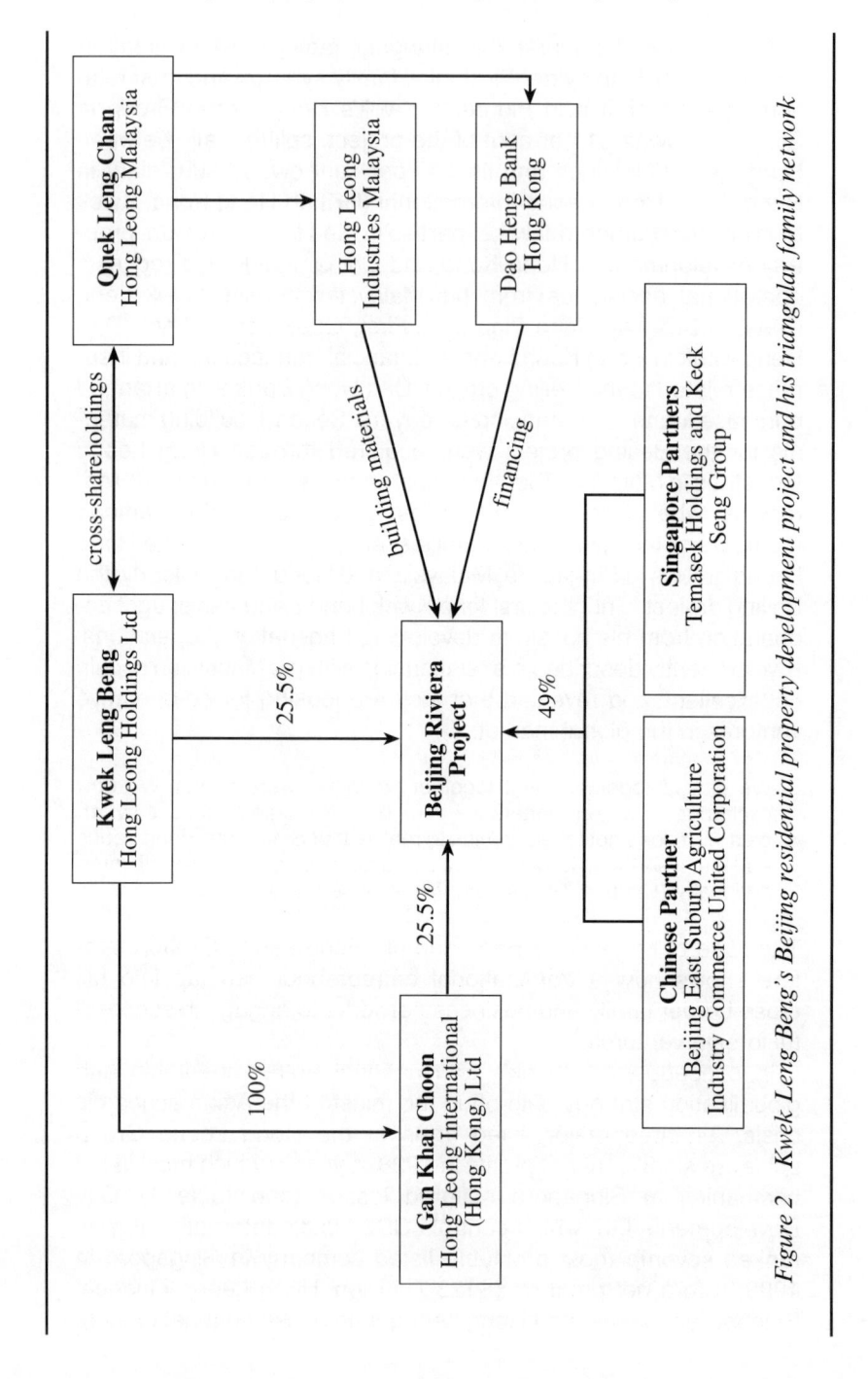

Figure 2 Kwek Leng Beng's Beijing residential property development project and his triangular family network

S$53.2 million, S$32.8 million, and S$17 million respectively. The performance of City Developments Ltd. was indeed way ahead of other listed property developers in Singapore. As shown in Table 1, among five top losing listed companies in 1998, four belonged to property developers (Keppel Land, DBS Land, Orchard Parade Holdings, and MCL Land). Four other property developers in Singapore also suffered losses in 1998.

Table 1 Performance of selected public listed companies in Singapore, 1997 and 1998

		Net Profit/(Loss) in S$million		Turnover in S$million	
Ranking	Company[a]	1998	1997	1998	1997
Profitable					
1	OCBC	425.3	581.1	4747.1	4079.1
2	UOB	367.8	502.1	3561.5	3331.2
3	DBS	222.7	436.4	5407.3	3689.0
4	OUB	180.4	254.8	2944.0	2723.6
5	ST Engineering	154.7	120.8	1661.7	1476.7
6	Asia Food & Properties	140.9	45.2	954.9	1432.8
7	**City Developments**	**123.7**	**409.2**	**2043.3**	**2470.4**
15	**Hong Leong Finance**	**53.2**	**72.9**	**422.8**	**374.9**
22	**Singapore Finance**	**32.8**	**34.8**	**153.1**	**135.9**
37	**Hong Leong Asia**	**17.0**	**(34.8)**	**456.3**	**616.0**
Loss-making					
1	NOL	(438.2)	(297.3)	6485.3	2672.5
2	Keppel Land	(350.6)	104.6	317.9	621.2
3	DBS Land	(239.0)	182.3	1419.8	1083.2
4	Orchard Parade Holdings	(196.2)	21.6	193.9	491.2
5	MCL Land	(188.5)	19.5	297.0	297.0
9	Tuan Sing	(83.9)	31.6	575.9	646.3
43	United Overseas Land	(4.1)	52.6	425.5	357.6
–	Wing Tai[b]	(99.8)	46.0	–	–
–	First Capital[b]	(17.8)	6.3	–	–

Notes:
[a] All Hong Leong Group Companies are in bold.
[b] Data refer to 6 months ended December 1997 and 1998.

Source: The Straits Times, 24 March 1999: 58; 2 April 1999: 86.

One of the major contributing factors to the relatively unscathed performance of City Developments Ltd was the net income from its global hotel operations, which exceeded that of its core property development business. In 1997, its hotel businesses in the UK and the USA were the most profitable operations and contributed some 71.8 per cent of profit before taxation of CDL Hotels International Ltd as shown in its annual report (1997: 75). In 1998, its hotel business turned in profits before interest and tax of S$237.9 million, not far behind the S$269.6 million from both property development and rental income from investment properties. Kwek Leng Beng said that '[t]his reflects the success of our group's strategy of diversification into international hotels embarked in the early 1990s to ensure a wider spread of earnings' (cited in *The Straits Times*, 24 March 1999: 58). My interview with a key Kwek family member in Hong Kong (11 June 1998) also shows that the Hong Leong Group had been prepared for cyclical fluctuations in the property markets well before the Asian economic crisis. All the foreign projects of Hong Leong are run as financially independent units and hedging is used to reduce foreign exchange risks. My interviewee also said that Kwek had been telling them that 'the market is not going up every day. We must also be prepared for the worst'.

Hong Leong's London-listed subsidiary, Millennium & Copthorne Hotels (M&C), was CDL Hotels International's star performer in 1998. M&C was listed in the London Stock Exchange on 25 April 1996, slightly more than one year before the outbreak of the Asian economic crisis. The listing attracted some £1.2 billion investor funds worldwide. Kwek commented a day before M&C's listing that '[w]e are very happy with the timing. It could not have been more perfect from the beginning up to the flotation' (cited in *The Straits Times*, 24 April 1996). Indeed, this comment could not have been more appropriate in the context of the crisis. The listing of M&C not only generated net proceeds of £174.5 million to relieve both M&C and its parent company CDL Hotels International from debt obligations, but also significantly raised the investment profile of Kwek in major global capital markets. This latter point proved to be important when Kwek needed to tap into these capital markets in the midst of the Asian economic crisis. In brief, what was initially an egg-spreading strategy pursued relentlessly by Kwek has turned out to be the key to shield the group from the severe impact of the Asian economic crisis.

Formation of Transnational Ventures

Chapter 3 has detailed the origins and rationales of transnational ventures by Singaporean firms. It does not differentiate, however, the formation of transnational ventures by the involvement of transnational entrepreneurs. This subsection aims to assess the extent to which the establishment of foreign operations by transnational entrepreneurs is influenced by structural conditions in home and host countries, as well as in the global economy. The statistically significant findings support the claim that pre-existing configurations of institutional structures in home and host countries have a significant influence on cross-border operations by transnational entrepreneurs (see Chapter 1).

Table 4.2 provides only statistically significant findings on the influence of *home country conditions* on foreign operations by transnational entrepreneurs. Our respondents were asked to evaluate the importance of seven home country conditions on their operations in five broad regions comprising Southeast Asia, East Asia, Europe, North America, and other regions (see also Table 3.8). Other than the two home country conditions shown in Table 4.2, there are no statistically significant differences in the influence of home country conditions on foreign operations by transnational entrepreneurs and non-transnational entrepreneurs.

In the first place, *intensified competition in Singapore* seems to be more important in driving non-transnational entrepreneurs to establish operations in Southeast Asia. Some 84 per cent of these non-transnational entrepreneurs cited the home country condition, compared with only 63 per cent of transnational entrepreneurs. This finding is important because Southeast Asia hosts some 46 per cent of all foreign subsidiaries of SINTNCs (see Table 3.7). The finding also implies that transnational entrepreneurs tend to be more able to handle intensified competition in Singapore and that their Southeast Asian operations are not a direct response to intensified competition in Singapore. Moreover, there is a statistically significant difference in the influence of *entrepreneurial vision* on North American subsidiaries established by transnational entrepreneurs and non-transnational entrepreneurs. Some 94 per cent of transnational entrepreneurs considered entrepreneurial vision as important in establishing their North American subsidiaries, compared with only 83 per cent in the case of non-transnational entrepreneurs. This difference can be attributed to the greater likelihood of transnational entrepreneurs to go beyond the immediate Asian region and to establish themselves in such highly competitive markets as North America.

The influence of *host country conditions* on the likelihood of foreign operations is shown in Table 4.3. There are six such conditions in the

Table 4.2 *Influence of home country conditions on the establishment of foreign operations by host region and transnational entrepreneurs*

Home Country Conditions	Entrepreneur	(%)	Non-entrepreneur	(%)	Total
Intensified competition on Southeast Asian subsidiaries					
Very important	14	17.3	15	30.0	29
Quite important	37	45.7	27	54.0	64
Neutral	13	16.0	1	2.0	14
Quite unimportant	10	12.3	4	8.0	14
Very unimportant	7	8.6	3	6.0	10
Total	81	100.0	50	100.0	131
$p<0.05$; chi-square=9.2; d.f.=4					
Entrepreneurial vision on North American subsidiaries					
Very important	10	58.8	10	83.3	20
Quite important	6	35.3	0	0.0	6
Neutral	0	0.0	2	16.7	2
Quite unimportant	1	5.9	0	0.0	1
Total	17	100.0	12	100.0	29
$p<0.05$; chi-square=8.4; d.f.=3					

Source: Author's survey.

original survey questionnaire (see Table 3.8). There are statistically significant differences in the influence of three host country conditions between transnational entrepreneurs and non-transnational entrepreneurs. They are (1) marketing strategies; (2) familiar operating environment; and (3) lower costs of operations. First, more transnational entrepreneurs establish cross-border operations in Southeast Asia (94 per cent) and Europe (100 per cent) because of *marketing strategies*. Only respectively 87 per cent and 83 per cent of non-transnational entrepreneurs cited the host country condition as important. This finding implies that transnational entrepreneurs tend to be more able to tap into business opportunities abroad by taking calculated risks (see Figure 1.1).

Second, *familiar operating environment* seems to play a more important role in establishing operations in East Asia. While it is almost equally important for transnational entrepreneurs and non-transnational entrepreneurs establishing their Southeast Asian operations (73 per cent), the condition is clearly more important to transnational entrepreneurs operating in East Asia (65 per cent). These findings show that both groups of respondents tend to be quite familiar with the host country conditions in other neighbouring Southeast Asian countries. Transnational entrepreneurs, however, may be more familiar with the host country conditions in

Table 4.3 *Influence of host country conditions on the establishment of foreign operations by host region and transnational entrepreneurs*

Host Country Conditions	Entrepreneur	(%)	Non-entrepreneur	(%)	Total
Marketing strategies on Southeast Asian subsidiaries					
Very important	30	32.3	21	39.6	51
Quite important	57	61.3	25	47.2	82
Neutral	4	4.3	1	1.9	5
Quite unimportant	2	2.2	4	7.5	6
Very unimportant	0	0.0	2	3.8	2
Total	93	100.0	53	100.0	146
$p < 0.08$; chi-square $= 8.2$; d.f. $= 4$					
Familiar operating environment on Southeast Asian subsidiaries					
Very important	5	5.4	11	21.6	16
Quite important	61	66.3	26	51.0	87
Neutral	10	10.9	10	19.6	20
Quite unimportant	11	12.0	2	3.9	13
Very unimportant	5	5.4	2	3.9	7
Total	92	100.0	51	100.0	143
$p < 0.01$; chi-square $= 13.2$; d.f. $= 4$					
Lower (labour) costs of operations on East Asian subsidiaries					
Very important	8	11.6	12	25.5	20
Quite important	26	37.7	15	31.9	41
Neutral	9	13.0	6	12.8	15
Quite unimportant	13	18.8	12	25.5	25
Very unimportant	13	18.8	2	4.3	15
Total	69	100.0	47	100.0	116
$p < 0.07$; chi-square $= 8.6$; d.f. $= 4$					
Familiar operating environment on East Asian subsidiaries					
Very important	7	7.7	8	13.8	15
Quite important	52	57.1	21	36.2	73
Neutral	13	14.3	18	31.0	31
Quite unimportant	10	11.0	9	15.5	19
Very unimportant	9	9.9	2	3.4	11
Total	91	100.0	58	100.0	149
$p < 0.02$; chi-square $= 11.8$; d.f. $= 4$					
Marketing strategies on European subsidiaries					
Very important	6	33.3	7	58.3	13
Quite important	12	66.7	3	25.0	15
Neutral	0	0.0	1	8.3	1
Quite unimportant	0	0.0	1	8.3	1
Total	18	100.0	12	100.0	30
$p < 0.09$; chi-square $= 6.5$; d.f. $= 3$					

Source: Author's survey.

East Asia, in particular China. This is an important finding, as China remains one of the top hosts of Singaporean investments (see Chapter 3). The relatively greater familiarity of Singaporean transnational entrepreneurs with China can facilitate their successful cross-border operations (see more case studies below and in Chapter 5).

Third, fewer transnational entrepreneurs from Singapore (49 per cent) establish their operations in East Asia because of *lower costs*. In fact, a majority of them do so in order to penetrate into emerging markets in East Asia. They are more likely to establish foreign operations to tap into growing markets and business opportunities. This tendency can be attributed to their greater access to entrepreneurial endowments and resources. This point will be supported by detailed case studies in the next subsection. Lower cost is a significantly more important host country condition in attracting non-transnational entrepreneurs from Singapore to operate in the East Asian region, an indication of their corporate mandates and pressures of cost reduction.

Finally, global conditions are found to have statistically different influences on the establishment of foreign operations by transnational entrepreneurs and non-transnational entrepreneurs. Table 4.4 shows that fewer transnational entrepreneurs establish their operations in East and Southeast Asia because of pressures from *growing global competition*. In fact, more non-transnational entrepreneurs tend to establish operations in the two regions to sustain their competitive advantages (e.g. lower costs). This finding is consistent with the above finding on the role of lower costs in influencing non-transnational entrepreneurs to establish operations in East Asia. Interestingly, however, many of these non-transnational entrepreneurs seem to be establishing operations in East Asia to tap into potential regional markets as well. This finding may be explained by the involvement of these non-transnational entrepreneurs in low-cost production that caters to the regional market in East Asia.

Successful Entry of Transnational Ventures

Once the decision to go regional or global has been made by transnational entrepreneurs, how then do they execute these decisions and make successful entry into foreign markets? What is the role of transnational entrepreneurship in ensuring the success of foreign operations? These critical issues are addressed in this subsection. In particular, empirical data will be presented to show how transnational entrepreneurs from Singapore are capable of tapping into the entrepreneurial endowments and resources institutionalised in their home country, and building new actor networks in host countries to facilitate such cross-border operations. The theoretical

Table 4.4 Influence of global conditions on the establishment of foreign operations by host region and transnational entrepreneurs

Global Conditions	Entrepreneur	(%)	Non-entrepreneur	(%)	Total
Growing global competition on Southeast Asian subsidiaries					
Very important	6	8.0	15	36.6	21
Quite important	39	52.0	14	34.1	53
Neutral	11	14.7	2	4.9	13
Quite unimportant	13	17.3	9	22.0	22
Very unimportant	6	8.0	1	2.4	7
Total	75	100.0	41	100.0	116
$p < 0.01$; chi-square = 17.7; d.f. = 4					
Growing global competition on East Asian subsidiaries					
Very important	7	9.0	14	29.8	21
Quite important	33	42.3	21	44.7	54
Neutral	12	15.4	2	4.3	14
Quite unimportant	19	24.4	7	14.9	26
Very unimportant	7	9.0	3	6.4	10
Total	78	100.0	47	100.0	125
$p < 0.01$; chi-square = 12.4; d.f. = 4					
Tapping potential regional market on East Asian subsidiaries					
Very important	26	29.5	24	41.4	50
Quite important	50	56.8	31	53.4	81
Neutral	1	1.1	3	5.2	4
Quite unimportant	3	3.4	0	0.0	3
Very unimportant	8	9.1	0	0.0	8
Total	88	100.0	58	100.0	146
$p < 0.03$; chi-square = 10.8; d.f. = 4					

Source: Author's survey.

issues of this institutional perspective on transnational entrepreneurship have already been examined in Chapter 1, in particular Figures 1.1 and 1.2.

To validate some of my theoretical claims in Chapter 1, survey data are presented in Table 4.5 to illustrate the mechanisms of foreign operations and the attributes of ongoing connections in successful cross-border operations (see also Chapter 3). Although data presented in Table 4.5 are not statistically significant, they are useful in highlighting some differences in the mechanisms of foreign operations between transnational entrepreneurs and non-transnational entrepreneurs. On the one hand, more transnational entrepreneurs tend to take suggestions from their major clients for overseas operations and to seek help from suitable local partners and/or persons. On the other hand, non-transnational entrepreneurs tend to favour expansion

Table 4.5 Mechanisms of establishing foreign operations and the role of entrepreneurial vision by transnational entrepreneurs

Mechanisms	Entrepreneur	(%)	Non-entrepreneur	(%)	Total
Mechanisms of foreign operations					
Decisions or suggestions from major clients	16	18.2	8	13.6	24
Expansion from existing operations elsewhere	15	17.0	17	28.8	32
Using established corporate procedures	15	17.0	13	22.0	28
Help from suitable local partner/persons	14	15.9	7	11.9	21
Importance of personal relations	8	9.1	9	15.3	17
Assistance from host government institutions	6	6.8	1	1.7	7
Sending staff from HQs	6	6.8	0	0.0	6
Direct merger or acquisition	3	3.4	0	0.0	3
Others	5	5.7	4	6.8	9
Total	88	100.0	59	100.0	147
$p < 0.12$; chi-square $= 12.8$; d.f. $= 8$					
Role of entrepreneurial visions					
Identifying the right markets	18	35.3	12	30.8	30
Assessing risks	13	25.5	7	17.9	20
Expanding globally	12	23.5	11	28.2	23
Being a pioneer	6	11.8	4	10.3	10
Making profits	1	2.0	4	10.3	5
Making personal contacts	1	2.0	1	2.6	2
Total	51	100.0	39	100.0	90
$p < 0.59$; chi-square $= 3.7$; d.f. $= 5$					
Attributes of ongoing connections					
High trust	41	19.3	37	15.7	78
Strong reputation and creditworthiness	36	17.0	27	11.4	63
Prior transactional relationships	33	15.6	25	10.6	58
Financial strength	25	11.8	23	9.7	48
Prior personal or family relationships	21	9.9	21	8.9	42
Involvement in established corporate networks	20	9.4	39	16.5	59

Table 4.5 (cont.)

Mechanisms	Entrepreneur	(%)	Non-entrepreneur	(%)	Total
Technological leadership	6	2.8	12	5.1	18
Strong backing by home country government/HQs	6	2.8	12	5.1	18
Privileged access to other markets and sources of capital	4	1.9	13	5.5	17
Others	20	9.4	27	11.4	47
Total	212	100.0	236	100.0	448

$p < 0.05$; chi-square = 17.4; d.f. = 9

Source: Author's survey.

of existing operations elsewhere and to use established corporate procedures as their main mechanisms of foreign operations.

Transnational entrepreneurs are more likely to be client- and market-driven in their foreign operations, a finding consistent with the institutional influence on marketing strategies described in the earlier subsection. The greater familiarity of transnational entrepreneurs with the host countries (e.g. in East Asia) also explains why they tend to seek help from suitable local partners in these host countries. As explained in the case studies below, these local partners and/or persons are highly important in helping transnational entrepreneurs to overcome the problems of information asymmetry and high risks in the host countries (see Figure 1.1). The enrolment of local partners and/or persons into the global actor networks of transnational entrepreneurs enables them to operate across borders relatively successfully (see Figure 1.2). The case of Kwek Leng Beng shows that he was able to organise his 'triangular family networks' to establish successful property development ventures in Beijing, China (see Box 4.1). A comparative case from Hong Kong (HKToys in Box 4.2) seems to lead to the same conclusion that personal networks provide the key mechanism to facilitate cross-border ventures by transnational entrepreneurs. These findings therefore have important implications for their modes of entry and market access (see below). They also offer a more nuanced interpretation of the general findings about the mechanisms of foreign operations described in Chapter 3.

With reference to entry modes, the globalisation of Chinese business firms takes a great variety of organisational forms. The choice of different modes of entry into foreign markets becomes an important issue not only in understanding their internationalisation processes (see Yeung, 1999d), but also in assessing their capabilities in meeting the challenges of the recent

BOX 4.2 HKTOYS, PERSONAL NETWORKS, AND CHINESE ENTREPRENEURSHIP

Founded in 1951, HKToys is a family business owned by its founding Chairman, Mr Chan, who was a Teochew emigrant from China in the 1940s (see Yeung, 1998a: Appendix Table 2). In 1967, HKToys expanded into Singapore to incorporate SINToys, which went into production in 1968. The key person in the establishment of SINToys was Mr Chiu who is now the Managing Director of SINToys. Mr Chiu was born in China and is also himself a Teochew. He also emigrated to Hong Kong in the 1940s, attending school in Hong Kong. He met Mr Chan even before the establishment of HKToys when Mr Chan was working for his relative's company in Hong Kong in the late 1940s. Several years later, Mr Chan founded HKToys and Mr Chiu was invited to work for HKToys. Regional ties among Teochews are claimed to be the strongest among the Hong Kong Chinese. Through years of hard work for HKToys, Mr Chiu had gained strong trust from Mr Chan, who later sent Mr Chiu, together with a few technicians, to establish SINToys as a joint venture with HKToys' local agent in Singapore. Mr Chiu recalled the early days:

> I came over to set up this factory from scratch ... At that time, we had altogether three people from Hong Kong, including myself. I was in charge of administrative work, e.g. overall management. We had a factory manager to take care of technical questions. Another staff from Hong Kong was deputy factory manager, something like that. It would be difficult to find similar staff with expertise here in Singapore. We did have some business with Singapore because we exported some toys to Singapore previously. At the beginning, we started as a joint venture with a local trading company who used to be our agent in Singapore. We were the majority shareholder and they were minority. They took care of local marketing because given so many years of experience, marketing in other countries would be taken care of by our operations in Hong Kong. You know, when we first came to this country, we were not familiar with the people and the legal environment. It would certainly be better if we could venture with someone we know of as a local partner. That's why we invited our local agent to come into a joint venture. Later on, since both were doing different businesses, we bought back all the shares of the company and the factory became 100% owned by us. (Interviewed in Singapore, 13 July 1994)

Today, Mr Chiu has been granted Singaporean citizenship and his children have all been brought up in Singapore. The initial entrepreneurial move to Singapore, despite great uncertainties in the 1960s when both Hong Kong and Singapore suffered from labour unrest, finally paid off when SINToys was awarded pioneer status and was proud to be one of the earliest toy manufacturers in Singapore. Today, Mr Chiu owns 15 per cent of SINToys while the remaining 85 per cent is owned by Mr Chan and his family. Most of the shareholders from early days have withdrawn because through reinvestment over the years, little dividend was paid to individual shareholders.

From HKToys' perspective, SINToys was not only a means of diversification from politically unstable Hong Kong during the mid-1960s, it was also a means of promoting entrepreneurship within the company because upward opportunities could be created through new (overseas) ventures. Even today, the family tradition and 'family-isation' are still very pervasive in the group as a whole. Educated in American universities, Mr Chan Jr., son of Mr Chan and Deputy Managing Director of HKToys, noted that:

> It's still a family business. In fact, the atmosphere of a family business is still very strong... You know the major difference between Chinese companies and foreigners' companies is that the latter are very much like a system. It's not that our companies do not have a system. We still have a very strong Confucian tradition. That is seniority: you will have seniority if you are the father. Your followers who have sacrificed a lot during the development of the company will be treated as seniors. There is such a thing as 'seniors'... We are close together because we are from the same blood. But we also treat our managers as family members. Family-orientation is our organisational culture. As I mentioned earlier, we follow the Confucian tradition. If you work here, you command 'respect'. I wonder whether such a thing as 'respect' exists in American companies! Our family attitude to this company is to treat everyone as our own. (Interviewed in Hong Kong, 20 January 1994)

1997/1998 Asian economic crisis. In general, there are many ways of organising transnational operations, from arm's-length market transactions (i.e. exports) to fully integrated vertical hierarchies. Before the Asian economic crisis, joint ventures and acquisitions were perhaps the most common organisational modes through which Chinese business firms internationalised their operations. In fact, many Chinese business firms in China joined hands with local enterprises and state institutions (e.g. the CP Group from Thailand; see Brown, 1998). The more opaque business environments in China and most Southeast Asian countries favoured joint ventures between Chinese business firms and indigenous enterprises/state institutions. These

Chinese business firms might also team up with Western firms in order to establish themselves in some Asian countries. For example, Chinese business firms from Singapore have long been promoting themselves as the 'gateway' to the East for the West.

Acquisitions were also preferred by large Chinese business conglomerates to control their foreign subsidiaries. When these firms globalised into regions outside Asia, acquisitions became an even more important instrument to enter these unfamiliar foreign markets. Rather than greenfield operations, acquisitions were preferred because of speed and risk factors. The open business environment in North America and Western Europe did not give these Chinese business firms the competitive advantage that they had previously enjoyed in the more opaque Asian business environments. Rather, these open business fields in the West (e.g. high-tech industries and hotel businesses) tended to promote intensified competition which accentuates the importance of economies of scale, technological innovations, and strong expertise, particularly for new entrants from Asia. Acquisitions of existing operations in these countries facilitated risk minimisation, experience building, and major subsequent investments in the host countries.

The best example is Kwek Leng Beng's inroads into global hotel businesses through a series of major acquisitions of hotels in the UK, the USA, and New Zealand (see Box 4.1). Through his CDL Hotels International, the transnational Chinese entrepreneur has built up a hotel empire within one decade, with 117 hotels spanning 13 countries in Europe, the USA, Australia, New Zealand, East and Southeast Asia. Reflecting on his successful pre-crisis acquisition strategy, Kwek commented that '[w]e have earned the distinction of being the first to export a British hotel brand [Copthorne chain] to countries outside Europe. I think it is also safe to say that this export is being done for the first time by a Singapore company' (Press Release by Hong Leong Group, 24 November 1998). To a certain extent, the Asian economic crisis has created more opportunities for Chinese business firms to acquire cheap assets as a part of their regionalisation drive. Referring to CDL Hotels International, Kwek Leng Beng said that '[w]e also intend to grow by acquiring hotels which fit the requirements of the Copthorne product. The regional crisis will provide ample opportunities' (Press Release by Hong Leong Group, 24 November 1998). This prospect for acquisitions, however, does not necessarily come without risks. Kwek further commented that 'the state of bankruptcy laws in certain Asian countries is a deterrent. So are the cultural differences' (*The Straits Times*, 25 November 1998). This view is also echoed in Backman's (1999) book in which he argued that those Asian countries with the weakest implementation of bankruptcy laws tended to be worst hit by the economic crisis.

In the context of the Asian economic crisis, direct investments through either greenfield operations or acquisitions may not be suitable modes of entry into highly risky regional markets because of financial constraints. Banks and financial institutions are more reluctant to finance major foreign acquisitions by Chinese business firms from Asia. Instead, they prefer these Chinese business firms to consolidate their positions and, sometimes, to repay their debts before incurring more new debts. Chinese business firms from Singapore therefore must look into other modes of *non-equity* investments abroad, including franchising, management contracts, co-operative agreements, licensing, subcontracting, strategic alliances, and so on. These non-equity modes of foreign market entry can reduce risk and capital commitment typical in other forms of direct investments. There is also sector-specificity in the use of these different non-equity modes of investments. Whereas manufacturing firms may prefer subcontracting, licensing and strategic alliances, service firms may find franchising and management contracts particularly attractive in both minimising capital outlays and securing market share in the host countries. SINFood, a leading Chinese dried-food manufacturing and retail family business, is using franchising as the key means for regionalising into Asia and eventually globalising into North America (see Box 4.3).

What then is the role of entrepreneurial vision in identifying and exploiting the mechanisms of foreign operations? Survey data in Table 4.5 show that transnational entrepreneurs are more capable than non-transnational entrepreneurs of capitalising on their entrepreneurial visions, of identifying the right markets for foreign operations, and of assessing risks in these foreign operations. The case of Hong Leong Group's Kwek Leng Beng best testifies to the importance of entrepreneurial vision in driving successful cross-border operations (see Box 4.1). In the case of Eu Yan Sang (see Box 4.4), the entrepreneurial vision of Richard Y.M. Eu and his cousins in revitalising the 120-year Chinese herbal medicine business is apparent. Without that entrepreneurial vision to globalise a traditional Chinese family business, Eu Yan Sang would not have been transformed into a modern business enterprise managed by family members in association with professional managers. Through this process, Richard Y.M. Eu has become a true transnational entrepreneur in that he has assumed risks in expanding and managing his business across borders. In a globalising era, he has successfully moved away from traditional practices in Chinese family business in which conservatism and ethnic closure are maintained (Olds and Yeung, 1999; Yeung, 2000b; Yeung and Olds, 2000).

As argued above, the successful execution of these entrepreneurial visions requires the formation and enrolment of global actor networks. As further illustrated in Table 4.5, over 50 per cent of transnational entrepreneurs

BOX 4.3   SINFOOD, THE ASIAN ECONOMIC CRISIS, AND CHANGING MODES OF FOREIGN MARKET ENTRY

Founded in 1945, SINFood is now owned and managed by the third generation of the Wong family. It had a relatively significant annual turnover of US$20.6 million, fixed assets of US$14.7 million, and a global workforce of more than 500 in 1997 (interview with Mr Wong in Singapore, 6 May 1998). Its long-term objective is 'to become not only the recognised leader in the [dried food] trade in Asia with an international chain of outlets, but also in other traditional Chinese delicacies' (Company Profile, 1995: 10).

By 1998, SINFood had a 35 per cent global market share in Chinese foodstuffs. This successful market penetration can be explained by the relentless pursuit of geographical diversification and franchising by the company under its third-generation leadership. Mr Wong, Managing Director of SINFood, is credited with introducing the concept of franchising as the key means of growing the company beyond the domestic market into Hong Kong, China, and Malaysia. Before he took over the management, his uncles had focused very much on retail business in the Singapore market. As he explained, '[w]e're a family business. So we didn't have a formal management. Our main business really took off from the third generation' (interviewed in Singapore, 6 May 1998). As envisioned in his company profile in 1995,

> With our experience and proven business system, we have begun realising this vision, by transferring our business know-how to other parts of the world through franchising. Our franchise marketing programme, initially targeted at Hong Kong and China, will eventually reach as far as Canada and the United States of America . . . Diversification and franchising are just the first steps in [SINFood's] corporate evolution, and we will continue to evolve our operations and products to suit the changing needs and tastes of our customers. In line with our globalisation strategy, we are also working toward listing [SINFood] on the stock exchange within this decade.

Our key concern here is with how SINFood managed the impact of the Asian economic crisis through transnational entrepreneurship and continuous engagement in franchising abroad. To overcome difficulties in the midst of a crisis, a transnational entrepreneur needs more than visions and foresight; he/she also needs perseverance and commitment to the foreign ventures. Mr

> Wong always wanted to go beyond his inherited business and establish a transnational empire of Chinese dried food outlets. Although the crisis put pressures on his operations abroad, he was determined to maintain his commitment to regional franchising business.
>
>> We didn't really help out much when the business initially started. The person who started it all told me that once we hang up our business name, we should never take it down. We don't play around with it. It made a deep impression on me. In Hong Kong, when we started out, we could have folded the business then. It was of no loss to me. But since we have started it there, we should stick it through. Even in China, we could have folded up too [in the midst of the crisis]. But since we do have some operations over there, we should continue. We wouldn't give up so easily unless there's something we really can't resolve. (Interviewed in Singapore, 6 May 1998)
>
> SINFood's franchising programme therefore not only enabled it to establish a strong foothold in the regional market, but also helped it narrowly to escape heavy capital write-off as a consequence of direct capital investments in retail outlets abroad. As Mr. Wong noted, '[t]his economic crisis changes predictions. For example, we predicted quite low figures for these 2 years because of low confidence. It's good enough if we could maintain the figures!'. Wong's entrepreneurial foresight, i.e. not over-stretching his financial resources abroad through aggressive direct investments, is clearly an important lesson for such Chinese family firms as SINFood in surviving the Asian economic crisis.

agreed that high trust, strong reputation and credit-worthiness, and prior transactional relationships are key attributes to enhance their ongoing connections with foreign partners, customers, and suppliers. However, only 38 per cent of non-transnational entrepreneurs identified these three attributes. They instead relied on involvement in established corporate networks, technological leadership, and support from home countries or corporate headquarters to engage in their foreign operations. These statistically significant findings show that there are major differences in the role of ongoing connections and actor network enrolment in facilitating foreign operations by transnational entrepreneurs and non-transnational entrepreneurs. We may tentatively conclude that both entrepreneurial visions and ongoing connections via global actor networks are key mechanisms to facilitate the cross-border operations of transnational entrepreneurs.

BOX 4.4 MANAGING TRADITIONAL CHINESE FAMILY FIRMS ACROSS BORDERS: FOUR GENERATIONS OF ENTREPRENEURSHIP IN EU YAN SANG

This case study examines the growth and transformation of Eu Yan Sang from a traditional Chinese medicine retail shop founded in 1879 to a modern transnational Chinese medicine and healthcare business group (Yeung, 2000g). Eu Yan Sang was first opened in Perak, Malaya in 1879 by Eu Kong, the father of Eu Tong Sen (a very famous philanthropist in Southeast Asia) and the great grandfather of Richard Y.M. Eu, now Managing Director of Eu Yan Sang International Holdings. From a small Chinese medicine shop in Perak some 120 years ago, Eu Yan Sang has now grown into a leading modern transnational corporation (TNC) specialising in the production and retailing of traditional Chinese herbs and medicines in Hong Kong, Malaysia, and Singapore. Today, Eu Yan Sang International Holdings has over 52 retail outlets in Hong Kong, Singapore, and Malaysia. It controls modern manufacturing facilities in Hong Kong and Malaysia, and exports its products worldwide to over 2000 supermarkets, retail shops, and pharmacies in Australia, Canada, China, Hong Kong, Indonesia, Malaysia, New Zealand, Singapore, Taiwan, the UK, and the USA. It has further plans to expand its operations into Europe and North America to become a truly global corporation specialising in Chinese traditional medicine.

Upon Eu Kong's unfortunate death in 1890 at the age of 38, his son, Eu Tong Sen, succeeded and diversified his businesses from a Chinese medicine shop into property, tin mining, and other businesses. By the turn of the century, Eu Tong Sen had become one of the two wealthiest Chinese in the field (the other was Loke Yew) (Yoshihara, 1988: 203). He invested some of his fortune from tin mining in rubber plantations, banking, real estate, and trading. Under his reign, Eu Yan Sang expanded rapidly within Malaya and across borders. Since the early 1930s, the third generation family members had succeeded to the ownership and control of Eu Yan Sang. Though having substantial ownership and control of Eu Yan Sang, the third generation Eu family members did not participate actively in its day-to-day management, which was handled by trusted employees. This early process of incorporating trusted employees who had been socialised into Eu Yan Sang's corporate family can be conceptualised as 'powers of attorney'. These 'attorneys' were professional managers who took care of Eu Tong Sen's vast business activities in Malaysia and Singapore. They would be equivalent to today's chief executive officers who report to the board of directors of a professionalised family firm, comprising the patriarch as the chairman and family members as directors. As recalled by Mr Richard Y.M. Eu,

> There was no formal corporate structure for these branches [of Eu Yan Sang]. So they were like proprietorships. Each branch would have been an individual proprietorship because they were not corporatised. So the employees were only responsible for the branch. After the second World War, because this was only one of the businesses that he [Eu Tong Sen] had, most of the businesses, the decision making, was probably made in Singapore, although they had companies which were incorporated in Malaysia, Hong Kong and Singapore. (Interviewed in Singapore, 24 November 1998)

This pattern of sole proprietorship in Eu Yan Sang lasted till 1955. In that year, Eu Yan Sang's operations in Malaysia and Singapore were converted from sole proprietorship to a limited company, with the establishment of Eu Yan Sang (Singapore) Pte. Ltd. on 13 October 1955. For the next 18 years until 1973 when Eu Yan Sang (Singapore) Pte. Ltd. was listed on the Stock Exchange of Singapore, the limited company continued to follow the management pattern that had prevailed during the early years when the shops were under sole proprietorship. During the 1970s and the 1980s, Eu Yan Sang Holdings Ltd. in Singapore was incorporated as a public listed company. Eu Yan Sang Hong Kong Ltd. was essentially a dormant shell company that was managed as a sole proprietorship under the responsibilities of the trustees of the Estate of Eu Tong Sen. Both companies used the same registered trademark inherited from Eu Tong Sen. But, there were by then clear differences in the management, growth, and evolution of these two entities in Hong Kong and Singapore.

The role of transnational entrepreneurship is critical in the recent transformation of Eu Yan Sang. In February 1990, Eu Yan Sang Holdings Ltd in Singapore was taken over by the Lum Chang Group, a local property developer. This acquisition ended the long history of family ownership and management of Eu Yan Sang Holdings Ltd in Malaysia and Singapore. The disintegration of Eu Yan Sang Holdings Ltd as a family firm, however, did not take place because of extraordinary efforts made by Dr Richard K.M. Eu, his son (Richard Y.M. Eu), and several family members. In fact,

Richard Y.M. Eu noted that since 1973, his immediate family had been buying back some of the shares of Eu Yan Sang Holdings Ltd. By 1990, he and his father comprised the single largest shareholder with up to 10 per cent of shareholding (author's interview in Singapore, 24 November 1998). Both of them agreed to stay on the board of directors as the chairman and an executive director. Dr Eu explained that:

> In a way it is sentimental reasons. I felt that it was a family company and outsiders came to take over the company. It is a great loss. These are the facts of life and I accept that. It was very good for them to offer me to carry on as chairman. (Interviewed in Singapore, 15 April 1999)

In 1993, members of the fourth generation of the Eu family, under the entrepreneurial leadership of Richard Y.M. Eu (currently managing director) and his four cousins (Joseph Eu, Winston Eu, Clifford Eu, and Robert Eu), acquired the Chinese medicine business from Eu Yan Sang Holdings Ltd in Singapore. This acquisition cost S$21 million (*The Straits Times*, 5 July 2000). In 1996, they consolidated Eu Yan Sang (Hong Kong) Ltd under Eu Yan Sang International Holdings Pte. Ltd, the holding company based in Singapore. The successful acquisition, which cost HK$230 million also led to the delisting of Eu Yan Sang (Hong Kong) Ltd from the Stock Exchange of Hong Kong. This ended the long separation of Eu Yan Sang's business operations in Hong Kong and Singapore/Malaysia. Since then, all Eu Yan Sang's operations in Hong Kong, Singapore, and Malaysia have been fully owned and managed by Eu Yan Sang International Holdings, which was listed again on the Stock Exchange of Singapore in July 2000. This process has completed the cycle and Eu Yan Sang is now returned to the hands of the fourth generation Eu family based in Singapore. This process has revitalised the family firm and prepared it for the future challenge as the leading transnational producer and retailer of traditional Chinese herbs and medicines in Asia.

Three specific reasons explain this acquisition of Eu Yan Sang's Hong Kong business by Richard Y.M. Eu and his four cousins. First, there was a serious dispute between Eu Yan Sang operations in Singapore and in Hong Kong over the usage of trademarks after the public listing in Hong Kong. A takeover bid by Eu Yan Sang International Holdings would end this trademark saga by merging all Eu Yan Sang's operations in Hong Kong and Singapore/Malaysia under one central holding company that would naturally own all Eu Yan Sang's registered trademarks. Second, the acquisition of Eu Yan Sang (Hong Kong) Ltd means that the Eu family can repossess Eu Yan Sang, a traditional family business handed from one generation to another. As reflected by Richard Y.M. Eu,

> The three of us were in agreement with the principle of doing it, keeping it within the family. It's tied up with the business reason. We wouldn't do this if it didn't make sense. But we could see that there were certain inefficiencies with the Hong Kong operations. We felt that, since we had some experience in operating the business here, we could help Hong Kong out by translating our experiences into the business there. (Interviewed in Singapore, 24 November 1998)

Third, the acquisition of Eu Yan Sang (Hong Kong) Ltd is the first step in the globalisation drive of Eu Yan Sang International Holdings. It reflects the vision and ambition of the fourth generation Eu family members led by Richard Y.M. Eu, who made a comment on the implications of the acquisition:

> That's a by-product. We want to grow the company. You need a certain base and by plugging into Hong Kong, our company base is so much bigger. So the next step in our globalisation would obviously have been much easier. Otherwise, we would be competing with the Hong Kong company all over the place, spending more time fighting with them than expanding the business. (Interviewed in Singapore, 24 November 1998)

After the acquisition, Eu Yan Sang in Hong Kong/China contributed over 50% of the group's turnover.

The entrepreneurial drive by Richard Y.M. Eu and his cousins has led to several important transformations in Eu Yan Sang's transnational business operations. First, the group's product developments and marketing have improved substantially, although a significant amount of capital investment has been put into this expansion. Second, the involvement of more fourth generation family members apparently has resolved some of the key problems associated with the lack of competent family members sufficiently interested in reviving the family business. Finally, a consolidated corporate management structure has also facilitated the implementation of a common corporate vision and strategy. This is a particularly important consideration for Eu Yan Sang's operations in Hong Kong.

Today, Richard Y.M. Eu leads an executive management team comprising 10 senior managers in Eu Yan Sang. Most of the decisions are based on consensus within this executive management team. Local general managers abroad report to Richard Y.M. Eu directly and local financial controllers report to the group finance manager based in Singapore. The control and reporting system has been streamlined to facilitate greater intra-group communication and co-ordination. By the end of 1998, the Eu Yan Sang group had become the single largest Chinese medicine retail chain in Hong Kong and Southeast Asia, with a turnover exceeding S$60 million, fixed assets of over S$30 million and worldwide employment of about 600. It is very much a family firm with regional operations and a vision to promote Chinese values and medicine. Building on its immense heritage, Eu Yan Sang's corporate vision is clear. It wants to 'promote herbal healthcare in order to reinforce family values and moral education' and hopes that 'every member in every family will be able to benefit from Chinese herbal healthcare' (http://www.euyansang.com, accessed on 20 November 1998). This vision, indeed, has never changed since the founding of Eu Yan Sang some 120 years ago by the pioneer Eu Kong.

Case Studies of Foreign Ventures by Transnational Entrepreneurs from Singapore

To understand better the processes of cross-border operations by transnational entrepreneurs from Singapore, I draw together nine additional case studies summarised in Table 4.6. These case studies are chosen on the basis of information available during personal interviews. They represent a variety of industries (e.g. manufacturing, financial, and infrastructural development), ownership background (e.g. Chinese family business and professionally managed business), and host countries (e.g. China and the UK). The objective here is to offer a variety of transnational entrepreneurial experiences rather than to identify some quantitative statistical regularities that can be used to generalise for all transnational entrepreneurs. Information in Table 4.6 originates from personal interviews with over 200 parent SINTNCs (see Chapter 1). The organisation of this qualitative information is based on the institutional perspective of transnational entrepreneurship developed in Chapter 1 (see Figure 1.1).

It is fairly obvious that all transnational entrepreneurs have developed some kind of *foreign actor networks*. These networks range from former clients (e.g. ChemicalCorp) and family members (e.g. the Hong Leong Group) to host country firms (e.g. PaperCorp) and host country governments (e.g. ChanEngin). Interestingly, some of the transnational entrepreneurs found their foreign joint venture partners through trade exhibitions (e.g. TexChemicals) and industrial shows (e.g. SemiTech). There are thus no specific ways to establish and develop these global actor networks. As argued in Chapter 1, transnational entrepreneurs who have better access to global actor networks tend to be more successful in establishing foreign operations. The personal relationships of these transnational entrepreneurs with many of their foreign partners and top local managers are equally important in enhancing the success of their foreign operations. Managing a family business with 24 subsidiaries in more than 18 cities around the Asia-Pacific region and an annual turnover of S$210 million, one Singapore entrepreneur noted that '[i]n order to continue branching out to other countries, I need to find many local business partners. It is hard to find long-term partners in the different countries; partners who are honest, hardworking and loyal, and who will contribute to the company's success. My fear is getting a dishonest business partner' (quoted in *The Straits Times*, 12 September 1996).

The successful enrolment of transnational entrepreneurs into these global actor networks, however, is insufficient to explain why they are capable of identifying the opportunities to go abroad in the first place. Their access to *entrepreneurial endowments and resources* (see Figure 1.1), which are highly influenced by home country institutional structures, becomes very important. In terms of *information asymmetry*, transnational entrepreneurs in Table 4.6 tend to engage in different practices to overcome the problem of information asymmetry when they operate in the host countries. These practices range from careful studies of foreign markets before entry (e.g. ChemicalCorp) and gathering information from business associates (e.g. the Pacific Group) to the use of beach-head strategies (e.g. PVCCorp) and the refusal to follow 'herd behaviour' (e.g. the Hong Leong Group). In PVCCorp's case, a manufacturing operation was established in Shanghai, China, in 1994 to test the local market. In extreme cases (e.g. PaperCorp), China ventures have had to be closed down due to lack of information about the behaviour of local partners. The Chairman of PaperCorp recalled that:

> Some [partners in China] I knew previously. Others I got to know in China. But there is little help in knowing a person as people change very quickly. For example, we had machinery meant for a joint venture project. But the market had changed and we left the machine for them to use. But they used the machine to produce goods for private sale. That's why I closed down the joint venture. On the other hand, if you can set up a profitable enterprise, they will also set up a similar company to 'eat' into your business. Then, you're dead. (Interviewed in Singapore, 3 March 1998)

There are clearly *risks and opportunities* associated with foreign operations by transnational entrepreneurs. There can be severe competition in

Table 4.6 Case studies of transnational entrepreneurs and their entrepreneurial endowments/resources

Name[a] and Sector	Transnational entrepreneur	Foreign actor networks	Information asymmetry	Risks and opportunities	Finance and capital	Experience in business	Customer and supplier relations
ChanEngin • mechanical engineering	Son of the founder and Chairman	• good host government in Tianjin, China	• strong in-house expertise • lack of marketing	• OBM in the US • looking for global markets	• severe constraints from home country banks	• meeting world class benchmarks	• more marketing needed
ChemicalCorp • chemicals and property development	Second generation family business and Executive Director	• Thailand with French client • China with foreign partners	• studied UK property market cycles	• withdrawal from Thailand • assuming risks in the UK	• public listed in Singapore • cash cows from selling chemicals	• some property projects done in Singapore	• secured customers in chemicals
Hong Leong • finance and property development	Son of the co-founder and Chairman	• extensive family business networks in Asia Foreign parties	• against herd behaviour • looking for good deals abroad	• high risks in developed countries • acquisitions at low prices	• public listed in Singapore • an integrated financial group • good relationship with global bankers	• big business family • trained in the UK and worked abroad for family business	• strong reputation • strong brand name after acquiring M&C Plc.
Pacific Group • finance and stockbroking	Son of the founder and Chairman	• many overseas JVs with foreign partners • trained in US banks	• lack of home government support • know major bankers in SIN	• inheritance: responsibility for growth • high risks in finance	• strong JV partners	• big business family • worked abroad for family business	• strong personal contacts
PaperCorp • paper trade and packaging	Son of the founder and Chairman	• approach by China's state-owned enterprise	• closure of joint ventures in China	• go China after Tiananmen Square Incident	• public listed in Singapore	• family business education in China	• good terms with agents

188

Company	Position	Strategy	Competitive factors	Finance	Experience	Other
PVCCorp — PVC pipe manufacturing and services	Founder and Managing Director	• bought over from JV partner in China	• use beach-head strategy in Shanghai, China	• trusted by Bank of China • public listed in Singapore	• long experiences • religious principles	• more marketing needed
ResourceCorp — power plant in China	• Founder and Managing Director	• doing business in China for 30 years	• risky in China • entrepreneurial X-factor • crucial commitment of Singapore partners	• difficult to borrow in Singapore • loans in China	• several previous JV experiences	• steady customers
SemiTech — semiconductor	Founder and CEO	• contacts via industrial shows • ex-colleagues	• information from past working for TNCs • shared with foreign partners	• investment from family members	• formerly top executive in a semiconductor TNC	• former clients from TNCs
SINFood — manufacturing and retailing of food	Grandson of founder and CEO	• use of local partners/managers	• proprietary knowledge in dried pork • use of franchising • local competitors in Malaysia	• finance from family and partners	• long history of family business	• strong brand names • good terms with suppliers
TechCorp — electronics components	Founder and CEO	• use local managers and given equity	• information from suppliers in Singapore • keep good staff abroad by using equity incentives	• not much costs from sales offices abroad	• long experience of dealing with leading TNCs	• follow clients in Singapore (global TNCs)
TexChemicals — textile dying chemicals	Founder and Managing Director	• JV partners in China via trade exhibitions	• reliance on local partners and Chinese expertise • highly competitive in Shanghai, China • lack of home country opportunities	• good JV partner	• previous employment in a Swiss chemical firm • trained as a chemist	• strong regional sales networks

Note: [a] With the exception of the Hong Leong Group, all names are disguised to maintain confidentiality and anonymity.

Source: Author's interviews.

host locations (e.g. CDL hotels in the UK and the USA; see Box 4.1). In the cases of both PVCCorp and TexChemicals, their operations in Shanghai, China, face significant local competition. But then transnational entrepreneurs are precisely endowed with the capacity for calculated risk-taking because market opportunities are often directly correlated with the extent of business risks and competition. For example, the Managing Director of PVCCorp explained why he decided to set up the PVC pipe manufacturing operation in Shanghai, instead of southern China and nearby Suzhou where the Suzhou-Singapore Industrial Park is located (see also Chapter 5).

> We were deciding between Shanghai and Shandong. We went to explore this part and left the South [of China] away on purpose. We felt that the South is, firstly, too crowded, and Hong Kong seems to be very strong there. There is no reason to go to the South to fight with them . . . We decided on Shanghai. And also, Shanghai is the driving force, the dragonhead, and the dragon force. Everything building and everything that is new always starts from Shanghai. So we thought, if we can survive in Shanghai, we can survive anywhere. We picked the toughest place. That is the place, in terms of technology edge and introduction of new products. If we get introduced in Shanghai, the other states and provinces will conveniently follow. Shanghai is the leader. Then we told ourselves, in Shanghai, there's the Singapore-China industrial park [in Suzhou]. Should we join them? When we saw them going by busload and planeload, I didn't like it, feeling like going in such a big group, and then call it entrepreneurship. It doesn't work that way. It doesn't fit my cup of tea. I'll rather learn on my own. Of course, when you go to Suzhou, you pay very high, but you don't have to learn everything to invent a wheel. That's not a life for an entrepreneur. Entrepreneur is someone who wants to learn something. You pay a bit more. However, in the end, you'll still pay less than going to Suzhou. In the process, we come into contact with Chinese partners, land negotiation and so on. We learn a lot by itself. If we go to Suzhou, we don't have to go through that learning curve. It's all done. You just need to pay a premium for the land. (Interviewed in Singapore, 31 August 1998)

He was clearly taking calculated risks to avoid southern China (unfamiliar territory) and the Suzhou Industrial Park (little scope for learning). Instead, he picked Shanghai because of its potential impact on market development for PVCCorp. Similarly, TexChemicals chose to locate its dyestuff manufacturing plant in Pudong, Shanghai, in 1990 because of the availability of strong textile traditions in Shanghai (see S.L. Wong, 1988). The founder thought that Shanghai's expertise in that industry was even better than TexChemicals in Singapore. Faced with institutional constraints in Singapore, he decided to establish a manufacturing operation right at the heart of China's textile industry. The institutional constraints in Singapore were related to the shortage of factory space and manpower. TexChemicals' application to its landlord in Singapore (a government statutory board) for more factory space had been consistently rejected because factory space was reserved for high-tech factories rather than textile dyestuff manufacturing. The Ministry of Manpower also refused to issue an employment pass to an Indonesian engineer who was supposed to be brought in for training in Singapore. These land and labour constraints are linked to the transformation of the Singapore economy into the high-tech manufacturing hub in Asia (see Chapter 2).

Another possible area of institutional constraint in Singapore refers to the poor availability of *finance and capital* for the globalisation of Singaporean firms and transnational entrepreneurs. Local banks in Singapore are extremely conservative in lending to Singapore firms for their foreign expansion. The Singapore government is also unable to provide much help and funding in this respect. This problem will be considered in greater detail in the next section. But it is useful to examine how transnational entrepreneurs in Table 4.6 are able to overcome the financial constraint on their foreign operations. Their capabilities to gather finance and capital are related to their access to entrepreneurial endowments and resources that are critical to the deployment and manipulation of resources for international business activities. Four transnational entrepreneurs (ChemicalCorp, the Hong Leong Group, PaperCorp, and PVCCorp) have their parent companies listed on the Stock Exchange of Singapore to attract investment funds for overseas expansion. Other private companies rely on investment funds from family networks (e.g. SemiTech and SINFood) and joint venture partners in the host countries (e.g. the Pacific Group and TexChemicals). In an exceptional case, ResourceCorp was able to secure loans from local banks in China to finance its 24-megawatt power plant established in 1993. The project cost US$10 million and a local bank in China agreed to finance 60 per cent of the project cost. The transnational entrepreneur managed to break even one year after the power plant went into operation in mid-1996 and has since been making good profits every year.

The ability of ResourceCorp to secure good returns to investments in the power plant in China goes beyond the local financing arrangement that reduces investment risks. As recognised by the founder and Managing Director, who has been doing business in China for 30 years, *experience in business and management* is crucial to successful operations in China.

> We know much more than other Singaporeans do. We have more experience and we have hands-on experience that is most important. Especially for myself since I've so much involvement in the various industries and cities. So I've a lot of cross-information and then I can compare and see. (Interviewed in Singapore, 1 July 1998)

His personal experience in China enables him to understand how to manage Chinese people who are working for his power plant. Instead of sending arrogant expatriate Singaporeans to manage the power plant, he paid a high salary to hire the right local Chinese manager. Referring to the failure of the Suzhou Industrial Park (see also Chapter 5), he noted that:

> Don't blame everything on the China side. Our Singapore side has also made a lot of mistakes. Part of it has to do with culture. Especially when we send all the young men there, they're too arrogant. They think that Singaporeans are superior to the Chinese. This is not true. In fact, the Chinese are much smarter and more experienced. And their exposure is international . . . I hire a Chinese to control the Chinese. I pay a high salary to get the right man. Then I let him run the show for us while I remain as the decision-maker. I put in another financial controller, also from China so as to balance. If you rely everything on one general manager, he might sell you out at the end. (Interviewed in Singapore, 1 July 1998)

Referring to Table 4.6 again, it appears that most heirs to Chinese family businesses have substantial experience in business and management. The early involvement of Kwek Leng Beng in his father's property development business in Singapore has equipped him with significant knowledge of property development and hotel investments (see Box 4.1). After his first employment in a US bank, the Chairman of the Pacific Group also experienced rotations of management posts within his family business in Indonesia (manufacturing), Hong Kong (financial services), Singapore (investment banking), and then back to Hong Kong (financial services). For those founding transnational entrepreneurs, they are more likely to have spun off from previous employment in related firms and/or industries. The founder of SemiTech used to work for National Semiconductor from the USA and rose to become one of its top executives in Singapore. His long experience in the semiconductor industry has helped him build up his clientele base and overseas business contacts. Similarly, the founder of TexChemicals used to work for a Swiss chemical firm. The experience of these transnational entrepreneurs in business and management is therefore a prerequisite to their success in domestic and international business ventures.

In some cases (e.g. ChemicalCorp, the Pacific Group, SemiTech, and TechCorp), transnational entrepreneurs are able to establish successfully international business ventures because of their strong *relationships with customers and/or suppliers* both in Singapore and abroad. For ChemicalCorp, its financial strength originates from its secure customer base in Singapore. It has such a strong established market position among Singapore's chemical industries that its sales have become the 'cash cow' to finance its overseas ventures in Thailand (chemicals), China (industrial estates), and the UK (property development). Its early establishment as a key chemical supplier to fuel Singapore's industrialisation programme since 1966 (see also Chapter 2) explains its market position. As its Executive Director explained,

> our industry is always traditionally considered as a basic building block in any country's industrialisation programme. So you will always be able to find similar operation in almost every country, especially countries that have a long-term view of wanting to industrialise the economy... So when you have played such a critical role, it is very unlikely that a country that is on an industrialisation program depends on an outside source or supply. (Interviewed in Singapore, 23 November 1998)

In fact, ChemicalCorp's property investment in the UK alone accounted for some 50 per cent of its entire group turnover by the end of 1998.

In other cases, transnational entrepreneurs have capitalised on their extensive relationships with customers and/or suppliers abroad. SemiTech, for example, is able to supply burn-in services to its major TNC clients in the USA (since 1993) and Taiwan (since 1994). Many of these clients are SemiTech's existing customers in Singapore. In another example, TechCorp established sales and training centres in Malaysia (1989), Taiwan (1989), China (1993), Thailand (1993), India (1994), and the Philippines (1995) at the request of major TNC clients that have manufacturing facilities in these Asian countries. These TNC clients include Intel, Motorola, Compaq, and Seagate. As explained by the founder and CEO,

> When TNCs move, two things happen. One is that they move because they are taking the lower end products, which Singapore can no longer sustain due to our higher labour cost. If you don't follow that trend, you'll end up losing the business opportunities. The second thing that MNCs try to do is that, as they move, they create supporting industries. If you go to Shenzhen or Shanghai, you'll find many supporting industries there due to the TNCs' investments. Supporting industries are subcontractors. These subcontractors are our customers as well. (Interviewed in Singapore, 10 July 1998)

To sum up my findings from these case studies, it is clear that the nature and extent of transnational entrepreneurs' access to endowments and resources vary significantly. There is obviously no single pathway to transnational entrepreneurship. Most of the transnational entrepreneurs in my survey are endowed with at least some resources to enable them to venture abroad. Measuring the exact impact of these endowments and resources (e.g. information asymmetry or experience) on transnational ventures is really a moot point. It all depends on the specific international business ventures that we are investigating. Once their international business ventures are established successfully, transnational entrepreneurs begin to manage these operations across borders. The issues remain as to how they compete with other domestic and international firms, and how they succeed in managing teething problems in the host countries.

MANAGING ACROSS BORDERS: TRANSNATIONAL ENTREPRENEURS IN ACTION

Does transnational entrepreneurship really matter in the performance and management of international business activities? Although there is no conclusive answer to this question, we can at least shed some light on the possibility that it may matter in international business. After all, a transnational corporation is only as good as its executives and managers who possess entrepreneurial tendencies. Table 4.7 summarises the main competitive advantages in establishing foreign operations by transnational entrepreneurs. It is statistically significant that more transnational entrepreneurs (75 per cent) than non-transnational entrepreneurs (52 per cent) agreed that they have competitive advantages over their local and foreign competitors in establishing their foreign operations. These competitive advantages include greater personal familiarity (23 per cent), better reputation (14 per cent), and better product quality and services (11 per cent).

Personal familiarity is important firstly because this competitive advantage tends to be *embodied* in specific transnational entrepreneurs, and therefore is unlikely to be transferable and imitated.

Secondly, personal familiarity in highly important in guiding successful international business ventures in Asia where the business environment in most host countries remains opaque and risky. For example, the successful operation of the power plant project in China by the founder of ResourceCorp (Table 4.6) is clearly an outcome of his long experience and familiarity of doing business in China. In another example, a transnational entrepreneur set up two paper mills in China in a US$500 million joint venture with the world's second largest paper producer from Finland. The competitive advantage of this transnational entrepreneur from Singapore is precisely his 30 years of experience in pulp and paper business in Asia. According to the Director of the Singapore firm,

> if the Finnish people want to go to China to set up the mill, first thing they're not familiar with the Chinese government, how to go about getting licences, getting all these things, anti-trust. The Chinese are still not opened up to an extent. They'll not be as skilful as Asian entrepreneurs who have done this business. They [Asian entrepreneurs] know how to take care and they know how to get things done. If you employ the local Chinese, they are not ready. They don't have this pool of talents there. It is still difficult to get good talented local managers in China itself . . . They can't conquer us in the sense that in Asia, the Asians know the place better, to get things done, rather than the Europeans. Why

Table 4.7   Competitive advantages in establishing foreign operations by transnational entrepreneurs

Competitive Advantages	Entrepreneur	(%)	Non-entrepreneur	(%)	Total
Presence of competitive advantages					
Yes	85	74.6	38	52.1	123
No	29	25.4	35	47.9	64
Total	114	100.0	73	100.0	187
$p < 0.01$; chi-square = 10.0; d.f. = 1					
Types of competitive advantages					
Greater personal familiarity and experience	50	23.0	17	18.3	67
Better reputation	31	14.3	19	20.4	50
Better product quality and services	24	11.1	6	6.5	30
Better managerial expertise	21	9.7	13	14.0	34
Better marketing expertise	20	9.2	4	4.3	24
Special contacts and connections	16	7.4	8	8.6	24
Higher technological edge	13	6.0	1	1.1	14
Possession of specialised materials and resources	13	6.0	6	6.5	19
Greater financial assets	12	5.5	5	5.4	17
Others	17	7.8	14	15.1	31
Total	217	100.0	93	100.0	310
$p < 0.13$; chi-square = 13.8; d.f. = 9					

Source: Author's survey.

do we say they aren't? In China especially because they don't understand the Chinese. We Singaporeans don't understand them either. So how do you expect the Finnish to do so? So it's very difficult and that's what sets us apart. A lot of people accept that. So the Finnish join with an Asian partner who knows the market and is willing to put their stake in it. (Interviewed in Singapore, 21 August 1998)

Given the high concentration of outward investments from Hong Kong and Singapore within Asia (see Chapter 3) and the institutional structures of many Asian host countries, there are thus unavoidable problems associated with international business operations in Asia and beyond. Table 4.8 summarises the main findings about problems encountered by Singapore companies and the solutions adopted, by region of operations. We asked

Table 4.8 Major problems faced and solutions adopted by indigenous companies from Singapore by region

Problems/Solutions	Southeast Asia	East Asia	Europe	North America	Other Regions
Problems (mean score)[a]					
1. high costs of operations	3.7	3.4	3.2	3.7	3.6
2. lack of technological edge	3.9	3.8	4.1	4.5	3.9
3. problems with local partners	3.4	3.2	4.2	4.5	3.8
4. lack of market information	3.7	3.3	4.0	4.3	3.5
5. lack of special connections with host countries	3.6	3.5	3.9	4.2	3.8
6. lack of personal experience	3.4	3.1	3.3	3.8	3.1
7. labour force problems	3.4	3.2	3.7	3.8	3.4
8. government regulations	3.7	2.5	3.7	4.2	3.0
9. lack of sufficient financial assets	3.7	3.5	3.8	4.0	3.9
10. lack of home government support	1.6	1.8	1.3	2.0	1.9
Solutions (cases)					
1. reliance on local partners/connections	47 (20%)	107 (43%)	4 (19%)	2 (12%)	9 (17%)
2. sending trusted executives from Singapore to manage	9 (4%)	11 (4%)	–	1 (6%)	3 (6%)
3. asking local governments for help	8 (3%)	35 (14%)	1 (5%)	–	4 (7%)
4. closing down the operations	29 (12%)	27 (11%)	1 (5%)	2 (12%)	3 (6%)
5. personal involvement of top executives/entrepreneurs	34 (14%)	16 (6%)	1 (5%)	2 (12%)	6 (11%)
6. established procedures	38 (16%)	14 (6%)	4 (19%)	4 (24%)	6 (11%)
7. encourage higher worker productivity/training of local staff	11 (5%)	9 (4%)	3 (14%)	1 (6%)	3 (6%)
8. adopt local practices/conform to local culture	41 (17%)	16 (6%)	3 (14%)	2 (12%)	11 (20%)
9. dismiss local staff/ change local partners	17 (7%)	14 (6%)	2 (10%)	2 (12%)	8 (15%)
10. others	3 (1%)	3 (1%)	2 (10%)	1 (6%)	–
Total cases (multiple answers allowed)	237 (100%)	252 (100%)	21 (100%)	17 (100%)	54 (100%)

Note: [a] The scale of importance ranges from Very Important [1] to Not Important At All [5].

Source: Author's survey.

respondents to evaluate 10 potential major problems they might have encountered during their global reach. We also allowed them to propose problems not included in this list. Several observations are clear from the corporate survey and personal interviews. Measured by importance, all 204 sampled SINTNCs considered the *lack of home government support* as the major problem in their global reach. Studies in international business have shown that strong home country government support is important for aspiring transnational corporations to overcome the initial disadvantages of entering and competing in foreign business environments (see Chapter 1). To a certain extent, the success of Japanese and Korean companies in Europe and North America can be attributed to the strong institutional and corporate support they have received from their respective home country governments.

This home country institutional constraint can be further understood in different aspects. First, it is related to the lack of home country support for entrepreneurship because the Singapore government has been wooing the most talented people to join the civil service or GLCs. For example, the CEO of an international commodity trader that operates in China, Myanmar, and Romania observed that:

> Why is it we are not there yet when we say Singapore is such a nice place to be in as a trading centre and yet our people have not emerged to that position? Because we have not seriously put into it that we have to develop conscientiously the core value of entrepreneurs. Then I ask the question: where have all our best talented people gone? All the President scholars, all the OMS scholars, GLCs, they come out and they go to the government-operated transnationals. Then you are neglecting your talented people to be entrepreneurs in the international scene. So you are left with people who feel that being a trader is skimming off somebody. That's the mental attitude out here. And then the career path is not seriously propagated and promoted. (Interviewed in Singapore, 13 July 1998)

Second, there is insufficient space within the home country economy for these transnational entrepreneurs to make their impact. This is related to the significant role of the developmental state in driving the Singapore economy (see also Chapters 2 and 3). Many transnational entrepreneurs interviewed felt that they are not given sufficient opportunities to prove themselves in Singapore. This lack of good job references poses a competitive disadvantage when they engage in international business activities. They find it hard to convince their prospective customers in the host countries that they are capable of performing up to the requirements of the contracts. The Managing Director of a healthcare equipment supplier pointed out that the company could not expand in Singapore because of the buying behaviour of government hospitals, which always look for global corporations as their suppliers of equipment.

For Singapore entrepreneurs, they will always treat us like we are small timers. And their confidence in buying from Singapore entrepreneurs like us is not that high, compared to transnationals like Philips, Siemens, General Electric etc. Their buying also more or less creates problems for us in the sense that we cannot sell very big systems to them. They are only interested in buying from big giants for some reasons that they feel more confident buying from these big organisations. That is a sad thing because our local hospitals are not supporting our local entrepreneurs. (Interviewed in Singapore, 15 July 1998)

Third, the problem is concerned with the lack of direct support from the Singapore government, compared to the direct involvement of Taiwanese and South Korean governments. This finding is surprising because of the recent official launch of Singapore's regionalisation programme in 1993 and the numerous schemes associated with this programme in helping Singapore companies to go regional and, in some cases, global (see Chapter 3). As noted by the Managing Director of a clean room equipment manufacturer and trader,

Say you want to go to a certain area in China. Where is the help and recognition from the Singapore government? We are on our own. For the Taiwanese, it's different. If the businessman identifies Shenzhen or Yangzhou or Zhuhai as a key area to grow, the [Taiwanese] government will go there first with an operating office. They will handle everything and help in contacts, evaluation and so on. (Interviewed in Singapore, 15 June 1998)

Probing further into the nature of this major problem, however, offers some clues. When asked whether their companies had benefited from the Singapore government's recent regionalisation programme, some 73.7 per cent of respondents replied 'No'. The rest of the 51 SINTNCs, which claimed to have benefited from the regionalisation programme, are spread among public listed companies ($N=12$), private companies ($N=20$), and GLCs ($N=19$). If we examine the relative proportion of different types of SINTNCs by ownership and their propensity to benefit from the regionalisation programme, we find an astonishing 19 GLCs out of 23 GLCs in our sample (82.6 per cent). The ratio for public listed and private SINTNCs are respectively 26.1 per cent and 14.8 per cent. In other words, a very high proportion of GLCs in our sample agreed that they have benefited from the Singapore government's regionalisation programme (see more in Chapter 5). In view of these findings, it is not surprising that most of the 204 sample SINTNCs found the lack of home government support as their major problem of global reach. What exactly are the main benefits of the Singapore government's recent regionalisation programme? Among those 51 SINTNCs which claimed to have benefited, some 30 (36.1 per cent) have received direct government assistance in the form of tax incentives and loans. Another 19 (22.9 per cent) rely on good inter-governmental relations with host countries to establish their presence abroad. Other major benefits cited by these SINTNCs include information access and connections (N = 14 or 16.9 per cent) and reputation from partnership with government agencies (N = 9 or 10.8 per cent).

Another major problem faced by some SINTNCs in their global reach is the role of *host government regulations* (see Table 4.8). This problem is particularly thorny in the case of SINTNCs operating in East Asia (mean score = 2.5). China, for example, is well known for its difficult operating environment. From interviews conducted with subsidiaries of SINTNCs in China, it appears that government regulations in China pose a serious threat to SINTNCs that are used to the relatively open and transparent home country regulatory regime. For these SINTNCs in China, the main problem rests with the *uncertainty* and *subjective interpretations* of government regulations, particularly at the local government level (see also the case of Suzhou Industrial Park in Chapter 5). For example, a transnational entrepreneur from Singapore established a computer furniture factory in Shenzhen, China, in 1994 to take advantage of perceived lower costs of production. The finished products were then exported to the European market. But the factory was shut down before the end of 1996 because of tremendous problems associated with host country institutional structures. These problems are related to different levels of authorities in China, corrupt practices by local officials, and labour control problems. As recalled bitterly by the transnational entrepreneur,

> We went there expecting that it is just like any other place where people need to work and make money and things like that. We were thinking that if we pay better and treat the workers better, and with all our machines, we should not have problems. Economically, it was very attractive, with the costs of the workers and rental seemed like a win-win situation where one cannot fail. Even if we encounter problems, with that much allowance from the profits, there would still be room for adjustments. But unfortunately, the hidden problems were too much. (Interviewed in Singapore, 1 August 1998)

To resolve these problems of host government regulations, most SINTNCs in East Asia resort to one of the following *localised measures* (Table 4.8):

- relying on local partners and connections to circumvent regulations (43 per cent);
- asking local governments for help (14 per cent); and
- adopting local practices or conforming to local regulations (6 per cent).

For example, many transnational entrepreneurs in Table 4.6 have co-operated with their local partners in the host countries to reduce risks and uncertainties. The senior manager of a large industrial enterprise from Singapore recognised the importance of its local joint venture partners in China.

> You always think that in China you just sell each one a bottle of Coke, and you can make so much. So based on the same logic we went into all these kinds of businesses. Then we realised that the people there are so different from us, in the way they think and all that. If you can get a very good partner in China, you should really treasure him. Just like the ones we have in Beijing and Tianjin. They are very good. Every year they make money for us and we don't bother them. (Interviewed in Singapore, 12 May 1998)

In other extreme cases (e.g. the computer furniture factor in Shenzhen, China), however, the factory had to be closed down in order to resolve the problem once and for all. Sometimes, the problem may be so insurmountable that the transnational entrepreneur has to give up the entire factory altogether. The Managing Director again explained that:

> I think we lost everything. Even the machines we left behind are lost too. We think when we moved back, we let go about S$300,000 to S$400,000. When we moved back, the custom did not allow us to bring the machines back. We had to apply for permits. As the machines went in without paying taxes, therefore we were not allowed to sell. So we would have to bring them out. But when we applied for the permits, they were disallowed. In other words, they wanted to keep the machines. (Interviewed in Singapore, 1 August 1998)

As shown in Table 4.8, transnational entrepreneurs from the headquarters in Singapore would also be personally involved in resolving problems in East Asian subsidiaries (6 per cent). In other regions of SINTNC operations, *established corporate procedures* were often used to resolve problems, indicating the extent of professional management systems. This reliance on established procedures tends to be more common among foreign subsidiaries in Europe and North America, again a reflection of the higher level of business trust and corporate governance in these host regions. The role of professional managers in ensuring successful international business operations is also related to the emergence of transnational entrepreneurs as will be detailed in the next chapter.

In the context of the recent 1997/1998 Asian economic crisis, *access to finance and capital* may pose a major problem for transnational entrepreneurs operating across borders. Compared to banks in Japan and South Korea, local banks in Singapore tend to be very conservative in financing overseas projects. In fact, a local entrepreneur wrote to Singapore's most read newspaper and openly complained that 'all of them [banks in

Singapore] were only interested in property business and trading – all heavily secured transactions. They had no desire to support a technical enterprise. The local banks also have limited experience in small and medium-sized enterprise (SME) operations and venture funding' (*The Straits Times*, 7 July 1999). Conservative banking practices in Singapore make it very difficult for transnational entrepreneurs to venture abroad for two reasons. First, the lack of venture capital in Singapore implies that transnational entrepreneurs have to raise their own funds for overseas operations through either the capital markets or internal reserves. Second, the Singapore government is unable to step in to fulfil such a role as a co-investor, unlike some other governments in Asia. The founder of a construction firm in Singapore with projects in Malaysia, China, and Australia commented on the conservatism of local banks in Singapore.

> You see, our bankers don't want to finance overseas projects, not like the Japanese and the others. The Koreans and the Japanese, their bankers are willing to finance their overseas projects. They [banks in Singapore] always say that it is because of the MAS [Monetary Authority of Singapore] rules that they cannot finance overseas projects. They also say that the Singapore dollar is not international. (Interviewed in Singapore, 26 June 1998)

Another transnational entrepreneur, who has ceramics manufacturing facilities in China, has suffered greatly from the conservative banking practices in Singapore.

> They [local banks in Singapore] will not lend the money because they say that any money borrowed in Singapore must be used in Singapore. In fact, from the beginning, I used an overdraft from my bank to invest overseas. Now, my bank is squeezing me because of the downturn. The problem is when I told them that I've the money in China, they told me that I was not supposed to send money to China. They said that the overdraft they gave me is for use in business in Singapore and not China. Therefore, it's better that you don't tell anybody about it . . . Many people do business like that because we're not a listed company whereby you simply issue some shares when you need funds. Therefore small companies like us are handicapped. (Interviewed in Singapore, 3 August 1998)

Tapping into global capital markets is another important strategy to expand one's access to financial resources. It is also a pre-emptive measure: those firms that implemented such a strategy tended to be less badly affected by the crisis of 1997/1998. To date, many Singaporean firms continue to rely on their social networks and personal ties in accessing funds and capital for investment. Indeed, many of today's renowned Chinese entrepreneurs in Asia started their businesses by pooling capital from various network sources (e.g. Redding, 1990; Chan and Chiang, 1994; Backman, 1999). As their business empires grow and their scales of operations extend beyond national boundaries, many of these transnational entrepreneurs no longer restrict their sources of capital exclusively to social and business networks embedded in their 'home' countries. The globalisation of their business activities is also fuelled by their abilities to tap into global capital markets. Though not many of these transnational Chinese entrepreneurs are successful in tapping into global capital funds (see Olds and Yeung, 1999; Yeung and Soh, 2000), those that managed to do so tended to weather the recent Asian economic crisis better. As such, the crisis presented golden opportunities for these transnational Chinese entrepreneurs to consolidate and expand their business empires within and outside the Asian region.

What then are the critical components of strategies for tapping into global capital markets? First, transnational Chinese entrepreneurs must be able to transfer the goodwill extensively developed in their 'home' countries. This goodwill often emanates from their strong embeddedness in domestic financial and business networks. Many of them are also involved in the banking and finance industry. They include Liem Sioe Liong (Bank Central Asia in Indonesia), Kwek Leng Beng (Hong Leong Finance in Singapore), Wee Cho Yaw (United Overseas Bank in Singapore), and Quek Leng Chan (Hong Leong Finance in Malaysia and Dao Heng Bank in Hong Kong). In some Southeast Asian countries, this goodwill also originates from their extensive involvement in political–economic alliances with leading politicians and military personnel (McVey, 1992; Brook and Luong, 1997; Hefner, 1998; Yeung, 1999e; 2000d). This strong embeddedness in goodwill of a domestic origin presents a significant problem for the globalisation of these business firms.

To what extent can this goodwill and its related competitive advantage be transferred to other geographical contexts (see also Hu, 1995)? Going back to the case study of Kwek Leng Beng's Hong Leong Group (see Box 4.1), it is clear that Kwek enjoyed tremendous goodwill transfer in his global operations. He has successfully listed many of his hotel businesses on stock exchanges in Hong Kong, London and New Zealand. As mentioned above, his successful placement of Millennium & Copthorne Hotels on the London Stock Exchange has not only brought him immediate financial gains, but also energised the London capital market for hotel investments (*The Straits Times*, 24 April 1996). In 1997, Prudential Client (MSS) Nominees Ltd was a substantial minority shareholder of M&C Hotels plc (Annual Report, 1997: 23). Kwek's CDL Hotels International, listed on the Hong Kong Stock Exchange, has also received very good support from major banks in Hong Kong (interview with a key Kwek family member in Hong Kong, 11 June 1998).

Second, those transnational entrepreneurs who hedged their long-term borrowings and diversified their bankers tended to manage better the major impact of the 1997/1998 Asian economic crisis. In the midst of the crisis, foreign exchange risks and liquidity squeeze were the major problems confronting many Asian firms. For the Korean *chaebols*, the problem rested with their high debt–equity ratios (Mathews, 1998; Wade and Veneroso, 1998; Chang, 2000). For many Indonesian firms, liquidity squeeze became a major problem when many Indonesian banks were put under the disciplinary programme imposed upon Indonesia by the International Monetary Fund (Bullard et al., 1998; Backman, 1999; Henderson, 1999). Similarly, rapidly falling stock market prices meant that these firms would be worth much less than their collateral, if there were ever such a thing as collateral! The important lesson here is that had these firms, particularly those with international business exposure, hedged and diversified their long-term borrowings, they would have been much better placed to ride out the crisis. In the case of CDL Hotels International, hedging of funds is always used as an important instrument to minimise foreign exchange exposure (interview with a key Kwek family member in Hong Kong, 11 June 1998). Its Annual Report in 1997 (p. 19) stated that:

> Care is exercised to ensure that borrowing facilities do not carry onerous or restrictive covenants, and that the terms of the facilities fulfil the underlying requirements. The Group's long-term debt consists of bank debts denominated in various currencies. As part of the hedging policy of the Group, the foreign net currency investments were hedged by borrowing funds in the currencies of the countries where the Group operates.

A breakdown of CDL Hotels International's long-term borrowings as at 31 December 1997 indicates that its HK$5.9 billion borrowings were denominated in the domestic currencies of the USA, the UK, New Zealand, Malaysia, Singapore, and Taiwan. Some 60 per cent of these borrowings were denominated in pounds sterling alone, indicating the importance of London-based financial institutions in supporting the globalisation of CDL Hotels International.

In addition to hedging long-term borrowings, Kwek has enjoyed a highly diversified portfolio of bankers for both his CDL Hotels International and M&C Hotels Plc. This diverse range of bankers for both listed companies in Hong Kong and London not only illustrates their strong financial support for Kwek's ambition to globalise his hotel business, but also reduces his risk of liquidity squeeze in times of economic crisis. For example, CDL Hotels International has amongst its bankers those from the UK, France, Japan, Hong Kong, Switzerland, Australia, and New Zealand. Its subsidiary, M&C Hotels plc, has also gained strong support from four major British banks – National Westminster Bank, ING Barings, HSBC, and Lloyds Bank. With diversified sources of capital, it is not surprising that both CDL Hotels International and M&C Hotels plc were able to weather major financial constraints in the midst of the Asian economic crisis. The case demonstrates that globalising into different capital markets is a key proactive strategy for the long-term expansion of transnational entrepreneurs across borders. The economic crisis of 1997/1998 has just made the point even clearer and more relevant.

Table 4.9 Attributes of entrepreneurship in overcoming problems in foreign operations by transnational entrepreneurs

Attributes	Entrepreneur	(%)	Non-entrepreneur	(%)	Total
Personal experience and expertise	58	18.6	32	17.9	90
Proactive adaptability to different environments	49	15.8	25	14.0	74
Strong vision and accomplishment	42	13.5	28	15.6	70
Abilities to capitalise on opportunities	35	11.3	15	8.4	50
Highly motivated and independent	34	10.9	17	9.5	51
Risk-taking	25	8.0	21	11.7	46
Abilities to plan and organise	21	6.8	6	3.4	27
Well-connected/well-resourced	12	3.9	10	5.6	22
Very creative and innovative	12	3.9	11	6.1	23
Good business acumen	10	3.2	2	1.1	12
Honesty, trustworthiness	9	2.9	5	2.8	14
Others	4	1.3	7	3.9	5
Total	311	100.0	179	100.0	484

$p < 0.27$; chi-square = 13.4; d.f. = 11

Source: Author's survey.

To sum up this section, the problems associated with international business activities are often enormous and sometimes insurmountable. It takes extraordinary entrepreneurial efforts to overcome these problems of international operations. The key attributes of these entrepreneurial efforts are summarised in Table 4.9. For transnational entrepreneurs, three attributes account for almost 50 per cent of total responses: (1) personal experience and expertise; (2) proactive adaptability to different environments; and (3) strong vision and accomplishment. As mentioned earlier, personal experience is critical in the establishment of cross-border activities by transnational entrepreneurs. In dealing with problems inherent in international business, those experienced transnational entrepreneurs tend to handle the situation better. Experience also implies that these transnational entrepreneurs may be able to adapt better to different environments in the host countries. For example, the founder of the construction firm explained how his China operation managed to overcome the problems of labour control and host government regulations.

> If you go to other countries, in the construction job, you've got to suit their way of doing it and not to get them to suit you. Because the practices have been there for donkey's years, if you want to change it suddenly it is not that easy. So we had to accommodate to their practices. (Interviewed in Singapore, 26 June 1998)

CONCLUSION

Transnational entrepreneurs are important drivers behind the globalisation of economic activities. Through both quantitative and qualitative analysis, this chapter has shown that these transnational entrepreneurs are often strongly embedded in, and therefore influenced by, home country institutional environments. Consistent with the institutional perspective proposed in Chapter 1, these home country conditions shape the access of transnational entrepreneurs to entrepreneurial endowments and resources. Though my findings are not very conclusive in statistical terms, they are at least useful in shedding light on *how* transnational entrepreneurship matters in the establishment and management of international business ventures.

As shown empirically in this chapter, transnational entrepreneurship is related to the strong vision, ability to capitalise on opportunities, risk-taking behaviour, personal experience, and proactive adaptability of transnational entrepreneurs. There are also many statistically significant differences between transnational entrepreneurs and non-transnational entrepreneurs in relation to the influence of institutional structures and ongoing connections and relationships on establishing their foreign operations. As illustrated in various detailed case studies, transnational entrepreneurs not only internalise these key attributes before they engage in international business activities, they must also be well endowed with entrepreneurial resources as defined in Figure 1.1. To ensure their successful cross-border operations, they enrol other actors into specific business and personal networks that span different host countries and/or regions.

Does it mean then that all business people who are involved in international business activities are known as transnational entrepreneurs? To be sure, the answer is far from that straightforward. As explained in the introduction to this chapter, there is a *prima facie* case to argue for a separate analysis of corporate managers who are mandated to establish and manage cross-border operations. Though they face a qualitatively different kind of risk profile, as compared to transnational entrepreneurs themselves, these transnational intrapreneurs can sometimes be exceptionally entrepreneurial in their international business behaviour. Their empowerment to engage in international business activities may unleash tremendous entrepreneurial tendencies. This is the analytical task for the next empirical chapter, which examines the role of transnational intrapreneurs in international business.

5. Empowered managers: intrapreneurs in international business

> You must have a passion to do everything yourself, do post and pre-acquisition or joint venture. After the deal is made, he [a transnational intrapreneur] is out there striking more deals like this; fundamentally a passion for this. (President of a major government-linked company in Singapore; interviewed on 18 May 1998)

> You've got to have the right CEO [abroad] who is interested in making friends. They have no choice but to be entrepreneurs since they are the top overseas managers and they are running the business all by themselves. Sometimes, you have to send your best managers overseas. You cannot keep all the good ones here [in Singapore]. Given the right incentives and environments, they are willing to go abroad. (Chairman of a major government-linked company in Singapore; interviewed on 25 July 1998)

INTRODUCTION

The ownership of capital distinguishes a transnational entrepreneur from a transnational intrapreneur, who is essentially a corporate manager empowered by the owners and/or shareholders of the transnational corporation (TNC) to engage in international business activities. Chapter 1 has reviewed some recent studies of corporate entrepreneurship and international business to understand the role of subsidiary initiatives in the global reach of TNCs. While their efforts are highly commendable, however, the understanding of subsidiary initiatives in the global networks of TNCs is insufficient because transnational intrapreneurs can operate both in parent headquarters and in foreign subsidiaries. Situated in the institutional perspective on transnational entrepreneurship in Chapter 1, transnational intrapreneurs should be understood as corporate managers who have taken exceptional initiatives to ensure successful cross-border operations. Though they may not own any operation in an equity sense, they are often bestowed with substantial autonomy in transnational management.

As implicit in the quotations above, there are therefore clearly two groups of transnational intrapreneurs. The first group includes those top executives in the corporate headquarters who make exceptionally entrepreneurial decisions about cross-border operations. They tend to be highly influenced by the institutional structures of their home countries. Sometimes, these top executives are also personally involved in establishing their cross-border operations. The second group of transnational intrapreneurs refers to those corporate managers who have been sent abroad to establish and manage foreign operations. They often encounter serious problems in managing these foreign operations. Their abilities to manage and overcome these problems of international business operations are highly important to the long-term viability of the corporate group as a whole. In managing their foreign operations, these transnational intrapreneurs are often compelled to come to terms with the institutional environments in the host countries. To manage across borders successfully, they require specific entrepreneurial skills and attributes.

My mode of analysing transnational intrapreneurs in this chapter is broadly similar to the preceding chapter. In particular, qualitative case studies are analysed in the next three sections to uncover the formation of their transnational ventures and their access to entrepreneurial endowments. The fourth section examines the role of transnational intrapreneurs in managing across borders. It not only offers analysis of the role of transnational entrepreneurship in determining parent–subsidiary relationships, but also shows how these transnational intrapreneurs are confronted with severe problems in the host countries, and how they manage to overcome barriers to internationalisation. The concluding section provides a brief summary of the main findings in this chapter.

PROFILES OF TRANSNATIONAL INTRAPRENEURS

In Table 4.1, 122 respondents agreed that they are transnational entrepreneurs. Some 73 of them are top executives of their companies, designated as either chairmen or CEO/managing directors/presidents. Due to constraints in the data collection, we are unable to ascertain how many of these 73 self-proclaimed transnational entrepreneurs are actually owners or major shareholders of their companies. Given the predominance of the owner-operated business system in Singapore (except government-linked companies), it is likely that a majority of them are owner-transnational entrepreneurs.

The remaining 49 respondents (40 per cent; N=122), however, are clearly neither owners nor majority shareholders of their respective companies. They occupy such corporate positions as executive directors, general managers, senior vice presidents, divisional managers, and so on.

They are best classified as *transnational intrapreneurs*. In comparison, some 52 or 68 per cent of those respondents who did not claim to be entrepreneurs (N = 76) hold similar positions in their respective companies. This finding implies that proportionately fewer corporate managers are entrepreneurial than top executives in SINTNCs. This may be explained by the relative lack of access to entrepreneurial endowments and resources experienced by these corporate managers.

If we examine in greater detail those Chinese family firms that are presumably the most entrepreneurial group of companies from Singapore, some interesting patterns emerge. There are not only such exceptional transnational Chinese entrepreneurs as Kwek Leng Beng and his family members who have been spearheading the internationalisation of Chinese business firms from Singapore (see Box 4.1). There is also apparently an increasing professionalisation of Chinese family business and the emergence of transnational intrapreneurs in these formerly ethnocentric organisations. Very often, transnational Chinese entrepreneurs are unable to manage all their operations abroad. They have to co-opt more professional and trusted managers who are then socialised into the corporate 'family'. First, I examine the survey data to find out how many of the respondents from 54 Chinese family firms in my sample of SINTNCs (N = 204) considered themselves as entrepreneurs. It turns out that only 31 of them (57.4 per cent) agreed that they could be considered entrepreneurs. Twenty-eight respondents were either chairmen or CEO/managing directors of the Chinese family firms. Virtually all of them were the patriarchs or their family members. Seventeen of these 28 respondents (61 per cent) claimed to be entrepreneurs. However, among the other 26 respondents who were not family members, only 14 (54 per cent) considered themselves to be entrepreneurs.

When I asked what constitutes entrepreneurship in their view, there seemed to be a major difference in the perceptions of family and non-family members. Those chairmen and CEO/managing directors who considered themselves as entrepreneurs cited 'abilities to capitalise on opportunities' as the most important (18 per cent) attribute of transnational entrepreneurship. Receiving equal emphasis at 13 per cent, other important attributes included: (1) risk taking; (2) strong vision and accomplishment; and (3) high motivation and independence. These four attributes are similar to those discussed in Chapter 4. Together, they accounted for 58 per cent of all responses from these 28 family members. On the other hand, non-family members or intrapreneurs tended to cite 'proactive adaptability to different environments' as the most important attribute (18 per cent) of transnational entrepreneurship. Other important attributes were similar to those cited by family members.

Based on these empirical observations, it can be argued that transnational intrapreneurs are much more concerned with adaptability issues than owner entrepreneurs, who are more opportunity-driven in their entrepreneurial behaviour. This observation is not surprising because the most trusted professional managers may be sent abroad to manage foreign operations. They have often been chosen because of their high adaptability to different business environments. Their performance is assessed on the basis of their success in managing and developing these foreign operations. Owner entrepreneurs, however, are less concerned with management issues since they can entrust their transnational intrapreneurs with management responsibilities. Rather, owner entrepreneurs are keen to expand the overall business activities of the group through capitalising on business opportunities that may arise in different countries and/or regions. The case of Teck Wah Paper in Box 5.1 shows how a transnational intrapreneur has been entrusted by the second-generation patriarch of a Chinese family firm to manage and develop the family's business interests in China. I will discuss the case further in the next section.

BOX 5.1   TECK WAH PAPER: TRUST AND INTRAPRENEURSHIP IN A CHINESE FAMILY FIRM

Founded in 1968 by its current Chairman, Mr Chua Seng Teck, Teck Wah Paper Products Pte Ltd. is a modern Chinese family firm from Singapore that specialises in creative printing and packaging. From its humble beginnings as a manufacturer of cardboard boxes, Teck Wah Seng Kee Company (later to be known as Teck Wah Paper Products Pte Ltd) was born out of a need to pursue a personal vision and a desire to fulfil an entrepreneurial calling. The Group has come a long way in this respect, with 14 subsidiary companies, and over 500 dedicated staff serving in an overseas business network that encompasses Singapore, Malaysia, China, Indonesia, and the USA (corporate web site: http://www.teckwah.com.sg). Today, the management of Teck Wah falls under second-generation family members, namely Mr Chua's two sons. Whereas his elder son (Thomas Chua) serves as Group Managing Director, the younger brother (James Chua) is the head of the sales and marketing division. However, the management of Teck Wah's overseas subsidiaries is entrusted to professional managers. As Mr Chua Seng Teck said, '[c]apital is important, but people are our most important asset'. This is a typical transformation in an entrepreneurial Chinese family firm during its internationalisation processes (see Yeung, 2000f). Key family members are kept within the home country so that they can be groomed to take over from the founder and/or patriarch when the time is ripe. Though these family members may be involved directly in the establishment and management of overseas subsidiaries, they are often required to take over more important group strategic management functions.

Here I want to consider specifically Teck Wah's joint venture in China and to show how an entrepreneurial decision to invest in China had turned into a management nightmare that could only be salvaged by sending an entrusted intrapreneur. In 1994, Teck Wah Paper entered into a majority joint venture (51 per cent) with a local town and village enterprise (TVE) in Wuxi, China, to set up Wuxi Teckwah Paper Products Co. Ltd (Wuxi Paper), a modern printing factory which had 63 staff by July 1998. While Wuxi Paper represented Teck Wah's long-term strategic vision to tap into the enormous market potential in China, the choice of Wuxi and the local partner was made on the basis of an introduction by a Mainland Chinese staff member employed in Teck Wah Paper in Singapore. The Wuxi relative of this Chinese staff member actually knew one new TVE project in Wuxi that had just built a new factory and brought in new printing machines. Though almost confirming a factory site in Shanghai at that time, Teck Wah Singapore decided to inject its 51 per cent equivalent of equity to enter into a joint venture with this Wuxi TVE, thinking that Wuxi Paper was a ready-made printing factory with an existing customer base. The investment was therefore opportunistic and entrepreneurial, reflecting the transnational entrepreneurship of second-generation family members (see also Chapter 4).

What the Chua brothers in Singapore did not realise, however, was that Wuxi Paper then was strapped with cash flow problems, which in turn led to significant management problems in view of obstacles from the local partner. My interviewee said that the initial cash flow problem was due to China's massive decentralisation of decision-making to local and village governments and the availability of easy credits from state banks to grow these TVEs during the early 1990s (see also Yeung, 2000h). In fact, the Chinese factory manager of Wuxi Paper knew nothing about printing at all before the formation of the joint venture and they had one state-owned enterprise in Wuxi as their only customer! The decision to construct the printing factory and to purchase new machinery and equipment was linked to potential personal gain by the factory manager and his cronies in the TVE. According to the joint venture agreement, Teck Wah Singapore would send one general manager and the local TVE would send three deputy general managers.

Significant management problems emerged soon after the joint venture was in operation. One deputy general manager was the former factory manager who had benefited personally from kickbacks during the establishment of the factory and acquisition of machinery. Once the joint venture was in operation, he clearly had neither intention nor incentives to make the joint venture work because he now had no control over the financial matters of Wuxi Paper and had to work with a 'foreign' general manager. He therefore put up formidable labour problems to confront the first general manager who was sent from Singapore. As recalled by my interviewee, who was the second general manager,

> He [first general manager] would just give any instructions and people would follow. But now he got no power at all. Everything he has to listen to the GM [sent by Teck Wah in Singapore]. So he does not like it. Then he would try to push the GM out and create problems for him. And after that, all subordinates boycotted the GM's instructions.

This Singaporean general manager was a bad choice insofar as Teck Wah Singapore is concerned. He only managed to survive as the general manager of Wuxi Paper for three months after the commencement of operations. As a result of mounting management pressures and lack of co-operation from his Chinese DGMs, he resigned and left the Teck Wah Group.

Faced with serious management problems in Wuxi Paper, the Chua brothers now had to do something to get the factory into operation. Since they were both very busy with Teck Wah Group's business activities, they had to entrust this difficult task to a faithful manager who could act as a transnational intrapreneur with strong adaptability and management mandates. This is how my interviewee, Mr Mah Kok Hui, was called upon to take over as the second general manager of Wuxi Paper. To start with, Mr Mah is a truly transnational intrapreneur. He first joined the Teck Wah Group in 1991, as the production director of Teck Wah Manufacturers Sdn Bhd in Malacca, Malaysia. Mah was offered the position and some shares in Teck Wah Malacca because of his trust relationships with Mr Thomas Chua (Group Managing Director) and Mr. Mok (then Executive Director). In fact, Mah was a classmate of both Thomas and Mok during their pre-university education. After joining Teck Wah Malacca, Mah demonstrated to both Thomas and Mok that he could be a truly transnational intrapreneur. Before Teck Wah, Mah was working for a Japanese oil company in Malaysia. In Teck Wah Malacca, Mah was able to contribute to the company's growth in at least two ways. First, he engineered some acquisitions of old machinery from his former Japanese employer that had since been closed down. Second, he developed a total packaging concept and advised that Teck Wah Malacca should not just specialise in printing, but should also develop capabilities to print, assemble, and pack products manufactured by leading foreign TNCs in Malaysia. His business strategy subsequently proved successful and the factory was well integrated with two existing Teck Wah manufacturing operations in Malacca. Mah was given virtually full autonomy by Thomas and Mok to run the Malacca operation.

Once Mah had demonstrated his transnational entrepreneurship and been socialised into the 'Teck Wah family', he was deemed an insider in the top executive elite group. After the general manager in Wuxi Paper had resigned, Teck Wah was looking for a replacement urgently. Several general managers of Teck Wah's other factories in Singapore and Malaysia turned down the offer because they lacked experience in China. Thomas Chua then asked his trusted lieutenant, Mah, to take over the troubled Wuxi Paper in 1994. Mah recalled:

> Because China project to them [Teck Wah] is very important. Then, they were in such a hurry at that time because the GM had resigned. Then they needed to get a person to replace. They actually asked all the subsidiary GMs: 'who wants to come?'. And then finally, I think when they talked to me at that time, those people requested to come didn't want to come . . . Actually, at that time, I could see that China was a good place and time to come because they were just starting. Then, I think we did know what was the problem here. (Interview in Wuxi, 6 July 1998)

It is clear that Mah has strong adaptability to different business environments and is proactive and pragmatic in his approach to problems in transnational operations. These are key attributes of transnational entrepreneurship as defined in Chapter 1. His positive attitude towards problem solving was important in addressing thorny labour and marketing problems in Wuxi Paper. When asked whether he had considered leaving Wuxi Paper, Mah said:

> No, I don't think that. Because I have faced all kinds of people even in Singapore. There are always good and bad people. Everywhere you go is the same, even in Thailand and Malaysia. You will face the same kind of problem . . . So, at that time we were facing a lot problems and we had to think of solving some of the main problems. So, we selected

some of the main problems we faced because the first problem that we faced was marketing. We needed to survive. All these [other] problems we can leave to one side first. (Interview in Wuxi, 6 July 1998)

First, Mah's approach to marketing and sales problems in Wuxi Paper was interesting. He did not believe in just forcing his Chinese sales staff to market Wuxi Paper's products without giving them sufficient training. His view was that employees must feel a sense of belonging to the company and that the company must provide good training and support to encourage staff to perform:

> Control means the people first. We had to push them to run business because all the salesmen didn't want to go out. But the other way is that as a GM, we should teach them how to do the marketing. If we just push them without teaching them and then just push them out to sell, they also will not know how to do. Because they have no experience. So after three months we got one Singapore marketing manager to come here and support for nine months and to help out and train the people here. (Interview in Wuxi, 6 July 1998)

Second, Mah reshuffled the original management team in Wuxi Paper. He was given substantial autonomy and trust in transforming the management team. In a period of four years, he has changed up to 70 per cent of top management positions in Wuxi Paper. There is now only one deputy general manager from the TVE partner. He has been put in charge of factory welfare and plays no effective role in shaping management decisions.

Mah's training and restructuring programme proved to be effective. Within the first year of his arrival, Wuxi Paper managed to attract several customers, compared to only one customer at the time of its establishment. Today, all customers of Wuxi Paper are 100 per cent foreign companies or joint ventures from Japan, Guangzhou, and local governments. It is the only printing company in China that supplies to all three top bubble gum manufactures in China. The company is also profitable if machine depreciation is excluded. These results are good in view of strong competition from state-owned enterprises in Shanghai that are endowed with strong local connections and good imported machines. Since the Chua family has strong faith in Mah's entrepreneurial performance, Teck Wah Singapore's stake in Wuxi Paper was increased from 51 per cent in 1994 to 90 per cent by June 1998. To sum up, Mah's transnational entrepreneurship played a critical role in turning Wuxi Paper around from a typical foreign investor's nightmare to a relatively profitable venture.

FOREIGN VENTURES BY TRANSNATIONAL INTRAPRENEURS FROM SINGAPORE: THE ROLE OF ACTOR NETWORKS

The role of home and host country institutional structures in influencing the tendencies to establish foreign ventures has been analysed in Chapter 4. Since it is reasonable to expect that there are no major differences in these influences on transnational entrepreneurs and transnational intrapreneurs, a similar analysis will not be repeated in this chapter. Instead, following the qualitative analysis in Chapter 4, this section draws upon a number of case studies to shed light on the processes of foreign ventures by transnational intrapreneurs. This analysis is conceptually based on the institutional perspective on transnational entrepreneurship explained in Chapter 1 (see Figure 1.1). In particular, the role of entrepreneurial endowments and resources in shaping the successful establishment of foreign ventures by these transnational intrapreneurs is examined.

In this analysis of transnational intrapreneurs, there is an important empirical distinction that must be made in relation to the types of firms to which these transnational intrapreneurs belong. In the context of home country institutional influence, we can separate these Singaporean firms into government and non-government linked companies. As explained in Chapter 2, government-linked companies (GLCs) in Singapore have rather peculiar ownership and governance structures that strongly influence their entrepreneurial tendencies. As Prime Minister Goh Chok Tong stated, 'what we are encouraging is corporate entrepreneurship. We get able people to be leaders of the company. If one or two of them have the extra entrepreneurial drive, they can recruit other people to join the company, and they can grow quicker than if there were no sustained efforts. The signal has been given' (*The Sunday Times*, 28 April 1996). Some top executives of GLCs are entrepreneurial in their foreign operations. They are therefore suitably identified as transnational intrapreneurs. Though their top executives may be encouraged to be entrepreneurial, these transnational intrapreneurs tend to face a lot of institutional constraints in practice that will be detailed below. On the other hand, non-GLCs include all private and publicly listed family firms, and non-family firms in Singapore that fall outside the state sector. Similarly to their counterparts in Chapter 4, it may be argued that these non-GLCs tend to be a lot more flexible and entrepreneurial in their governance structures and business practices. These differences will be more apparent as the analysis proceeds.

In Tables 5.1 and 5.2, the entrepreneurial endowments and resources of transnational intrapreneurs from GLCs and non-GLCs are summarised in accordance with Figures 1.1 and 1.2. These 11 case studies originate from personal interviews with top executives in parent companies and, in some cases, their foreign subsidiaries in Hong Kong and China. In all these 11 cases, the top executives, who are based either in parent companies or in host countries, reflect key attributes of transnational intrapreneurs defined earlier. They are, of course, subject to different institutional influences in relation to their access to entrepreneurial endowments and resources. Similarly to the case studies of transnational entrepreneurs in Chapter 4, these case study firms represent a variety of industries (e.g. manufacturing, telecommunications, and infrastructural development), ownership background (e.g. Chinese family business, professionally managed business, and government-linked business), and host countries (e.g. China, Southeast Asia, the USA, and the UK). Because of the peculiar nature of GLCs in Singapore (see Chapter 2) and the role of transnational entrepreneurship in their international business operations, the following analysis places more emphasis on the entrepreneurial endowments and resources of these GLCs, and compares them with transnational intrapreneurs from non-GLCs.

Transnational Intrapreneurs in Government-linked Companies

To begin my analysis, transnational intrapreneurs require access to and enrolment into *foreign actor networks* in order to engage in international business ventures successfully. Among the GLCs mentioned in Table 5.1, this access and enrolment can be analysed in three dimensions: political entrepreneurship, provision of information, and strong reputation. First, there is no doubt that the Singapore government has been instrumental in developing foreign business opportunities for GLCs. In general, this may take the forms of foreign business missions and inter-governmental relations with host country governments. Indeed, one of the earliest GLC investments in China started off with the Singapore government taking the lead in 1981. One GLC top executive, who was involved in putting together the deal for negotiations with the Chinese, recalled that:

> in 1981, the government led the way with a mission. It was up to the individual businessman to identify what business they wanted to be in. So we said: 'Why don't we do this business?' The government said 'Okay, let's hedge the risk of this. Let's get a few other government companies to join in'. So we had a consortium of 5–8 major Singapore companies to join in. They were mainly state-owned enterprises. Those were the days when we had to take the lead [from the Singapore government]. (Interviewed in Singapore, 18 May 1998)

This investment in China was a minority joint venture (30 per cent ownership by the Singapore consortium) worth US$20 million in 1984. The Singapore government intended to test the China market and to assess future business opportunities in China. As explained by a top executive sent from Singapore to manage the joint venture in China,

> It's a little bit of politics. Singapore was very interested then in China and it's not so easy to do business in China. Everyone was very sceptical about whether the China market could be secured. Under that kind of situation, the Singapore government wanted somebody to test the market. They formed a consortium, comprising eight companies . . . For US$20 million, I think many would call it big. The government expected the eight companies to use this investment as a bingo to try the China market. Of course, no one wanted to take all the risk and everyone wanted to share the risk. (Interviewed in China, 12 June 1998)

The Singapore government therefore led a mission to China to introduce several GLCs to local authorities in China and to build inter-governmental relations. In fact, the lead GLC in the consortium was a trading company and had prior business relations with several state-owned enterprises in China that eventually turned out to be the key local partners in the joint venture. One of them was China Merchant Holdings, the fourth largest state-owned enterprise in China in terms of assets and resources. The enrolment of the lead GLC and other GLCs in the Singapore consortium into the actor networks of these Chinese state-owned enterprises via the Singapore government's investment mission and prior business relations is crucial to the success of the joint venture. As shown in Chapter 4, local partners in China can make or break a joint venture, which is virtually the *de facto* entry mode of international business activities in China (Pearson, 1991; Child, 1994; Child and Lu, 1996; Luo, 2000). As the top executive from Singapore explained, China Merchant Holdings was very supportive in ensuring the success of the joint venture because of its capitalist orientation, compared with many other state-owned enterprises in China that have all kinds of other hidden motives and agendas.

> China Merchant owns banking, insurance, shipping, and all the rest of it. I think there are some marked differences between dealing with Chinese companies in the south and in the north, because the exposure to international business by companies in the south is much more than in the north. In the south, you are dealing with businessmen who have been exposed to Hong Kong businessmen. So they are more ahead than their cousins up north, who are mostly bureaucrats. Coming back to the south, we were lucky to have China Merchant Holdings. We were lucky in their style and we were lucky that they have offices in Hong Kong which appreciated the intention is to make money and not to do national service of any sort. Making money basically, you know. Today we have a public listed company that makes US$6 to 8 million per year, which is great. I think we succeeded because of the formula. (Interviewed in Singapore, 18 May 1998)

Table 5.1 Case studies of transnational intrapreneurs from government-linked companies and their entrepreneurial endowments/resources

Name[a] and Sector	Transnational intrapreneur	Foreign actor networks	Information asymmetry	Risks and opportunities	Finance and capital	Experience in business	Relations with home country
JTC International • development of industrial estate	Top executive	• use local partners in the Philippines and Thailand		• risky to develop industrial parks abroad	• strong backing from JTC, the parent GLC	• experienced in the civil service and private sector	• some constraints as a GLC
Keppel FELS • marine engineering	Top executive	• formed as part of ASEAN projects • go regional with other GLCs		• strong support from host governments	• strong backing from the Keppel Group, the parent GLC • public listed in Singapore	• technical experience before joining Keppel FELS	• some influence from Temasek Holdings
Natsteel Ltd • steel and electronics manufacturing	Senior executives	• joint venture partners in steel business • prior transactions	• knew JV partners via business connections • help from government agencies (TDB and EDB)	• steel as a protected industry • JVs to produce and market in host countries	• strong shareholders in Singapore • public listed in Singapore • strong JV partners	• national company in steel since independence	
Pidemco Land • property development (London and China)	Senior executive in charge of international operations	• invited by a transnational entrepreneur from Singapore (HPL) • information from other GLCs	• some help from local partners • use local consultants (UK) • sent own team to China	• share risks with HPL and local partners	• strong stream of income from rentals in Singapore • public listed in Singapore	• used to be the largest landlord in Singapore	• some constraints as a GLC

218

Company	Position of interviewee				
Sembawang Marine • marine engineering • offshore oil platform • port operations	Top executive and General Manager (China)	• connections with state-owned enterprises in China and Malaysia • connections with an entrepreneur in Indonesia	• strong government support • quick decision and information • depend on host country rules and transparency	• commitment from JV partners (Malaysia) • joined investment missions by the Singapore Government (China)	• public listed in Singapore • co-invest with other GLCs	• strong company experience since the 1960s • personal experience in port operations	• some national restrictions • not much intervention from Temasek Holdings • no bailing out
Singapore Telecom • telecommunication	Senior executive in charge of international operations and country managers in Hong Kong and China	• unrelated local partners due to strong competition from incumbent operators	• strong local partners	• high risk investments • host government regulation	• strong home market share (monopoly until recently) • largest public listed company in Singapore	• strong foothold and technology in Singapore	• current CEO is the brother of Deputy Prime Minister and son of former Prime Minister Lee Kuan Yew
Singapore Technologies Group • engineering and technology • infrastructure and property • finance	Senior executive in Singapore and country manager in China	• approached by JV partners • go for reputable JV partners	• lots of affiliates in host countries • use of resources from the Singapore Government	• focus on core businesses • use established corporate procedure	• government funding in some areas • several public listed subsidiaries	• set up in 1967 to engage in high-tech manufacturing	• current CEO is the wife of Deputy Prime Minister and daughter-in-law of former Prime Minister Lee Kuan Yew

Note: "Since there are not many government-linked companies in Singapore (see Table 2.10), it is difficult to maintain their anonymity. The real names of various GLCs are used here. However, the designations of interviewees are disguised to protect their confidentiality. The names of these GLCs will not be cited in each chapter's analysis.

Source: Author's interviews.

Table 5.2 *Case studies of transnational intrapreneurs and their entrepreneurial endowments/resources*

Name[a] and Sector	Transnational intrapreneur	Foreign actor networks	Information asymmetry	Risks and opportunities	Finance and capital	Experience in business	Customer and supplier relations
CraftCorp • design and manufacturing of paper-based stationery	CEO	• buyer-driven demands (e.g. Hallmark and Walmart)	• reliance on the US/UK buyers to distribute	• not much fixed investment in host countries • large market shares in some major markets	• public listed in Singapore	• packaging and manufacturing background	• strong reputation • strong brand name
PackwayCorp • packaging for manufacturers	Executive Director and General Manager (China)	• TNC clients moved to China • personal connections	• from TNC clients	• secured business from existing clients • challenge of managing China operations	• equities and loans • public listed in Singapore	• employed since 1969 • Chinese languages • experience in project management	• customer driven operations abroad
Teck Wah Group • paper and printing	General Manager (China)	• contacts via an employee from China	• false reliance on local partners	• low risks and new machinery from local partners • potential clients in China	• public listed in Singapore	• long history of printing in Singapore awarded ISO9002 certificate	• stable in Singapore • must develop new markets in China
UnitedCorp • shipping and ship repair	Managing Director in a Chinese family firm	• known via earlier appointment as CEOs as many listed firms	• personal contacts via the family patriarch	• more cautious than the family patriarch	• public listed in Singapore to finance port development in China	• very experienced in professional management	

Note: [a] All names are disguised to maintain confidentiality and anonymity.

Source: Author's interviews.

On the other hand, the political entrepreneurship of the Singapore government does not always succeed. As shown in the case of the infamous Suzhou-Singapore Industrial Park (SSIP) in China (Figure 5.1 and Box 5.2), strong inter-governmental relations might be an important factor in enticing many GLCs into the mega joint venture. This idea of developing a township and bringing the Singaporean style of economic management to China was first mooted by Singapore's former Prime Minister Lee Kuan Yew when he met China's senior leader Deng Xiaoping during his visit to Singapore in 1978. It involved the Singapore government taking the lead to develop an industrial township in China (Economic Development Board, 1995: 20–1). With the strong personal involvement of so many top leaders from both countries, it is not difficult to imagine how leading GLCs from Singapore (e.g. the Keppel Group and the Singapore Technologies Group) got enrolled into the project's highly-charged actor networks and had a slice of one of the biggest foreign-led infrastructural developments in China. In this case, the entrepreneurial resources originated from the Singapore government and its vast networks of GLCs (see Chapter 2). These resources are clearly beyond the reach of any single transnational entrepreneur, not even those mentioned in Chapter 4 (e.g. Kwek Leng Beng). In other words, while transnational entrepreneurs and intrapreneurs from non-GLCs have to rely on private inter-personal relationships to enrol into foreign actor networks (see below), their counterparts from GLCs can rely on inter-personal relationships at the state level. Similarly, the kinds of entrepreneurial attributes in the SSIP project are highly unlikely to be found in many other countries, given the strong involvement of the developmental state in Singapore in the project. Of course, precisely because of the institutional structures underscoring the project, there are peculiar problems associated with the project that are clearly beyond management and will be analysed in the next section.

Second, the *provision of information* from various government ministries and statutory boards is clearly important to GLCs that are making inroads into the global economy. This information provision can be in the form of timing or location of foreign investments. As mentioned briefly in Chapter 2, many GLCs have very close links with the Singapore government. Some of their board directors and senior executives are not only former civil servants, but also still sit on the boards of various other government and/or affiliated institutions. In fact, the CEOs of the two largest GLCs in Singapore (Singapore Telecom and Singapore Technologies) are members of the immediate family of the former Prime Minister Lee Kuan Yew. They are respectively the brother and wife of the current Deputy Prime Minister Lee Hsien Loong (elder son of Lee Kuan Yew). Their access to a wide range of information and advice is beyond doubt. Key transnational intrapreneurs

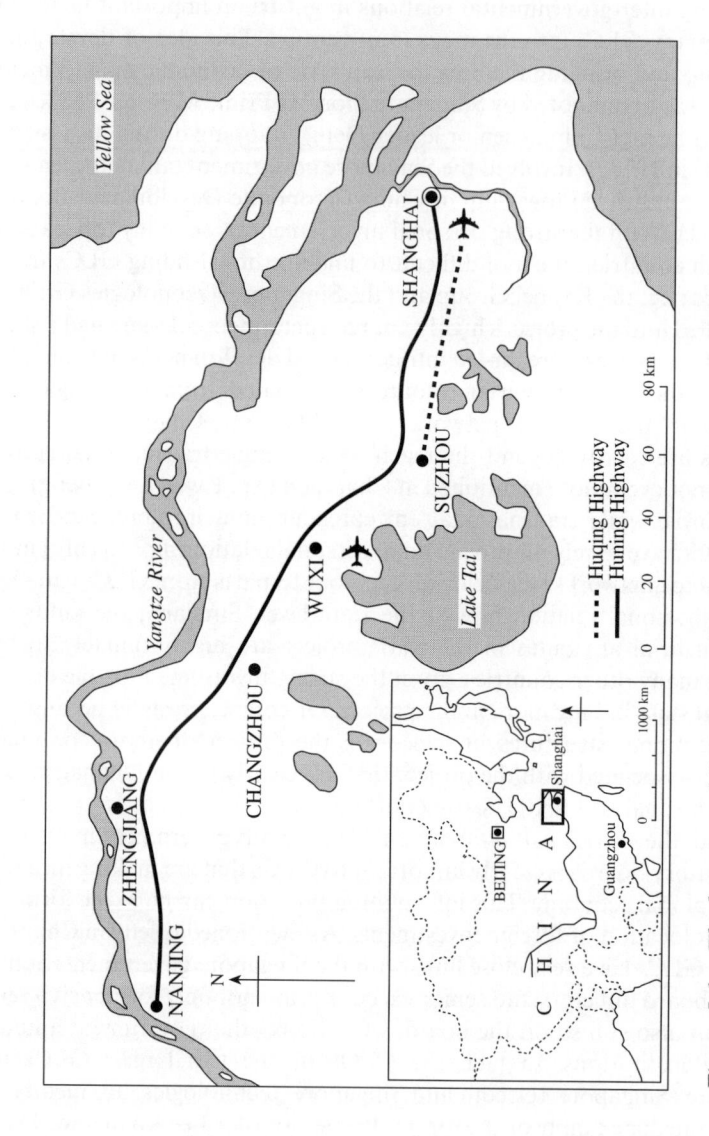

Figure 5.1 The location of Singapore industrial parks in Wuxi and Suzhou in Jiangsu Province, China

BOX 5.2 SUZHOU-SINGAPORE INDUSTRIAL PARK: 'POLITICAL ENTREPRENEURSHIP' IN CHINA

The high-profile China-Singapore Suzhou Industrial Park (CSSIP) had the symbolic support of top Chinese statesmen (e.g. the late Deng Xiaoping, Jiang Zemin, Li Peng, Qiao Shi, and Li Lanqing) and top Singapore statesmen (e.g. Lee Kuan Yew, Ong Teng Cheong, Goh Chok Tong, and Lee Hsien Loong) (see Yeung, 1998d; 2000h). The project started in May 1994 when Keppel Corporation, a major government-linked company with a shipyard background, led a consortium of 24 Singapore companies to form the Singapore-Suzhou Township Development Company (SSTD). Ten of these 24 Singapore companies were government-linked companies and statutory boards and their share was S$115 million (US$67.6 million) (*The Straits Times*, 15 January 1998). The China-Singapore Suzhou Industrial Park Development Company (CSSD) was a S$75 million (US$44 million) joint venture between the Singapore consortium, SSTD (65 per cent), and its Chinese counterpart, China Suzhou Industrial Park Company (CSIPC), which comprised 11 state-owned enterprises mainly from Suzhou (35 per cent). It aimed to develop an industrial township covering an area of approximately 70 square kilometres. The total cost of the township was estimated to be S$30 billion (US$17.6 billion) and it would take about 20–30 years to complete. When fully developed, the township could support a population of 600000 and provide employment for more than 360000 people.

By early 1997, the CSSIP project which was officially inaugurated slightly later than the Waxi-Singapore Industrial Park (WSIP), on February 1994, began to face mounting pressures from poor profitability and slow implementation. By June 1998, four years after the initial launch of the Suzhou township project, it became clear that the loss-making developer CSSD could not expect to make money in the near future (*The Straits Times*, 18 April 1998; 19 June 1998; *Far Eastern Economic Review*, 4 March 1999). The park has experienced yearly losses, averaging US$23–24 million, since establishment and is further expected to chalk up accumulated losses of US$90 million by the end of 2000 (*The Straits Times*, 15 September 1999). Although by the end of March 2000, cumulative contractual investment in the China-Singapore Suzhou Industrial Park (CSSIP) reached US$7 billion (*The Straits Times*, 18 April 2000), it was still far below the US$20 billion target. About US$3.5 billion of these investment commitments were realised and it was unclear how much more would be utilised in the context of the Asian economic crisis. In term of physical development, the CSSD had prepared 11 square kilometres (about 15.7 per cent of the total master plan) for occupation by tenants. On 28 June 1999, the Singapore government signed a memorandum of understanding with the Jiangsu government to cut its stake in the Suzhou Industrial Park project from 65 per cent to 35 per cent. It also agreed to hand over the management and control of the project to the Chinese government on 1 January 2001 (*The Straits Times*, 29 June 1999). Both governments reassured investors that the new management would be committed to the CSSIP and would continue to provide the same high level of services that investors had come to expect. It was apparent, however, that the strongest selling point of the CSSIP, i.e. 'the Singapore experience', would vanish by 2001.

According to a top executive from the CSSD interviewed in Suzhou on 3 July 1998, two main problems confronted the CSSD and the CSSIP project: (1) differences in partners' objectives and (2) complex involvement of different levels of governments. The first main problem of the SIP originated from *the different and conflicting objectives* held by key partners of the Singapore Suzhou township (interviewed in Suzhou, 3 July 1998). As noted by Singapore's Senior Minister Lee Kuan Yew (*The Straits Times*, 1 October 1999), the mutual identity of interests of the central governments in Beijing and Singapore was not shared by the working parties on the ground (i.e. local governments). On the one hand, the central government in Beijing wanted Singapore to help transfer its software or know-how in developing a township, replete with factories, commercial complexes, housing and social amenities that could then be replicated throughout China. On the other hand, the major local partner, the Suzhou municipal government, was interested in the hardware and took profit making as the top priority of the township project. SM Lee further commented that 'Suzhou does not want to go around to build 100 industrial parks in China. They just want more factories, more jobs, more money, and more promotions in Suzhou ... *There was no identity of goals at that level*' (quoted in *The Straits Times*, 1 October 1999; emphasis added). This conflict of partners' interest at the local level was clearly an institutional outcome of 'fiscal politics' in a shifting central–local relationship during an era of decentralisation and local autonomy in China (Naughton, 1995; Walder, 1995; Pearson,

1997; Oi, 1999). It also explains the rivalry between local states in China and foreign states/TNCs.

From Singapore's perspective, however, the township represented the first ever transfer of Singapore's economic management 'software' to another country. As evident in the high level of personal involvement by leading statesmen from Singapore, the Singapore government had staked its reputation and credibility on the CSSIP project. Comparing the CSSIP with the WSIP, my interviewee from the CSSD noted that:

> No. It is not even similar. Wuxi one [WSIP] is GLC-led [government-linked company] and a joint venture. There is no direct government involvement. In that sense, you know, you don't have to deal with the government. It is a pure commercial deal. Whatever decision is needed, the board of directors will settle. Here in CSSIP, whatever decision needs approval from not only the board, there is a wider perspective. In that sense it makes the project more complicated. (Interviewed in Suzhou, 3 July 1998)

Profitability, though an important objective, was not the most important concern (compared with the WSIP). Rather, it was the reputation and credibility of the Singapore government's track record in township development and management that had to be guarded at all costs.

> We are quite different from any other companies. I guess some things are quite sensitive because we are unlike any normal company. In the sense that your ultimate objective is to make profit and whatever means you use, it doesn't matter. So long as you do not cause embarrassment to the company. You can be above table, under table, back door, front door or whatever you can think of, but not for us. Number one we cannot embarrass the Singapore government... The [CSSIP] project represents the country [Singapore]. But the company [CSSD] doesn't. But yet people will associate the company with the country. (Interviewed in Suzhou, 3 July 1998)

The strict adherence to the Singapore government's guidelines has resulted in a very responsible and accountable institutional set-up in the CSSIP. For example, an article by China's official Xinhua News Agency in December 1998 noted that '[t]hrough strict laws and regulations, and drawing on Singapore's experience of honest and clean government, not a single civil servant in the [CSSIP] park's administrative committee has broken the law or committed a crime. This has earned the committee the high acclaim of the Central Commission for Discipline Inspection' (quoted in *The Straits Times*, 11 December 1998). The subtle and yet crucial difference in objectives accounted for major perception differences by the two parties, contributing to protracted conflicts and slow implementation of the project.

The second main problem confronting the CSSIP was *the complex involvement of different government authorities* at different spatial scales, further complicating the park's business development. My interviewee commented that:

> It is a complex thing. And here is not just the local government because it is between the two countries. So Beijing is involved. Jiangsu [provincial government] and Nanjing [provincial government] are involved. So people here are under microscopic examination. So you can imagine. When you are under microscopic examination, what do you do? Your behavior is different. Again it is no more like a private company and the local government kind of relationship [e.g. WSIP]. In that kind of business sense, I do whatever I can to please the local government and it will provide whatever to facilitate my business. (Interviewed in Suzhou, 3 July 1998)

Because so many levels of government (central, provincial, municipal, and district) were involved in the CSSIP, it became very difficult to please everybody and delay in the project implementation was inevitable (compared with the WSIP). Whereas the central government wanted to show its commitment to Singapore's kind offer of 'software transfer', local government authorities preferred to squeeze as much from the CSSIP project as possible in order to fulfil their capital accumulation objectives. One of the main sources of tension was the diversion of promotional efforts and resources of the Suzhou municipal government from the CSSIP to a rival industrial park, the Suzhou New District (SND). This was clearly perceived by the Singapore government as a sign of a lack of commitment by local Chinese partners. Interestingly, the SND had existed since 1989, long before the proposal to establish SIP in 1994. As a competitor of the SIP, the SND received land and infrastructure investments on special terms (*The Straits Times*, 7 April 1998). It was also given the same official status as the SIP by local authorities. This contrasts with the official instruction from President Jiang to Jiangsu's provincial party secretary and Suzhou's city mayor that the SIP is the 'top priority of all priorities' as a national and government-to-government project (*The Straits Times*, 10 March 1998).

The problem of the tussle between the central and provincial governments over the CSSIP is best captured in SM Lee's comment that '[w]hen dealing with the Chinese bureaucracy at middle and local levels, one needs not only patience but also determination, so as not to be deflected from an objective both sides have originally agreed upon at the Beijing level' (quoted in *The Straits Times*, 7 April 1998). The real problem here is that the Singapore side does not really know whether *local* Chinese partners shared the same objectives from the beginning of the project. My interviewee agreed that even by 1998, they still were not sure of the commitment of their *local* Chinese partners. In a recent interview, Singapore's Deputy Prime Minister, Lee Hsien Loong, admitted that 'we under-estimated the length of the chain of command between the centre and the locals, and the extent to which the locals have latitude' (*The Straits Times*, 10 July 1999). He said that if Singapore had known that local perspectives in China often prevail over those of the central government in Beijing, 'we might have made a different calculation'. Interestingly, two GLCs, Straits Steamship Land and Natsteel, experienced similar problems some six years ago with their S$25 million marine theme park project in Qingdao. Seven months after signing their memorandum of understanding with the Qingdao Tourism Bureau in early 1993, the two GLCs learnt that 'the Qingdao city authorities have approved two competing projects, contrary to the undertaking given to the Singapore parties that they have the exclusive rights to develop such a marine theme park in the city' (quoted in *The Straits Times*, 12 November 1993). The other project was led by Hong Kong interests and approved just prior to the construction of the Singapore project. The two GLCs therefore felt 'cheated' and decided to withdraw from the Qingdao venture. It is clear that the CSSIP project has *not* learnt from the experience of Straits Steamship Land and Natsteel.

Because of its significantly lower charges and favourable attention granted by the Suzhou government, the SND became a formidable competitor to the CSSIP. As late as March 1999, Singapore was still submitting a detailed proposal to the Chinese central government on how to resolve the outstanding conflicts in Suzhou (*The Straits Times*, 14 May 1999). By June 1999, it was clear that the Singapore government had lost faith in the commitment on the part of the Chinese and decided to complete only a portion of the SIP, leaving the rest of the project to its Chinese partners. Senior Minister Lee Kuan Yew openly declared that '[o]bviously we are not happy because we are not getting the kind of attention, which we were assured that we would get, special attention. Indeed, what we

> are getting now is competition. Having learnt how we are doing it, they can always duplicate it and offer it at a lower rate of land' (quoted in *The Straits Times*, 10 June 1999; 11 June 1999; 4 August 1999). The Singapore government's lack of understanding of the importance of local politics in China has led to a significant loss in both financial costs and international reputation. As of 1 August 1999, Singapore's statutory boards and government-linked companies invested some US$147 million in equity and loans. Other Singaporean companies also invested another US$65.5 million. An additional US$24.2 million investment in the SIP came from non-Singaporean TNCs in the Singapore consortium, CSSD.

from GLCs are therefore more likely to receive administrative guidance and advice from government agencies and statutory boards. Among the government agencies that are most active in supporting the regionalisation of GLCs, the Economic Development Board (EDB) and the Trade Development Board (TDB) are at the forefront.

The EDB provides both information on specific host country business environments, and investment grants to local companies in Singapore, including the GLCs. In fact, the Chairman of the EDB has been also the chairman of several GLCs and sits on the boards of several other GLCs. It is quite possible that these GLCs benefit from the personal insights and experience of the EDB Chairman. As one top executive from a GLC mentioned,

> We've been very lucky in [GLC name] by way of having [EDB Chairman] as the chairman. Because I think it is very important that the leader sets the example. The head man must show he is true to entrepreneurship and not be afraid to make decisions. If you've got a chairman who says everything in a memo, then that kills it. In that way, [he] has been over the past 5–6 years very gung-ho. We've been very much on our own. This is shown in the past four years that the group has expanded very much notwithstanding the debt we've incurred. But we've grown! (Interviewed in Singapore, 18 May 1998)

Because of its highly successful role in attracting inward investments into Singapore, the EDB has access to very high-level contacts with top global corporations and host country governments. It can help GLCs to open important doors. For example, a GLC was allowed to bid for a project in a highly sensitive and protected industry in the USA after the EDB had stepped in to give credits to the GLC as a leading company in that support industry in Singapore. According to its Vice President, 'EDB is often approached by big companies at very high levels and they would look at the companies' requirements and aspirations in the area. Wherever possible, we find that they [EDB] would try to channel the contact to us to see whether we are interested to pursue that jointly with them and they would facilitate meetings' (interviewed in Singapore, 3 August 1998).

In another GLC, its relationship with the EDB and the TDB has grown to the extent that both government agencies would consult the GLC for information related to the host country in which this GLC operates. This is the kind of trust relationship that is established between top civil servants in these two government agencies and the top executive of the GLC. As the senior vice president of the GLC noted, 'we have certainly had a lot of assistance from EDB and TDB in terms of where and how to invest overseas. At the same time now, such assistance has gradually been transformed into a symbiotic relationship whereby they will come to us and ask what is the situation in [a host country]' (interviewed in Singapore, 7 January 1999).

Third, the *strong reputation* of many leading GLCs in their respective industries has attracted a large number of potential 'suitors' who may be foreign or local enterprises. Many of the GLCs listed in Table 2.10 have billion dollar turnovers. Since most of them did not begin globalising their business operations until the late 1980s and the early 1990s, it is fair to assume that their domestic size and market position does help them in gaining recognition from potential foreign partners when they go abroad. This special 'GLC effect' in building entrepreneurial resources and access to foreign actor networks is *not* likely to be replicated among non-GLCs, with the exception of a very few large and financially powerful business groups (e.g. the Hong Leong Group in Chapter 4). Such is the case of at least two GLCs that have manufacturing operations abroad. Their foreign actor networks are developed on the basis of their strong reputation in the respective industries in which they have gained worldwide recognition. In the first case, the GLC has a group turnover of S$2.7 billion, a worldwide workforce of 19 000, and operations in 15 countries. One of its core businesses has five manufacturing operations in Asia that were established in the early 1990s. Recently, it entered into a minority joint venture with a South American company in the same industry. The GLC's strategy is that it will take a stake and always partner with a local company. According to a senior executive from the GLC,

> Because of our many years in the industry and our reputation, we are constantly solicited in all kinds of businesses. Through our government links, we are able to identify the potential ones. The [South American] company had been supplying us for the past decade before we decided to take a stake in it. There are lots of business links and they are complex. These partners often introduce us to different businesses and these contacts will begin to re-appear in our industrial division. You can say that the initial [core business] set-up has been transformed into other diversified business areas in the host countries. (Interviewed on 7 January 1999)

The second GLC has a very large turnover of S$5.4 billion, a worldwide workforce of 22000 people, and over 200 companies abroad. It has different modes of international business operations, ranging from greenfield investments to joint ventures with local partners and other GLCs. As its Director of Strategic Development explained, 'we are flexible. We can form partnerships with another statutory board or another GLC or private companies to go overseas or we can find partners overseas. [GLC] in the Asian region is quite established in terms of reputation and name. It is not too difficult to find partners' (interviewed in Singapore, 21 July 1998). Although it prefers to work with the bigger and more established companies abroad, the GLC also works with smaller companies because of their flexibility and entrepreneurial tendencies.

In some instances, the nature of the industry determines the ways in which foreign actor networks develop. In the telecommunications and airlines industry, there are two unique constraints that Singapore Telecom and Singapore Airlines have to face in their foreign ventures. First, many Asian host country regulations protect domestic telecommunications and airline companies, and require foreign firms to enter into joint ventures with local partners. Second, many incumbent telecommunications and airline companies in respective host countries tend to enjoy established market share in their home countries. They are therefore unlikely to enter into joint ventures with such foreign companies as Singapore Telecom or Singapore Airlines. These GLCs from Singapore therefore have to develop rather different foreign actor networks *vis-à-vis* unrelated partners that may not have much experience in the same industry as their Singapore partners. As the top executive of a GLC explained,

> unfortunately, my business is like that. Because in this business, you know you normally go there and compete against the incumbent. The incumbents are normally people who know. But there is little opportunity for you to invest in an incumbent because they know the business and they are probably as skilled as we are in terms of [core business]. The opportunity is working with people who are not in the industry to go in and compete with the incumbent. Since we don't have many dealings with people outside of the industry, then in most cases, the question is to know them just to do this special project. So we have to take the risk and you have to make a proper assessment that these people would be good long-term partners. (Interviewed in Singapore, 4 May 1998)

The reputation of GLCs in the domestic business scene in Singapore can also attract potential joint venture partners from Singapore. These partners can be other GLCs, as mentioned earlier, or non-GLCs. In fact, some of the GLCs listed in Table 2.10 continue to have significant involvement of private entrepreneurs in their management such that the Singapore government, through its holding company Temasek Holdings, remains a shareholder. In other cases, however, private transnational entrepreneurs, who have identified good investment opportunities and inter-group synergies, may approach a GLC to co-invest abroad in specific projects and/or ventures. For example, a GLC ventured into London's Canary Wharf project with a smaller property firm from Singapore that is owned and managed by a truly transnational entrepreneur. The opportunity came when the GLC was looking into investment opportunities in London and the transnational entrepreneur had already established some presence in London. When he asked the GLC to join hands, the partnership clicked instantly and a joint venture was formed to that effect. As the senior vice president of the GLC noted,

> I think in any industry, the industry circle is always very small. Once you are in the circle, everybody knows that this is what you want to do and this is where your interests are. This is because you have the brokers, you have the banks, and you have a lot of information flowing all over the place. Once you are in the market, everyone knows who wants to do what. So as far as the [London] project is concerned, it fits into what we wanted and people know that we are interested in this type of project. That's the first reason. Secondly, why [us]? I think the second question is partly an issue of chemistry and by and large, everyone wants to be friends with everybody else. So there's a lot of sharing, especially in property, where the investment amount is so big that nobody swallows everything by itself anyway . . . I think GLCs are always perceived to be stronger financially. So, I think that the combination with [the transnational entrepreneur] is quite interesting because you know, you have a smaller company but much more entrepreneurial. I mean if you look at their history and then you have [us], a steady partner. That kind of combination and we are much more structured and we are much more organised in the way we do things. I mean, there's a lot of synergy when you have two partners like this. (Interviewed in Singapore, 12 November 1998)

Moreover, many transnational intrapreneurs from GLCs felt that because of their reputation abroad, it was preferable to enter into ventures with foreign partners also of good reputation. As the senior vice president quoted above explained, 'if we want to go to Hong Kong, we are more likely to work with Cheung Kong and Sun Hung Kai [the two largest property developers in Hong Kong] than the individual guys. Although Cheung Kong is owned by the entrepreneur [Li Ka-shing], we are more likely to work with them than with somebody who happens to own 200 square feet of land' (interviewed in Singapore, 12 November 1998).

From the above analysis of qualitative case studies, it appears that GLCs in Singapore have formidable access to local and foreign actor networks that greatly facilitate their international business operations. One may argue that this access to actor networks abroad is embedded in institutional rather than personal interrelationships. In other words, there is no significant role played by transnational intrapreneurs in these GLCs to develop and find access to these actor networks because they are established at the institutional level. While this perspective has some validity, it fails to recognise the important role of individual transnational intrapreneurs in these GLCs in making key decisions to enrol into these actor networks and to engage in international business activities. It also fails to appreciate the importance of key transnational intrapreneurs who manage to resolve major problems confronting the international operations of these GLCs.

Transnational Intrapreneurs in Non-GLCs

What then is the access of transnational intrapreneurs from *non-GLCs* to foreign actor networks? As shown in Table 5.2, although all four non-GLCs are public listed on the Stock Exchange of Singapore, they are highly unlikely to enjoy the same access to foreign actor networks as their GLC counterparts. In particular, these transnational intrapreneurs have to rely very much on existing personal contacts or clients to develop foreign actor networks. They are unlikely to receive much help or direct introductions from government agencies such as the EDB or the TDB. In fact, the case of the Teck Wah Group shows that the contact with a town and village enterprise (TVE) in Wuxi, China, came from a Chinese employee who was then working in Teck Wah's parent company in Singapore (see Box 5.1). The lack of access to foreign actor networks explains why Teck Wah faced tremendous problems with operational matters and joint venture partners. This finding partially confirms the fact that transnational entrepreneurship is not so well developed among the two Chua brothers who are the successors to the patriarch of the family firm in Singapore. Instead, Mr Mah should be conceived of as a transnational intrapreneur who has helped to turn around the Wuxi factory to become a profitable venture. I will re-examine this case in the next section.

On the other hand, both CraftCorp and PackwayCorp seem to be relatively successful in gaining access to foreign actor networks through their existing or newly developed clientele networks. CraftCorp was originally established as a trader and manufacturer of paper-based stationery in 1978. It now has a 70 per cent market share in Australia, 40 per cent in the UK, and Walmart and Staples as its distributors in the USA. The success of CraftCorp is attributed to several factors. First, it set up a creative design and research facility in London immediately after it became publicly listed on the Stock Exchange of Singapore in 1994. This facility provides CraftCorp with highly creative, customised, and therefore competitive, products. Second, the current CEO, who joined CraftCorp right after its public listing in 1994, managed to persuade a famous British publisher to sell its brand name to be used in CraftCorp's paper-based stationery. Third, the CEO convinced two giant American retailers, Walmart and Staples, to distribute its paper-based stationery products in the USA.

In short, as described by its CEO, 'we fundamentally changed the nature of the company from being OEM [original equipment manufacturer] – you know the typical Asian company where you make it cheaper than the guy down the road. We've now changed to a design, publishing business, and a knowledge-based company. Where manufacturing is important, it's not the primary money and profit generator. Distribution is a key thing in developed economies. The cost [there] is very high and that's what the developed economies are all about' (interviewed in Singapore, 24 November 1998). This case shows that the key to CraftCorp's success in major markets in Australia, the USA, and the UK was related to its enrolment into global actor networks and commodity chains. In these networks and chains, major retailers in the USA and the UK are playing an increasingly important role (see Gereffi and Korzeniewicz, 1994; Gereffi, 1996; 1999). Its successful design facility in London further enables its products to have global appeal. Its current CEO should be credited for his entrepreneurial abilities in enrolling CraftCorp into these very important global actor networks.

Similarly, PackwayCorp's foreign actor networks are also driven predominantly by its major clients who are mostly global electronics manufacturers. PackwayCorp was established in 1969 to provide interior protective packaging services to major electronics TNCs. It has a group turnover of about S$60 million, and over 1000 employees worldwide. It has packaging operations in Indonesia, Malaysia, Thailand, and China. Its enrolment into the actor networks of these major electronics TNCs is facilitated by the strong supplier relationships developed in Singapore. PackwayCorp subsequently benefits from information about when its major clients are going to establish manufacturing operations elsewhere in the Asian region. As described by its Executive Director, 'if you want to be a dominant regional player, we must be there where the market is. So we have strategically figured out where the bulk of demand in the region is and the timing of all that is often coincidental with the set up of these big companies there. This is especially if we know them from here and so we can get the exact timing' (interviewed in Singapore, 24 April 1998). The Director and General Manager of the company's China facilities also echoed his views.

> We moved out of Singapore to Malaysia only to follow the major customers. We moved to Thailand on the same basis and we moved to China also on the same basis. Our major customers set up plants and we would just follow them. Usually in our business, they don't sign a contract with you. They just give you an indication: 'Hey, we are there. Would you like to come?' 'Ah, yes!'. That's how we get business. (Interviewed in China, 30 June 1998)

The director in China further explained that the referral business from Singapore accounts for at least 85 per cent of the company's total business in Shanghai and Suzhou. This case shows that its successful enrolment into the supplier networks of global corporations in Singapore has enabled PackwayCorp to establish its China operations.

TRANSNATIONAL INTRAPRENEURS FROM SINGAPORE AND THEIR ENTREPRENEURIAL ENDOWMENTS

The above case studies demonstrate that transnational intrapreneurs from both GLCs and non-GLCs are well-enrolled into selective foreign actor networks. Although the exact nature of their enrolment may differ in relation to the role of home country government support and information provision, these foreign actor networks tend to facilitate their international business operations. As explained in Figure 1.1, however, one has to raise some further questions concerning the role of entrepreneurial endowments and resources in preparing these transnational intrapreneurs to engage in international business activities. In Figure 1.1, five key dimensions of these endowments and resources have been conceptualised. This section probes further into the embeddedness of transnational intrapreneurs in these endowments and resources. Because of the vast amount of information from these case studies, the analysis will be brief and succinct.

First, it is obvious from Tables 5.1 and 5.2 that transnational intrapreneurs are capable of overcoming the problems of *information asymmetry* inherent in their international business operations. Among the GLCs analysed above, many have sought specific information from their contacts in government ministries and statutory boards (e.g. the EDB and the TDB) in Singapore. Because of their prior experience in the civil service or related businesses, they tend to develop some personal contacts with key actors abroad as well. This endowment enables transnational intrapreneurs from GLCs to operate quite successfully abroad. For example, as the senior vice president of one GLC described it, 'because everybody goes out, you have many more people to talk to. So if I talk to Temasek Holdings or Government Investment Corporation, or Singaporean companies for that matter, I've a lot of additional sources of information which I may not have if we are the only company going overseas' (interviewed in Singapore, 12 November 1998). Since most of the GLCs tend to be very large corporations, their transnational intrapreneurs tend to implement and follow established corporate procedure in their assessment of the viability of foreign projects. In more recent years, these GLCs have been operated in relatively more autonomous ways, particularly in their globalisation processes. As the Director of Strategic Development from one large GLC explained,

> We are a lot more business-oriented than we were 10 years ago. A lot of decisions are done very independently as against 15 years ago when it was still very much influenced by ministries and government officials. There are corporate guidelines, yes, and so different levels of decision making. If it's a big investment, you go to a certain level and if it's small, you just make your own decision. Some of these systems . . . sometimes it's not that you don't trust the person. More so because since it's a significant investment, you would like to have a few opinions of it before you finally make the decision. Information sharing or comments given can be very useful. And we actually tap a lot of external parties on the board to help us take a second and sometimes third look. (Interviewed in Singapore, 21 July 1998)

Among the non-GLCs, however, information about host countries often comes from existing clients in Singapore or personal contacts with business people abroad. They are unable to access the wide repertoire of information enjoyed by transnational intrapreneurs from most GLCs. For example, UnitedCorp in Table 5.2 is involved in a port city project in China that commenced operations in April 1997. According to its Group Managing Director (interviewed in Singapore, 4 August 1998), the project came about through personal contacts of the patriarch of the family firm. The patriarch happened to know someone who was offered the land in China to establish a manufacturing facility. But due to problems of importing raw materials, the other party decided to withdraw from the investment and offered the land to the patriarch of UnitedCorp.

Second, transnational intrapreneurs have to identify *business opportunities* and take *calculated risks* when they enter into foreign operations. There are, of course, major differences between transnational intrapreneurs from GLCs and those from non-GLCs. The former group of transnational intrapreneurs tends to be backed up by the immense financial and information strength of their GLCs. As mentioned earlier, they are also more likely to be approached by foreign partners and private or public companies from Singapore to engage in international business. Their business opportunities are more institutionalised because they are major GLCs and they have representatives from their holding company, Temasek Holdings, and other statutory boards involved in their boards of directors. While it is true that these transnational intrapreneurs have to take calculated risks, they tend to receive strong support from home and host country governments. For example, one large GLC encourages its senior executives to look for business opportunities on their own and put propositions to the board of directors for approval. The establishment of corporate procedures to govern investment decisions tends to safeguard against too much risk-taking behaviour by these executives of the GLC. As its Director of Strategic Development explained, 'if they went through company procedure, then chances are less likely. Quite often it is when people take risk, they overlook certain company procedures' (interviewed in Singapore 21 July 1998). Its CEO and President once commented that '[i]f the group is too full of mavericks, it will become anarchic. But if we have a flavour of the unusual, then we may see something which conventional wisdom would overlook. That is why we tolerate quirks all over the place, as long as the price is not the failure of the whole ship' (quoted in *The Straits Times*, issue withheld to maintain anonymity).

Of course, calculated risk-taking does matter in international business precisely because of the many unpredictable variables. But whether key executives in the GLC will take calculated risks in their foreign investments depends very much on the 'entrepreneurial climate' of the company. If established corporate procedures are too rigid and top-down, it is highly unlikely that individual executives will raise high-risk proposals for fear of retribution or adverse performance assessment. The top executive of one GLC, however, has managed to build a corporate culture that strongly encourages entrepreneurial behaviour among its key executives. Two particular examples are sufficient to show how this President of the GLC managed to build strong entrepreneurial endowments in his GLC. In the first case, the GLC has been involved in a China venture with other GLCs since 1981. After 15 years of operations, only one Deputy General Manager has been sent from the parent GLC in Singapore to manage the China operation. The President of the GLC gives this Deputy General Manager in China a lot of freedom and autonomy to manage the China operations, in association with the General Manager from the joint venture partners. As described by the Deputy General Manager in China, his main motivation to stay in China for 15 years is the autonomy given by his President in Singapore.

> I'll still attribute it to the freedom I'm given to run the company. And to job satisfaction and I don't think I would want to venture to work for anybody even though I'm leaving. That's enough. I think my boss is a really good boss. I think he has given me a lot of respect and a lot of freedom so I won't want to disturb him. There's that kind of mutual understanding that we have. I don't demand ... A lot of things I approve and I say 'just give me the forms', as long as you know you're doing these things for the sake of the company. I bought a vehicle worth about half a million renminbi [Chinese currency]. I don't have to go through a lot of procedures. That's the kind of base that we're going to in China. Of course we have the system here, a good financial system. I have a financial controller. A good financial system almost covers the loopholes where people can misappropriate funds. The pace of getting things approved is so fast that we can serve our customers well. (Interviewed in China, 12 June 1998)

On the other hand, however, too much risk-taking may be detrimental to corporate performance. The President of the GLC relates another example of how a maverick executive circumvented all corporate procedures and took excessive risks that cost the GLC S$8 million. This individual was transferred from a related company of the GLC and the President moved him to the Middle East. This person went into a joint venture in December one year when there was a slight lapse in management and many senior executives were on holidays. The President was on leave and the person circumvented the Acting President. As the President recalled, this person made a mistake in his judgement for two reasons. First, he did not understand the joint venture business well enough. Second, he lacked the guidance and advice of senior executives who had been in business long enough. Despite this failure in the joint venture and the loss to the GLC, the President did not fire this person for making a mistake.

> Some people say he ought to have been sacked, but I know from my heart that this man wanted to do the project. Don't forget that there were other business deals that he did put through which were successful. Unfortunately, he went for a S$1.5 million deal that costs us S$8 million. So, I think the only way to learn was to make mistakes. Unfortunately, the Singapore government is very unforgiving. I had the opportunity and I made mistakes with my previous boss and I learned from it. But in Singapore, it is very unforgiving. You make a mistake and you are condemned. I gave him that wonderful opportunity to start [again] and not many people have that. You must be able to see where you went wrong and learn to do a better job next time... I think he must have the passion. No point to fool me and say 'I am interested in something' and I know that you haven't done enough. (Interviewed in Singapore, 18 May 1998)

If we examine the case studies of non-GLCs in Table 5.2, it is interesting to observe that transnational intrapreneurs from these non-GLCs tend to be more cautious in their international operations. It may firstly be due to their relatively weaker financial position *vis-à-vis* the GLCs. For example, the Group Managing Director from UnitedCorp, a transnational intrapreneur himself, observed that 'like most entrepreneurs, you don't have all these [foreign investments] documented. I was quite surprised that a lot of these investments were made with entrepreneurial acumen [by the family patriarch], but there was not a lot of due diligence. That is not to say that I'm critical of the investments, but perhaps if more due diligence had been undertaken, some of the projects would have been viewed with a lot more caution' (interviewed in Singapore, 4 August 1998). Second, transnational intrapreneurs from many of these non-GLCs tend to engage in smaller and lower-risk operations in host countries. As shown in the case of Teck Wah's joint venture in Wuxi (see Box 5.1), it went into the venture because the local partner had already built a brand new factory and imported new machinery for printing jobs. In view of this commitment of fixed assets by local partners, it was thought that the investment carried not much risk.

Third, there is no doubt that transnational intrapreneurs from GLCs are very well endowed with *capital and financial resources*. Most of them are publicly listed on the Stock Exchange of Singapore. Their holding company, Temasek Holdings, is a giant corporate entity established in 1974 to manage formerly state-owned enterprises that have been privatised into GLCs today (see Chapter 2). Apart from having representatives on the board of directors of respective GLCs, Temasek Holdings also encourages GLCs to be competitive in their respective industries. Some top executives of these GLCs noted that as a rule, Temasek Holdings does not bail out failed GLCs. This implies that GLCs have to take risks and be accountable for their actions. An unintended consequence of this governance structure is that GLCs may enter into similar fields in Singapore and abroad, and compete fiercely against each other. As the Chairman of one GLC observed, 'some GLCs are more ambitious and therefore we may be competing alongside in the same business. There used to be a lot of competition between the GLCs, even until now. Even within the group, there is competition. It is more like two brothers chasing after the same girl, but it is not designed this way. It is done unconsciously. There are no directives from Temasek Holdings on what you can or cannot do' (interviewed in Singapore, 25 July 1998).

In addition, some of these GLCs have very strong footholds in specific industries and/or sectors in Singapore, for example, JTC International in industrial estates, Natsteel Ltd. in steel, Pidemco Land in property development, Singapore Telecom in telecommunications, and Singapore Technologies in semiconductors and engineering. According to theories of international business, this strong ownership-specific advantage based in the home country allows the GLC to internationalise successfully. One question, however, is whether this availability of finance and capital is fully exploited by entrepreneurial executives in these GLCs. It may well be argued that transnational intrapreneurs in these GLCs do not take many risks because they do not own the capital and financial resources. While this argument has some validity, transnational intrapreneurs in GLCs do have to take risks because of the sheer scale and diversity of their overseas investments. Sometimes, these transnational intrapreneurs have to confront the very institutional system that supports their GLCs. They are taking a personal risk to challenge the institutional system in Singapore. For example, one GLC managing director is frustrated by the conservatism of the ministry to which its parent statutory board belongs. While the GLC was making S$5–7 million profit abroad before the 1997/1998 Asian economic crisis, it suffered a loss of S$1–2 million in 1998. This immediately drew the attention of conservative bureaucrats from the ministry who questioned the viability of the GLC.

> But you must understand that the statutory board mindset and confining only to Singapore's experience does not lend themselves to doing international projects very well. As a statutory board, I think you can set a lot of rules and regulations. When you go overseas, you are actually working in other people's country and other people's regulations . . . You want me to build a company? You want me to be an entrepreneur? You want me to do something for the future? If you want, shut up about the $1–2m loss. Better still, help cover me by allowing me to do some of the consultancy work in Singapore. No, no, no, but that is a statutory board; we cannot be used to be private operation. Then allow me to make the $1–2m loss. No, no, no. You cannot make a loss. So the Singapore government, by the last 20 years of saying everything must break even, I think is causing this problem. And I'm not sure that the government actually means to cause this problem. It's just that down the line people are afraid to break this general rule. (Interviewed in Singapore, 13 August 1998)

While such conservatism can equally exist in the private sector among non-GLCs, one may argue that their deployment and manipulation of financial resources tends to be much more flexible and responsive to market and investment conditions. This flexibility and responsiveness is possible because these non-GLCs do not have to get clearance from different levels of governance and decision-making. Their boards of directors are the ultimate decision-making bodies able to endorse the proposals of transnational intrapreneurs in these companies. In a typical shareholder company (e.g. CraftCorp and PackwayCorp), the corporate governance is similar to Anglo-Saxon practice in which the CEO is responsible to the boards of directors who in turn are accountable to shareholders. Once the CEO gets board approval, he or she will be able to proceed with the proposed foreign investment. In a typical Chinese family firm (e.g. the Teck Wah Group and UnitedCorp), however, transnational intrapreneurs must have very strong personal relationships with the patriarch and other family members who are likely to be well represented on the boards of directors. In other words, whether a transnational intrapreneur from a Chinese family firm will succeed in securing capital and funding for foreign operations depends on the endorsement of a few selected members of the family. The relationship between this transnational intrapreneur and the family becomes highly important in determining his/her access to entrepreneurial resources. As such, it is quite possible that trusted professional managers can gain quick access to a large pool of family capital to execute international business ventures (see the case of HKToy in Box 4.2).

Finally, transnational intrapreneurs require strong *personal experience* and/or good *relationships with customers and suppliers*. It is almost inconceivable that a professional manager can become a transnational intrapreneur without these important endowments. For transnational intrapreneurs of GLCs, their previous experience in the civil service is important in helping them navigate the administrative system of the Singapore government and secure key resources for their international business operations. For example, the Managing Director of one GLC used to serve in the Singapore Armed Forces together with his current Chairman. The personal trust relationship between them is highly significant in the support that this Chairman renders him in international operations. The Managing Director also worked for a number of other public and private organisations before taking over the top post in the GLC. According to him, he learnt how to manage and operate in a big organisation through his eight years in the Armed Forces. He learnt legal skills and international business experience from his work with an international marine construction company. He also experienced business development and general management skills after working for an automobile distribution firm and a bank (interviewed in Singapore, 13 August 1998). The President of another GLC used to work for a private entrepreneur and the Economic Development Board of Singapore. He is therefore experienced in both entrepreneurial and bureaucratic institutions. As he recalled,

> So I got a balance of both worlds. Very institutional and bureaucratic organisation and, on the other extreme, shooting from the hip. And I put the two together and see how it balances out. So, a lot of my overseas operations, the general managers are quite free to run the operations they want. But when it comes to investments and when you need to pay some capital up, I'll get them to speak to me and talk to me. (Interviewed in Singapore, 18 May 1998)

On the other hand, transnational intrapreneurs from non-GLCs often have very strong experience in business and management. Since they are professional managers, they are required not only to be entrepreneurial in developing business opportunities in Singapore and abroad, but also experienced in managing their local and foreign operations. All four transnational intrapreneurs described in Table 5.2 have previous experience in professional management. In some cases (e.g. PackwayCorp and the Teck Wah Group), they possess strong skills in Chinese languages that are highly important in their abilities to communicate with their local joint venture partners in China. The Director of PackwayCorp's China operations remembered how his CEO in Singapore entrusted to him the task of managing in China.

> He realised that China's not the place to come. So the CEO at that time was chatting to me about China. And knowing that I'm a Chinese educated person, I speak good Chinese, so he was saying that, 'You think you have some interest there?' I said 'Why not? I always consider there'. That's how it got started. I had never come to China before I came to Shanghai. But I knew China very well

because I have been reading Chinese newspapers and magazines about China. Even back in 1986, when I was doing my MBA in the University of Southern California, we did an international marketing project for one of the companies in California. (Interviewed in China, 30 June 1998)

Some of these transnational intrapreneurs also rely on congenial relationships with their customers and suppliers in their international operations.

THE ROLE OF TRANSNATIONAL INTRAPRENEURS IN MANAGING ACROSS BORDERS

In their cross-border operations, transnational intrapreneurs are confronted with all kinds of problems. Some of these problems are similar to those experienced by transnational entrepreneurs. The capabilities and resourcefulness of transnational intrapreneurs in managing these problems abroad are the essential defining attributes of transnational entrepreneurship. A similar section in Chapter 4 has already explained in detail some generic problems faced by transnational entrepreneurs from Singapore (see also Table 4.8). This section aims to focus on three specific problems and illustrate how entrepreneurial tendencies in key transnational intrapreneurs help resolve these problems. More specifically, transnational intrapreneurs from GLCs and non-GLCs may face problems associated with (1) their embeddedness in the home country institutional environment; (2) their relations to the Singapore government; and (3) their manpower problems.

The first two problems are clearly more applicable to GLCs because of their predominance and peculiar institutional origins in Singapore. They can also be very serious because they can undermine the entrepreneurial efforts of transnational intrapreneurs from these GLCs. When GLCs venture abroad, they unavoidably come into contact with host country institutional structures that are very different from those in Singapore. As many of these GLCs are strongly *embedded in home country institutional structures and mindsets*, it is sometimes difficult for their top executives to adjust and adapt to host country conditions (cf. transnational entrepreneurs described in Chapter 4). As shown in the case of the Suzhou-Singapore Industrial Park (see Box 5.2), the Singapore government and its various GLCs have clearly underestimated the importance of local politics in China. The political process in Singapore is characterised by its undifferentiated scale politics (see Yeung, 1998d; 1999c; 2000h). There is virtually no difference between the national and the local scale in Singapore's political process because it is a city-state with a long-standing domination of the Peoples' Action Party (PAP) in national–local politics (see Chapter 2). Because Singapore is a city-state in its own right, both the national and the urban/local scales are juxtaposed to explain Singapore's political economy. In other words, what happens to Singapore as a nation is also applicable to Singapore as a locality or city (Yeung and Olds, 1998). This undifferentiated scale politics also allows the PAP state to engage in developmentalism to legitimise its existence. The Singapore state is highly successful in operationalising developmentalism at the national scale. When they engage in cross-border investments, the state and its affiliated companies (GLCs) find it difficult to understand the rescaling of political economy in host countries (e.g. China). This results in a mismatch of scale politics in the context of Singapore's government-led investments in China.

Even ventures strongly supported by the Singapore government, in particular those ventures by GLCs, may not necessarily lead to immediate success in China because of the significant influence of local politics and Singapore's failure to understand the relatively recent rescaling of China's political economy. Some of these ventures have also received top priority mandates from China's central government (cf. earlier studies of foreign firms in China; Shenkar, 1990; Yan and Gray, 1994; Walsh et al., 1999). The existence of local politics reveals one of the main difficulties confronting joint ventures of foreign firms in China – the different objectives of local partners. Many foreign partners hold a *long-term* view of their joint ventures in China. To them, entering into joint ventures in China is more than just a statutory requirement. Very often, they view joint ventures as facilitating their access to Chinese markets and securing location-specific resources. Their local Chinese partners, however, may have different objectives that are primarily *short term*. For example, Child (1994) noted that Chinese managers are often motivated to seek specific local advantages, such as greater managerial autonomy, higher salaries, and operating privileges. They also have a strong interest in achieving short-term profits because profitable projects bring tax revenues and prestige to the local municipality, city, or village. These attitudes and behaviour on the part of the Chinese local partners are an institutional outcome of restructured central–local politics. Consequently, there are significant differences in the business and production objectives of Chinese partners and foreign firms (see another example of an automobile joint venture in Aiello, 1991).

Transnational intrapreneurs from some GLCs are able to pre-empt these potential problems if they appreciate peculiar host country institutional structures and manage to disembed from government influence in their foreign operations. For example, another infrastructural project in Wuxi, China, led by one GLC is much more successful than the Suzhou-Singapore Industrial Park because of the alignment of mutual interests and interdependence between the Singapore and the Chinese partners in the project. Located at the economic heart of Jiangsu Province in China (see Figure 5.1), the Wuxi-Singapore Industrial Park (WSIP) offers good infrastructure facilities and an ideal environment for high-tech manufacturing. According to a senior executive from the WSIP (interviewed in Wuxi, 29 June 1998), the WSIP had already completed Phase I of development in 1998, equivalent to 10 per cent of the 1000 hectare master plan. Phase II was almost completed, with another 131 hectares of factory space. The occupancy rate was about 70 per cent with at least 35 foreign firms, many of which are such leading TNCs as Siemens, Seagate, National/Panasonic, Sumitomo Electric, KEC, ALPS, and so on. This was considered good performance in the midst of the 1998/1999 Asian economic crisis.

According to my interviewee, the success of the WSIP has been attributed to two factors. First, Singapore's strong track record in the efficient building and operating of industrial parks (see Rodan, 1989; Low, 1998), that is, the 'Singapore label', proved to be a strong brand name when foreign firms chose specific industrial parks for their manufacturing operations. My interviewee believed that '[h]aving the Singapore presence is a plus point. A number of tenants are here because this park has the Singapore image. This is the main reason why they preferred to come here. They believed in Singapore's management and we've developed it here'. Second and more importantly, the role of the Singapore government in the WSIP has gradually reduced over time. This proved to be very useful in allowing the WSIP management to develop flexibly their full commercial capabilities and to match their interests with those of local governments and business partners.

One key dimension of this relative autonomy and independence from the Singapore government is that it allows the local partner of the WSIP, the Wuxi municipal government, to benefit fully from the joint venture. Instead of viewing the WSIP as a top-down venture agreed at the Singapore–Beijing level, the Wuxi municipal government has been fully supportive in the initial conception and the subsequent implementation of the industrial park project. Because of the absence of vested interests in similar infrastructural projects in the Wuxi municipality at the beginning of the WSIP, the local partner has taken the project seriously and given the WSIP management a lot of support and autonomy. To the local partner, the success of the WSIP will bring in both financial rewards and symbolic prestige. In financial terms, the WSIP venture can be an important source of revenue for the Wuxi municipal government in an era of decentralisation and economic reform. In symbolic terms, the success of the WSIP will further enhance the political position of Wuxi cadres at the levels of provincial and central governments. This mutual satisfaction is an important dimension of the good performance by the WSIP.

The second major problem confronting transnational intrapreneurs from GLCs is that these companies are often seen as part of the Singapore state apparatus. This poses a significant problem for GLCs operating in countries that have strong nationalistic feelings. In other words, GLCs may face *nationalism* and its negative repercussions in the host countries because of their relations to the Singapore government. For example, Singapore Telecom's recent failed attempt to acquire a controlling stake in Hong Kong's incumbent telecommunications company, Cable & Wireless HKT, from its parent company based in London is a good case in point (see Box 5.3). As explained earlier, Singapore Telecom tends to face more problems in international business ventures because of the protected nature of the industry. Its ownership link with the Singapore government makes its foreign ventures even more conspicuous, in particular to the host countries (see also *Asiaweek*, 24 March 2000: 44–6). The alleged intervention of the Hong Kong SAR government in the deal to enable the success of a private entrepreneur from Hong Kong, Richard Li, in his acquisition of Cable & Wireless HKT is highly instructive. The intervention is widely seen as an expression of China's concern about the possibility that Hong Kong's telecommunications industry may be dominated by its rival in Singapore. It may be argued that Cable & Wireless HKT would have been successfully acquired by Singapore Telecom if the latter company had not been linked to the Singapore government. Contrary to the earlier analysis of GLCs' privileged access to entrepreneurial endowments, this case shows that such access and privilege can be as much an asset as a liability in international business activities. The Director of Strategic Development of another GLC also confirmed such an experience with foreign nationalism.

> Let's say you go to Malaysia and you say you are [GLC's name], they won't want to do anything with you! If you go to China, they still think that government connections are important. Being a Singapore body would be disadvantageous because they [the Malaysian government] don't like to do business with the Singapore government. I think in Malaysia, they are very aware of us. They envy what we can do. But it's because of the political inclination that makes it a little awkward. I mean if we tender for Malaysian government contracts, most likely we will be disqualified. (Interviewed in Singapore, 21 July 1998)

However thorny this problem is, some transnational intrapreneurs are capable of resolving it by engaging in certain 'creative solutions'. For example, one GLC went into London's Canary Wharf project with a transnational entrepreneur from Singapore. This partnership enabled the project to be recognised in the UK as a regular foreign investment project that does not compromise national concerns.

Third, most transnational intrapreneurs from GLCs and non-GLCs are

BOX 5.3 SINGAPORE TELECOM: TRANSNATIONAL ENTREPRENEURSHIP IN A GOVERNMENT-LINKED COMPANY

One of the hottest corporate manoeuvres among three global cities in recent years was the merger bid involving Singapore's Singapore Telecom (SingTel), Hong Kong's Cable & Wireless HKT (C&W HKT), which is 54.4 per cent owned by Cable & Wireless Plc based in London, and Hong Kong's Pacific Century CyberWorks Ltd (CyberWorks). SingTel is a former telecommunications monopoly in Singapore. Despite its privatisation in the mid-1990s, SingTel is still 76 per cent owned by the Singapore government's official holding company, Temasek Holdings (*The Straits Times*, 15 February 2000: 68). Its CEO and President, 42-year-old Lee Hsien Yang, is the second son of Singapore's former Prime Minister and current Senior Minister Lee Kuan Yew. His elder brother, Lee Hsien Loong, is currently Deputy Prime Minister of Singapore and has been named by Prime Minister Goh Chok Tong as his successor in the near future. In a very similar kinship way, CyberWorks is founded and run by the 33-year-old Richard Li, the second son of Hong Kong's most famous Chinese multi-billionaire Li Ka-shing. However, as a 10-month-old internet set-up, CyberWorks certainly has no specific ownership and control relationships with the Hong Kong government or the Chinese government. It only wants to set its sights on becoming the largest internet company in Asia. So much for the suitors.

The 'prey' – C&W HKT – has more than 100 years of experience in providing telecommunications services in Hong Kong. It was a colonial monopoly set up by the British giant, Cable & Wireless Plc. It was being ditched by its parent company in London because Cable & Wireless Plc wanted to refocus on the internet and corporate data segments in Europe and to sell off all its 'non-core' assets in Asia. While the merger talks started between SingTel and Cable & Wireless Plc in November 1999 and a deal was almost sealed in early February 2000, CyberWorks surprised the industry by announcing plans to merge with C&W HKT on 11 February 2000. A merger bidding war was initiated. By 29 February 2000, the verdict was out. The board of directors of Cable & Wireless Plc held a meeting in London on 28 February 2000 and CyberWorks got the deal to take over their 54.4 per cent of the C&W HKT shares (*The Straits Times*, 29 February 2000).

This story has a key message for understanding the problems confronting the globalisation of government-linked companies from Singapore. The Singapore government had denied any political motives in the deal, and sent a high-level official delegation to Hong Kong to explain this to Chief Executive Tung Chee Hwa and his senior government officials (*The Straits Times*, 4 February 2000). The dissociation of the Singapore government from the merger talks, however, was not convincing, particularly given the ownership and management links between SingTel and the Singapore government. The now failed merger between SingTel and C&W HKT illustrates the determination and capabilities of Singapore, a global city-state, in reaching out to other global cities and/or regions. It also underscores the role of the developmental state in driving Singapore's global reach (see Chapter 3). On the other hand, Singapore's global reach does not always go smoothly without counter-resistance in the host cities and/or countries. On 13 and 14 February 2000, both the Hong Kong and Chinese governments denied reports that they were trying to influence the outcome of merger talks between SingTel and C&W HKT for 'political reasons'.

Given the close personal links between Li Ka-shing, father of CyberWorks' Richard Li, and the highest level of authority in China, it is hard to believe that China did not intervene in the merger process. In fact, the Beijing-controlled newspaper *Wenhui Daily* reported on 13 February 2000 that China had 'indirectly expressed its disapproval' of the merger between SingTel and C&W HKT. This intervention from China did not come as a surprise for several reasons (*The Straits Times*, 28 February 2000: 56–7). First, a successful merger between SingTel and C&W HKT would give Singapore a significant stake in one of Hong Kong's oldest and most respected companies. Second, there was fear that Hong Kong's position as a key regional telecommunications hub would be diminished, given the intense rivalry between the two global city-states. In this regard, Singapore has recently further liberalised its telecommunications industry to welcome global competition (*The Straits Times*, 22 January 2000). Third, China Telecom, the state monopoly in China, holds a 10 per cent indirect stake in C&W HKT. It would clearly like someone closer to Beijing to take over C&W HKT, rather than a rival government-linked company from Singapore.

confronted with *severe manpower problems*. They have great difficulties in identifying and sending entrepreneurial managers abroad to run their foreign operations. This problem is of course not unique to Singaporean firms; it is indeed a common problem faced by global corporations. It may be argued, however, that given Singapore's pre-existing configurations of institutional structures, as described in Chapters 2 and 3, the problem may be aggravated by the nearly full employment status of Singapore's labour markets. Professional managers in Singapore also seem to lack any strong personal desire to venture abroad and to become transnational intrapreneurs who make or break foreign ventures. As the Chief Operating Officer of a large GLC explained, 'the biggest problem that we face today is still very much with us. That is the problem of sending our people overseas, people with children overseas because they have a big problem with the education system there [in Singapore]' (interviewed in Singapore, 4 May 1998). This relative lack of interest in engaging in international business activities may be explained by the hierarchical governance structures of most large corporations, particularly GLCs and statutory boards. As the case of Teck Wah Paper in Wuxi shows, a transnational intrapreneur can exist in a traditional Chinese family firm. He was able to perform his entrepreneurial duties very well and resolved major operational problems confronting Teck Wah's Wuxi operation. In fact, some of the interviewees from GLCs and non-GLCs went to the extent of arguing that they should send their best managers to manage international business operations, both in Singapore and abroad.

In another example cited earlier, the Deputy General Manager of a GLC spent 15 years managing a joint venture in China and making it work. His initiative to take on the job in China was motivated very much by his desire to gain exposure to managing across borders and to achieve autonomy in professional management. As he recalled, 'I knew for sure that when the door is opened for China, the world will be there. A lot of investments would be done in China. I felt that if I can expose myself in China, it'd do me good and gain further development. Not many people were experienced in China at that time [in 1984] and I felt it was good to act as a pioneer especially when one is young' (interviewed in China, 12 June 1998). Although the Singapore consortium has since been making steady profits from its US$20 million investment, the joint venture has also generated some problems over its 15 years of existence. In dealing with human resource management, a generic problem confronting all foreign joint ventures in China, this transnational intrapreneur is highly experienced. Instead of applying the standard management methods practised in Singapore, he adapts his management mindset to the Chinese context and thereby successfully avoids major misunderstanding.

I seldom say to my local Chinese 'hey, we in Singapore, we do this way'. I just tell them how things are done, but I've never compared it with them. That's very important. You must respect them and their country. You can tell them that this could be a better way to do it. What you've done is not wrong, but this is a better way. You explain to them why so, and the implications behind and they will take it. If you compare, you'll get confrontations. They'll go out of your office unconvinced and they will wonder. It's probably because Singapore is so small, but China is so big! Why must they follow you? (Interviewed in China, 12 June 1998)

More importantly, he understands management in China and is able to communicate directly with his Chinese partners and staff. As he reasoned, 'You're the general manager of the company and you don't get the feel of talking to your staff. That's a sin. I can talk to my manager and I can feel whether he has something on his mind, whether he's talking sense or whether he's with you. Then you've to start asking what's wrong. Then you can empathise with his problems and the next few days you deal with him softly. Then they're appreciative. It's a tough job' (interviewed in China, 12 June 1998). These good qualities in transnational intrapreneurs, however, are not found in many professional managers in Singapore. Most top executives from GLCs and non-GLCs in the survey have complained about the lack of entrepreneurial managers who can be sent abroad to manage their foreign operations (see also Willis and Yeoh, 1998; Yeung, 1999b; Yeoh et al., 2000).

CONCLUSION

The qualitative findings presented in this chapter clearly show that transnational intrapreneurs are highly important to the success of international business operations. In their embodiment of transnational entrepreneurship, these professional managers are empowered and entrusted by their shareholders and/or ultimate owners to engage in and manage foreign operations. Although they are not owners of the companies themselves, transnational intrapreneurs have privileged access to specific foreign actor networks to facilitate the establishment of their foreign operations. Their endowment in entrepreneurial resources also allows them to overcome information asymmetry, initiate and capitalise on business opportunities, deploy substantial financial resources, benefit from personal experience, and develop further customer and supplier relationships. Their entrepreneurial attributes are also critical in enabling them to resolve key problems associated with managing across borders.

Not all professional managers, however, can become transnational intrapreneurs. This chapter has shown that there are major differences between transnational intrapreneurs from GLCs and non-GLCs in Singapore. The former group of transnational intrapreneurs tends to be well endowed in entrepreneurial resources, whereas the latter group has to rely on a limited pool of these entrepreneurial resources. Moreover, home and host country institutional structures may significantly shape the formation and activation of these entrepreneurial tendencies *embodied* in transnational intrapreneurs. The peculiar institutional structures in Singapore explain why transnational intrapreneurs, while enjoying good entrepreneurial endowments and resources, tend to find it more difficult to operate within the ownership and governance structures of GLCs. As shown in various case studies, transnational intrapreneurs in GLCs must take exceptional initiatives to gain operational autonomy and to make entrepreneurial decisions. Among non-GLCs, however, transnational intrapreneurs tend to be able to stand on their own terms and operate flexibly to accomplish their missions in international business. But they are much less well endowed *vis-à-vis* their counterparts from GLCs.

On the other hand, host country conditions can shape the activation of transnational entrepreneurship among these intrapreneurs. In other words, whether these professional managers are really transnational intrapreneurs depends significantly on their abilities to develop and manage international business activities. As explained in Chapter 1, international business activities are primarily about resolving the inherent problems of operating in 'foreign' business environments and institutional conditions. The capacity of specific professional managers to overcome these problems of international business operations enables them to become successful transnational intrapreneurs. What then are the policy implications of this study for developing transnational entrepreneurship? These are the key issues to be addressed in the final chapter.

6. Conclusion: developing entrepreneurship in international business

> Changes in the rules and other attendant circumstances can, of course, modify the composition of the class of entrepreneurs and can also alter its size ... But if what is required is the adjustment of rules of the game to induce a more felicitous allocation of entrepreneurial resources, then the policymaker's task is less formidable, and it is certainly not hopeless. The prevailing rules that affect the allocation of entrepreneurial activity can be observed, described, and, with luck, modified and improved. (William Baumol, 1990: 894)

ENTREPRENEURSHIP AND THE INTERNATIONALISATION OF ASIAN FIRMS: A SUMMARY

In Chapter 1, three analytical questions are raised to set the research agenda of this book. These questions concerned the rationales, mechanisms, and successes of cross-border operations by transnational entrepreneurs and/or intrapreneurs. These questions emanate from an institutional perspective on entrepreneurship in international business. This institutional perspective argues that significant variations in the institutional structures of home countries explain variations in the entrepreneurial endowments and resources of prospective transnational entrepreneurs and intrapreneurs. These structures also form and enforce conventions, values, views, norms, practices, and 'rules of the game' to shape the logic governing economic decision-making and actions, and market processes. Once embedded in these institutional structures, transnational entrepreneurs and/or intrapreneurs have differential abilities and access to make use of their entrepreneurial endowments and resources for international business activities. Home country institutional structures and business systems significantly shape these endowments and resources. Moreover, whether specific transnational entrepreneurs and/or intrapreneurs succeed in establishing themselves in foreign markets depends on their enrolment into transnational actor networks. These networks and relations tend to span national boundaries and different business systems. They are therefore not peculiar to specific home countries and business systems, and provide specific mechanisms to enable international business operations by transnational entrepreneurs and intrapreneurs.

To accomplish this task of understanding entrepreneurship in international business, I have chosen for empirical analysis two Asian city-states with similar historical and geographical contexts, but very different developmental outcomes – Hong Kong and Singapore. In Chapter 2, I have compared the key institutional features of economic development in both Hong Kong and Singapore. I have shown that they have indeed very different dominant forms of economic organisation in relation to business organisations, industrial structures, labour organisations, and capital markets. These institutional differences are an outcome of the differential role of the state and entrepreneurship in driving economic development. Whereas Hong Kong's post-war economic development can be largely explained by neoliberal laissez-faire economic ideologies that favour the role of private entrepreneurship in economic development, Singapore seems to have taken a significantly different pathway to economic development. In particular, Singapore's developmental state has taken over the primary responsibility for economic development from private entrepreneurs. The state has therefore become a public entrepreneur in its own right and invited global corporations to locate their production facilities in Singapore. Put in their different historical contexts, the two city-states have evolved into very different business systems in which pre-existing configurations of institutional structures have differential impacts on entrepreneurial activities. Transnational entrepreneurs and/or intrapreneurs in both city-states therefore enjoy differential access to entrepreneurial endowments and resources.

These institutional differences in home country business systems are directly translated into quantitative and qualitative differences in outward investments and transnational corporations from Hong Kong (HKTNCs) and Singapore (SINTNCs). In Chapter 3, I have drawn upon extensive primary and secondary data to show that outward investments from Hong Kong tend to have a longer history and geographical reach, compared with those from Singapore. This may be explained by the state-directed preoccupation with nation building and domestic economic development in Singapore. There is either insufficient encouragement for outward investments from Singapore or a lack of transnational entrepreneurship to take business across borders. Indeed, both economies have developed very different external presences. In the case of Hong Kong, the domestic economy is dominated by small and medium enterprises (SMEs) in most industries and sectors. When these vibrant and entrepreneurial SMEs grow into large firms, they begin to internationalise their operations into Asia and beyond. There is thus a natural process of conversion from private and domestic entrepreneurship to transnational entrepreneurship when these entrepreneurs and intrapreneurs tap into their entrepreneurial endowments and resources.

This process, however, is less evident in Singapore where the state has taken a lead in domestic economic development, mainly via the establishment of government-linked companies (GLCs). These GLCs were known as state-owned enterprises before major privatisation initiatives took place in the late 1980s and the early 1990s. The dominant role of GLCs (and global corporations) in Singapore's domestic economy has had two consequences. First, they account for a large proportion of outward investments from Singapore. Second, private entrepreneurs from Singapore have to look for new markets elsewhere for their products and/or services. Their relative lack of access to entrepreneurial endowments and resources in Singapore has effectively forced them to engage in international business activities. These private entrepreneurs do not progress naturally from domestic to transnational entrepreneurs. Instead, they have reluctantly become transnational entrepreneurs because of limited business opportunities in their home country. In fact, most respondents in the survey of 204 transnational corporations from Singapore have chosen market-related motives as the most important set of reasons to explain the establishment of their foreign operations. Many private-sector SINTNCs in the sample felt that business and commercial laws in Singapore tend to favour bigger companies, i.e. GLCs and foreign firms. Due to these laws, financial institutions and capital markets in Singapore also tend to favour big companies in their lending policies. This phenomenon disadvantages the global reach of SMEs from Singapore.

Given the peculiar constraints faced by entrepreneurs from Singapore, how then do they operate successfully across borders to become truly transnational entrepreneurs? This issue has been fully taken up in Chapter 4, which examines how transnational entrepreneurs engage in international business. Drawing upon extensive survey data, I have shown that there are indeed statistically significant differences between transnational entrepreneurs and non-transnational entrepreneurs in terms of their key attributes, the influence of institutional structures, and their mechanisms of foreign market entry. Transnational entrepreneurs are found to have strong vision, abilities to take risks, and abilities to capitalise on opportunities. They are also more familiar with certain host country business environments in Asia and elsewhere. Through analysis of qualitative case studies, I have demonstrated that successful transnational entrepreneurs are often well endowed with the entrepreneurial resources outlined in Chapter 1. In particular, they are able to overcome the problems of information asymmetry and high risks through their enrolment into foreign actor networks. Through these actor networks, transnational entrepreneurs are also able to tap into host country business opportunities swiftly, and to deploy good pools of capital and finance. Many of these transnational entrepreneurs are highly experienced in business and management, and enjoy strong relationships with their customers and/or suppliers. Their entrepreneurial tendencies are best demonstrated when they have to resolve thorny operating problems in the host countries. They not only have to draw upon their entrepreneurial endowments and resources, but also need to enrol into strategic actor networks to enhance and strengthen further these endowments and resources.

While recognising the primary role of individual entrepreneurs in driving transnational entrepreneurship, however, entrepreneurship in international business is surely about more than just transnational entrepreneurs. It is also concerned with professional managers who have taken exceptional initiatives to ensure the successful establishment and management of international business operations. These transnational intrapreneurs and their exceptionally entrepreneurial activities are analysed in Chapter 5. Following closely the analytical format in the earlier chapter, I have examined the role played by these transnational intrapreneurs in the global reach of GLCs and non-GLCs from Singapore. The institutional perspective on transnational entrepreneurship is again highly relevant here because these two groups of TNCs have differential embeddedness in home country institutional structures. Transnational intrapreneurs from GLCs and non-GLCs therefore are subject to opportunities and constraints from different internal management practices, competitive pressures in the home market, parent–subsidiary relationships, firm–state relations, and interaction with host country firms and governments.

Drawing upon detailed qualitative case studies, I have shown that transnational intrapreneurs from GLCs tend to enjoy privileged access to information about host countries through government agencies and statutory boards in their home country. They are more likely to be able to assess accurately foreign risks and opportunities. They also have better access to finance and capital, and stronger relationships with customers and suppliers. Enjoying these competitive advantages, GLCs are theoretically better positioned than non-GLCs to perform well in international business ventures. The reality, however, does not necessarily correspond to our theoretical postulations because of the inherent constraints faced by transnational intrapreneurs from GLCs. In fact, precisely because of their historical and ownership links to the Singapore government, GLCs may face problems of nationalism and extra institutional constraints in the host countries. Successful transnational intrapreneurs from these GLCs are able to appreciate peculiar host country institutional structures and manage to disembed from the home country state's influence on their foreign operations.

Transnational intrapreneurs from non-GLCs, on the other hand, do not face the institutional constraints peculiar to GLCs in the host countries. Similar to transnational entrepreneurs analysed in Chapter 4, their major disadvantage in international business operations is related to the limited access to entrepreneurial endowments and resources. My analysis of qualitative case studies has revealed that transnational intrapreneurs from non-GLCs are in fact suffering from a lack of access to finance and capital, and the problem of manpower. These problems are related to the study of corporate intrapreneurship and subsidiary initiatives reviewed in Chapter 1. For corporate intrapreneurship to thrive, transnational intrapreneurs must be given not only strong mandates and management autonomy, but also strong financial and manpower support by their parent companies and/or home countries.

The separate, yet interrelated, analysis of transnational entrepreneurship in relation to transnational entrepreneurs and intrapreneurs in Chapters 4 and 5 implies that there are observable differences between these two groups of international business actors. This final chapter aims to draw together some common threads from these analyses, and proposes some policy implications for business and government. While many scholars of entrepreneurship argue that entrepreneurship is inborn and cannot be taught, there are still important lessons to be learnt from the analysis presented in this book. In today's globalising era, many countries and companies are particularly interested in developing entrepreneurship in their people and/or managers in order to compete effectively in the global economy. More specifically, I argue that there are significant differences in the nature and attributes of transnational entrepreneurship between entrepreneurs (owners) and intrapreneurs (managers). Put in the institutional perspective outlined in Chapter 1, these differences are significantly shaped by peculiar home and home business systems. The differences between transnational entrepreneurs and intrapreneurs are therefore highly relevant for our understanding of the underlying factors that condition their entrepreneurial tendencies. Although we cannot be very precise in comparing and explaining their differences, we can at least draw some important implications for policy and research purposes.

The following section compares and contrasts the key findings of this study on transnational entrepreneurs and intrapreneurs. It also explains these findings in relation to different factors and conditions, in particular institutional influences. Some general lessons for developing entrepreneurship in international business are then offered. The final section examines the policy implications for developing transnational entrepreneurship in Asian business.

A COMPARATIVE INSTITUTIONAL ANALYSIS OF TRANSNATIONAL ENTREPRENEURSHIP

Differences in Transnational Entrepreneurship: Entrepreneurs vs. Intrapreneurs

The analyses in Chapters 4 and 5 have been conducted on the assumption that there are significant differences in the access and deployment of entrepreneurial endowments between transnational entrepreneurs and intrapreneurs. This subsection summarises these differences (see Table 6.1) and the next subsection attempts to provide some explanations of such differences. In the first place, transnational entrepreneurs and intrapreneurs are enrolled into *foreign actor networks* through different mechanisms and networks. Whereas transnational entrepreneurs tend to attach greater significance to the role of personal and family networks, transnational intrapreneurs tend to ride on established corporate/client relationships and their strong reputation in order to enrol foreign actors into their international business operations. Institutional introduction, for example via the Economic Development Board of Singapore, also plays some role in the enrolment of transnational intrapreneurs from Singapore into foreign actor networks.

The role of personal networks and experience in overcoming the problem of *information asymmetry* is also highly significant. Most transnational entrepreneurs depend on personal networks established through many years of business and family experience and, in some cases, host country partners to secure information about potential operations in host countries. Very often, they have to visit the prospective host countries regularly to establish their repertoire of information and to gain first-hand understanding of host country operations. Their corporate counterparts in government-linked companies (GLCs) and non-GLCs, however, rely on established procedures to gain access to information about foreign operations. These professional managers are not entrepreneurial because they do not have first-hand information about business opportunities in foreign countries. For example, in the case of a GLC having problems with its local partners in China who have not fulfilled their agreements in the joint venture contract, the General Manager pointed out painstakingly that 'my boss keeps telling me, we must go down to that level. That was what we agreed on. But I know if we do that, this is not like Singapore. If it's another [similar project] in Singapore, you can do that. But this is not Singapore. You can't do that. This is the problem with commanders who sit in [GLC] pushing toy tanks and generals who're fighting the war in the field. The generals and all these; they all fall out with commanders who push toy tanks

Table 6.1 Comparison of transnational entrepreneurs and transnational intrapreneurs

Category	Transnational Entrepreneurs	Transnational Intrapreneurs
Foreign actor networks	• strong personal relationships • family business and linkages	• corporate/client relationships • reputation of established business • introduction from third party institutions
Information asymmetry	• personal networks • past experience • host country partners	• help from established subsidiaries and other institutions (e.g. government agencies) • client networks
Risks and opportunities	• high risks • quick decisions and deployment of resources • personalised business opportunities	• risk minimisation strategy • assessment through established corporate procedures • joint or consensual decision-making • tapping into client networks
Finance and capital	• severe constraints from home and host country banks • reliance on local partners • reliance on personal or family networks • some successful public listing	• strong support from parent companies • mostly listed in the stock exchanges • little dependence on host country partners or personal networks
Experience in business & management	• significant personal experience in business • more hands-on approach to international operations • more centralisation of authority	• mostly corporate management experience • more delegation of authority • more professional management practices
Customer and supplier relationships	• strong personal contacts • personal marketing practices • secured business in some cases	• established brand names and/or client networks • dedicated marketing units or departments • strong home country market shares

256

Conclusion: developing entrepreneurship in international business 257

in [headquarters]' (interviewed in Singapore, 24 July 1998). Those truly transnational intrapreneurs, however, are able to benefit from strong client networks built on the basis of inter-firm linkages. In some cases (e.g. GLCs), transnational intrapreneurs have privileged access to information collected and processed by home government agencies.

In relation to these different situations of information asymmetry and corporate procedures, there are important differences in their attitudes to *risk and business opportunities* (cf. Ray, 1994; Teoh and Foo, 1997). Transnational entrepreneurs take a highly personalised approach to business development and risk-taking. As owners of capital, they are more likely to exercise authoritative control and make quick decisions. They are also able to deploy personal and corporate resources in a speedy manner. For example, Kwek Leng Beng in Box 4.1 was able to tap into a vast network of personal, family, and market resources to acquire the London-based Millennium & Copthorne Hotels via his public listed vehicle in Hong Kong – CDL Hotels International. In making important decisions to acquire or to establish foreign operations, transnational entrepreneurs have to take significant risks that may result in the loss of their business fortunes in the event of major failures. Although such negative outcomes of high risk-taking are not reported in this book, one may still find some evidence in the case studies of ChemicalCorp and PaperCorp (see Table 4.6). These companies withdrew, respectively, their Thai and China operations after unsuccessful co-operation with the French joint venture partner in Thailand and increasing risks in the host country environment in China. On the other hand, transnational intrapreneurs tend to pursue a risk-minimisation strategy and assess their foreign projects through established corporate procedures. They are also likely to engage in joint or consensual decision-making in order to tap into the wider information pool of other top executives in the companies. In some cases, they consult their vast networks of clients and local subsidiaries in order to reduce the risks of international business activities and to develop new business opportunities in the host countries.

To a certain extent, the different risk-taking behaviour of transnational entrepreneurs and intrapreneurs is influenced by their access to *finance and capital*. With a few exceptions (e.g. Kwek Leng Beng), most transnational entrepreneurs in this study tend to suffer from severe constraints if they borrow from home country financial institutions. They are even more unlikely to secure financing from host country financial institutions. As a consequence, these transnational entrepreneurs have to rely on their local or foreign partners and their personal and family networks for finance. While some of them are successful in gaining access to home country capital markets, most transnational entrepreneurs are unable to gain, or actually prefer to stay away from, public listing because of perceived constraints imposed on their entrepreneurial behaviour by public shareholders. These constraints in capital and finance essentially imply that transnational entrepreneurs are in fact highly risk-taking precisely because they have to maximise their returns from limited financial resources. Transnational intrapreneurs, nevertheless, are much less constrained by financial resources. On the contrary, they receive strong support from parent companies (e.g. Temasek Holdings) or their companies are public companies listed on the Stock Exchange of Singapore. They also depend less on host country partners or personal networks for financial resources. One may argue that these transnational intrapreneurs incur much less risk when they engage in international business activities.

The extent of transnational entrepreneurship between the two groups of transnational actors, of course, depends significantly on their *experience in business and management*. From the analyses presented in Chapters 4 and 5, transnational entrepreneurs and intrapreneurs both appear to be highly experienced in business and management. The notable difference between them, however, is that transnational entrepreneurs tend to have more *personalised* experience in international business activities. They are more likely to take a hands-on approach to their international operations. But they are also likely to manage their own businesses through the centralisation of authority and control. In contrast, transnational intrapreneurs have mostly corporate management experience. Their likely lack of personalised experience in cross-border operations implies that they have to delegate more control and authority to managers in the parent companies and in their foreign subsidiaries. These managers abroad are often granted specific mandates to operate local subsidiaries. This parent–subsidiary relationship has been termed 'dispersed corporate entrepreneurship' by Birkinshaw (1997; 2000).

Finally, transnational entrepreneurs and intrapreneurs also differ in their *relationships with customers and/or suppliers*. As transnational entrepreneurs are less endowed with financial and corporate resources, they need to develop strong personal relationships with their customers and/or suppliers. Sometimes, they have to establish foreign operations to serve major customers in the host countries. This 'personal touch' in market development gives transnational entrepreneurs an advantage in competing with established corporations because of their flexibility and responsiveness. In certain sectors (e.g. property development and consultancy services), personal relationships with customers are highly important in international business development. In comparison, transnational intrapreneurs enjoy established brand name and/or client networks. Their companies often have dedicated units or departments to take care of relationships with customers and/or suppliers. These transnational intrapreneurs can therefore focus their atten-

Conclusion: developing entrepreneurship in international business 259

tion on such strategic issues as the formation and management of international business operations. In some cases, transnational intrapreneurs from GLCs ride on the strong home country market shares of their companies. These home market positions contribute to ownership-specific advantages that in turn enable the success of companies' cross-border operations.

Accounting for Differences in Transnational Entrepreneurship

How then do we explain these differences in transnational entrepreneurship? To answer this question, we have to revert to the various perspectives in entrepreneurship studies (see Chapter 1). It appears that three key factors are particularly relevant in explaining why transnational entrepreneurs differ from their counterparts from the corporate sector. First, *personal and psychological factors* clearly account for some of the major differences in transnational entrepreneurship. Although both groups of individuals favour autonomy and adventure, it may be argued that transnational entrepreneurs are significantly more risk-taking than transnational intrapreneurs. This may be related to the personal experience of individual transnational entrepreneurs. Some have been born into business families and are therefore unlikely to want to work for corporations. Indeed, most transnational entrepreneurs described in Table 4.6 are either founders themselves or second-generation offspring of founding entrepreneurs.

On the other hand, most transnational intrapreneurs have been working in government-related ministries and statutory boards, or in private-sector corporations. They have been professional managers virtually throughout their careers. Indeed, almost no transnational intrapreneurs in my study had previous experience of setting up their own businesses. On the other hand, most transnational entrepreneurs who founded their own companies would have worked for other corporations previously. A tentative conclusion is that transnational entrepreneurs are not only born with certain entrepreneurial tendencies (those from family businesses), they can also acquire such tendencies through their experience (those founding new companies). A related conclusion is that transnational *intra*preneurs do not remain professional managers forever. They may indeed venture into their own businesses eventually to become truly transnational *entre*preneurs.

Second, the nature of their *access to entrepreneurial resources* plays an equally important role in shaping the entrepreneurial behaviour of transnational entrepreneurs and intrapreneurs. A successful transnational entrepreneur requires not only risk-taking abilities, but also significant resources to exploit those abilities across borders. In fact, many of the transnational entrepreneurs in Chapter 4 managed to draw upon a wide repertoire of entrepreneurial endowments and resources before they were able to engage in international business activities. To cite just one example (see Box 4.1), without the strong financial position of his family business, Kwek Leng Beng may not have been able to realise his entrepreneurial potential. Under his father's personal tutelage, Kwek has not only learnt the key secrets of property development and hotel investments, but also developed strong personal and business networks with financiers in Singapore and in global financial markets (see also the case of Eu Yan Sang in Box 4.4). A transnational entrepreneur cannot succeed by trial-and-error methods. Those that do succeed on the basis of these methods are lucky, but they are not really entrepreneurial. Truly transnational entrepreneurs must be experienced, and able to take calculated risks based on certain 'gut feelings' and specific business opportunities.

Access to entrepreneurial resources is equally important for transnational intrapreneurs. This is particularly the case for transnational intrapreneurs from GLCs in Singapore who are well endowed with the financial resources of GLCs and the Singapore government. Some respondents in the survey have argued that the best way to test the entrepreneurial tendencies of those top executives in GLCs is to ask them to co-invest their own capital with that from GLCs. In this way, the top executives of GLCs will have to be more risk-taking in their investment behaviour. This in turn will change their management strategy from risk-minimisation to calculated risk-taking. Having said that, however, it is equally true that some top executives from GLCs are entrepreneurial in their international business behaviour. Indeed, they are able to exploit their resource endowments in those GLCs to globalise their business operations. Through their entrepreneurial decisions, these top GLC executives are able to generate good returns for their shareholders, including both Temasek Holdings and the general public in Singapore.

Third and perhaps most significantly, a businessperson born with entrepreneurial tendencies is unlikely to become a truly transnational entrepreneur (or transnational intrapreneur for that matter) if the home country business system does not favour such entrepreneurial tendencies. As conceptualised in Chapter 1, the pre-existing configurations of *institutional structures* in this business system are critical in shaping the ways in which entrepreneurial tendencies in a businessperson can be realised. My analyses in both Chapters 4 and 5 show that significant institutional differences between different business systems account for the inherent problems of international business activities. Businesspersons who are unable to grapple with these differences are likely to fail in their international business ventures (e.g. the Suzhou-Singapore Industrial Park project and Teck Wah Paper in Wuxi). The entrepreneurial culture of specific business systems also explains why businesspersons from some home countries are more entrepreneurial (see also Tiessen, 1997; Daly, 1998). In Chapter 4, I have described the entrepreneurial culture of the Chinese business system that prevails in certain sectors in Singapore and Hong Kong. This entrepreneurial culture is strongly embedded in the peculiar institutional structures and business systems of home countries. As a kind of 'atmosphere' in a typical Marshallian sense (Marshall, 1961), entrepreneurial culture is a key driving force behind the success of transnational entrepreneurs from Chinese family business. It also explains why many of the transnational entrepreneurs in Table 4.6 are owners of Chinese family firms.

The same institutional explanation can be applied to the understanding of the entrepreneurial behaviour of transnational intrapreneurs. While it is true that top executives in most GLCs have very privileged access to entrepreneurial resources and thereby should be more entrepreneurial in their international business behaviour, the fact remains that only a selected number of them become truly transnational intrapreneurs. This phenomenon of 'selective adaptation' occurs because only a few of these top executives are able to break out of the 'institutional entrapment' that can be defined as the constraints on mindset and behaviour imposed by bureaucratic and institutional peculiarities in Singapore. These emerging transnational intrapreneurs are able to adapt their personal entrepreneurial attributes to such bureaucratic organisations as giant GLCs, thereby transforming their business and organisational practices. Revisiting an example in Chapter 5, the President of one GLC was able to save a manager from being fired for making a loss of S$8 million in the Middle East. This is inconceivable in most GLCs where failure is not tolerated. But the GLC's President was able to justify his decision that this maverick manager should be given another chance for taking risks and being entrepreneurial.

The above analysis demonstrates not only that there are important differences between transnational entrepreneurs and intrapreneurs in their international business endowments and behaviour, but also that these differences can be accounted for by three interrelated factors: personal attributes, access to resources, and institutional structures. In the next two sections, I consider some lessons and policy implications of these findings for engaging in international business activities.

LESSONS FOR DEVELOPING ENTREPRENEURSHIP IN INTERNATIONAL BUSINESS

Why Bother with Transnational Entrepreneurship?

This book has so far implicitly assumed that entrepreneurship plays a positive role in economic development and international business activities (see also McDougall and Oviatt, 2000). Before determining any lessons for developing entrepreneurship in international business, it is perhaps important to ask a fundamental question: is entrepreneurship necessarily a good thing? While not engaging in a 'glorification' of transnational entrepreneurs or intrapreneurs *per se*, I argue that it is important to develop and promote the process of entrepreneurship itself. To do so, we need to go beyond Schumpeter (1934) and Leibenstein (1966), who saw entrepreneurs as merely fulfilling some pre-determined functions in economy and society:

> It may, therefore, not be superfluous to point out that our analysis of the role of the entrepreneur does not involve any 'glorification' of the type, as some readers of the first edition of this book seemed to think. We do hold that entrepreneurs *have* an economic function as distinguished from, say, robbers. But we neither style every entrepreneur a genius or a benefactor to humanity, nor do we wish to express any opinion about the comparative merits of the social organisation in which he plays his role, or about the question whether what he does could not be effected more cheaply or efficiently in other ways. (Schumpeter, 1934: 90; original emphasis).

Strangely enough, we do not need to glorify transnational entrepreneurs and intrapreneurs as geniuses for them to play an important role in economy and society. This is particularly the case in an era of accelerated globalisation and global competition during which cross-border operations by transnational entrepreneurs and intrapreneurs are increasingly common in the global marketplace. In his historical context, while recognising the dynamic role of entrepreneurs in economic development, Schumpeter (1934) ironically took a functionalist view of these entrepreneurs and overlooked their other important contributions to society.

We also need to go beyond thinking of entrepreneurs as necessarily constructive in economy and society (cf. Baumol, 1990; 1993). The institutional perspective in this book demonstrates that entrepreneurship varies in time and place. In other words, a business system pre-configured with certain institutional features and structures can significantly stimulate or inhibit the outburst of entrepreneurship, domestically and internationally. This structural influence is itself shaped by broader processes beyond specific national territories. These broader processes are peculiar to different historical episodes in contemporary capitalism. There is thus a time period to each significant outburst of entrepreneurship because entrepreneurial endowments and/or resources are highly dependent on the interaction between institutional structures in business systems (place-specific) and the formation of global actor networks by transnational entrepreneurs or intrapreneurs (time-specific).

For established businesses, it is perhaps more important to focus on growing transnational intrapreneurship because professional management and corporatised procedures in these corporations leaves little room for entrepreneurial activities by individual managers. To Duncan et al. (1988: 17), corporate intrapreneurship is seen as 'a pain in the neck' for two reasons. First, it disrupts the established order when intrapreneurs keep 'asking questions and experimenting with new ways of doing things when well established procedures are available to provide direction' (Duncan et al., 1988: 17–18). This tendency is important in challenging the corporation to seek new directions and strategic reorientation to compete effectively in the global economy. Some case studies in Chapter 5 have shown that transnational intrapreneurs are not mere followers of corporate procedures and directives from above. They are also capable to inventing new rules within the transnational corporation, provided that they have strong support from the top management and access to entrepreneurial resources. Granted support and resources, transnational intrapreneurs can make a significant contribution to the success of international business operations.

Second, there is a need to reinvent the corporation to provide a better context for developing intrapreneurship. Duncan et al. (1988: 18) argued that '[t]he person who is capable of intrapreneuring is as rare as the type of business it takes to nurture him or her. If this rare breed is to procreate, a genuine reinvention of the corporation is not merely desirable; it is essential'. An entrepreneurial corporation cannot remain static for too long. The intrapreneur is almost as entrepreneurial as the corporation itself. In other words, while corporate intrapreneurship is desirable, it is more important to provide an appropriate corporate context in which such entrepreneurial tendencies thrive. One specific way to do so is to build certain institutional structures within an economy and inside a corporation to enhance the outburst of such entrepreneurial tendencies.

Building Institutions for Developing Transnational Entrepreneurship

If entrepreneurship is inherently good for the economy and society, it opens up another question in relation to its time- and place-specificity. Schumpeter (1934: 78) argued that the time- and place-specificity of entrepreneurship implies that entrepreneurs cannot be a lasting class of their own. In his later work, Schumpeter (1942: 132–3) commented that over time, the social function of the entrepreneur will lose importance because of the routinisation of innovations and the bureaucratisation of economic change in the hands of large corporations. Schumpeter's pessimistic assessment of entrepreneurship in the age of giant corporations perhaps underestimates the importance of the very essence of entrepreneurship itself – making differences. Since entrepreneurship is a spur of human individuality to do things *differently*, it will always remain important in economy and society. There are always entrepreneurs who want to explore new and different ways of doing business (e.g. international business). There are thus always important policy implications for developing entrepreneurship. This is precisely the point overlooked by Schumpeter because of his premature closure of the subject of developing entrepreneurship.

In the field of economics, Baumol (1968: 71) also argued that '[w]ithout awaiting a change in the entrepreneurial drive exhibited in our society, we can try to learn how one can stimulate the volume and intensity of entrepreneurial activity, thus making the most of what is permitted by current mores and attitudes'. Some 20 years later, Baumol (1990) recognised the policy silence of Schumpeter's analysis of entrepreneurship, and extended Schumpeter's analysis by arguing that it is possible to nurture such a class of social actors by reconfiguring the institutional structures in which they are embedded. Similarly, Van de Ven (1995: 48; emphasis omitted) argued that '[a]n infrastructure for entrepreneurship does not emerge by a few discrete events involving a few key enterpreneurs. Instead, it emerges through the accretion of numerous institutions, resources, and proprietary events involving many entrepreneurs located in the public and private sectors over an extended period of time.'

While entrepreneurship may be stimulated through institution building at the level of the economy itself, intrapreneurship can be developed by specific initiatives within the corporation. First, early work by Burgelman (1983; 1984) and Duncan et al. (1988) suggests that strategic context analysis can be carried out within corporations to uncover the obstacles to corporate intrapreneurship. In the context of developing transnational entrepreneurship, it may be argued that such an analysis should be extended to the international business context within transnational corporations (see Birkinshaw, 2000). For example, it is important for top management in major corporations to recognise the strategic importance of international business units/divisions, and to devise specific corporate structures to enhance the development of entrepreneurial tendencies in those units and divisions. In one of the GLCs in the survey, the President attempted to promote transnational entrepreneurship among its top managers by ensuring that those with successful international business experience were almost always promoted faster and rewarded handsomely. The President was also trying to develop an incentive system that rewards these transnational intrapreneurs by allowing them to be minority shareholders of foreign subsidiaries (interviewed in Singapore, 18 May 1998).

Second, other general policy suggestions include 'intracapital', a form of capital that is derived from the added net income from intrapreneurs' contributions. Duncan et al. (1988: 18) suggested that some portion of this intracapital should be reserved to support intrapreneurs' future creativity. There are also suggestions for increasing intensity in certain strategic management practices, e.g. scanning intensity, planning flexibility, and employee participation in planning. For example, Barringer and Bluedorn (1999: 436) studied the relationships between entrepreneurial intensity and five strategic management practices (scanning intensity, planning flexibility, planning horizon, locus of planning, and control attributes). They concluded that 'the fundamental practice of scanning the environment to recognize opportunities and threats should be a principal concern of entrepreneurially minded firms'. Hisrich (1990: 217–19) suggested a series of other programmes to enhance entrepreneurship and intrapreneurship.

POLICY IMPLICATIONS FOR TRANSNATIONAL ENTREPRENEURSHIP IN ASIAN BUSINESS

Theoretically informed social science often has a natural distaste for policy prescriptions. This problem is particularly important to the field of (transnational) entrepreneurship because, as argued above, entrepreneurial tendencies cannot be imparted and can only be experienced. On this issue of the difficulties of describing and prescribing (transnational) entrepreneurship, Baumol (1993: 15) suggested that

> there is a sort of Heisenberg principle that holds for entrepreneurial acts. The very process of describing them can transmute pioneering entrepreneurial undertakings into routine managerial activities. The same problem, of course, besets the schools of business, which would like to be able to train at least some of their students in the ways of the entrepreneur, but which usually succeed in imparting only the skills of the manager. That is accomplishment enough, and certainly calls for no apology; for these schools, like any other entity, find it difficult to achieve the impossible.

In the context of the proposed institutional perspective on transnational entrepreneurship, however, it may be argued that certain policy initiatives can be enhanced for developing transnational entrepreneurship in global business. While we cannot prescribe policies to impart entrepreneurial tendencies to specific individuals, we can at least initiate changes to the business systems and pre-existing configurations of institutional structures to enable better access to entrepreneurial endowments and resources. This task is particularly critical in Asia in an era of globalisation and global competition (see Yeung, 2000b). In this final section, I consider five major policy implications of my empirical analysis for developing transnational entrepreneurship in Asian business: (1) access to capital; (2) internal management structures and processes; (3) transnational entrepreneurship and family control; (4) sources of dynamic competitive advantage; and (5) changing public policy in home countries.

Access to Capital

As evidenced by the recent 1997/1998 Asian economic crisis, sources of capital play a significant role in influencing how transnational entrepreneurs and/or intrapreneurs can meet the challenges of globalisation, both from local competitors and from globalising firms. It is clear that many transnational entrepreneurs and/or intrapreneurs in Asia have not only invested a lot in *network capital*, but that they have also become dependent on these networks and connections. For example, intra-corporate financial transactions and insider trading are often cited as the 'dark side' of Asian business (Backman, 1999). Many entrepreneurs and intrapreneurs in Asian firms have pursued aggressive expansionary programmes at the expense of minority shareholders in their public listed companies. Before the outbreak of the Asian economic crisis, this heavy dependence on networks and connections did not seem to matter much because everything remained rather rosy, and investors, including fund managers, in these Asian firms did not concern themselves with these irregular business practices. If these Asian entrepreneurs and intrapreneurs tapped into cross-border business networks and connections, it became even more difficult for minority investors to notice these irregularities. Many leading conglomerates from Southeast Asia, for example, managed to expand rapidly within two decades to become major regional competitors just before the Asian economic crisis. Their internationalisation processes were largely embedded in wider social and business networks at a regional scale (see Yeung, 1999d). Sound corporate governance across borders was not an issue. Rather, these transnational entrepreneurs were concerned with building up their transnational 'network capital' and expanding their operations in almost every industry in every other Asian country.

At the beginning of the twenty-first century, we have seen the powerful unfolding of the 1997/1998 Asian economic crisis and its negative impact on the social organisation of Asian capitalism in East and Southeast Asia. It is true that many firms investing heavily in those Asian economies with least corporate governance and business regulation standards tended to suffer most. This is primarily because many of these firms and their entrepreneurs relied on personal connections and political alliances with ruling elites to make their investment decisions. They often invested in host country companies on the basis of a potential windfall gain because of a licence or a monopoly right granted by their political 'allies'. This phenomenon is best seen in the case of the collapse of Peregrine Investment Holdings from Hong Kong in January 1998 because of a controversial unsecured 'bridge loan' granted to PT Steady Safe taxicab company in Indonesia with the personal blessing of ex-President Suharto's daughter (see Yeung, 1999e).

For researchers, it is therefore important to go beyond a study of how traditional entrepreneurs and/or intrapreneurs pool capital based on locally constituted social and business networks (e.g. bank financing). We need to examine how transnational entrepreneurs and/or intrapreneurs are tapping into capital markets outside their home countries. We need to know more about how they transfer their goodwill to other localities and how they embed themselves in business networks abroad. Empirical studies of how a top transnational entrepreneur from Hong Kong – Li Ka-shing – managed to transfer his goodwill to tap into local business networks in Vancouver are clearly a good starting point (see Mitchell, 1995; Olds, 1998; 2001; Mitchell and Olds, 2000).

For practitioners in Asian business, a change in attitude is required in order to embrace globalisation and international business successfully. Actors in Asian business need to go beyond a view of public listing on stock exchanges as a kind of 'vacuum cleaner' operation to absorb fresh capital from minority shareholders to fund their own private businesses (Backman, 1999). Increasingly, this kind of operation will no longer be welcome by well-informed investors in an information-intensive era. Rather, transnational entrepreneurs and/or intrapreneurs must see public listing as a learning experience through which they may gain a better understanding of and access to *global* capital markets. The case of CDL Hotels International in Chapter 4 has shown vividly how a transnational entrepreneur can grow his global business through strategic acquisitions and carefully tapping into global capital markets. In view of the fact that access to capital is perhaps the most important constraint on cross-border entrepreneurial activities (see Chapters 4 and 5), other transnational entrepreneurs and/or intrapreneurs must put this capital market learning into practice. This brings us to the next major policy implication.

Internal Management Structures and Processes

Globalising trust and credibility of transnational entrepreneurs and/or intrapreneurs requires a lot more attention to internal management structures and processes than would be the case in domestically-oriented Asian firms. To date, very few transnational entrepreneurs and/or intrapreneurs have tapped into global capital markets and gained the trust and favour of major investment houses based in global financial centres outside Asia.

This access requires significant improvement in corporate governance and the accounting transparency of Asian firms, implying that they need to drop their 'old habits' and develop modern management systems (see Yeung and Soh, 2000).

During the 1997/1998 Asian economic crisis, many Asian firms failed because they were so poorly managed that even cheap sale of their assets did not attract foreign investors. For example, the Zurich Group, which originally agreed to take a 24.1 per cent stake in Peregrine Investment Holdings in November 1997, had decided to pull out by January 1998 as the depth of Peregrine's problems became apparent (Yeung, 1999e: 18). Many of these ailing Asian firms were also family firms managed by entrepreneurs, though the phenomenon might not be exclusive to family businesses. Embracing globalisation and international business implies more than buying and selling assets in other countries beyond the home turf of transnational entrepreneurs and/or intrapreneurs. It is also about how they can manage these foreign assets and/or advantages better than their competitors.

Being a family business does not necessarily mean that it cannot be professionalised. Indeed, there are no inherent limits to the growth and professionalisation of family business (see Yeung, 2000f). For researchers of Asian business, the challenge is to identify the best management practices that can contribute to successful international business operations by these once highly patriarchal firms. We must also situate these best practices in their social and institutional contexts. For example, is a professional CEO always a good thing for Asian family firms run by entrepreneurial patriarchs (see the case of UnitedCorp in Chapter 5)? Must capable family members participate in business? How much separation between ownership and management is required?

For practitioners in Asian business, one crucial implication to be reckoned with is that engaging in international business requires much more streamlined operations and management than the kind of 'corporate omelettes', defined as 'quite flat and with each of the constituent parts intermingled with the others' (Backman, 1999: 67). True enough, venturing abroad necessitates a lot more transnational entrepreneurship than domestic operations, as pointed out in Chapter 1. But this requirement for entrepreneurial decisions and insights does not negate the importance of professional management systems that must be put in place to ensure that any sustainable foreign ventures are workable. In this sense, I agree with Backman's (1999: 79) assessment that 'in the era of the global marketplace, cultural idiosyncrasies belong anywhere but in the boardroom. Ramshackle corporate structures and patriarchal management might be quaint, but they come at an enormous cost'.

Transnational Entrepreneurship and Family Control

While transnational entrepreneurship seems to be a highly positive and desirable attribute for international business success, it should not be forgotten that a highly entrepreneurial individual tends to assume too much control and to take risks without due diligence. If the bottom line turns out to be fine, the transnational entrepreneur's judgement will not be questioned. This is particularly so if he/she owns much of the company. As the Asian economic crisis has demonstrated, however, rogue decisions can lead to significant corporate disasters that culminate in serious losses by minority shareholders. Poor bankruptcy laws in some Asian countries mean that the majority shareholders (who are most likely the CEOs) may get away with their wrong decisions. Events such as these have happened not because minority shareholders and/or professional managers did not object to the majority shareholder's 'entrepreneurial' decisions, but rather because there was simply no way for them to control the irrational and stubborn behaviour of the patriarch.

One lesson that we should learn from the crisis is that many Asian firms need to professionalise their management systems and corporate governance. This is easier said than done because one may argue that the very existence of Asian family firms is to provide for *the family*. But surely there is a big difference between providing for the family and managing a huge conglomerate with diverse business interests in different regions and countries. While simple ownership of shares would satisfy the former requirement, it takes a long time to professionalise the management of a sound conglomerate.

While not advocating the separation of ownership and management as in the case of the emergence of American corporations and managerial capitalism (Chandler, 1977; 1990), I believe that any family firm today must have an explicit strategy for succession (see also Handler, 1994; Morris et al., 1996). By succession, I mean a clear system for promoting good intrapreneurs to senior executive positions on the basis of some rational criteria, even though kinship relations may be one key criterion. There are two options, either grooming family members (typically sons and nephews) to become successful transnational entrepreneurs, or socialising capable professional intrapreneurs into the 'family' and grooming them as future heirs to top management. On the first option, many family patriarchs send their children to be educated in top universities and business schools. They also get their children involved as interns in leading global corporations before they return to manage family businesses (Yeung, 2000b; 2000f; see also Magretta, 1998 for the case of Victor Fung from Li & Fung; and Olds, 1998; 2001 for the case of Victor Li from Cheung Kong Holdings). These new generation successors of Asian family business tend to gain better recognition among bankers, financiers, and analysts based in major global financial centres. In Chapter 4, I have already shown how the Hong Leong Group's late founder groomed his son, Kwek Leng Beng, to become a transnational entrepreneur in his own right. The case of fourth generation family members – Richard Eu and his cousins – in revitalising the family business of Eu Yan Sang is also instructive (see Box 4.4).

On the other hand, it is true that as a family business empire expands across regions and countries, the firm will eventually run out of family members. There is thus a strong need to develop a modern management system in order to identify significant entrepreneurial managers who can be delegated important management functions. An intrapreneurship programme is required in these Asian family firms so that they can survive beyond, for example, S.L. Wong's (1985; 1988) dilemma of three generations of Chinese family business (cf. Yeung, 2000g). In Chapter 5, I have shown how in the case of Teck Wah Paper, a trusted classmate can be a very useful transnational intrapreneur to assist in the internationalisation of the family business. Taken together, the successful professionalisation of management in Asian family firms not only enables them to gain better recognition from worldwide business communities, but also reduces the necessity for too much personal control by founders and patriarchs. In today's era of accelerated global competition, the Asian economic crisis may have been the last wake-up call for these family firms to reform themselves. Whether such reforms and transformations in Asian capitalism will enable it to survive the new millennium is quite another story, and one that depends largely on the dynamics of competitive advantage in the global economy.

Sources of Dynamic Competitive Advantage

The point of sustainability is important in understanding the dynamic competitive advantage of Asian firms. With globalisation, Asian firms must actively search for new sources of dynamic competitive advantage (cf. Mascarenhas et al., 1998). Many of these firms have grown from imperfect and relatively monopolistic domestic markets. Their entrepreneurs have often enjoyed tremendous advantages in these domestic markets because of their special connections and relationships with ruling politicians and/or key business elites. Special licences and monopoly rights have been granted to these entrepreneurs and these privileges have become their major 'cash cows'. When these entrepreneurs venture into foreign markets, the scenario is almost completely different. The field of competition becomes much more open and level; only the fittest and most competitive firms will survive. This tendency towards global competition was accentuated by the

Asian economic crisis. Many entrepreneurs and/or intrapreneurs from Asian firms not only lost premium monopolistic positions in their ailing domestic economies but, more importantly, they had to look beyond their home turf for the future growth and prosperity of the firms. In the context of growing global competition, we need to understand and cultivate the sources of dynamic competitive advantages for transnational entrepreneurs and/or intrapreneurs to establish themselves successfully in foreign markets. While most entrepreneurs and/or intrapreneurs are facing serious problems such as entry barriers and lack of competitiveness, others (e.g. Kwek Leng Beng in Chapter 4 and Pidemco Land in Chapter 5) have managed to penetrate the once-invincible markets in Europe and North America.

Changing Public Policies in Home Countries

If competition is increasingly operating at the regional and global scale, and Singapore companies must globalise to survive, what then are the implications of this study for public policies in Singapore? First, the *needs of entrepreneurial firms* must be further developed by appropriate government policies. As explained in Chapter 3, saturation of domestic markets in Singapore is a key driving force behind Singapore's global reach. This is especially the case for transnational entrepreneurs from Singapore. In their global reach, however, these transnational entrepreneurs may require significant assistance from the Singapore government to establish themselves successfully. Their needs result primarily from their relative lack of resources and/or capital to operate across borders. The government can play a role here by establishing institutional support to facilitate the global reach of Singapore's transnational entrepreneurs. This support can take the form of 'business incubators'. For example, Arcasia Land, a privatised spin-off from Jurong Town Corporation, has developed Gateway@SV in San Jose, California, capital of the Silicon Valley, to provide business space and services to aspiring transnational 'technopreneurs' from Singapore. Similar 'business incubators' can be set up in major technological centres of the world to support the global reach of technopreneurs from Singapore. In the commercial sector, the Singapore government can assist the establishment of chambers of commerce in selected strategic host countries to enhance the global networking capabilities of transnational entrepreneurs from Singapore.

In the midst of the 1997/1998 Asian economic crisis, Singapore's Trade Development Board (TDB) stepped up efforts to help Singapore companies venture beyond the Asian region (see Table 6.2). These Singaporean firms leveraged early-to-market entry advantages to establish a foothold in

Table 6.2 Activities by the Trade Development Board to promote Singapore's trade and investments outside Asia, 1993–1998

Host	Priority Markets	Activities
Africa	• tourism, manufacturing, infrastructure development and resource-mining industries • furniture trade with South Africa	• mission to western Africa in March 1998 • Business Opportunities Conference on Africa in November 1998
Central Asia	• Azerbaijan and Kazakhstan: political stability and no foreign exchange control • trading in foodstuffs, commodities, consumer electronics and household goods • real-estate boom: building material supplies, furniture and fixtures	• two infrastructure fairs in Azerbaijan in 1999 • taking part in Aspat 98 (food fair) and InterFood Kazakhstan in late 1998
Middle East	• United Arab Emirates: redistribution hub of the Middle East • Saudi Arabia: Singapore's biggest trading partner for the region • Lebanon: reconstruction and building materials industries • Iran and Turkey: sources for building materials	• several food, infrastructure and building materials missions planned
Central and Eastern Europe	• Russia: consumer electronics, food and beverages • Czech Republic, Hungary, Poland and Slovenia: electronics, food industry and property development • contract manufacturing and outsourcing for IT industry	• two trips to the Baltics since January 1998 • trade promotion with Russia and the European Union
Latin America	• Brazil, Argentina, Chile and Mexico: top trading partners with Singapore in the region • growing consumer markets: lower tariffs and privatisation	• 3 electronics missions to Mexico and two business seminars there since September 1997 • a multi-sectoral mission to Brazil, Argentina and Chile in April 1997: companies from consumer products, food and beverage, textile and timber sectors • two more missions to be held by end 1998

Source: Collated from *The Straits Times*, 8 August 1998: 17.

potential markets that were relatively untouched by the crisis (*The Straits Times*, 8 August 1998). To create the momentum, the TDB increased its grants from 30 per cent to 50 per cent for Singaporean companies to move into new markets. It undertook the common group expenses of trade missions and overseas fair participation. The TDB also helped companies contact the right authorities and business partners abroad.

Second, the government may need to *educate and finance transnational entrepreneurship* further. Since the mid-1990s, there has been a series of government-led drives to develop entrepreneurship and, lately, technopreneurship in Singapore. While these are clearly laudable projects, it remains to be seen how things as intangible as entrepreneurship and technopreneurship can be intentionally groomed. Insofar as foreign operations are concerned, this study has demonstrated that many transnational entrepreneurs from Singapore found business and commercial environments in the home country rather restrictive. Some of their foreign operations are *de facto* outcomes of this 'crowding out' effect where they felt helpless in a domestic economy dominated by GLCs and foreign transnational corporations. Having worked closely with Microsoft's founder, Paul Lovell, the managing director of Microsoft Singapore, responded to Senior Minister Lee Kuan Yew's observation that such entrepreneurs as Microsoft's Bill Gates are born, not made.

> Even if you think you can't make a Bill Gates, you could stop one. Bill Gates was born with a great deal of natural ability, but the lion's share of his success is what he did with it in an environment that offers opportunities and rewards personal effort and initiative . . . So the right environment is important. (Quoted in *The Straits Times*, 17 August 1996)

Singapore's Prime Minister, for example, also noted that 'we have to change our attitude towards entrepreneurs. Our society must be more tolerant of those who tried and failed. We may have to review bankruptcy laws to see how they can be more forgiving to those who failed in business and to give them a second chance' (quoted in *The Straits Times*, 3 February 1999).

As shown in this study, this inevitable orientation towards the global market among transnational entrepreneurs from Singapore can be turned into an opportunity for Singapore to prosper through developing a significant external economy. While many of these private companies are owned and managed by entrepreneurs, their transnational entrepreneurship cannot be taken for granted. Doing business in foreign lands is always more risky and uncertain than in the domestic economy. This need to cultivate and nurture transnational entrepreneurship has two further implications. We need to educate students and individuals better to appreciate the geographical complexity of a world in which venturing abroad is both exciting and risky. These aspects of transnational entrepreneurship need to be ingrained in students through a syllabus sensitive to the differences of the geographical world we live in. Furthermore, transnational entrepreneurs from Singapore cannot venture abroad without favourable financial and capital support. It is even more difficult for them to raise capital in host countries (see above). The government can help by relaxing financial regulations and providing direct financial assistance to aspiring transnational entrepreneurs who, if successful, will contribute significantly to Singapore's global reach.

Third, the *formation of business associations abroad* may enhance transnational entrepreneurship from Singapore. To globalise successfully, transnational entrepreneurs from the USA, Japan, and the UK (three top global direct investors) often organise their foreign operations through the formation of business associations and industry institutions abroad. These organisations help companies to overcome initial barriers to market entry, and to appreciate better the competitive and regulatory dynamics of host countries. As a relatively small economy, transnational entrepreneurs from Singapore cannot be expected to form similar kinds of business associations in all major markets abroad. But this economies-of-scale argument should not stop us from thinking about industry- or trade-specific organisations in selected host countries. For example, a Singapore chamber of commerce has been established in Hong Kong. It has been serving the commercial interests of Singapore companies in Hong Kong very well.

Last but not least, the *provision of social support* may be crucial to the development of transnational entrepreneurship in Singapore. Through various personal interviews with Singaporean transnational entrepreneurs in Hong Kong and China, I found that their main worry was not business *per se*, but rather their families, children's education, and future in Singapore. This is termed a 're-entry problem' because many of these Singaporeans abroad felt that upon returning home, their children might not fit into Singapore's education system and, for that matter, Singapore in general. Recently, the Singapore government has initiated a programme – Singapore 21 – to keep Singaporeans global in their orientation and local in their loyalty. In view of this initiative, it becomes imperative for the government to continue its provision of support for family and education of Singaporeans abroad (see also Willis and Yeoh, 1998; Kong, 1999; Yeoh and Willis, 1999; Yeoh et al., 2000). The government's effort to establish Singapore clubs and schools in Hong Kong and China, for example, should be highly commended. In tune with the government's drive towards Singapore's global reach, it is perhaps time to think more about such initiatives as social and family support of Singaporeans *outside* Asia. Japan, for example, has been quite successful in ensuring Japanese education for its citizens in Europe and North America. This process also helps Japanese abroad to internalise the Japanese culture.

CONCLUSION

This book has shown that there is indeed much to be learnt from the study of transnational entrepreneurship within an institutional perspective. It has also raised more questions than it can provide answers for. Setting the future research agenda in entrepreneurship and international business studies can be a rather difficult pursuit (see Cox et al., 1993; Brewer and Guisinger, 2000; Casson, 2000; McDougall and Oviatt, 2000). But what this book on entrepreneurship and the internationalisation of Asian firms has plainly demonstrated is that enrolment into foreign actor networks provides an important social and institutional mechanism for transnational entrepreneurs and intrapreneurs to engage in international business activities. Summing up their research agenda for strategic management, Gulati et al. (2000: 213) argued in a special issue of *Strategic Management Journal* that there is an 'enormous promise that lies in incorporating a deeper understanding of strategic networks into the mainstream of strategy research. The points of opportunity we have identified are but the tip of the iceberg. We believe there is much more to be learned by adopting such a relational perspective in strategy research'. Such a network-specific institutional analysis therefore promises to open up many new avenues for researchers in entrepreneurship and international business studies. It helps these researchers not only to be more aware of the wider social and institutional relations that govern firm-specific activities, but also to recognise that transnational actors have an important role to play in the formation, enrolment, and manipulation of these relations. Entrepreneurship in international business is clearly concerned with more than comparative entrepreneurship in different international contexts (cf. international entrepreneurship studies). More importantly, it is about why and how transnational actors (entrepreneurs and intrapreneurs) take exceptional risks and initiatives to overcome the immense difficulties inherent in operating and managing foreign business systems. The study of transnational entrepreneurship is only the beginning of an important intellectual endeavour to appreciate better the real world of international business *and* the people who make this world possible.

References

Aharoni, Yair (ed.) (1993), *Coalitions and Competition: The Globalization of Professional Business Services*, London: Routledge.

Aiello, Paul (1991), 'Building a joint venture in China: the case of Chrysler and the Beijing Jeep Corporation', *Journal of General Management*, Vol. 17(2), pp. 47–64.

Aldrich, Howard E. and Waldinger, Roger (1990), 'Ethnicity and entrepreneurship', *Annual Review of Sociology*, Vol. 16, pp. 111–35.

Amin, Ash and Thrift, Nigel (eds) (1994), *Globalization, Institutions, and Regional Development in Europe*, Oxford: Oxford University Press.

Amsden, Alice (1989), *Asia's Next Giant: South Korea and Late Industrialization*, New York: Oxford University Press.

Aoki, Masahiko (2001), *Towards a Comparative Institutional Analysis*, Cambridge, MA: MIT Press.

Appelbaum, Richard P. and Henderson, Jeffrey (eds) (1992), *States and Development in the Asian Pacific Rim*, Newbury Park, CA: Sage.

Asiaweek, 24 March 2000.

Au, Kevin, Peng, Mike W. and Wang, Denis (2000), 'Interlocking directorates, firm strategies, and performance in Hong Kong: towards a research agenda', *Asia Pacific Journal of Management*, Vol. 17(1), pp. 29–47.

Backman, Michael (1999), *Asian Eclipse: Exposing the Dark Side of Business in Asia*, Singapore: John Wiley.

Barringer, Bruce R. and Bluedorn, Allen C. (1999), 'The relationship between corporate entrepreneurship and strategic management', *Strategic Management Journal*, Vol. 20, pp. 421–44.

Baumol, William J. (1968), 'Entrepreneurship in economic theory', *American Economic Review*, Vol. 58(2), pp. 64–71.

Baumol, William J. (1990), 'Entrepreneurship: productive, unproductive, and destructive', *Journal of Political Economy*, Vol. 98(5), pp. 893–921.

Baumol, William J. (1993), *Entrepreneurship, Management, and the Structure of Payoffs*, Cambridge, MA: MIT Press.

Baumol, William J. (1995), 'Formal entrepreneurship theory in economics: existence and bounds', in Ivan Bull, Howard Thomas and Gary Willard (eds), *Entrepreneurship: Perspectives on Theory Building*, Oxford: Pergamon, pp. 17–33.

Beamish, Paul W. and Killing, J. Peter (eds) (1997), *Cooperative Strategies*, 3 volumes, San Francisco, CA: The New Lexington Press.
Berger, Suzanne and Dore, Ronald (eds) (1996), *National Diversity and Global Capitalism*, Ithaca, NY: Cornell University Press.
Berger, Suzanne and Lester, Richard K. (eds) (1997), *Made by Hong Kong*, Hong Kong: Oxford University Press.
Best, Michael H. (1990), *The New Competition: Institutions of Industrial Restructuring*, Cambridge: Polity Press.
Biggart, Nicole Woolsey and Guillén, Mauro F. (1999), 'Developing difference: social organization and the rise of the auto industries of South Korea, Taiwan, Spain, and Argentina', *American Sociological Review*, Vol. 64, pp. 722–47.
Birkinshaw, Julian M. (1997), 'Entrepreneurship in multinational corporations: the characteristics of subsidiary initiatives', *Strategic Management Journal*, Vol. 18(3), pp. 207–29.
Birkinshaw, Julian M. (2000), *Entrepreneurship in the Global Firm: Enterprise and Renewal*, London: Sage.
Birley, Sue (1985), 'The role of networks in the entrepreneurial process', *Journal of Business Venturing*, Vol. 1, pp. 107–17.
Birley, Sue and MacMillan, Ian C. (eds) (1995), *International Entrepreneurship*, London: Routledge.
Birley, Sue and MacMillan, Ian C. (eds) (1997), *Entrepreneurship in a Global Context*, London: Routledge.
Björkman, Ingmar and Forsgren, Mats (eds) (1997), *The Nature of the International Firm*, Copenhagen: Copenhagen Business School Press.
Block, Zenas and MacMillan, Ian C. (1993), *Corporate Venturing: Creating New Business within the Firm*, Boston, MA: Harvard Business School.
Bond, Michael Harris (ed.) (1986), *The Psychology of the Chinese People*, Hong Kong: Oxford University Press.
Braverman, Harry (1974), *Labor and Monopoly Capital*, New York: Monthly Review Press.
Brewer, Thomas L. and Guisinger, Stephen E. (eds) (2000), *The New Economic Analysis of Multinationals: An Agenda for Management, Policy and Research*, Cheltenham: Edward Elgar.
Bridge, Simon, O'Neill, Ken and Cromie, Stan (1998), *Understanding Enterprise, Entrepreneurship and Small Business*, London: Macmillan.
Brook, Timothy and Luong, Hy V. (eds) (1997), *Culture and Economy: The Shaping of Capitalism in Eastern Asia*, Ann Arbor: University of Michigan Press.
Brown, Jonathan and Rose, Mary B. (eds) (1993), *Entrepreneurship, Networks, and Modern Business*, Manchester: Manchester University Press.

Brown, Rajeswary Ampalavana (1994), *Capital and Entrepreneurship in South-East Asia*, London: Macmillan.

Brown, Rajeswary Ampalavana (1998), 'Overseas Chinese investments in China – patterns of growth, diversification and finance: the case of Charoen Pokphand', *The China Quarterly*, No.155, pp. 610–36.

Brüderl, Josef and Preisendörfer, Peter (1998), 'Network support and the success of newly founded businesses', *Small Business Economics*, Vol. 10(3), pp. 213–25.

Brush, Candida G. (1995), *International Entrepreneurship: The Effect of Firm Age on Motives for Internationalization*, New York: Garland Pub.

Buckley, Peter J. and Ghauri, Pervez (eds) (1993), *The Internationalization of the Firm: A Reader*, London: Academic Press.

Bull, Ivan, Thomas, Howard and Willard, Gary (eds) (1995), *Entrepreneurship: Perspectives on Theory Building*, Oxford: Pergamon.

Bullard, Nicola, Bello, Walden and Mallhotra, Kamal (1998), 'Taming the tigers: the IMF and the Asian crisis', *Third World Quarterly*, Vol. 19(3), pp. 505–55.

Burgelman, Robert A. (1983), 'Corporate entrepreneurship and strategic management: insights from a process study', *Management Science*, Vol. 29, pp. 1349–64.

Burgelman, Robert A. (1984), 'Designs for corporate entrepreneurship in established firms', *California Management Review*, Vol. 26(2), pp. 154–66.

Cantwell, John (1989), *Technological Innovation and Multinational Corporations*, Oxford: Basil Blackwell.

Cantwell, John (1995), 'The globalisation of technology: what remains of the product cycle model?', *Cambridge Journal of Economics*, Vol. 19, pp. 155–74.

Casson, Mark (1982), *The Entrepreneur: An Economic Theory*, Oxford: Basil Blackwell.

Casson, Mark (1985), 'Entrepreneurship and the dynamics of foreign direct investment', in Peter J. Buckley and Mark Casson (eds), *The Economic Theory of the Multinational Enterprise: Selected Papers*, London: Macmillan, pp. 172–91.

Casson, Mark (ed.) (1990a), *Entrepreneurship*, Aldershot: Edward Elgar.

Casson, Mark (1990b), *Enterprise and Competitiveness: A Systems View of International Business*, Oxford: Clarendon Press.

Casson, Mark (1995), *Entrepreneurship and Business Culture: Studies in the Economics of Trust*, Aldershot: Edward Elgar.

Casson, Mark (2000), *Economics of International Business: A New Research Agenda*, Cheltenham: Edward Elgar.

Census and Statistics Department (various years a), *Annual Digest of Statistics*, Hong Kong: Government Printer.
Census and Statistics Department (various years b), *External Investments in Hong Kong's Non-manufacturing Sectors*, Hong Kong: Government Printer.
Census and Statistics Department (various years c), *Report on Annual Survey of Industrial Production*, Hong Kong: Government Printer.
Census and Statistics Department (1969), *Hong Kong Statistics 1947–1967*, Hong Kong: Government Printer.
Census and Statistics Department (1998), *Estimates of Gross Domestic Product 1961–1997*, Hong Kong: Government Printer.
Census and Statistics Department (2000a), *Hong Kong Annual Digest of Statistics 1999*, Hong Kong: Government Printer.
Census and Statistics Department (2000b), *External Direct Investment Statistics of Hong Kong 1998*, Hong Kong: Government Printer.
Census and Statistics Department (2000c), *Report on 1998 Annual Survey of Industrial Production*, Hong Kong: Government Printer.
Chan, Kwok Bun (ed.) (2000), *Chinese Business Networks: State, Economy and Culture*, Singapore: Prentice Hall.
Chan, Kwok Bun and Chiang, See-Ngoh Claire (1994), *Stepping Out: The Making of Chinese Entrepreneurs*, Singapore: Simon and Schuster.
Chandler, Alfred D. Jr. (1977), *The Visible Hand: The Managerial Revolution in American Business*, Cambridge, MA: Harvard University Press.
Chandler, Alfred D. (1990), *Scale and Scope: The Dynamics of Industrial Capitalism*, Cambridge, MA: Harvard University Press.
Chang, Ha-Joon (2000), 'The hazard of moral hazard: untangling the Asian crisis', *World Development*, Vol. 28(4), pp. 775–88.
Chang, Ha-Joon and Kozul-Wright, Richard (1994), 'Organizing development – comparing the national systems of entrepreneurship in Sweden and South Korea', *Journal of Development Studies*, Vol. 30(4), pp. 859–91.
Chell, Elizabeth, Haworth, Jean and Brearley, Sally (1991), *The Entrepreneurial Personality: Concepts, Cases and Categories*, London: Routledge.
Chen, Edward K.Y. (1979), *Hyper-growth in Asian Economies: A Comparative Study of Hong Kong, Japan, Korea, Singapore and Taiwan*, London: Macmillan.
Chen, Edward K.Y. (1984), 'The economic setting', in David G. Lethbridge (ed.), *The Business Environment in Hong Kong*, 2nd edition, Hong Kong: Oxford University Press, pp. 1–51.
Chen, Edward K.Y. (1989), 'Hong Kong's role in Asian and Pacific economic development', *Asian Development Review*, Vol. 7(2), pp. 26–47.

Chen, Edward K.Y. and Wong, Teresa Y.C. (1995), 'Economic synergy – a study of two-way foreign direct investment flow between Hong Kong and mainland China', in *The New Wave of Foreign Direct Investment in Asia*, Singapore: Nomura Research Institute and Institute of Southeast Asian Studies, pp. 243–77.

Chen, Edward K.Y., Nyaw, Mee-kau and Wong, Teresa Y.C. (eds) (1991), *Industrial and Trade Development in Hong Kong*, Hong Kong: Centre of Asian Studies, University of Hong Kong.

Chen, Min (1995), *Asian Management Systems: Chinese, Japanese and Korean Styles of Business*, London: Routledge.

Cheng, L.K. (1995), 'Strategies for rapid economic development – the case of Hong Kong', *Contemporary Economic Policy*, Vol. 13(1), pp. 28–37.

Cheng, Yuk-shing, Lu, Weiguo and Findlay, Christopher (1998), 'Hong Kong's economic relationship with China', *Journal of the Asia Pacific Economy*, Vol. 3(1), pp. 104–30.

Chew, Yoke-Tong and Yeung, Henry Wai-chung (2001), 'The SME advantage: adding local touch to foreign transnational corporations in Singapore', *Regional Studies*, Vol. 35(5), pp. 431–48.

Chia, Siow Yue (1993), 'Foreign direct investment in the Singapore economy', in Ippei Yamazawa and Fu-Chen Lo (eds), *Evolution of Asia-Pacific Economies: International Trade and Direct Investment*, Kuala Lumpur: Asian and Pacific Development Centre, pp. 183–232.

Chia, Siow Yue (1997), 'Singapore: advanced production base and smart hub of the electronics industry', in Wendy Dobson and Chia Siow Yue (eds), *Multinationals and East Asian Integration*, Canada: IDRC, pp. 31–61.

Child, John (1994), *Management in China during the Age of Reform*, Cambridge: Cambridge University Press.

Child, John and Lu, Yuan (eds) (1996), *Management Issues in China: International Enterprises*, 2 volumes, London: Routledge.

Chiu, Stephen W.K. (1996), 'Unravelling Hong Kong's exceptionalism: the politics of laissez-faire in the industrial takeoff', *Political Power and Social Theory*, Vol. 10, pp. 229–56.

Chiu, Stephen W.K., Ho, Kong Chong and Lui, Tai-Lok (1997), *City-states in the Global Economy: Industrial Restructuring in Hong Kong and Singapore*, Boulder, CO: Westview.

Choi, Alex Hang-Keung (1994), 'Beyond market and state: a study of Hong Kong's industrial transformation', *Studies in Political Economy*, Vol. 45(1), pp. 28–65.

Clark, Gordon L. and Kim, Won Bae (eds) (1995), *Asian NIEs in the Global Economy*, Baltimore: Johns Hopkins University Press.

Clark, Gordon L., Felman, Maryann A. and Gertler, Meric S. (eds) (2000),

The Oxford Handbook of Economic Geography, Oxford: Oxford University Press.

Coe, Neil M. and Kelly, Philip F. (2000), 'Distance and discourse in the local labour market: the case of Singapore', *Area*, Vol. 32(4), pp. 413–22.

Cooke, Philip N. and Morgan, Kevin (1998), *The Associational Economy: Firms, Regions, and Innovation*, Oxford: Oxford University Press.

Cox, Howard, Clegg, Jeremy and Ietto-Gillies, Grazia (1993), 'The growth of global business: three agendas', in Howard Cox, Jeremy Clegg and Grazia Ietto-Gillies (eds), *The Growth of Global Business*, London: Routledge, pp. 1–16.

Crawford, Darryl (2001), 'Globalisation and guanxi: the ethos of Hong Kong finance', *New Political Economy*, Vol. 6.

Crouch, Colin and Streeck, Wolfgang (eds) (1997), *Political Economy of Modern Capitalism: Mapping Convergence and Divergence*, London: Sage.

Dacin, M. Tina, Beal, Brent D. and Ventresca, Marc J. (1999), 'The embeddedness of organizations: dialogue and directions', *Journal of Management*, Vol. 25(3), pp. 317–56.

Daly, George G. (1998), 'Entrepreneurship and business culture in Japan and the U.S.', *Japan and the World Economy*, Vol. 10, pp. 487–94.

Dana, Leo Paul (ed.) (1999), *International Entrepreneurship*, Singapore: NTU-Entrepreneurship Development Centre.

Davies, Stephen N.G. (1989), 'The changing nature of representation in Hong Kong politics', in Kathleen Cheek-Milby and Miron Mushkat (eds), *Hong Kong: The Challenge of Transformation*, Hong Kong: Centre of Asian Studies, University of Hong Kong, pp. 36–76.

Department of Statistics (various years a), *Statistical Yearbook of Singapore*, Singapore: DOS.

Department of Statistics (various years b), *Foreign Equity Investment in Singapore*, Singapore: DOS.

Department of Statistics (various years c), *Report on the Census of Industrial Production*, Singapore: DOS.

Department of Statistics (various years d), *Report on the Census of Services*, Singapore: DOS.

Department of Statistics (various years e), *Report on Wholesale and Retail*, Singapore: DOS.

Department of Statistics (various years f), *Report on the Labour Forces Survey*, Singapore: DOS.

Department of Statistics (various years g), *Report on the Census of Population*, Singapore: DOS.

Department of Statistics (various years h), *Singapore's Investment Abroad*, Singapore: DOS.

Department of Statistics (1991), *Singapore's Investment Abroad 1976–1989*, Singapore: DOS.

Department of Statistics (1992), *Singapore's Corporate Sector: Size, Composition and Financial Structure*, Singapore: DOS.

Department of Statistics (1997), *Profile of Growing Small and Medium Enterprises in Singapore*, Singapore: DOS.

Department of Statistics (2000), *Singapore's Corporate Sector 1996–1997*, Singapore: DOS.

Dery, R. and Toulouse, Jean Marie (1996), 'Social structuration of the field of entrepreneurship: a case study', *Canadian Journal of Administrative Sciences*, Vol. 13(4), pp. 285–305.

Deyo, Frederic C. (ed.) (1987), *The Political Economy of the New Asian Industrialism*, Ithaca, NY: Cornell University Press.

Dicken, Peter and Kirkpatrick, Colin (1991), 'Services-led development in ASEAN: transnational regional headquarters in Singapore', *Pacific Review*, Vol. 4(2), pp. 174–84.

Dicken, Peter and Yeung, Henry Wai-chung (1999), 'Investing in the future: East and Southeast Asian firms in the global economy', in Kris Olds, Peter Dicken, Philip Kelly, Lily Kong and Henry Wai-chung Yeung (eds), *Globalisation and the Asia-Pacific: Contested Territories*, London: Routledge, pp. 107–28.

DiConti, Michael A. (1992), *Entrepreneurship in Training: The Multinational Corporation in Mexico and Canada*, Columbia: University of South Carolina Press.

DiMaggio, Paul J. and Powell, Walter W. (eds) (1991), *The New Institutionalism in Organizational Analysis*, Chicago: University of Chicago Press.

Douglass, Mike (2000), 'The rise and fall of world cities in the changing space-economy of globalization', *Political Geography*, Vol. 19(1), pp. 43–9.

Doz, Yves L. and Hamel, Gary (1998), *Alliance Advantage: The Art of Creating Value through Partnering*, Boston, MA: Harvard Business School Press.

Duncan, W. Jack, Ginter, Peter M., Rucks, Andrew C. and Jacobs, T. Douglas (1988), 'Intrapreneurship and the reinvention of the corporation', *Business Horizons*, Vol. 31(3), pp. 16–21.

East Asia Analytical Unit (1995), *Overseas Chinese Business Networks in Asia*, Parkes, Australia: Department of Foreign Affairs and Trade.

Economic Development Board (various issues), *Annual Report*, Singapore: EDB.

Economic Development Board (1993), *Growing with Enterprise: A National Report*, Singapore: EDB.

Economic Development Board (1995), *Regionalisation 2000: Singapore Unlimited*, Singapore: EDB.
Eisenhardt, Kathleen M. (1989), 'Building theories from case study research', *Academy of Management Review*, Vol. 14(4), pp. 532–50.
Eng, Irene (1997), 'Flexible production in late industrialization: the case of Hong Kong', *Economic Geography*, Vol. 73(1), pp. 26–43.
Enright, Michael J., Scott, Edith E. and Dodwell, David (1997), *The Hong Kong Advantage*, Hong Kong: Oxford University Press.
Etzioni, Amitai (1988), *The Moral Dimension: Toward a New Economics*, New York: Free Press.
Evans, David S. and Leighton, Linda S. (1989), 'Some empirical aspects of entrepreneurship', *American Economic Review*, Vol. 79(3), pp. 519–35.
Far Eastern Economic Review, various issues.
Federation of Hong Kong Industries (1992), *Hong Kong's Industrial Investment in the Pearl River Delta: 1991 Survey among Members of the Federation of Hong Kong Industries*, Hong Kong: Federation of Hong Kong Industries.
Feenstra, Robert C., Yang, Tzu-Han and Hamilton, Gary G. (1999), 'Business groups and product variety in trade: evidence from South Korea, Taiwan and Japan', *Journal of International Economics*, Vol. 48(1), pp. 71–100.
The Financial Times, various issues.
Fröbel, Folker, Heinrichs, Jurgen and Kreye, Otto (1980), *The New International Division of Labour*, Cambridge: Cambridge University Press.
Fukuyama, Francis (1995), *Trust: The Social Virtues and the Creation of Prosperity*, London: Hamish Hamilton.
Fulop, Liz (1991), 'Middle managers: victims or vanguards of the entrepreneurial movement', *Journal of Management Studies*, Vol. 28(1), pp. 25–44.
Fung, Victor (1997), 'Evolution in the management of family enterprises in Asia', in Gungwu Wang and Siu-lun Wong (eds), *Dynamic Hong Kong: Business and Culture*, Hong Kong: Hong Kong University Press, pp. 216–29.
Garavan, Thomas N., Cinnéide, Barra Ó. and Fleming, Patricia (1997), *Entrepreneurship and Business Start-ups in Ireland*, Dublin: Oak Tree Press.
Garnsey, Elizabeth (1998), 'A theory of the early growth of the firm', *Industrial and Corporate Change*, Vol. 7(3), pp. 523–56.
Gartner, William B. (1988), '"Who is an entrepreneur?" is the wrong question', *American Journal of Small Business*, Vol. 12(4), pp. 11–32.
Geisler, Eliezer (1993), 'Middle managers as internal corporate entrepreneurs: an unfolding agenda', *Interfaces*, Vol. 23(6), pp. 52–63.

Gereffi, Gary (1996), 'Global commodity chains: new forms of coordination and control among nations and firms in international industries', *Competition and Change*, Vol. 1(4), pp. 427–39.

Gereffi, Gary (1999), 'International trade and industrial upgrading in the apparel commodity chain', *Journal of International Economics*, Vol. 48(1), pp. 37–70.

Gereffi, Gary and Korzeniewicz, Miguel (eds) (1994), *Commodity Chains and Global Capitalism*, Westport, CT: Praeger.

Ghoshal, Sumantra and Bartlett, Christopher A. (1990), 'The multinational corporation as an interorganizational network', *Academy of Management Review*, Vol. 15(4), pp. 603–25.

Grandori, Anna (ed.) (1999), *Interfirm Networks: Organisation and Industrial Competitiveness*, London: Routledge.

Granovetter, Mark (1985), 'Economic action, and social structure: the problem of embeddedness', *American Journal of Sociology*, Vol. 91(3), pp. 481–510.

Granovetter, Mark and Swedberg, Richard (eds) (1992), *The Sociology of Economic Life*, Boulder, CO: Westview Press.

Gulati, Ranjay (1995), 'Does familiarity breed trust? The implications of repeated ties for contractual choice in alliances', *Academy of Management Journal*, Vol. 38(1), pp. 85–112.

Gulati, Ranjay (1998), 'Alliances and networks', *Strategic Management Journal*, Vol. 19(4), pp. 293–317.

Gulati, Ranjay (1999), 'Network location and learning: the influence of network resources and firm capabilities on alliance formation', *Strategic Management Journal*, Vol. 20(5), pp. 397–420.

Gulati, Ranjay and Gargiulo, M. (1999), 'Where do interorganizational networks come from?', *American Journal of Sociology*, Vol. 104(5), pp. 1439–93.

Gulati, Ranjay, Nohria, Nitin and Zaheer, Akbar (eds) (2000), 'Special issue: strategic networks', *Strategic Management Journal*, Vol. 21(3), pp. 191–425.

Guth, William D. and Ginsberg, Ari (1990), 'Special issue on corporate entrepreneurship', *Strategic Management Journal*, Vol. 11 (Special Issue), pp. 5–179.

Haggard, Stephen (1990), *Pathways from the Periphery: The Politics of Growth in the Newly Industrializing Countries*, Ithaca, NY: Cornell University Press.

Hamilton, Gary G. (ed.) (1991), *Business Networks and Economic Development in East and South East Asia*, Hong Kong: Centre of Asian Studies, University of Hong Kong.

Hamilton, Gary G. (1994), 'Civilizations and the organization of economies', in Neil J. Smelser and Richard Swedberg (eds), *The Handbook of Economic Sociology*, Princeton: Princeton University Press, pp. 183–205.

Hamilton, Gary G. (1996), 'Overseas Chinese capitalism', in Wei-ming Tu (ed.), *Confucian Traditions in East Asian Modernity: Moral Education and Economic Culture in Japan and the Four Mini-Dragons*, Cambridge, MA: Harvard University Press, pp. 328–42.

Hamilton, Gary G. (1997), 'Hong Kong and the rise of capitalism in Asia', in Gungwu Wang and Siu-lun Wong (eds), *Dynamic Hong Kong: Business and Culture*, Hong Kong: Hong Kong University Press, pp. 118–48.

Hamilton, Gary G. and Feenstra, Robert (1995), 'Varieties of hierarchies and markets', *Industrial and Corporate Change*, Vol. 4(1), pp. 93–130.

Hamilton-Hart, Natasha (2000), 'The Singapore state revisited', *Pacific Review*, Vol. 13(2), pp. 195–216.

Hamlin, Michael Alan (1998), *Asia's Best: The Myth and Reality of Asia's Most Successful Companies*, Singapore: Prentice Hall.

Handler, Wendy C. (1994), 'Succession in family business: a review of the research', *Family Business Review*, Vol. 7(2), pp. 133–57.

Hébert, Robert F. and Link, Albert N. (1988), *The Entrepreneur: Mainstream Views and Radical Critiques*, 2nd edition, New York: Praeger.

Heenan, David A. and Keegan, Warren J. (1979), 'The rise of third world multinationals', *Harvard Business Review*, January-February, pp. 101–9.

Hefner, Robert W. (ed.) (1998), *Market Cultures: Society and Values in the New Asian Capitalisms*, Singapore: Institute of Southeast Asian Studies.

Henderson, Jeffrey (1989a), 'The political economy of technological transformation in Hong Kong', *Comparative Urban and Community Research*, Vol. 2, pp. 102–55.

Henderson, Jeffrey (1989b), *The Globalisation of High Technology Production*, London: Routledge.

Henderson, Jeffrey (1991a), 'The political economy of technological transformation in the Hong Kong electronics industry', in Edward K.Y. Chen, Mee-Kau Nyaw and Teresa Y.C. Wong (eds), *Industrial and Trade Development in Hong Kong*, Hong Kong: Centre of Asian Studies, University of Hong Kong, pp. 57–115.

Henderson, Jeffrey (1991b), 'Urbanization in the Hong Kong–South China Region: an introduction to dynamics and dilemmas', *International Journal of Urban and Regional Research*, Vol. 15(2), pp. 169–79.

Henderson, Jeffrey (1999), 'Uneven crises: institutional foundations of East Asian economic turmoil', *Economy and Society*, Vol. 28(3), pp. 327–68.

Hill, Michael and Lian, Kwen Fee (1995), *The Politics of Nation Building and Citizenship in Singapore*, London: Routledge.

Hisrich, Robert D. (1990), 'Entrepreneurship/intrapreneurship', *American Psychologist*, Vol. 45(2), pp. 209–222.

Hisrich, Robert D., McDougall, Patricia P. and Oviatt, Benjamin M. (1997), *Cases in International Entrepreneurship*, Boston, MA: Irwin/McGraw-Hill.

Ho, Kong Chong (1993), 'Industrial restructuring and the dynamics of city-state adjustments', *Environment and Planning A*, Vol. 25(1), pp. 47–62.

Ho, Kong Chong (1994), 'Industrial restructuring, the Singapore city-state, and the regional division of labour', *Environment and Planning A*, Vol. 26(1), pp. 33–51.

Ho, Kong Chong and So, Alvin (1997), 'Semi-periphery and borderland integration: Singapore and Hong Kong experiences', *Political Geography*, Vol. 16(3), pp. 241–59.

Ho, Yin-Ping (1992), *Trade, Industrial Restructuring and Development in Hong Kong*, London: Macmillan.

Hodgson, Geoffrey M. (1988), *Economics and Institutions: A Manifesto for a Modern Institutional Economics*, Cambridge: Polity Press.

Hodgson, Geoffrey M. (1994), *Economics and Evolution: Bringing Life Back into Economics*, Cambridge: Polity Press.

Hodgson, Geoffrey M. (2000), *Evolution and Institutions: On Evolutionary Economics and the Evolution of Economics*, Cheltenham: Edward Elgar.

Hodder, Rupert (1996), *Merchant Princes of the East: Cultural Delusions, Economic Success and the Overseas Chinese in Southeast Asia*, Chichester: John Wiley.

Hollingsworth, J. Rogers (1998), 'New perspectives on the spatial dimensions of economic coordination: tensions between globalization and social systems of production', *Review of International Political Economy*, Vol. 5(3), pp. 482–507.

Hollingsworth, J. Rogers and Boyer, Robert (eds) (1997), *Contemporary Capitalism: The Embeddedness of Institutions*, Cambridge: Cambridge University Press.

Holmes, Thomas J. and Schmitz, James A. (1990), 'A theory of entrepreneurship and its application to the study of business transfers', *Journal of Political Economy*, Vol. 98(2), pp. 265–94.

Hong Kong Government (1984), *A Draft Agreement between the Government of the United Kingdom of Great Britain and Northern Ireland and the Government of the People's Republic of China on the Future of Hong Kong*, Hong Kong: Government Printer.

Hong Kong Industry Development Board (1991), *Techno-economic and*

Market Research Study on Hong Kong's Electronics Industry 1988–1989, Hong Kong: Industry Development Board.

Hu, Yao-Su (1995), 'The international transferability of the firm's advantages', *California Management Review*, Vol. 37(4), pp. 73–88.

Huff, W.G. (1994), *The Economic Growth of Singapore: Trade and Development in the Twentieth Century*, Cambridge: Cambridge University Press.

Huff, W.G. (1995), 'The developmental state, government, and Singapore's economic development since 1960', *World Development*, Vol. 23(8), pp. 1421–38.

Huff, W.G. (1999), 'Turning the corner in Singapore's developmental state?', *Asian Survey*, Vol. 39(2), pp. 214–42.

Hughes, Helen and Sing, You-poh (eds) (1969), *Foreign Investment and Industrialization in Singapore*, Madison: University of Wisconsin.

Hui, Weng-Tat (1997), 'Regionalization, economic restructuring and labour migration in Singapore', *International Migration*, Vol. 35(1), pp. 109–30.

Hymer, Stephen H. (1976), *The International Operations of National Firms: A Study of Foreign Direct Investment*, Cambridge, MA: MIT Press.

Industry Department (various years a), *Hong Kong's Manufacturing Industries*, Hong Kong: Government Printer.

Industry Department (various years b), *Survey of External Investment in Hong Kong's Manufacturing Industries*, Hong Kong: Industry Department.

Jarillo, J. Carlos (1988), 'On strategic networks', *Strategic Management Journal*, Vol. 9, pp. 31–41.

Jessop, Bob and Sum, Ngai-ling (2000), 'An entrepreneurial city in action: Hong Kong's emerging strategies in and for (inter) urban competition', *Urban Studies*, Vol. 37(12), pp. 2287–313.

Jesudason, James V. (1989), *Ethnicity and the Economy: The State, Chinese Business and Multinationals in Malaysia*, Singapore: Oxford University Press.

Johanson, Jan and Vahlne, Jan-Erik (1977), 'The internationalization process of the firm: a model of knowledge development and increasing foreign commitments', *Journal of International Business Studies*, Vol. 8(1), pp. 23–32.

Johnson, Chalmer (1982), *MITI and the Japanese Economic Miracle*, Stanford: Stanford University Press.

Kanai, Takao (1993), 'Singapore's new focus on regional business expansion', *Nomura Research Institute Quarterly*, Vol. 2(3), pp. 18–41.

Kao, John (1993), 'The worldwide web of Chinese business', *Harvard Business Review*, March-April, pp. 24–36.

Kirzner, Israel M. (1973), *Competition and Entrepreneurship*, Chicago: University of Chicago Press.

Kirzner, Israel M. (1985), *Discovery and the Capitalist Process*, Chicago: University of Chicago Press.

Kohn, Tomas Otto (1989), 'International entrepreneurship: foreign direct investment by small U.S.-based manufacturing firms', Unpublished DBA Thesis, Harvard University, Ann Arbor, MI: University Microfilms International.

Kong, Lily (1999), 'Globalisation and Singaporean transmigration: re-imagining and negotiating national identity', *Political Geography*, Vol. 18, pp. 563–89.

Kyle, David (1999), 'The Otavalo trade diaspora: social capital and transnational entrepreneurship', *Ethnic and Racial Studies*, Vol. 22(2), pp. 422–46.

Landa, Janet T. (1991), 'Culture and entrepreneurship in less-developed countries: ethnic trading networks as economic organizations', in Brigitte Berger (ed.), *The Culture of Entrepreneurship*, San Francisco: ICS Press, pp. 53–72.

Landstrom, Hans, Frank, Hermann and Veciana, Jose M. (eds) (1997), *Entrepreneurship and Small Business Research in Europe: An ECSB Survey*, Aldershot: Avebury.

Larson, Andrea (1992), 'Network dyads in entrepreneurial settings: a study of the governance of exchange relationships', *Administrative Science Quarterly*, Vol. 37(1), pp. 76–104.

Lau, Siu-kai and Kuan, Hsin-chi (1988), *The Ethos of the Hong Kong Chinese*, Hong Kong: Chinese University Press.

Lazonick, William (1991), *Business Organization and the Myth of the Market Economy*, Cambridge: Cambridge University Press.

Lee, Kuan Yew (2000), *From Third World to First: The Singapore Story: 1965–2000*, Singapore: Times Editions.

Lee, Tsao Yuan (1994), *Overseas Investment: Experience of Singapore Manufacturing Companies*, Singapore: McGraw-Hill.

Lee, Tsao Yuan and Low, Linda (1990), *Local Entrepreneurship in Singapore: Private and State*, Singapore: Times Academic Press.

Leff, Nathaniel H. (1978), 'Industrial organization and entrepreneurship in the developing countries: the economic groups', *Economic Development and Cultural Change*, Vol. 78, pp. 661–74.

Leff, Nathaniel H. (1979), 'Entrepreneurship and economic development: the problem revisited', *Journal of Economic Literature*, Vol. 17(1), pp. 46–64.

Leibenstein, Harvey (1966), 'Allocative efficiency vs. "X-efficiency"', *American Economic Review*, Vol. 56(3), pp. 392–415.

Leibenstein, Harvey (1968), 'Entrepreneurship and development', *American Economic Review*, Vol. 58(2), pp. 72–83.

Leung, Chi-kin (1993), 'Personal contacts, subcontracting linkages, and development in the Hong Kong–Zhujiang Delta region', *Annals of the Association of American Geographers*, Vol. 83(2), pp. 272–302.

Leung, Chi Kin and Wu, Chung Tong (1995), 'Innovation environment, R&D linkages and technology development in Hong Kong', *Regional Studies*, Vol. 29(6), pp. 533–46.

Lewis, Jordan D. (1995), *The Connected Corporation: How Leading Companies Win Through Customer-Supplier Alliances*, New York: Free Press.

Lim, Linda Y.C. (1996), 'The evolution of Southeast Asian business systems', *Journal of Southeast Asian Business*, Vol. 12(1), pp. 51–74.

Lim, Linda Y.C. (2000), 'Southeast Asian Chinese business: past success, recent crisis and future evolution', *Journal of Asian Business*, Vol. 16(1), pp. 1–14.

Lim, Linda Y.C. and Gosling, L.A. Peter (eds) (1983), *The Chinese in Southeast Asia*, Singapore: Maruzen Asia.

Lim, Mah-hui and Teoh, Kit-fong (1986), 'Singapore corporations go transnational', *Journal of South East Asian Studies*, Vol. 17(2), pp. 336–65.

Lin, Justin Yifu and Chen, Chien-Liang (1996), 'Dutch disease, Taiwan's success and "the China boom"', in Linda Fung-Yee Ng and Chyau Tuan (eds), *Three Chinese Economies – China, Hong Kong and Taiwan: Challenges and Opportunities*, Hong Kong: Chinese University Press, pp. 53–75.

Livesay, Harold C. (ed.) (1995), *Entrepreneurship and the Growth of Firms*, Aldershot: Edward Elgar.

Lovas, Bjorn and Ghoshal, Sumantra (2000), 'Strategy as guided evolution', *Strategic Management Journal*, Vol. 21, pp. 875–96.

Low, Aik Meng and Tan, Wee Liang (eds) (1996), *Entrepreneurs, Entrepreneurship and Enterprising Culture*, Singapore: Addison-Wesley.

Low, Linda (1998), *The Political Economy of a City-state: Government-made Singapore*, Singapore: Oxford University Press.

Low, Linda, Ramstetter, Eric D. and Yeung, Henry Wai-chung (1998), 'Accounting for outward direct investment from Hong Kong and Singapore: who controls what?', in Robert E. Baldwin, Robert E. Lipsey and J. David Richardson (eds), *Geography and Ownership as Bases for Economic Accounting*, Chicago: University of Chicago Press, pp. 139–68.

Low, Linda, Toh, Mun Heng, Soon, Teck Wong, Tan, Kong Yam and Hughes, Helen (1993), *Challenge and Response: Thirty Years of the Economic Development Board*, Singapore: Times Academic Press.

Low, M.B. and McMillan, Ian C. (1988), 'Entrepreneurship: past research and future challenges, *Journal of Management*, Vol. 14(2) pp. 139–61.

Lu, Ding and Zhu, Gangti (1995), 'Singapore direct investment in China: features and implications', *ASEAN Economic Bulletin*, Vol. 12(1), pp. 53–63.

Lui, Tai Lok and Chiu, Stephen (1993), 'Industrial restructuring and labour market adjustment under positive non-intervention', *Environment and Planning A*, Vol. 25(1), pp. 63–79.

Lui, Tai Lok and Chiu, Stephen (1994), 'A tale of two industries: the restructuring of Hong Kong's garment making and electronics industries', *Environment and Planning A*, Vol. 26(1), pp. 53–70.

Lui, Tai-lok and Chiu, Stephen W.K. (1996), 'Merchants, small employers and a non-interventionist state: Hong Kong as a case of unorganized late industrialization', in John Borrego, Alejandro Alvarez Bejar and K.S. Jomo (eds), *Capital, the State, and Late Industrialization: Comparative Perspectives on the Pacific Rim*, Boulder, CO: Westview, pp. 221–46.

Lundvall, Bengt-Åke (ed.) (1992), *National Systems of Innovation: Towards a Theory of Innovation and Interactive Learning*, London: Pinter.

Luo, Yadong (2000), *Multinational Corporations in China: Benefiting from Structural Transformation*, Copenhagen: Copenhagen Business School Press.

Lynn, Pann (ed.) (1998), *The Encyclopedia of Chinese Overseas*, Singapore: Archipelago Press.

Magretta, Joan (1998), 'Fast, global, and entrepreneurial: supply chain management, Hong Kong style: an interview with Victor Fung', *Harvard Business Review*, Vol. 76(5), pp. 103–14.

Mair, Andrew (1994), *Honda's Global Local Corporation*, New York: St. Martin's Press.

Marshall, Alfred (1961), *Principles of Economics*, 9th edition, London: Macmillan.

Martinsons, Maris G. (1998), 'Hong Kong government policy and information technology innovation: the invisible hand, the helping hand, and the hand-over to China', *IEEE Transactions on Engineering Management*, Vol. 45(4), pp. 366–78.

Mascarenhas, Briance, Baveja, Alok and Jamil, Mamnoon (1998), 'Dynamics of core competencies in leading multinational companies', *California Management Review*, Vol. 40(4), pp. 117–32.

Mathews, John A. (1998), 'Fashioning a new Korean model out of the crisis: the rebuilding of institutional capabilities', *Cambridge Journal of Economics*, Vol. 22(6), pp. 747–59.

Mathews, John A. and Snow, Charles C. (1998), 'A conversation with the

Acer Groups' Stan Shih on global strategy and management', *Organizational Dynamics*, Vol. 27(1), pp. 65–74.
McClelland, David (1961), *The Achieving Society*, Princeton, NJ: Van Nostrand.
McDougall, Patricia P. (1989), 'International versus domestic entrepreneurship – new venture strategic behavior and industry structure', *Journal of Business Venturing*, Vol. 4(6), pp. 387–400.
McDougall, Patricia P. and Oviatt, Benjamin M. (1996), 'New venture internationalization, strategic change, and performance: a follow-up study', *Journal of Business Venturing*, Vol. 11(1), pp. 23–40.
McDougall, Patricia P. and Oviatt, Benjamin M. (2000), 'International entrepreneurship: the intersection of two research paths', *Academy of Management Journal*, Vol. 43(5), pp. 902–906.
McDougall, Patricia P., Shane, Scott and Oviatt, Benjamin M. (1994), 'Explaining the formation of international new ventures: the limits of theories from international business research', *Journal of Business Venturing*, Vol. 9(6), pp. 469–87.
McVey, Ruth (ed.) (1992), *Southeast Asian Capitalists*, Ithaca: Cornell University Southeast Asia Program.
Menkhoff, Thomas (1993), *Trade Routes, Trust and Trading Networks – Chinese Small Enteprises in Singapore*, Saarbrucken, Germany: Verlag breitenback Publishers.
Meyer, David R. (2000), *Hong Kong as a Global Metropolis*, Cambridge: Cambridge University Press.
Ministry of Finance (1993a), *Interim Report of the Committee to Promote Enterprise Overseas*, Singapore: MOF.
Ministry of Finance (1993b), *Final Report of the Committee to Promote Enterprise Overseas*, Singapore: MOF.
Ministry of Foreign Trade and Economic Cooperation (various years), *Almanac of China's Foreign Economic Relations and Trade*, Beijing: Ministry of Foreign Trade and Economic Cooperation.
Ministry of Trade and Industry (1998), *Committee on Singapore's Competitiveness*, Singapore: MTI.
Mirza, Hafiz (1986), *Multinationals and the Growth of the Singapore Economy*, London: Croom Helm.
Mitchell, Katharyne (1995), 'Flexible circulation in the Pacific Rim: capitalism in cultural context', *Economic Geography*, Vol. 71(4), pp. 364–82.
Mitchell, Katharyne and Olds, Kris (2000), 'Chinese business networks and the globalisation of property markets in the Pacific Rim', in Henry Wai-chung Yeung and Kris Olds (eds), *The Globalisation of Chinese Business Firms*, London: Macmillan, pp. 195–219.

Monetary Authority of Singapore (various years), *Annual Report*, Singapore: MAS.

Moon, H. Chang and Peery, Newman S. Jr. (1997), 'Entrepreneurship in international business: concept, strategy, and implementation', *Entrepreneurship, Innovation, and Change*, Vol. 6(1), pp. 5–20.

Morris, Michael H., Williams, Roy W. and Nel, Deon (1996), 'Factors influencing family business succession', *International Journal of Entrepreneurial Behaviour & Research*, Vol. 2(3), pp. 68–81.

Mosakowski, Elaine (1998), 'Entrepreneurial resources, organizational choices, and competitive outcomes', *Organization Science*, Vol. 9(6), pp. 625–43.

Mourdoukoutas, Panos (1999), *Collective Entrepreneurship in a Globalizing Economy*, Westport, CT: Quorum Books.

Nachum, Lilach (1999), *The Origins of International Competitiveness of Firms: The Impact of Location and Ownership in the Professional Service Industries*, Cheltenham: Edward Elgar.

Nafziger, E. Wayne (1986), *Entrepreneurship, Equity, and Economic Development*, Greenwich, CT: JAI Press.

Naughton, Barry (1995), *Growing Out of the Plan: Chinese Economic Reform, 1978–1993*, New York: Cambridge University Press.

Nelson, Richard R. and Winter, Sidney G. (1982), *An Evolutionary Theory of Economic Change*, Cambridge, MA: Harvard University Press.

Ng, Linda Fung-Yee and Tuan, Chyau (eds) (1996), *Three Chinese Economies – China, Hong Kong and Taiwan: Challenges and Opportunities*, Hong Kong: Chinese University Press.

Nooteboom, Bart (1996), 'Trust, opportunism and governance: a process and control model', *Organization Studies*, Vol. 17(6), pp. 985–1010.

Nooteboom, Bart (1999), *Inter-firm Alliances: International Analysis and Design*, London: Routledge.

North, Douglass (1990), *Institutions, Institutional Change, and Economic Performance*, New York: Cambridge University Press.

Numagami, Tsuyoshi (1998), 'The infeasibility of invariant laws in management studies: a reflective dialogue in defense of case studies', *Organization Science*, Vol. 9(1), pp. 2–15.

Nyaw, Mee-kau (1991), 'The experiences of industrial growth in Hong Kong and Singapore: a comparative study', in Edward K.Y. Chen, Mee-Kau Nyaw and Teresa Y.C. Wong (eds), *Industrial and Trade Development in Hong Kong*, Hong Kong: Centre of Asian Studies, University of Hong Kong, pp. 185–222.

Ohmae, Kenichi (1990), *The Borderless World: Power and Strategy in the Interlinked Economy*, London: Collins.

Oi, Jean C. (1999), *Rural China Takes Off: Institutional Foundations*

of Economic Reform, Berkeley, CA: University of California Press.
Okposin, Samuel Bassey (1999), *The Extent of Singapore's Investments Abroad*, Aldershot: Ashgate.
Olds, Kris (1998), 'Globalization and urban change: tales from Vancouver via Hong Kong', *Urban Geography*, Vol. 19(4), pp. 360–85.
Olds, Kris (2001), *Globalization and Urban Change: Capital, Culture and Pacific Rim Mega Projects*, Oxford: Oxford University Press.
Olds, Kris and Yeung, Henry Wai-chung (1999), '(Re)shaping "Chinese" business networks in a globalising era', *Environment and Planning D: Society and Space*, Vol. 17(5), pp. 535–55.
Olds, Kris and Yeung, Henry Wai-chung (2000), 'Global cities and developmental states: globalising the city-state', Paper presented at the 96th Annual Meeting of the Association of American Geographers, Pittsburgh, Pennsylvania, 4–8 April.
Oviatt, Benjamin M. and McDougall, Patricia P. (1994), 'Toward a theory of international new ventures', *Journal of International Business Studies*, Vol. 25(1), pp. 45–64.
Pang, Eng Fong (1995), 'Staying global and going regional: Singapore's inward and outward direct investments', in *The New Wave of Foreign Direct Investment in Asia*, Singapore: Nomura Research Institute and Institute of Southeast Asian Studies, pp. 111–29.
Patel, Pari (1995), 'Localised production of technology for global markets', *Cambridge Journal of Economics*, Vol. 19, pp. 141–53.
Patel, Pari and Pavitt, Keith L.R. (1991), 'Large firms in the production of the world's technology: an important case of "non-globalisation"', *Journal of International Business Studies*, Vol. 22(1), pp. 1–21.
Pauly, Louis W. and Reich, Simon (1997), 'National structures and multinational corporate behavior: enduring differences in the age of globalization', *International Organization*, Vol. 51(1), pp. 1–30.
Pearson, Margaret M. (1991), *Joint Ventures in the People's Republic of China: The Control of Foreign Direct Investment under Socialism*, Princeton, NJ: Princeton University Press.
Pearson, Margaret M. (1997), *China's New Business Elite: The Political Consequences of Economic Reform*, Berkeley, CA: University of California Press.
Penrose, Edith (1995), *The Theory of the Growth of the Firm*, Revised Edition, Oxford: Oxford University Press.
Perry, Martin (1991), 'The Singapore growth triangle: state, capital and labour at a new frontier in the world economy', *Singapore Journal of Tropical Geography*, Vol. 12(2), pp. 138–51.
Perry, Martin (1992), 'Promoting corporate control in Singapore', *Regional Studies*, Vol. 26(3), pp. 289–94.

Perry, Martin (1995), 'New corporate structures, regional offices and Singapore's new economic directions', *Singapore Journal of Tropical Geography*, Vol. 16(2), pp. 181–96.
Perry, Martin and Yeoh, Caroline (2000), 'Singapore's overseas industrial parks', *Regional Studies*, Vol. 34(2), pp. 199–206.
Perry, Martin, Kong, Lily and Yeoh, Brenda (1997), *Singapore: A Developmental City State*, London: John Wiley.
Perry, Martin, Poon, Jessie and Yeung, Henry (1998a), 'Regional offices in Singapore: spatial and strategic influences in the location of corporate control', *Review of Urban and Regional Development Studies*, Vol. 10(1), pp. 42–59.
Perry, Martin, Yeung, Henry and Poon, Jessie (1998b), 'Regional office mobility: the case of corporate control in Singapore and Hong Kong', *Geoforum*, Vol. 29(3), pp. 237–55.
Pinchot, Gifford III (1985), *Intrapreneuring: Why You Don't Have to Leave the Corporation to Become an Entrepreneur*, New York: Harper & Row.
Porac, Joseph F. and Ventresca, M. (eds) (1999), *The Social Construction of Markets and Industries*, Oxford: Pergamon.
Porter, Michael E. (1990), *The Competitive Advantage of Nations*, London: Macmillan.
Rajan, K. Sreenivas and Pangarkar, Nitin (2000), 'Mode of entry choice: an empirical study of Singaporean multinationals', *Asia Pacific Journal of Management*, Vol. 17(1), pp. 49–66.
Ray, Dennis M. (1994), 'The role of risk-taking in Singapore', *Journal of Business Venturing*, Vol. 9(2), pp. 157–77.
Redding, S. Gordon (1990), *The Spirit of Chinese Capitalism*, Berlin: De Gruyter.
Redding, S. Gordon (1994), 'Competitive advantage in the context of Hong Kong', *Journal of Far Eastern Business*, Vol. 1(1), pp. 71–89.
Redding, S. Gordon (1995), 'Overseas Chinese networks: understanding the enigma', *Long Range Planning*, Vol. 28(1), pp. 61–9.
Redding, S. Gordon (1996), 'The distinct nature of Chinese capitalism', *Pacific Review*, Vol. 9(3), pp. 426–41.
Régnier, Philippe (1991), *Singapore: City-state in South-East Asia*, Hawaii: University of Hawaii Press.
Régnier, Philippe (1993), 'Spreading Singapore's wings worldwide: a review of traditional and new investment strategies', *Pacific Review*, Vol. 6(4), pp. 305–12.
Reich, Robert B. (1991), *The Work of Nations: Preparing Ourselves for 21st-Century Capitalism*, London: Simon & Schuster.
Ripsas, Sven (1998), 'Towards an interdisciplinary theory of entrepreneurship', *Small Business Economics*, Vol. 10(2), pp. 103–15.

Rodan, Garry (1989), *The Political Economy of Singapore's Industralization: Nation State and International Capital*, Kuala Lumpur: Forum.

Rothwell, Roy and Zegueld, Walter (1982), *Innovation and the Small and Medium Sized Firm: Their Role in Employment and in Economic Change*, London: Pinter.

Sabel, Charles F. (1993), 'Studied trust: building new forms of co-operation in a volatile economy', *Human Relations*, Vol. 46(9), pp. 1133–70.

Sabel, Charles F. and Zeitlin, Jonathan (eds) (1996), *Worlds of Possibility: Flexibility and Mass Production in Western Industrialization*, Cambridge: Cambridge University Press.

Sako, Mari (1992), *Prices, Quality and Trust: Inter-firm Relations in Britain and Japan*, Cambridge: Cambridge University Press.

Sassen, Saskia (1991), *The Global City: New York, London, Tokyo*, Princeton, NJ: Princeton University Press.

Sauvant, Karl P. and Mallampally, Padma (eds) (1993), *Transnational Corporations in Services*, United Nations Library on Transnational Corporations, Vol. 12, London: Routledge.

Saxenian, Anne (1994), *Regional Advantage: Culture and Competition in Silicon Valley and Route 128*, Cambridge, MA: Harvard University Press.

Scaperlanda, Anthony (1994), 'Schumpeterian entrepreneurship and multinational enterprises: implications for social economics', *Review of Social Economy*, Vol. 52(4), pp. 338–52.

Schumpeter, Joseph A. (1934), *The Theory of Economic Development: An Inquiry into Profits, Capital, Credit, Interest and the Business Cycle*, Cambridge, MA: Harvard University Press.

Schumpeter, Joseph (1942), *Capitalism, Socialism and Democracy*, New York: Harper and Brothers.

Scott, Allen J. (1987), 'The semi-conductor industry in Southeast Asia', *Regional Studies*, Vol. 21, pp. 143–60.

Scott, Allen J. (1988), *New Industrial Spaces: Flexible Production, Organisation and Regional Development in North America and Western Europe*, London: Pion.

Scott, Allen J. (1998), *Regions and the World Economy: The Coming Shape of Global Production, Competition and Political Order*, Oxford: Oxford University Press.

Shenkar, Oded (1990), 'International joint ventures' problems in China: risks and remedies', *Long Range Planning*, Vol. 23(3), pp. 82–90.

Simon, Herbert (1957), *Models of Man*, New York: John Wiley.

Simon, Herbert (1961), *Administrative Behavior*, 2nd Edition, New York: Macmillan.

Singh, Kulwant and Ang, Siah Hwee (1998), 'The strategies and success of government linked corporations in Singapore', Research Paper Series No. 98–06, Faculty of Business Administration, National University of Singapore, Singapore.

Sit, Victor F.S. and Wong, Siu Lun (1989), *Small and Medium Industries in an Export-Oriented Economy: The Case of Hong Kong*, Hong Kong: Centre of Asian Studies, University of Hong Kong.

Sloane, Patricia (1999), *Islam, Modernity and Entrepreneurship among the Malays*, London: Macmillan.

Smelser, Neil and Swedberg, Richard (eds) (1994), *The Handbook of Economic Sociology*, Princeton, NJ: Princeton University Press.

Smith, Ken G., Carroll, Stephen J. and Ashford, Susan J. (1995), 'Intra- and interorganizational cooperation: toward a research agenda', *Academy of Management Journal*, Vol. 38(1), pp. 7–23.

Snape, Ed and Chan, Andy W. (1997), 'Whither Hong Kong's unions: autonomous trade unionism or classic dualism?', *British Journal of Industrial Relations*, Vol. 35(1), pp. 39–63.

Speeches, Ministry of Information and the Arts, Singapore, May–June 1993, p. 15.

Storper, Michael (1997), *The Regional World: Territorial Development in a Global Economy*, New York: Guilford Press.

Storper, Michael and Salais, R. (1997), *Worlds of Production: The Action Frameworks of the Economy*, Cambridge, MA: Harvard University Press.

The Straits Times, Singapore, various issues.

Sum, Ngai-Ling (1995), 'More than a "war of words": identity, politics and the struggle for dominance during the recent "political reform" period in Hong Kong', *Economy and Society*, Vol. 24(1), pp. 67–100.

Sun, Haishun (1998), 'Macroeconomic impact of direct foreign investment in China: 1976–96', *World Economy*, Vol. 21(5), pp. 675–94.

The Sunday Times, Singapore, various issues.

Sung, Yun-wing (1991), *The China-Hong Kong Connection: The Key to China's Open-Door Policy*, Cambridge: Cambridge University Press.

Tan, Chwee Huat (1995), *Venturing Overseas: Singapore's External Wing*, Singapore: McGraw-Hill.

Tan, Hock (1991), 'State capitalism, multi-national corporations and Chinese entrepreneurship in Singapore', in Gary G. Hamilton (ed.), *Business Networks and Economic Development in East and South East Asia*, Hong Kong: Centre of Asian Studies, University of Hong Kong, pp. 201–16.

Teoh, Hai Yap and Foo, See Liang (1997), 'Moderating effects of tolerance for ambiguity and risk-taking propensity on the role conflict-perceived performance relationship: evidence from Singaporean entrepreneurs', *Journal of Business Venturing*, Vol. 12(1), pp. 67–81.

Thoburn, John T., Leung, H.M. Chau, Esther and Tang, S.H. (1990), *Foreign Investment in China under the Open Policy: The Experience of Hong Kong Companies*, Aldershot: Avebury.
Thomas, Anisya S. and Mueller, Stephen L. (2000), 'A case for comparative entrepreneurship: assessing the relevance of culture', *Journal of International Business Studies*, Vol. 31(2), pp. 287–301.
Thompson, Paul (1989), *The Nature of Work: An Introduction to Debates on the Labour Process*, 2nd edition, Basingstoke: Macmillan.
Thornton, Patricia H. (1999), 'The sociology of entrepreneurship', *Annual Review of Sociology*, Vol. 25, pp. 19–46.
Thrift, Nigel (1996), *Spatial Formations*, London: Sage.
Thrift, Nigel (1998), 'The rise of soft capitalism', in Andrew Herod, Gearóid Ó Tuathail and Susan M. Roberts (eds), *An Unruly World: Globalization, Governance and Geography*, London: Routledge, pp. 25–71.
Thrift, Nigel (1999), 'The globalisation of business knowledge', in Kris Olds, Peter Dicken, Philip Kelly, Lily Kong and Henry Wai-chung Yeung (eds), *Globalisation and the Asia Pacific: Contested Territories*, London: Routledge, pp. 57–71.
Thrift, Nigel and Leyshon, Andrew (1994), 'A phantom state? The detraditionalisation of money, the international financial system and international financial centres', *Political Geography*, Vol. 13, pp. 299–327.
Tiessen, James H. (1997), 'Individualism, collectivism and entrepreneurship: a framework for international comparative research', *Journal of Business Venturing*, Vol. 12(5), pp. 367–84.
Toh, Mun Heng and Low, Linda (eds) (1993), *Regional Cooperation and Growth Triangles in ASEAN*, Singapore: Times Academic Press.
Tomer, John F. (1998a), 'Beyond the machine model of the firm: toward a holistic human model', *Journal of Socio-economics*, Vol. 27(3), pp. 323–40.
Tomer, John F. (1998b), 'Beyond transaction markets, toward relationship marketing in the human firm: a socio-economic model', *Journal of Socio-Economics*, Vol. 27(2), pp. 207–28.
Tremewan, Christopher (1994), *The Political Economy of Social Control in Singapore*, London: Macmillan.
Tsang, Eric W.K. (1999a), 'Internationalization as a learning process: Singapore MNCs in China', *Academy of Management Executive*, Vol. 13(1), pp. 91–101.
Tsang, Eric W.K. (1999b), 'The knowledge transfer and learning aspects of international HRM: an empirical study of Singapore MNCs', *International Business Review*, Vol. 8(5/6), pp. 591–609.
Tuan, Chyau and Ng, Linda Fung-Yee (1995a), 'The turning point of the

Hong Kong manufacturing sector: impact of outward investment to Pearl River delta', *Journal of International Trade and Economic Development*, Vol. 4(2), pp. 153–70.

Tuan, Chyau and Ng, Linda Fung-Yee (1995b), 'Manufacturing evolution under passive industrial policy and cross-border operations in China: the case of Hong Kong', *Journal of Asian Economics*, Vol. 6(1), pp. 71–88.

UNCTAD (1996), *World Investment Report 1996: Investment, Trade and International Policy Arrangements*, New York: United Nations.

UNCTAD (1999), *World Investment Report 1999: Foreign Direct Investment and the Challenge of Development*, New York: United Nations.

Uzzi, Brian (1997), 'Social structure and competition in interfirm networks: the paradox of embeddedness', *Administrative Science Quarterly*, Vol. 42, pp. 35–67.

Uzzi, Brian (1999), 'Embeddedness in the making of financial capital: how social relations and networks benefit firms seeking financing', *American Sociological Review*, Vol. 64(4), pp. 481–505.

Van de Ven, Andrew H. (1995), 'The development of an infrastructure for entrepreneurship', in Ivan Bull, Howard Thomas and Gary Willard (eds), *Entrepreneurship: Perspectives on Theory Building*, Oxford: Pergamon, pp. 39–63.

Wade, Robert (1990), *Governing the Market: Economic Theory and the Role of Government in East Asian Industrialization*, Princeton: Princeton University Press.

Wade, Robert and Veneroso, Frank (1998), 'The Asian crisis: the high debt model versus the Wall Street-Treasury-IMF complex', *New Left Review*, No. 228, pp. 3–23.

Walder, Andrew G. (1995), 'Local governments as industrial firms: an organizational analysis of China's transitional economy', *American Journal of Sociology*, Vol. 101(2), pp. 263–301.

Walsh, J.P., Wang, E.P. and Xin, K.R. (1999), 'Same bed, different dreams: working relationships in Sino-American joint ventures', *Journal of World Business*, Vol. 34(1), pp. 69–93.

Weber, Max [1904] (1992), *The Protestant Ethic and the Spirit of Capitalism*, New York: Routledge.

Weidenbaum, Murray and Hughes, Samuel (1996), *The Bamboo Network: How Expatriate Chinese Entrepreneurs Are Creating a New Economic Superpower in Asia*, New York: The Free Press.

Wenger, Etienne (1998), *Communities of Practice: Learning, Meaning, and Identity*, Cambridge: Cambridge University Press.

Wenger, Etienne (2000), 'Communities of practice and social learning systems', *Organization*, Vol. 7(2), pp. 225–46.

Werbner, Pnina (1999), 'What colour "success"? Distorting value in studies of ethnic entrepreneurship', *Sociological Review*, Vol. 47(3), pp. 548–79.

Westhead, Paul and Wright, Mike (eds) (2000), *Advances in Entrepreneurship*, Cheltenham: Edward Elgar.

Westney, D. Eleanor (1987), *Imitation and Innovation: The Transfer of Western Organisational Patterns to Meiji Japan*, Cambridge, MA: Harvard University Press.

Whitley, Richard (1992a), *Business Systems in East Asia: Firms, Markets and Societies*, London: Sage.

Whitley, Richard (ed.) (1992b), *European Business Systems: Firms and Markets in their National Contexts*, London: Sage.

Whitley, Richard (1994), 'The internationalization of firms and markets: its significance and institutional structuring', *Organization*, Vol. 1(1), pp. 101–24.

Whitley, Richard (1998), 'Internationalization and varieties of capitalism: the limited effects of cross-national coordination of economic activities on the nature of business systems', *Review of International Political Economy*, Vol. 5(3), pp. 445–81.

Whitley, Richard (1999), *Divergent Capitalisms: The Social Structuring and Change of Business Systems*, New York: Oxford University Press.

Whitley, Richard and Kristensen, Peer Hull (eds) (1996), *The Changing European Firm: Limits to Convergence*, London: Routledge.

Whitley, Richard and Kristensen, Peer Hull (eds) (1997), *Governance at Work: The Social Regulation of Economic Relations*, Oxford: Oxford University Press.

Whyte, Martin King (1996), 'The Chinese family and economic development: obstacle or engine?', *Economic Development and Cultural Change*, Vol. 45(1), pp. 1–30.

Willcocks, Leslie and Choi, Chong Ju (1995), 'Co-operative partnership and "total" IT outsourcing: from contractual obligation to strategic alliance?', *European Management Journal*, Vol. 13(1), pp. 67–78.

Williamson, Oliver E. (1975), *Markets and Hierarchies: Analysis and Antitrust Implications*, New York: Free Press.

Williamson, Oliver E. (1985), *The Economic Institution of Capitalism*, New York: Free Press.

Williamson, Oliver E. (1986), *Economic Organization: Firms, Markets and Policy Control*, Brighton: Wheatsheaf Books.

Williamson, Oliver E. (1993), 'Calculativeness, trust, and economic organization', *Journal of Law and Economics*, Vol. 36, pp. 453–86.

Williamson, Oliver E. (1999), 'Strategy research: governance and competence perspectives', *Strategic Management Journal*, Vol. 20, pp. 1087–108.

Williamson, Oliver E. and Winter, Sidney G. (eds) (1991), *The Nature of the Firm: Origins, Evolution, and Development*, New York: Oxford University Press.

Willis, Katie D. and Yeoh, Brenda (1998), 'The social sustainability of Singapore's regionalisation drive', *Third World Planning Review*, Vol. 20(2), pp. 203–21.

Wong, Bernard (1998), *Ethnicity and Entrepreneurship: The New Chinese Immigrants in the San Francisco Bay Area*, Boston: Allyn and Bacon.

Wong, Gilbert K.K. (1991), 'Business groups in a dynamic environment: Hong Kong 1976–1986', in Gary Hamilton (ed.), *Business Networks and Economic Development in East and Southeast Asia*, Hong Kong: Centre of Asian Studies, University of Hong Kong, pp. 126–54.

Wong, Siu-lun (1985), 'The Chinese family firm: a model', *British Journal of Sociology*, Vol. 36, pp. 58–72.

Wong, Siu-lun (1988), *Emigrant Entrepreneurs: Shanghai Industrialists in Hong Kong*, Hong Kong: Oxford University Press.

Wong, Siu-lun (1993), 'Business and politics in Hong Kong during the transition', in *Hong Kong in Transition 1992*, Hong Kong: One Country Two Systems Economic Research Institute, pp. 488–514.

Wong, Siu-lun (1995), 'Business networks, cultural values and the state in Hong Kong and Singapore', in Rajeswary Ampalavana Brown (ed.), *Chinese Business Enterprise in Asia*, London: Routledge, pp. 136–53.

Wright, Richard W. and Ricks, David A. (1994), 'Trends in international-business research: 25 years later', *Journal of International Business Studies*, Vol. 25(4), pp. 687–701.

Wu, Friedrich (1997), 'Hong Kong and Singapore: a tale of two Asian business hubs', *Journal of Asian Business*, Vol. 13(2), pp. 1–17.

Wu, Friedrich and Duk, Sin Yue (1995), 'Hong Kong and Singapore: "twin capitals" for overseas Chinese capital', *Business and the Contemporary World*, Vol. 7(3), pp. 21–33.

Yan, Aimin and Gray, Barbara (1994), 'Bargaining power, management control, and performance in United States–China joint ventures – a comparative case study', *Academy of Management Journal*, Vol. 37(6), pp. 1478–517.

Yeh, Anthony G.O. and Ng, M.K. (1994), 'The changing role of the state in high-tech industrial development – the experience of Hong Kong', *Environment and Planning C: Government and Policy*, Vol. 12(4), pp. 449–72.

Yeoh, Brenda S.A. (1999), 'Global/globalizing cities', *Progress in Human Geography*, Vol. 23(4), pp. 607–16.

Yeoh, Brenda S.A. and Willis, Katie (1999), '"Hear" and "wing", nation and diaspora: gendered discourses in Singapore's regionalisation process', *Gender, Place and Culture*, Vol. 6(4), pp. 355–72.

Yeoh, Brenda S.A., Huang, Shirlena and Willis, Katie (2000), 'Global cities, transnational flows and gender dimensions, the view from Singapore', *Tijdschrift voor Economische en Sociale Geografie*, Vol. 91(2), pp. 147–58.

Yeung, Henry Wai-chung (1994a), 'Hong Kong firms in the ASEAN region: transnational corporations and foreign direct investment', *Environment and Planning A*, Vol. 26(12), pp. 1931–56.

Yeung, Henry Wai-chung (1994b), 'Transnational corporations from Asian developing countries: their characteristics and competitive edge', *Journal of Asian Business*, Vol. 10(4), pp. 17–58.

Yeung, Henry Wai-chung (1995), 'Qualitative personal interviews in international business research: some lessons from a study of Hong Kong transnational corporations', *International Business Review*, Vol. 4(3), pp. 313–39.

Yeung, Henry Wai-chung (1996), 'Sectoral specialization and competitive advantage: Hong Kong investments in the ASEAN region', *ASEAN Economic Bulletin*, Vol. 13(1), pp. 74–94.

Yeung, Henry Wai-chung (1997a), 'Business networks and transnational corporations: a study of Hong Kong firms in the ASEAN region', *Economic Geography*, Vol. 73(1), pp. 1–25.

Yeung, Henry Wai-chung (1997b), 'Cooperative strategies and Chinese business networks: a study of Hong Kong transnational corporations in the ASEAN region', in Paul W. Beamish and J. Peter Killing (eds), *Cooperative Strategies: Asia-Pacific Perspectives*, San Francisco, CA: The New Lexington Press, pp. 22–56.

Yeung, Henry Wai-chung (1998a), *Transnational Corporations and Business Networks: Hong Kong Firms in the ASEAN Region*, London: Routledge.

Yeung, Henry Wai-chung (1998b), 'Competing for transnational corporations? The regional operations of foreign firms in Hong Kong and Singapore', in Ian G. Cook, Marcus A. Doel, Rex Y.F. Li and Yongjiang Wang (eds), *Dynamic Asia: Business, Trade and Economic Development in Pacific Asia*, Aldershot: Ashgate, pp. 78–119.

Yeung, Henry Wai-chung (1998c), 'Transnational economic synergy and business networks: the case of two-way investment between Malaysia and Singapore', *Regional Studies*, Vol. 32(8), pp. 687–706.

Yeung, Henry Wai-chung (1998d), 'The political economy of transnational corporations: a study of the regionalisation of Singaporean firms', *Political Geography*, Vol. 17(4), pp. 389–416.

Yeung, Henry Wai-chung (1998e), 'Capital, state and space: contesting the borderless world', *Transactions of the Institute of British Geographers*, Vol. 23(3), pp. 291–309.

Yeung, Henry Wai-chung (ed.) (1999a), *The Globalisation of Business Firms from Emerging Economies*, 2 volumes, Cheltenham: Edward Elgar.

Yeung, Henry Wai-chung (1999b), *Singapore's Global Reach: An Executive Report*, Singapore: Department of Geography, National University of Singapore. http://courses.nus.edu.sg/course/geoywc/publication/report.pdf.

Yeung, Henry Wai-chung (1999c), 'Regulating investment abroad? The political economy of the regionalisation of Singaporean firms', *Antipode*, Vol. 31(3), pp. 245–73.

Yeung, Henry Wai-chung (1999d), 'The internationalization of ethnic Chinese business firms from Southeast Asia: strategies, processes and competitive advantage', *International Journal of Urban and Regional Research*, Vol. 23(1), pp. 103–27.

Yeung, Henry Wai-chung (1999e), 'Under siege? Economic globalisation and Chinese business in Southeast Asia', *Economy and Society*, Vol. 28(1), pp. 1–29.

Yeung, Henry Wai-chung (1999f), 'Managing crisis in a globalising era: the case of Chinese business firms from Singapore', CAS Research Papers Series No.14, Centre for Advanced Studies, National University of Singapore, Singapore

Yeung, Henry Wai-chung (2000a), 'A crisis of industrial and business networks in Asia?', *Environment and Planning A*, Vol. 32(2), pp. 191–200.

Yeung, Henry Wai-chung (2000b), 'The dynamics of Asian business systems in a globalising era', *Review of International Political Economy*, Vol. 7(3), pp. 399–432.

Yeung, Henry Wai-chung (2000c), 'Neoliberalism, *laissez-faire* capitalism and economic crisis: the political economy of deindustrialisation in Hong Kong', *Competition and Change*, Vol. 4(2), pp. 121–69.

Yeung, Henry Wai-chung (2000d), 'Economic globalisation, crisis, and the emergence of Chinese business communities in Southeast Asia', *International Sociology*, Vol. 15(2), pp. 269–90.

Yeung, Henry Wai-chung (2000e), 'State intervention and neoliberalism in the globalising world economy: lessons from Singapore's regionalisation programme', *Pacific Review*, Vol. 13(1), pp. 133–62.

Yeung, Henry Wai-chung (2000f), 'Limits to the growth of family-owned business? The case of Chinese transnational corporations from Hong Kong', *Family Business Review*, Vol. 13(1), pp. 55–70.

Yeung, Henry Wai-chung (2000g), 'Managing traditional Chinese family firms across borders: four generations of entrepreneurship in Eu Yan Sang', in Leo Douw, Cen Huang and David Ip (eds), *Chinese Transnational Enterprise in Prosperity and Adversity*, Surrey, UK: Curzon.

Yeung, Henry Wai-chung (2000h), 'Local politics and foreign ventures in China's transitional economy: the political economy of Singaporean investments in China', *Political Geography*, Vol. 19(7), pp. 809–40.

Yeung, Henry Wai-chung and Olds, Kris (1998), 'Singapore's global reach: situating the city-state in the global economy', *International Journal of Urban Sciences*, Vol. 2(1), pp. 24–47.

Yeung, Henry Wai-chung and Olds, Kris (eds) (2000), *The Globalisation of Chinese Business Firms*, London: Macmillan.

Yeung, Henry Wai-chung and Soh, Tse Min (2000), 'Corporate governance and the global reach of Chinese family firms in Singapore', *Seoul Journal of Economics*, Vol. 13(3), pp. 301–34.

Yeung, Henry Wai-chung, Poon, Jessie and Perry, Martin (2001), 'Towards a regional strategy: the role of regional headquarters and regional offices in the Asia Pacific', *Urban Studies*, Vol. 38(1), pp. 157–83.

Yeung, K.Y. (1991), 'The role of the Hong Kong Government in industrial development', in Edward K.Y. Chen, Mee-Kau Nyaw and Teresa Y.C. Wong (eds), *Industrial and Trade Development in Hong Kong*, Hong Kong: Centre of Asian Studies, University of Hong Kong, pp. 48–56.

Yeung, Yue-man (1973), 'National policy and urban transformation in Singapore: a study of public housing and the marketing system', Research Paper No.149, Department of Geography, University of Chicago.

Yin, Robert K. (1994), *Case Study Research: Design and Methods*, 2nd edition, Thousand Oaks, CA: Sage.

Yoshihara, Kunio (1976), *Foreign Investment and Domestic Response: A Study of Singapore's Industrialization*, Singapore: Eastern University Press.

Yoshihara, Kunio (1988), *The Rise of Ersatz Capitalism in South East Asia*, Singapore: Oxford University Press.

Yu, Fu-Lai Tony (1997), *Entrepreneurship and Economic Development in Hong Kong*, London: Routledge.

Yu, Fu-Lai Tony (1998), 'Adaptive entrepreneurship and the economic development of Hong Kong', *World Development*, Vol. 26(5), pp. 897–911.

Yu, Fu-Lai Tony (2000), 'Hong Kong's entrepreneurship: behaviours and determinants', *Entrepreneurship and Regional Development*, Vol. 12(3), pp. 179–94.

Zucker, Lynne G. (1987), 'Institutional theories of organisation', *Annual Review of Sociology*, Vol. 13, pp. 443–64.

Index

Acer 36
acquisitions 161–3, 177–9, 183–4, 212–3, 267
adaptability 209–10, 212, 239
agglomeration 29
alliances 32
Argentina 115
ASEAN 114
Asia-Pacific region 50, 57, 62, 99–100, 104–5, 141
Asian economic crisis 45, 58, 61, 84, 112, 165, 168, 177–9, 200, 202–4, 224, 238, 243, 266–71
Australia 38, 114, 131, 161, 178, 182, 201, 203, 232–3
authority systems 33
automobiles 20, 240, 242

banks 25, 85, 88–9, 126, 155, 179, 191, 200, 211, 240
Baumol, William J. 3–4, 11–12, 15, 17, 250, 262, 264–5
Belgium 114
Bermuda 106
bounded rationality 26
Brazil 115
Britain 19, 25, 67–9, 71, 104, 117, 159, 161
  see also UK
British Virgin Islands 106
business groups 20, 24, 28
business history 5
business schools 38, 269
business systems 4, 19, 26, 29–38, 74, 100, 149, 151, 208, 250, 254, 260, 262
  definition 3
  Chinese 98 99, 261
  institutional structuring 19, 25, 91, 135, 149, 265
business ventures 2, 5, 21, 30–32, 99, 152

foreign 17–18, 82, 151, 155–6, 164–5, 169–72, 247, 268
buyer uncertainty 28

Cable & Wireless HKT 244–6
California 29, 271
Canada 180, 182
Cantillon, Richard 7
capitalism
  Chinese 153
  co-operative 24, 32
  laissez-faire 63, 66
  varieties of 19–20, 262, 269
case study method 46, 205, 208, 231, 234
Cayman Islands 106
CDL Hotels International 159–68, 178, 202–4, 257, 267
Cheung Kong Holdings 38, 269
China 36, 43, 45–6, 50–51, 57, 71, 79, 82, 98–9, 104–8, 112–14, 124–6, 131–2, 136–8, 143–4, 159, 172, 177, 180, 182, 186, 191, 193–4, 197, 199–201, 205, 210–17, 223–8, 233–6, 242, 255, 257
  Beijing 117, 164–5, 175, 224, 227, 246
  Fujian 159
  Guangdong province 45, 105–6
  Jiangsu province 45, 242
  Pearl River Delta 51
  Qingdao 227
  Shanghai 50, 105, 187, 190, 193, 211, 214, 224
  Shenzhen 193, 199–200
  Suzhou 143, 190, 223–8, 224
  Wuxi 211, 232, 237, 242–3, 247, 260
China Merchant Holdings 217
China-Singapore Suzhou Industrial Park 190, 192, 199, 221–8, 241–2, 260

China-Singapore Wuxi Industrial Park 221–8, 242–3
Chinese 68–9, 97, 99, 117, 153
  business elites 68–9
  community 68
  entrepreneurs 72, 98, 154–5, 201, 209
  family firms 79, 99, 156, 163, 178–86, 192, 209–14, 216, 232, 235, 239, 247, 261, 270
Chua Seng Teck 210
City Developments Ltd. 159–68
city-states 42, 49–50, 57, 72, 74, 92, 97, 100, 103, 115, 117, 135, 149, 241
Compaq 193
comparative advantage 140, 144
competitive advantage 34, 141, 154–5, 172, 178, 194, 197, 202, 270–71
contracts 28, 33
construction 20, 44, 90, 114, 201, 205, 227, 240
corporate
  finance 21
  governance 21, 84, 129–32, 154, 185, 200, 234–7, 239, 266, 268
  heterarchy 16
  hierarchy 16, 177
  managers 25, 152, 157, 206–9
credit-rating agencies 37
creative destruction 2
culture 9, 29, 192, 236, 260–61, 275
customer relationships 26, 32, 36, 98, 157, 192–3, 240, 258

Dao Heng Bank 161, 165, 202
decision-making 9, 18, 31, 39, 152, 154, 164, 192, 211, 239, 250, 257
Deng Xiaoping 221, 223
Denmark 20
developing countries 30, 66, 69, 104, 115–17, 135
direct investments 17, 42, 51, 58, 103–14, 154, 179
diversification 168, 177, 180–81

economic
  development 5, 9, 11, 20, 42, 67, 71, 79, 98, 103, 139, 261–2
  institutions 20
  structures 14
  systems 5
economics 5, 9, 12, 26
  institutional 28
  transaction costs 17, 24, 26, 28, 33, 40
education 31, 38
electronics 20, 51, 57–8, 70, 105, 138, 233
embeddedness 4, 18–19, 21, 202, 234, 241
entrepreneur 2–4, 9–10, 28, 40, 127, 144, 149, 152
  definition 11–14
entrepreneurial endowments 18–19, 25–32, 74, 85, 91–2, 98, 151, 157, 172, 187, 191, 205, 208–9, 215, 229, 234–41, 244, 250, 255–62, 265
entrepreneurship 1–3, 24, 28–33, 71–2, 75, 91–101, 144, 197, 209, 261–75
  comparative analysis 9, 39, 42, 75, 255–61
  corporate 7, 15, 25, 132, 207
  definition 2, 11, 157
  disadvantage model 14, 25
  domestic 7, 17, 26, 34, 36–7, 75, 79, 91, 97–101, 139–42
  ethnic 14, 25, 30
  'great person' school 12
  misfit model 14, 25
  studies 4–5, 9–11, 21, 41–2, 259, 275
  X-efficiency theory 24
ethnic groups 14
Eu Kong 182, 186
Eu, Richard K.M. 183–6
Eu, Richard Y.M. 179, 182–6, 270
Eu Tong Seng 182–3
Eu Yan Sang 179, 182–6, 260, 270
expatriation 36, 124–5, 192
experience 16, 26, 30–31, 36, 39, 98, 129, 133, 142, 157, 159, 163, 178, 185–6, 191, 194, 204–5, 213, 228, 239, 258–60
  see also learning

family 30
  business 30, 38, 156, 159–68, 176–7, 179–86, 259, 268–75
  ties 30, 155–6

'family-isation' 155–6, 177, 213, 269
firms 9–10, 12, 16, 20, 25, 215
   Asian 2–3, 250, 265–75
   American 21, 269
   boundary of 28
   Germany 21
   Japanese 21
   national 21, 36, 144
   ownership of 21, 24
   stock-broking 37
financial services 20, 37, 54, 57, 79–80, 84–5, 92, 98, 112, 120, 155, 165, 192
financial systems 33, 37, 85, 90–91, 98, 186
Finland 194
'first-mover' advantages 17, 33
foresight 17, 156, 204
foreign exchange 168, 203
France 203, 257
franchising 179–81
Fung, Victor 151, 269

Gan Khai Choon 164–5
gender 157
geography 7, 100, 117, 123, 125, 142, 149, 154, 273–4
Germany 20, 58
global cities 37, 103, 141, 246
global corporations 9, 21, 73, 126, 197, 228, 247, 269
   see also transnational corporations
global competition 17, 38, 62, 136, 139–40, 172, 262, 265, 270
global economy 31, 37, 103, 115, 117, 122, 136, 140–41, 169, 221, 254, 263, 270
globalisation 4–5, 34, 36, 44, 117, 125–30, 136–7, 154, 165, 175, 180, 185, 202, 205, 235, 246, 262, 265–6
   see also internationalisation
Goh Chok Tong 139, 141, 143, 215, 223, 245
goodwill 202, 267
governance structures 28, 238
Granovetter, Mark 4
Guoco Group 159

hedging 168, 202–3
Honda 36

Hong Kong 4, 38–9, 42–6, 58, 108, 153–6, 159, 180, 182, 192, 216, 227, 244–6, 251, 274
   capital markets 85–91, 202
   colonial state in 62–9, 79, 85, 90, 97, 135, 138
   companies from 42–4, 51, 79, 104–8, 115–21, 176–7, 182–6, 267
   economic development 49–57, 63–9, 74–9, 98
   foreign ownership 74–9, 244
   industrial restructuring 51, 79, 105, 136–9
   outward investments from 104–8, 136–9, 195
   Sino-British Joint Declaration 105
   small and medium enterprises 63–6, 79, 90, 144
   Stock Exchange 79, 120, 161, 184, 202
Hongkong and Shanghai Banking Corporation 203
Hong Leong Group 159–60, 179, 186–7, 191, 202, 229, 270
Hopewell Holdings 38
hotels 159–68, 178
Hymer, Stephen 7

immigrants 14, 25
India 193
Indonesia 44, 61, 82, 106, 112, 117, 125, 131, 140, 153, 182, 192, 202–3, 210, 233, 267
industrialisation 21, 51, 58, 63, 67–8, 72, 79–80, 85, 92, 97–9, 115, 139–40
industry
   association 29, 149, 274
   structure 10
information 15–16, 28–9, 32, 39, 66, 98, 221, 228–9, 233–5
   asymmetry 26, 28–31, 98, 157, 159, 175, 187, 234, 255
   impactedness 28
   see also knowledge
ING Barings 203
innovation 9, 14, 20–21, 66, 136, 178, 263
   see also R&D

international business 1–3, 5, 15–16, 19, 25–6, 33–40, 152, 159, 191, 194, 197, 200, 204, 217, 234–6, 239–40, 244, 247, 250–54, 257–8, 261, 264–75
   studies of 4–5, 7–10, 40–42, 46, 152, 197, 207, 238, 275
international entrepreneurship 5, 10–11, 33, 275
   see also transnational entrepreneurship
international finance 36
International Monetary Fund 203
internationalisation 2, 9, 33, 40–42, 98, 101, 135, 175, 208–11, 250, 266, 270
   see also globalisation
Institute for Scientific Information 10
institutional
   context 2–3, 5, 7, 28–33, 40–42, 137, 149, 153
   perspective 3–4, 7, 18–42, 205, 215, 250–54, 275
   relations 3, 231, 275
   resources 2, 15, 152
   structures 18–21, 25, 28–32, 40–42, 72, 74, 99–100, 149, 151, 169, 187, 195, 199, 208, 215, 241–2, 247–54, 260–75
   thickness 31
Intel 193
intrapreneur 30, 127, 149, 152, 207–49
intrapreneurship 12, 16, 254, 262–5

Japan 20, 25, 29, 36, 51, 57–8, 66, 164, 200, 203, 214, 274
   investments abroad 61, 105
   keiretsu 32
   Tokyo 103
Jiang Zemin 223, 226
joint ventures 131, 135, 143, 164, 176–7, 186, 194, 211–2, 214, 217, 221, 223, 229–31, 237, 242–3, 247
   partners 39, 130, 164, 186, 191, 200, 224–6, 229–30, 232, 236, 240

Keppel Corporation 223
knowledge 15–16, 32, 34, 36, 39, 66, 129, 137
   see also information

Kuok, Robert 156
Kwek Hong Lye 159
Kwek Hong Png 159, 161–2
Kwek Leng Beng 159–68, 175, 178–9, 192, 202, 209, 221, 257, 260, 270–71

labour 58, 191
   employment relations 20, 25, 29, 95, 199, 205, 212
   market 14, 21, 70, 73, 95, 247
   processes 20, 63
   productivity 57, 70, 137
learning 16, 31, 36, 66, 190, 237, 240, 267
   see also experience
Lee Hsien Loong 221, 223, 227, 245
Lee Hsien Yang 245
Lee Kuan Yew 49, 72, 97, 99, 103, 141, 143, 221, 223–4, 226–7, 245, 273
Li Ka-shing 245–6, 267
Li Lanqing 223
Li Peng 223
Li, Richard 244–6
Liberia 114
Liem Sioe Liong 202
Lloyds Bank 203
local partners 130, 173, 175–6, 187, 199–200, 211, 217, 224, 227, 230, 237, 242–3, 255, 257
Lum Chang Group 183–4

Malaya 159, 182
Malaysia 44, 57, 61, 105–6, 108, 112, 124, 139–40, 153, 159, 161, 164–5, 180, 182–6, 193, 201–3, 210, 212–3, 233
management
   bureaucratic 31
   financial 24
   intra-firm 25, 31
   studies 9, 12, 14–15
manufacturing 20, 44, 51–8, 69, 74, 79–80, 84–5, 92–5, 98–9, 105–6, 112–14, 120–21, 126–7, 135–9, 179, 182, 186, 190, 192–3, 198, 201, 229, 233, 243
market 162
   capital 21, 24, 30, 37–9, 85–91, 155, 168, 201–4, 251–2, 257, 267

contracting 20
diversification 136, 203
domestic 17, 270
financial 37, 155
foreign 17, 127, 135
opportunity 15, 29, 39, 127, 159, 172, 187, 190, 193, 235
saturation 29
stock 30, 203, 267
methodological individualism 9
Mexico 115
Microsoft 273
Millennium & Copthorne Hotels 159–68, 202–4, 257
Morgan Stanley 37
Motorola 193
Myanmar 112, 197

Natsteel 227, 238
national development 31, 117
National Westminster Bank 203
nationalism 244, 253
neoliberalism 63, 66–69, 97, 136, 138–9
Netherlands 58, 114, 142
Netherlands Antilles 114
networks 4, 10, 15, 20, 24, 32, 98, 126, 135, 176–7, 266
  actor 18–19, 33–9, 152, 175, 179, 181, 186–7, 215–34, 250, 255, 262
  business 3, 15, 25, 38, 99, 130, 151–6, 164–5, 202, 210, 266–7
  inter-firm 32, 152, 257
  intra-firm 16, 152
  social 3, 15, 30, 127, 130, 154, 156, 191, 201–2, 266–7
new international division of labour 58, 73, 127
new ventures 9–10
New Zealand 114, 131, 161, 178, 182, 202–3
Newly Industrialised Economies 4, 55, 57, 61, 66, 69, 104, 108, 136, 142, 144
North America 38, 57, 105, 108, 122, 124, 126–33, 154–5, 169, 178–9, 182, 197, 200, 271, 275

Ong Teng Cheong 223
opportunism 32

organisational
  analysis 40
  behaviour 9–10
  capacity 20, 117, 133
Original Equipment Manufacturing 126

Pacific Century Cyberworks Ltd 245–6
Panama 106
Peregrine Investment Holdings 267–8
personal interview method 44–6, 186, 197, 216
personal relationships 130, 155–6, 175, 187, 221, 231, 239, 258
Philippines 61, 122, 131, 161, 193
political economy 135–49, 242
political structures 5, 71, 202
professional managers 16, 20, 36, 38, 84, 117, 156, 179, 183, 200, 209, 216, 239–40, 247–8, 255, 259, 269–70
profit 26, 32, 162, 164, 191, 214, 224, 238, 242, 247
Protestant ethic 14
Prudential Client (MSS) Nominees Ltd 202
psychology 12, 14–15

Qiao Shi 223
quantitative methodology 9
Quek Leng Chan 161, 164–5, 202

R&D 20–21, 29
  see also innovation
regional divisions of labour 61, 140
regulation 130, 199, 205, 274
resource-based view 7, 15
resources
  control 15, 17–18, 28, 39, 98, 191
  cross-border 16–17, 221
  ownership 15, 143, 229
  strategic 34
risk 16, 24, 26, 29–31, 37, 39, 82, 98, 130, 142–3, 152, 154–9, 162–3, 168, 170, 175, 178–9, 187, 190, 194, 200, 203, 207, 209, 217, 235–8, 257, 259–60, 269
Romania 197

Schumpeter, Joseph 1–3, 11, 14–17, 30, 262–4
Seagate 193, 243
Silicon Valley 29, 271
Singapore 4, 39, 42, 45–6, 153–6, 191, 251–4, 271–5
  capital markets 85, 201, 203
  Central Provident Fund 91
  companies from 36, 42, 44–5, 115–35
  Development Bank of Singapore 85, 90
  developmental state 43, 69–73, 97, 99, 139–49, 197, 216–7, 221, 242, 246, 271–4
  economic development 49, 57–62, 72–9, 142
  entrepreneurs from 151–206
  Economic Development Board 72, 144, 148–9, 228–9, 232, 240, 255
  foreign investments in 58–62, 72, 79–80, 108
  foreign workers in 70–71
  government-linked companies 81, 85, 95, 99, 117, 121, 140–43, 152, 163, 197–8, 207–49, 252
  Jurong Town Corporation 72, 238, 271
  National Wage Council 70
  National Trade Union Congress 97
  outward investment and regionalisation 43, 62, 70, 81–2, 99–100, 108–14, 124, 139–49, 162, 169–72, 191, 195, 197, 228, 271–4
  People's Action Party 71–3, 97, 140, 241
  Stock Exchange 82, 117, 142, 183, 191, 232, 238, 258
  Temasek Holdings 81–4, 143, 163–4, 230, 234–5, 238, 245, 258, 260
  Trade Development Board 228–9, 232, 271–3
Singapore Airlines 82, 142, 230
Singapore-Indonesia-Malaysia Growth Triangle 139–40
Singapore Telecom 230, 238, 244–6
small and medium enterprises (SMEs) 63–6, 84–7, 98, 121, 144, 149, 201

Social Sciences Citation Index 10
socialisation 16
sociology 12, 14–15, 41
Sony 36
South Africa 105
South Korea 55, 85, 115, 136–8, 198, 200
  chaebol 32, 203
  war 51
Southeast Asia 44, 57, 61, 79, 99, 104–6, 112, 124, 127–8, 130, 133, 136, 144, 153, 161, 169–70, 177–8, 186, 216, 266
spatial scales 34, 39, 104, 152, 226
Standard and Poor's 37
state 33, 42, 67–73
  agencies 21
  bureaucratic 67
  control 28, 244–6
  developmental 62, 69–73, 103, 136, 246
  ideologies of 32
  ownership 24
Straits Steamship Land 227
strategic
  choices 132, 141, 144
  behaviour 10, 25
  infrastructure 15
  management 15, 17–18, 24, 31, 39, 41, 152, 211, 265, 275
strategies 24, 129–30, 168, 185, 201, 269
  competitive 20
  innovative 20
  marketing 127–8, 133, 138, 170, 175, 185
subcontracting 66, 179, 193
supplier relationships 24, 26, 31–2, 36, 98, 133, 157, 192–3, 233, 240, 258
Switzerland 142, 203, 268

Taiwan 36, 55, 57, 66, 85, 105, 124, 131, 136–8, 153, 164, 182, 193, 198, 203
technology 127, 133, 136–9, 155
Teck Wah Paper 210–14, 232, 237, 239–40, 247, 260, 270
Thailand 44, 61, 106, 131, 153, 192–3, 233, 257

trade 57, 67–8, 71, 74, 79–80, 84, 92–5, 120, 129, 159, 198, 217, 273
trade unions 29, 73, 95
transaction costs 28
transnational corporations 4, 7, 9–10, 16, 42, 101, 104, 108, 149, 152, 194, 197, 207, 264
  entry modes 130, 135, 175–86, 197, 217, 230
  from Asia 115–17
  headquarter-subsidiary relations 16, 125, 131–3, 152, 200, 208, 258, 264
  regional headquarters 61, 140
  subsidiary initiatives 7, 152, 207
transnational entrepreneur 2–3, 5, 10, 19, 31, 33, 39–40, 74, 98, 101, 152, 157–206, 250–54
  definition 3, 15–18
  see also entrepreneur
transnational entrepreneurship 2, 4, 10–11, 40, 101, 157–206, 209, 241, 248, 250–53
  definition 5, 15–16
  institutional perspective 18–39, 151, 186, 207
  institutionalisation 19, 26, 33–9, 98, 153–6
  policy implications 261–75
  see also entrepreneurship
transnational intrapreneurs 16, 19, 152, 156, 207–54

trust 32–3, 154–5, 165, 181, 200, 212, 214, 229, 240, 267
Tung Chee Hwa 246

UK 20, 57, 67, 106, 108, 112, 114, 142, 168, 178, 182, 186, 190, 192, 203, 216, 232–3, 244, 274
  London 67, 103, 117, 161, 168, 202–3, 231–3, 244–5, 257
  see also Britain
USA 14, 20, 24–5, 29–30, 51, 57–8, 106, 137, 164, 168, 178, 180, 182, 190, 192–3, 203, 210, 216, 228, 232–3, 274
  investments abroad 61, 105
  New York 103, 161
United Overseas Bank 202

value creation 14
Vancouver 38, 267
Venture capital 201
Vietnam 112

Weber, Max 14
Wee Cho Yaw 202
Western Europe 38, 57–8, 105, 108, 114, 122, 124–33, 154–5, 161, 164, 169–70, 178, 182, 197, 200, 245, 271, 275
Whitley, Richard 3, 36
World Economic Forum 50